A QUEST IN THE MIDDLE EAST

Aftershadows of colonialism remain in the minds of both – former masters and former subjects.
Clifford Gertz, *After the Fact*

A QUEST
IN THE MIDDLE EAST

Gertrude Bell
and the Making of Modern Iraq

LIORA LUKITZ

I.B. TAURIS
LONDON · NEW YORK

Published in 2006 by I.B.Tauris & Co Ltd
6 Salem Road, London W2 4BU
175 Fifth Avenue, New York NY 10010
www.ibtauris.com

In the United States of America and Canada
distributed by Palgrave Macmillan a division of St Martin's Press
175 Fifth Avenue, New York NY 10010

ISBN 1 85043 415 8
EAN 978 1 85043 415 3

A full CIP record for this book is available from the British Library
A full CIP record is available from the Library of Congress

Library of Congress Catalog Card Number: available

Typeset in Galliard by JCS Publishing Services
Printed and bound in Great Britain by MPG Books Ltd, Bodmin

Contents

List of Illustrations

Illustrations 1–2 and 4–8 reproduced with the kind permission of the curators of Gertrude Bell's photographic collection at the School of Historical Studies, University of Newcastle

Acknowledgements

This project started many years ago when I was a fellow at the Center for Middle Eastern Studies at Harvard University and a recipient of a grant from the H. F. Guggenheim Foundation in New York. My thanks go to both institutions for the opportunity and the support. The project had been inspired, however, much earlier, by a comment from the late Professor Elie Kedourie who, seeing me digging in a pile of documents on Iraq of the 1920s, suggested a glance into Gertrude Bell's letters 'in order to catch the atmosphere' of those days. The discovery of Gertrude Bell's unpublished papers was a revelation. Not only did her personality come across in her writings, but also the beauty of a long-forgotten Middle East pervaded the documents with most colourful images.

In a leap of imagination, I saw the numerous bits of information therein contained taking shape in the form of a book. It took me several years, however, before I could concretise this vision. The task was so absorbing and fascinating that I decided to pursue it, in spite of the difficulties I found during its materialisation. My thanks go foremost to the friends and colleagues who kept encouraging me, among them young Iraqi friends who understood Gertrude's dilemmas so well. Their names are not mentioned here, but they know they deserve my gratitude for all I learned from them. I am also especially indebted to Professors Roy Mottahedeh and William Graham, the successive directors of the Center for Middle Eastern Studies at Harvard during my stay there, both staunch supporters of the project from its very beginning. Without their help this project wouldn't have been completed. My thanks also go to Professor Bernard Lewis whose encouragement will never be forgotten.

My thanks are also extended to Lynne Gay, who grew as fond of Gertrude Bell as I was already, when I started writing. Lynne Gay's editorial skills and sensitivity helped me preserve the beauty of Gertrude Bell's writings in the text. Dalia Geffen touched it with her renowned editorial elegance. Haya Naor and Daniela Korem brought the manuscript to its final version with their usual skills and endless dedication. My thanks also go to Dr Katherine Prior and Professor Angela V. John, who amazed me with their wide knowledge of the period. A very special reverence goes to a friend, the late St John Armitage, one of the leading authorities on T. E. Lawrence and his times. His deep knowledge and personal acquaintances made him a most reliable source and an outstanding contributor in any writing of the region's annals. His advice will be greatly missed. The book wouldn't have taken its actual shape without the help, vision, fairness and enthusiasm of Dr Lester Crook, the academic editor at I.B. Tauris. My thanks go to him and also to Kate Sheratt who, with infinite patience and sympathy, led me through the sometimes thorny editorial process.

Dr James Crow, the curator of Gertrude Bell's photographic material at the Department of Archaeology at the University of Newcastle, was a long-term supporter, and a sharp and knowledgeable reader. The late Dr Lesley Gordon, with her intimate knowledge of the collection, skilfully delineated Gertrude Bell's life to me and heartfully answered my endless queries.

I was also helped by the staffs of the Middle East Archives at the India Office Collections, the Sudan Archive at the University of Durham, the Fales Library at the New York University, the Public Records Office, the British Library, and the Geographical Society. Lieutenant General P. A. Crocker, the curator of the Regimental Museum of the Royal Welch Fusiliers at Caernafon, Wales, helped me by making available to me, from long distance, Lieutenant Colonel Doughty-Wylie's diaries, and Diana Ring, the librarian at St Antony's College, Oxford, helped me handle C. J. Edmonds' Papers. Jane R. Hogan, the assistant keeper of the Sudan Archive at Durham kindly and patiently helped me solve seemingly unsolvable mysteries. However, the dedication of all the above could not avoid the remaining errors, for which I alone am responsible.

A special acknowledgement also goes to Sir Geoffrey Trevelyan and the late Lady Bridget Plowden, who were immensely kind and understood my need to touch and write about the more personal aspects of Gertrude Bell's life. Their hospitality and openness in talking about their Aunt Gertrude remains one of the most vivid experiences I had when working on this project. The same should be said about my encounter, in East Jerusalem, with Dame Val Vester, whose insights and accounts enliven the text itself.

My stay at Harvard also endowed me with two very dear friends: Britt Ahlfert, whose hospitality and encouragement remained a constant while the project matured; and the late Milton A. Steinmetz, to whom this project owes much more than I can express. His music remains an unforgettable source of joy and inspiration, and his support helped me get through with this project when the difficulties seemed insurmountable.

During the period of self-involvement required by the process, I especially missed the irreplaceable presence of my late father, Moshé Lokiec, a

writer and poet of another still vivid era. The echoes of years of encouragement by other greatly missed members of the family, Marcus Lokiec and
Benjamin Migdal, rekindled my courage when it waned. I believe that they
would have enjoyed Gertrude and the 'omen'. My young cousin, Lina Kre-
icmer, whose life was nipped in the bud, would perhaps have followed in
Gertrude Bell's footsteps, endowed as Lina was with a remarkable intelligence, a very focused scientific curiosity, and a witty sense of humor.

In difficult moments, I drew much strength from the family's younger
generation: Alex, Michal, Amit, Yael, Roni, Gili and now Elai, Imri and
Yochai, growing so confidently into a hoped-for more peaceful future.

My thanks also go to the four 'musketeers' – Irad and Hili, Yanai and
Mali – who gave back so much more than I ever dared to expect. And to
my brother Franklin who, once more, understood and kept believing.

Above all, my gratitude goes to my late mother, Esther Lokiec who,
years ago, gave me her blessing expressed, again, in the form of a wish. 'You
will be happy', she once said, 'because you have your books . . .'. The refer-
ence was to books in general, the treasures and hidden messages one can
always find in their pages.

It is only natural that, reverentially, and very tenderly, I dedicate this one
to her.

To my mother,
ESTHER MIGDAL LOKIEC,

Who taught me so much about women's courage
and people's dignity.

Preface

It would have been better for our country and perhaps for the world if Doughty, Lawrence and Gertrude Bell had not been such admirable and persuasive writers.
Colonel Richard Meinertzhagen, *Middle East Diary: 1917–1956*

Charles Doughty's classic book, *Travels in Arabia Deserta* (1888) inspired T. E. Lawrence's and Gertrude Bell's travels across the lands of the Ottoman Empire and shaped their images of it. During and after the First World War, together and in association with other players on the Middle Eastern stage, these two charismatic individuals helped draw the lines of the contemporary Middle East, sometimes with problematic consequences for the states themselves. Lawrence and Bell worked against the backdrop of the First World War, which erupted after years of tension in Europe. A major source of tension was Germany's rise as an economic and industrial power forcing the realignment of Britain, France and Russia, both within and outside Europe. The alliances formed at the time were an attempt to preserve the shaky balance of power in the continent, which also had profound ramifications for Europe's territorial and economic interests in Asia and Africa. However, some of the Allied Powers' territorial targets were still in the domain of the Ottoman Empire. Pressured by the Powers from without and by his subjects from within, Sultan Abdul Hamid II (1876–1909) was compelled to put into effect administrative and judicial reforms that had started in 1839 with the Tanzimat. But the restoration in 1908 of the previous constitution was insufficient to prevent the outburst of a simmering movement for autonomy among the empire's non-Muslim subjects. Having been promulgated in December 1876 and practically abrogated in February 1878 after the dissolution of the Chamber by the sultan as a reaction to the deputies' confrontation with the ministers, the constitution was again seen as the solution for the empire's difficulties.

Britain, which, in the years preceding the First World War, still clung to strategic and political considerations dating from the nineteenth century, was reluctant to call for the dismemberment of the Ottoman Empire. Instead, it continued to focus on the Persian Gulf and the Suez Canal – both strategic assets along the passage to India. Britain's presence in Egypt, dating from 1882, gained France's recognition with the signing in April 1904 of the 'Entente Cordiale', which also acknowledged France's designs on Morocco. In another pre-war arrangement of 1907, Britain achieved a tacit understanding with Russia, in accordance with which, Persian's northern provinces would come under Russia's influence and the southern under Britain's. However, in 1911, Field Marshal Horatio Herbert Kitchener, the British agent in Egypt – the 'Great K' as he was known to his soldiers – began toying with the notion of freeing the Arabs from Turkish hegemony, an idea first conceived by a group of British experts on the Middle East, led by the famous Oxford archaeologist D. G. Hogarth. This proposal was in response to the Arabs' desire for autonomy as expressed by the Arabs themselves, a claim made before the Young Turks rose to power; after their rise, the Arab secret societies continued their activities until more open advances by Arab representatives to British authorities in Cairo and India took place some years later.[1]

In fact, three years elapsed before a more intensive channel of communication was opened with Sharif Husayn of Mecca with the intent of winning him over to the Allies' side during the war. Two parallel sets of negotiations were then initiated: one between Britain and the Arabs that would become famous as the Husayn–McMahon correspondence, and the other between Britain, France and Russia, that would result in a secret agreement disclosed in early 1918 by the Bolsheviks. The Sykes–Picot agreement, as it became known, divided the Middle East into zones of influence that would become effective after the Arabs were liberated from the Turks. Although open and implied pledges in both agreements recognised the right of the Arabs to create an independent Arab state, promised by Britain to the sharif in exchange for his wartime collaboration, there were controversies over its exact boundaries and configuration.

Gertrude Bell and T. E. Lawrence were among the British experts actively promoting Britain's hegemony in the area, but they became personally infatuated with the Arab cause in the process. Both penned their adventures, experiences, accomplishments and opinions on their mission, not only in their official reports and publications, but also in lively correspondence and detailed diaries.

Colonel Richard Meinertzhagen, General Allenby's intelligence officer who served with Lawrence in the Middle East and in the Colonial Office, held a different view of the confluence of interests between the British and the Arabs and, according to some authorities, downplayed, *ipso facto*, the significance of Lawrence's desert campaign to promote the Arab national movement. Although not as friendly with Gertrude Bell as he was with Lawrence, Meinertzhagen treated both as if they held definite and identical opinions. While defending the Arabs in their negotiations with the Powers at the 1919 Versailles peace conference and acting to promote these views in London's corridors of power during the decisive years preceding the 1921 Cairo conference, Bell and Lawrence took different stands on many occasions. This book attempts, among other things, to reappraise Meinertzhagen's comments, at least concerning Gertrude Bell and her insights about the future of the Middle East.

Much more nuanced in her opinions than Lawrence, Gertrude Bell was able to see 'the frayed edges and the holes in the weaving' of Middle Eastern politics. 'Gifted writer, intrepid traveller, skilful archaeologist, oriental scholar',[2] Gertrude Bell was the sum of many complex and sometimes conflicting parts. Extremely intelligent, courageous and outspoken, she was the only woman appointed by the British Foreign Office as a political officer after British troops landed in Basra in November 1914, and later she served as the Oriental Secretary to the Civil Commissioner in Baghdad. She was also the sole woman delegate to the 1921 Cairo peace conference, which outlined Britain's policy in the Middle East for decades to come. Back in Baghdad, she helped lay the foundations of modern Iraq and draw the country's boundaries. The last two years before her death in 1926 were dedicated to archaeological work: the discovery of Iraq's 'buried past' and the founding of the British School of Archaeology in Baghdad. Not only was Gertrude Bell extraordinary in her scholarship, political insights, and physical endurance, she was also a multifaceted character in her personal dealings with other players in the Middle East political arena.

Sir Mark Sykes (the schemer, with George Picot, of the 1916 Anglo-French agreement), with whom Gertrude Bell developed a life-long rivalry, once described her as a 'flat-chested, man-woman, globe-trotting, rump-wagging, blathering ass', while T. E. Lawrence (her fellow archaeologist and partner in the planning of an independent Arab state) saw her rather as 'exciting but unpredictable . . . for you never knew how far she would leap in any direction when attracted by new intellectual challenges'. Lawrence, like other male colleagues, saw her as more driven by emotion than by depth of mind, 'changing her directions each time as a weathercock'. According to their standards of feminine behaviour she was 'not very like a woman', yet they certainly recognised her grasp of politics and knowledge of the area. With Lawrence himself, Gertrude Bell had many confrontations, describing him once as 'an angel' and later, when suddenly upset for some minor or major reason, as 'possessed by the devil'.[3]

One can get a better perspective of Gertrude Bell's life and deeds by tracing her encounters with fellow travellers in her voyages over time and through different places. The comparison of her views with those of people who agreed with her or opposed her ideas on some of the central issues of her time will help define her life. Among them were Sir Mark Sykes and T. E. Lawrence, with whom Gertrude Bell debated extensively on the Middle East and Britain's role in the region. Other snapshots of intercepting lives will focus on Gertrude Bell's debates with Elizabeth Robins, a London-based American actress and a personal friend of the Bells – she became a leader in the struggle for women's suffrage in England during the years preceding the First World War. As a complementary contrast, there was also Yasin al-Hashimi, the leading Iraqi nationalist and ardent opponent of Britain's mandate over Iraq.

However, the remarkable thing about Gertrude Bell was not just her ability to stand up for her ideas, but also the wit with which those debates were described and the humour underpinning her letters. Her diaries allow the reader to enter a world of very personal thoughts, while getting a glimpse of the broad spectrum of impressions that marked her journey. Unmatched in seizing these meaningful moments, Gertrude Bell managed, in many cases, to win over her reader, even if momentarily, to the points she wanted to make. Her writing reflected a combative spirit but also great vulnerability, her views extending sometimes to subjects she did not always master in a strictly academic way.

In memoranda and in official documents, Gertrude Bell's writing was at once descriptive and analytical, and as accurate as possible for someone in her position and at her time. Although grounded in her intimate knowledge of the geography, history and archaeology of the Middle East, and pervaded with details and subtleties that made the reader feel part of the historic moment described, she was, one must admit, also very opinionated, letting personal views affect even the norms of objectivity that prevailed at the time. And yet, her brilliantly worded analyses of particular situations, infused with complex historical meanings, offered a broad and unique view of the way in which her deep understanding of the area helped her to fulfil her political mission; at least as she understood it. However, the mission itself already had, even then, controversial aspects.

Gertrude still manages to make the magic of the world she creates influence her readers. Most of them are enticed by her writings and follow her through events, cultures and places, while enjoying the atmosphere she describes so well. Engaging in the adventure (even if knowing that much of it is an interpretation of history, and that there was certainly more to it by today's standards), we still fall under the spell. It would always be easier to return to the view that the study of Middle Eastern history is never a purely academic exercise. Yet, this attempt is, perhaps more than others, an interpretative version of Gertrude Bell's story and her search for the 'good omen', the promised event that would change her life.

*   *   *

Gertrude Bell's story bridges two worlds: the Northumbria of her youth and the Middle East of her adulthood. The contrasts between the two could not be more marked. From the dark skies of industrial England to the sunny mornings in Middle Eastern deserts; from Middlesbrough's furnaces, where iron and coke were used to make steel, to the fields and marshes along the Tigris and the Euphrates, still tilled with wooden ploughs; from London's salons to the desert's *mudhifs*, Gertrude's story evolves by encompassing these contrasts. While becoming an exponent of the European misrepresentation of the East and the illusory and romantic vision of it, Gertrude herself fell prey to the distorted notions of romance and excitement, the indelible memories of exotic places and unexpected encounters that could, so she came to believe, take place only in the East.

For her, as for other travellers before her, the East also symbolised unconformity, an individual quest for unconventionality and, at the bottom of it, an attempt to fill in needs and absences whose roots and reasons run way back to early childhood. By following Gertrude's footsteps, from her first archaeological mission in Asia Minor in 1904 to Carchemish in 1911, where D. G. Hogarth's archaeological team excavated, and some years later to Ha'il, the city fortress in central Arabia, we discover the first signs of the difficulties she and others found when trying to bridge the gap and connect between West and East. Considering themselves messengers of the British Crown, the bearers of the civilisatory mission of an empire that ruled lands and waves, they became in fact the victims of a misconceived enterprise launched by an empire riddled with contradictions and prejudices. In tracing Gertrude in her wartime assignments in Europe and the Middle East, in her mission to Basra, where she was sent to 'pull things straight between

Delhi and Cairo', we discover the price paid for the illusions of racial supremacy and political dominance.

Although concealing the natural arrogance that was part of the myth she lived by, Gertrude's writing is so endearing that one could best quote her own words when choosing the titles of the book's chapters, hoping that they would better convey the flavours, colours and scents of her two worlds. 'On the Edge of Important Things' is a line taken from one of Gertrude's letters home, describing her feelings when taking part in the events that marked Iraq's beginnings. This feeling of renewal came after periods of rupture and after times of solitude during which she felt like 'A Shadow of a Stone . . .', wheeling in the bare desert. It also came with the painful disappointment at the death of Lieutenant Colonel Doughty-Wylie ('Dick' in her letters), with whom Gertrude Bell shared similar thoughts and feelings. In some ways, the two were closer than people involved in lengthy and consummated love affairs. These new beginnings, encapsulating all the previous chapters of her life, heralded a new part, which was mainly dedicated to scholarly work and political activity. In 'Making Kings and Inventing Kingdoms . . .' she shared with 'Ken' Cornwallis (fondly defined by her as 'a tower of strength and wisdom') a partnership that lasted during the years in which they were both engaged in helping create a modern Iraq. Once her task was completed she fell prey to the emptiness and melancholy that come in the aftermath of accomplished missions. The mission, as she saw it, could never be entirely completed, however.

The vastness and vagueness of the empire, the illusions regarding the possible change of patterns in the territories conquered by sword or by persuasion, the difficulty of connecting cultures and beliefs, led the mediator, almost invariably, to fall into the gap he or she was trying to bridge. Gertrude Bell's apprehensions, often voiced with the plea 'absit omen', a line taken from Ovid's *Amores*: 'procul omen abesto' (let the bad omen be far away from us) became a premonition, sometimes a warning. The search for the 'good omen', for the right solution, for those things she wanted to see happen or those she hoped could be prevented, appears therefore, more often than not, as a wish. The book's focus on Gertrude Bell's 'omen' does not indicate, however, a hidden attempt to change the Middle East 'Gertrude's way', but rather a journey of quest and discovery of the different interpretations and often clashing aspirations that re-emerge over time, carrying readjusted meanings.

Unveiling Gertrude Bell's life while unravelling the subtleties and nuances of Gertrude Bell's vision leads us from ancient Mesopotamia and its intertwining languages, cultures and religions to the dealings of Iraq's daily administration. Her vision of the country emerged from her knowledge of its past, its origins, its historical roots and their different ways of going, of searching underneath, in the darkness of hidden layers, for some of the answers to its entangled present. What emerges is a colourful picture that encompasses 'Dust . . .' and 'Flood . . .' two opposites, pointing to Gertrude's personal changing moods as well as to the two extremes that characterise Iraq's perennial cycle of life.

A last caveat to the reader: do not be fooled by Gertrude's flamboyant style of writing, 'a style that conceals much more than it reveals but still reveals much more than she initially intended', as Seton Dearden rightly observed. Only when an intimate knowledge of Gertrude Bell develops, can one discern the sharp insights and deep thoughts cloaked in her subtle and witty remarks. Gertrude Bell's lightness of writing does not reflect a lightness of being or observing. On the contrary, although her delicacy of touch presents history as a treat, her own story is far from being a fairy tale. It is a true story presented by her in the form and style of a fairy tale and I felt that it had to be told that way.

The book leads to many new questions but also, so I hope, teaches some lessons. Gertrude Bell's impact on what was considered a male domain demonstrates that women, given the right circumstances, knowledge and opportunity, can defy barriers of sex, culture and age, sometimes far more easily than men. The fact that she was a woman and not a pretty one, nourished Gertrude's initial ambition to concentrate in political matters. Her knowledge made her an equal partner to men no less ambitious than she was. Some recognised her value, others didn't, but even the latter were drawn to her by her character and personality. Her knowledge found expression in her deep feelings for the Middle East and its peoples, feelings rarely found in the writings of her male colleagues. It is therefore, her 'feminine touch' that makes her writings appear to some as less erudite or objective than those they are used to reading.

When adopting what is called an interpretative approach, one that brings much of the worldview of the author into the story he/she wants to tell, I also have, for the sake of fluency, slightly edited some of the quotations without, so I hope, affecting their accuracy or meaning. The quotations from Gertrude Bell's writings were here selected, pulled together, and finally woven into a tapestry that aims to render as coherent a picture of the period as possible. It should be noted here that when I chose the storytelling approach to relate Gertrude Bell's life, I also believed that it would permit me to highlight themes and motifs that would, otherwise, be over-shadowed by less important events that usually form the skeleton of strictly chronological accounts. In sum, I felt privileged to have discovered some of the hidden layers of Gertrude Bell's story and to present them to an audi-ence wider than the usual circle of scholars and students of the modern Middle East, while following her very personal way of approaching history: with a twinkle in her eye and a lush palette of chromatic tones to flesh out her descriptions of life itself.

Not much has been said yet about her most remarkable feature – her immense energy – and the way she used it to project herself into the British and the Iraqi political arenas – promulgating what seemed to her to be con-nected interests. Without admitting it in her vivacious and gossip-laden letters, she saw these interests as compatible, positioning herself in the role of a bridging factor between both worlds and, to some extent, as a 'shaper of history'.

Was she suitable for the role? In spite of the different opinions regarding her personal virtues and failures, and the controversial debate on the role of individuals in shaping history, there is much to say about the pretentious-ness and, for some, the arrogance of the 'carriers of civilisation' when attempting to impose their views and thoughts on the local population. One can say that her finest act – her input in the creation of a modern Iraq – also reflected in her zig-zagging positions, which revealed an acute need of approval, and a behaviour that revealed a haughty and sometimes too severe criticism of men and situations. For, as much as she was cultured, articulate, and overtly strong, she was also vulnerable and excessively romantic at times, and too convinced of the validity of her mission to always make the right choices and decisions. She was, one could still argue, ill equipped for failure; unable, sometimes, to correctly visualise the differ-ences between history and mythology, and the way they could affect the judgement of agents in history. One could even say that she overestimated their role without internalising their limitations.

Her letters turned, with time, into documents where the meaning seems to have shifted through the decades. That is because her writing touches the later reader at different levels, the rational and the emotional, giving the illusion of closeness, of almost active participation in the events described. And as a result, her descriptions and opinions give rise to more genuine and intensive reactions.

Underneath the hard-core political opinions, Gertrude Bell's 'orientalist' vision of the East[4] emerges once again, rekindling mixed views and renewing debates. However, the magic of her writing seems to have lasted, skipping two or three generations and connecting again, unexpectedly, with the younger among us, the generation that grew up and matured in its views between and after the Gulf wars. Younger women rediscover Gertrude Bell and connect to her great courage and skilful ability to make things happen, qualities that seem so naturally feminine to them today.

While revisiting Gertrude Bell's unedited letters and documents that contain information and quotations that do not appear in the edited texts on line and in print, I stumbled across the snapshots of a life. While trying to assemble them into some coherent form, I could not but reconsider the meaning of biography as we understand it today, and refer to it not just as the resolution of a subject's life but rather, as Elie Kedourie (*The Anglo-Arab Labyrinth*, 1978) saw it, as 'another product of the historian's craft that seeks to restore . . . the meanings, thoughts and actions, now dead and gone, which once upon a time were the designs and choices of living [women and] men'.[5]

Prologue

Gertrude Bell's childhood and youth coincided with the last three decades of the Victorian era, years marked in Britain's history by a growing awareness that the formerly idealised Pax Britannica was taking on new meanings. Britain's command of the sea, its direct and indirect control of ports, straits, and hinterlands, had endowed the British with a sense of pride and responsibility.

The idea of the world as a reflection of Europe's designs and a mirror of its flickering moods filled the hearts of the men and women assembled in the vicinity of Hyde Park on that sunny morning in June 1897. For the participants in the festivities marking Queen Victoria's Diamond Jubilee, there still was the feeling of a common destiny displayed by the embroidered jackets of the British officers serving in the overseas colonies. For them, imperialism was more than a political mission. It was a collective state of mind.[1] This colourful parade of exotic uniforms marching to the sound of military bands and popular cheering seemed to be the climax of an era of worldwide British influence spanning almost a century.

The popular sense of a common purpose, of the universal acceptance of Britain's dominion was an illusion, however. The territories assembled under the British Crown (spreading from Africa to the Middle East, India, Afghanistan, Singapore, Australia, some Pacific islands and Canada) were a kaleidoscope of languages and creeds, and the conviction that Britain retained the secret of good governance was a long-lived fallacy. The belief that a delicate equilibrium between the heterogeneous populations in the colonies could be reached only through Britain's mediation, and that the presence of Britain's officers prevented the colonies from sinking into chaos, had already been challenged. The export of British standards to different societies, considered the sacred mission of the Pax Britannica, had been overshadowed by the roughness of the imperial enterprise. The excessive romantic idea behind it stood in contrast with the feelings it aroused. Either ruled by Britain's soldiers, or by the arrogance of British officials, the populations' reaction outweighed all the initial intentions that Britain might have had. Seeds of discontent in the colonies contrasted with the idea of the enterprise as a whole. And yet, the British authorities refused to consider the alternative to their presence. Infatuated by their self-image as carriers of progress, they still believed that Britain's economic and strategic interests took precedence over the needs, the feelings and the pride of the peoples themselves. But all these considerations had been forgotten in the turmoil of the festivities on that sunny morning in June.

The export of British capital in the form of investments in gold mines, plantations and railroads was still viewed by the believers in Britain's superiority not only as an outlet for British investors, but as a blessing for the colonies themselves. The diffusion of European technology – an outgrowth of the flourishing applied sciences in Britain and Europe – was also seen by them as a proof of Britain's keen desire to offer assistance to less-technically advanced societies. This version of imperialism as a lever for progress disguised, though, its true motivation: the search for new sources of raw materials, of oil for the navy, and of new markets for manufactured goods that had dominated Britain's overseas economic activities during generations.[2] This simplistic vision, which attempted to validate imperialism per se, in fact carried the seeds of its own failure.

However, the export of capital that led British investors to finance the exploration of gold mines and plantations, lending money through modern banking and insurance services, represented only one side of the coin. Britain's need to guarantee exclusive trade rights in Asia, Africa and the Pacific pushed Britain to gradually drop the notion of 'unofficial empire'[3] (based on the new territories' dependence on Britain's economic supremacy) and opt for a more direct form of political intervention.[4] In other words, Britain coupled economic penetration with tighter political dominance. This idea of 'new imperialism' would also alter Britain's vision of the best way to protect the route to India. India's importance in the eyes of the British grew after 1877, when Disraeli bestowed on Queen Victoria the title of Empress of India, an act that implied Britain's permanent presence in the subcontinent. Believing that Britain would remain the world's greatest power as long as it ruled over India, British policy makers subordinated all other imperial interests to a fluent communication with the 'jewel in the crown'.[5]

The opening of a shorter sea route to India with the completion of the Suez Canal in 1869 had refocused Britain's attention on Egypt.[6] The control of this section of the route to India then became as important as Britain's economic interest in Egypt. Without formally annexing the country after its invasion in 1882 on behalf of the canal's creditors, Britain started running the country through an agent and consul general in spite of Egypt's formal allegiance to the sultan. Britain's idea of imperialism had repercussions for generations of young Westerners who saw the East as a 'career'.[7] For many, the East represented a range of opportunities, of temporary escapes or of permanent evasions to the boundless vastitudes of an empire where the sun never sets.[8] Questions of personal status and prestige were more easily resolved abroad than in a rigidly structured society like the British one.

The idea of the empire as a personal and collective adventure became even stronger when members of the ascendant middle classes began to share the pleasures and responsibilities offered by Britain's overseas campaigns. The empire's wide horizons also provided a sense of freedom indispensable to the personal and collective equilibrium of such secluded islanders as the British. The British were thrilled by the opportunities abroad as described in the classics of the time: Sir Charles Dilke's *Great Britain* (1870), Sir John Seeley's *The Expansion of the Empire* (1883), the novels of Rider Haggard (1856–1925) and the verse and prose of Rudyard Kipling (1865–1936).[9] However, this romantic view of the East concealed a false sense of power and cultural superiority that, from then on, characterised the relations between West and East, becoming the very cause for further clashes between both worlds.

But again, it did not seem to affect the optimism of the participants in the festivities of Queen Victoria's Diamond Jubilee. They seemed to overlook the palpable threats to Britain's sense of superiority and, in a larger measure, to Europe's political equilibrium: Germany's technical progress, France's increasing political influence and the emergence of the USA as a big player in the international arena.

Changes were also felt in the domestic arena where new elites rose to positions of power and responsibility. In fact, from 1860, the India Office, the Colonial Office, the Home Office, the Treasury and finally the Foreign Office opened up to members of these new elites who had gradually conquered position in the tight system of patronage and privilege, challenging the aristocracy's monopoly of the role of 'shapers' of England's future.[10] More attuned to technology, to private initiative, the members of the new elites approached Britain's policy abroad with a more direct and assertive personal style.

Riding the wave of economic expansion, the new elites pervaded the imperial enterprise with a sense of political and economic urgency. This gradual shift, which distinguished the final decades of the Victorian era from earlier ones was linked, among others, to the collapse of land values[11] that undermined the aristocracy's territorial base and diminished their assurance of being the owners of the Earth and history makers.[12] Gradually, members of the rising classes engaged in the imperial mission, adopting the idea of the empire as an expression of the 'special genius of the Anglo-Saxon race'.[13] It was an idea that implied excellence, performance, physical fitness and endurance, and some well-mannered arrogance. Originally an affectation of the aristocracy, the 'stiff upper lip', along with other acquired mannerisms, was adopted by the rising elites and carried with them to the colonies.

*   *   *

Gertrude Margaret Lowthian Bell, the daughter of one of the most eminent members of the rising elites, was a vivid example of the new spirit of enterprise that spilled over from the aristocracy to Britain's financial and industrial upper classes. Imbued with a sense of responsibility for national causes and possessing enough personal confidence to contest inherited privilege, Gertrude Bell was to perform one of the most audacious tasks in the Middle East. Her double legacy, a reflection of the supreme confidence with which she started her mission and of the delusion that shaped the end of her career should now be explained in slightly different terms. Not just a 'child of fortune' but an ambitious woman who craved for affection, that, so she thought, would only be earned by measuring up in new challenges. But the higher the aspirations, the lower the deceptions. While embodying – perhaps better than others – the need to understand, conquer and in some way dominate the East, Gertrude Bell was also trapped in the belief that her identity depended on her ability to participate in the imperial adventure.

Born at Washington Hall in the county of Durham on 14 July 1868, Gertrude Margaret Lowthian Bell was descended from one of the richest and most enlightened families of her time. She was the granddaughter of Sir Isaac Lowthian Bell, a pioneer in England's steel industry, and the daughter of Hugh Bell and Maria Shield Bell of Newcastle upon Tyne. The marriage of a scion of Durham's steel industry and a daughter of Newcastle's merchant bourgeoisie represented another knot in the expanding social net of the rising classes.

Maria Bell, a young woman of 'delicate health and frail beauty',[14] died in April 1871 after the birth of her second child, Maurice Hugh Lowthian Bell. Gertrude was not yet three years old, and the full effect that her mother's premature death had on her remains unknown. At first glance one could imagine that her personal loss at such a sensitive period of life increased her sense of independence and self-reliance. It would take a closer look into Gertrude's life as it unfolded to see that other, less effective personality traits resulted from it.

Hugh Bell's second marriage, six years later, to Florence Evelyn Eleonore Oliffe, the daughter of Sir Joseph Oliffe, the physician of the British Embassy in Paris, forced young Gertrude to confront new familial situations and cope with new, contradictory, emotions. Living with her father, her aunt Ada Bell, and her brother Maurice at Redcar, on the Yorkshire coast, young Gertrude used to send short letters to Florence Oliffe, telling her of her and Maurice's adventures. Signing her letters to Florence 'your affectionate little friend', young Gertrude seemed eager to bring Florence closer to the family's circle. Hoping, intuitively, that Florence would fill the void left by her mother, Gertrude seemed apparently open and receptive. The birth of Florence's children – Hugo, Elsa and Mary (or Molly) – changed the familial scenery, however. Now the eldest of five children,[15] Gertrude had to excel in all kind of activities in order to retain a position of leadership. Determined and strong-willed, she would climb trees, jump from walls and challenge the younger members of her family to other courageous adventures.

In 1883, at the age of fifteen, Gertrude was sent to Queen's College in London, a high school for upper-class girls. Three years later, she enrolled as a student of history at Lady Margaret Hall in Oxford, and was amongst the first women students to attend one of Oxford's most-praised men's colleges. From her writings and the written opinions of her colleagues it appears that she was not intimidated by gender differences. Gertrude Bell was 'the most brilliant creature who ever came amongst us', wrote Janet Hogarth, Gertrude's close friend at the time. Gertrude was noted for 'her timeless energy, splendid vitality, her unlimited capacity for work, for talk, for play'.[16] She was 'brilliant and opinionated, childlike and mature' and, as Janet Hogarth observed then, naive and enthusiastic when dealing with ideas but sceptical and self-assured when interacting with people.

With her quick mind and sure command of facts, Gertrude Bell immediately stood out in class and in all sport activities. She swam, rowed and played tennis, danced, acted and yet managed to obtain a 'first' in history and archaeology. This drive for excellence became her personal trademark. Unusually intense and assertive for a woman of her time, Gertrude tempered an otherwise serious demeanour with sprinkles of humour and irony.

1. Gertrude Bell, a serious and very intense twelve-year-old.

Never tongue-tied or shy, she used to challenge the highest authorities when her opinion differed from theirs. She 'shocked' Oxford's dons at her *viva voce* examination when she dared to contest the opinion of Professor S. R. Gardiner on his estimate of Charles I and the Stuarts. Not less were they impressed, so Florence reported later, by her assurance and by her 'crossed slender feet in neat brown shoes'.[17] As there are no recorded or published versions of Gertrude's views on the issue, one can deduce that Florence's observations pointed mainly at Gertrude's courage and at the fact that she dared to speak her mind and challenge one of the leading experts in the field in a head-on, unconventional way.

Although she subscribed to the social conventions of the late Victorian years, Gertrude did not hesitate to circumvent them when it served her purposes. Too daring on certain occasions and rather manipulative on others, Gertrude's tendency to question authority without breaking with convention seemed a characteristic of the ascendant elites who had made their way to the top of the social pyramid without, so it seemed then, disturbing its equilibrium. While teasing colleagues and her teachers with witty remarks, Gertrude Bell matured into a strong-willed and intellectually courageous young woman. There were, however, very few professional opportunities for educated young women like her at the time. Tall and slim, with a sensitive face, thick light-auburn hair, and piercing grey eyes, Gertrude conveyed strength and vivacity, some intensity as well as fragility. Without corresponding to an ideal of beauty, she shone with intelligence and humour. Her preoccupation with physical fitness – corresponding to the dictates of physical and intellectual excellence prevalent at the time – only added to her attractiveness by striking a 'supra-gender' chord. Like her male colleagues, she would display bravery, discipline and a sense for fair play, but she was already then a solo player. Her concealed fragility appeared, however, as a haughty and patronising attitude. An antithesis to her sisters, Gertrude developed, with the years, a scorn for the ideal of femininity they represented. This contempt for other women's traditional role in society seemed to indicate a difficulty in conforming with a woman's low expectations at that time.

The years at Oxford helped Gertrude to grow in 'her judgement of men and affairs'[18] and sharpened her perception of the changes occurring in Britain at the time. Among them were ideas that spread from the natural sciences to the social domain. Without having expressed herself specifically on the issue, her life story seems to indicate that the idea of 'the survival of the fittest', the basic assumption of social Darwinism, first applied to the domain of human activities and later translated to competition between nations, could have appealed to her.

Class conflicts had also brought the 'discovery' of poverty and the predicament of the working classes. Some of these themes inspired the works of Charles Dickens, George Meredith and Thomas Hardy. At the time, Britain's overseas colonies were also depicted as recipients of the lower classes, who found in exile a solution to their plights at home, as Coketown's inhabitants in Dickens' *Hard Times*. Some decades earlier, the struggle of the lower classes had been explored in Karl Marx's *Manifest de Kommunistischen Partei* (*The Communist Manifesto*) (1848) and *Das Kapital* (*Capital*) (1867), two works that would gather momentum at the turning of the century.

New ideas enlivened the debates in London's intellectual circles, where Gertrude Bell mixed in her post-Oxford years. Following the expansion of academic life in Britain and its growing influence on society, this intellectual outburst, which grew in the last decades of the Victorian era, culminated in 1895 with the establishment of the London School of Economics (LSE). The spirit of free enquiry and open reflection that characterised this modern institution, in defiance of the rigidity of Oxford, Cambridge and Durham, spilled over into the debates taking place outside university walls in which Gertrude Bell was particularly active.

On the other hand, this flowering of liberal ideas and rational thought also inspired mystic and totalitarian threads. Appealing to the instinctive and the emotional, notions of racial purity and national character emerged in embryonic works such as *The Foundations of the Nineteenth Century* (1899), by Houston Stewart Chamberlain, Richard Wagner's son-in-law. These dissonant chords would grow louder and eventually shatter the illusions of political harmony at home and in the continent.

Gertrude Bell's exposure to these trends enhanced her ability to reassess assumptions and to meet new intellectual challenges. During her first visit to Europe in 1888 at the invitation of Lady Lascelles, Florence Bell's sister and wife of Sir Frank Lascelles, Britain's minister in Bucharest, Gertrude sensed the tension inherent in an artificially maintained peace. The cheerfulness and glamour that ostensibly characterised Europe at the end of the nineteenth century now seemed to her nothing more than a veneer, barely disguising the unrest simmering underneath. In one of her characteristic unsolicited interventions, Gertrude Bell amazed the Lascelles by adventuring her opinion on the dangers awaiting Central Europe. '. . . Il me semble, Monsieur, que vous n'avez pas saisi l'esprit du peuple Allemand',[19] she reportedly exclaimed, alluding to the possibility of an armed conflict in Europe.

In fact, Bismarck's fall in 1890, and with it the illusion of a pacified and self-contained Germany, brought to an end a whole system of alliances and counter-alliances engineered to prevent France's political and military ascendance. In parallel, France's designs on Alsace-Lorraine, together with the flamboyance of its republican appeal, spilled over from the long Franco-German conflict, turning Europe into a major arena of confrontation. Moreover, the crumbling in 1887 of the Dreikaiserbund (the imperial alliance between Germany, Austria-Hungary and Russia), the rapprochement of France and Russia, and the formation in 1882 of the Triple Alliance (in which Italy replaced Russia), polarised Europe's political system, sowing the seeds of a general discontent that would in the end lead to war.

Discerning the nationalistic feelings simmering beneath the exaggerated *joie de vivre* she had found in Bucharest, and sensing the effects of an artificially contained Eastern Question, Gertrude also seized the possible implications of an unresolved situation in the Balkans. The rivalries created by a series of nationalistic uprisings increased the tensions in Europe. The Christian subjects of a faltering Ottoman Empire (Serbs, Greeks, Romanians and Bulgarians) appealed to Russia and Austria, two neighbouring empires that were just waiting to take advantage of the Ottomans' weakness and shatter their position in Europe. Their ambitions were countered by Britain's opposition to any attempts to dismantle the Ottoman Empire without, however, becoming directly involved in Europe's political conflicts.

Britain's 'splendid isolation', the outcome of Lord Salisbury's pragmatic policy of non-interference was, though, considered by some an unaffordable luxury. Although capable of appraising the real significance of the historic moment and of its political possibilities, young Gertrude was still reluctant to believe, in the early 1890s, that war was imminent. The ripening of conditions that would lead to political upheaval in Europe would correspond to her own personal growth and maturation. When the First World War finally broke out, she was ready to play a definitive role in channelling its after-effects.

The dismemberment of three empires – the German, the Austria-Hungarian and the Ottoman – and the aspirations of new nations to statehood counted among the war's consequences. This book is an account of Gertrude Bell's role in shaping a new Middle East following the crumbling of the Ottoman Empire. More specifically, it follows her personal adventure that started with her visit to Ha'il, Central Arabia in 1913, and culminated in 1926 when Iraq had already become a political reality.

As we follow Gertrude Bell through her thoughts, beliefs and aspirations, as documented in her letters and diaries, we discover a process of a dual creation: the 'invention' of modern Iraq and Gertrude Bell's 'reinvention' of herself. Viewed and reinterpreted from today's perspective they acquire a new, multifaceted, meaning. Fascinating as it is in its own right, Gertrude Bell's adventure also reveals a forgotten aspect of 'Orientalism' – one that tells the stories of the agents of the imperial idea and the personal price they paid for their belief in their ability to change the course of history. Caught up in the process, they were condemned for the excesses of their ideals. More often than not, they themselves misunderstood the real purpose of their actions, manipulated as they were by their own governments.

For the agents of the Great Powers the Orient was 'an idea that had a history, a tradition of thought, and imagery'.[20] The idea was, in fact, more powerful than their perception of it. Admired at times, emulated at others, but rarely tolerated by the peoples in the territories coveted by the Crown, the representatives of the British empire almost invariably left the Middle East embittered and disillusioned.

Gertrude Bell never left. She preferred to stay and die in Iraq, where she had become so close to the people of the state she had helped to create. By following Gertrude Bell in her double adventure, we rediscover Iraq and its peoples, their conflicts, failed attempts, forgotten roads. And we find again the Middle East in its incessant search for national expression.

PART I

THE JOURNEY

CHAPTER 1

'Light of Mine Eyes and Harvest of My Heart'

Gertrude saluting at parting – very gallantly she stands there.
All one's life to remember.

Elizabeth Robins

The caravan left Damascus on 16 December 1913, heading for Ha'il in Central Arabia. 'We shall need seventeen camels, at the cost of £13 a piece, £50 for food, £50 for presents (clocks, keffiyehs, and cotton clothes), that comes together to £321 . . . £80 to take with me, and £200 to give to a Najd merchant who lives here in return for a letter of credit which will permit me to draw the sum in Ha'il', Gertrude wrote to her father before leaving.[1] The total was £600. She had no more than £250, so she had to ask her father's help to borrow the sum and discount it from the next year's allowance.

What had compelled her to start this voyage is not so clear. Many reasons combined: curiosity, a taste for challenge and adventure and a need to fly away – to escape. And so Gertrude found herself heading for Ghadir and Qasr al-Burqa, the first stops on the south-eastern route to Ha'il, the Banu Rashid's city-fortress in the midst of the barren desert.

This was another world. Silent and colourful, with predominant yellow, amber and auburn tones and subtones. The colour spectrum of the desert differed hugely from England's summer hues. Memories of English summers – the patchwork of fields – followed Gertrude in the desert. She missed the contrasts: the richness of colourful fields and the nakedness of Northumberland's shores, the wilderness, the thin grass and the scant turfs bending in the wind. She remembered Hadrian's Wall, the last vestige of the Roman defences on England's soil, a vivid monument of Rome's lost military power; past glories that 'dwindled to the shadow of a shadow'[2] and reminded the visitor of other failed invasions and of the precariousness of military adventures carried to foreign countries. Less concerned with the history lessons that could be drawn from the abandoned Roman ruins, Gertrude related now mainly to the sense of emptiness they aroused in her. This sense of void was also connected to the memories of the then Captain Charles Hotham Montagu Doughty-Wylie ('Dick' as he was known to his friends) and his visit in August to Rounton, the Bells' residence near Northallerton. From this previous summer, she had retained some memories that were not easy to carry. These memories remained as vivid and pertinent as the squawk of crows and the grunt and gurgle of the camels. Dick had found her in the garden, where she often took refuge – the garden where colours ranged from white to red, purple, and near black. A garden where yellow crocuses and primroses sprout in winter and where the white clematis gracing the old pinkish bricks of the garden walls set off the purple irises that emerged from behind the rocks during summers. These were the black irises of Moab, brought back from one of her visits to the East. In spring the rose-pink buds of the Japanese cherry trees contrasted with the climbing roses that scrambled over the archway. Farther away there was the tower, the way to which was paved with pots, spilling over with yellow, orange and red seasonal flowers.

To walk through the garden was to walk through time, to connect with other summers, those of her childhood. The grass was green then, the birds had nested and the swallows seemed to have forgotten to return to the south, not sensing the change of season. The foliage was full and intense, spilling moisture and freshness. Gertrude knew that it was Dick's coming to the garden and their walking to the tower that had led her to seek refuge in the desert.

But even in the desert, the colours and sounds of Rounton's days and the visions and fears of its nights invaded the surroundings. There she was – the journey planned, the itinerary traced, the direction chosen. But she had the feeling that the desert was an interim choice. Unlike her previous journeys to the desert, this voyage involved introspection, 'fleeting impressions caught and hardened out of all knowing', as she wrote in the journal she would later send to Dick. These images connected her with her first voyage to the desert around Teheran when she was a young woman. In the desert of her youth, 'a garden suddenly sprang from a little pool of cool water, [and] a tiny house stood with slabs of looking-glass, blue-tiled, as if echoing the colours and sounds of running water and fountains'. This was the house where she first discovered eastern hospitality.[3]

The Najd of Arabia – to which she headed now – was different from Teheran's desert. 'Grave and circumspect, it was not given to distractions', she would later explain. Containing only sand, and 'white stretches of salt . . . and sand again, the Najd was the real thing'. Solitude and nothingness. The Najd also differed from the Syrian Desert, where the ruins of Palmyra, 'with masses of columns ranging into long avenues . . . lying broken on the sand, or pointing one solitary finger to Heaven', hinted at the existence of a previous life. Images of a remote and vivid past also sprang into her mind when she recalled the ruins of Petra, where 'temples cut out of a rose red rock seemed transparent when touched by the sun'.[4] Compared to all these, the Najd was 'hard and insolent, rude, contemptuous, and invincible'. It defied men, inspired legends, created myths. All religions had emerged from its empty spaces. The Najd she traversed, heading toward the Rubʿ al-Khali – the Empty Quarter – seemed to her now not just a place but a state of mind. 'The Najd was defiance, while the Rubʿ al-Khali was solitude and the longing for it', as Dick had said in one of his letters.

Dick's visit to Rounton was meant to be a visit of courtesy. 'In between duties', he then explained, a break between missions. It became, she now knew, a turning point. Their first meeting in Turkey two years earlier had been no more than an encounter between two British wanderers far away from home. Gallant and reserved, Captain Doughty-Wylie (as she had then addressed him) radiated strength and pride, the understated attributes of his uniform – captain of the Royal Welch Fusiliers. Captain Doughty-Wylie reflected the confidence born of accomplished missions. His roughness was tempered, however, by a shyness that Gertrude could easily detect.

Tales of his courage were well known. She herself had heard the details of the military operation he had led that had stopped a massacre of the Armenians in 1908. Taking command of a battalion of Turkish soldiers, he had managed to halt the turbulent Turkish mobs that were about to attack the Christian refugees abandoned by the Ottomans and ignored by the Young Turks. He had handled the affair with confidence and with the certainty that the destinies of others were dependent on his own. The awards he received – the CMG (Companion of the Order of St Michael and St George) and the Turkish Order of Mejidiye – left him indifferent, however. It was his duty, he then explained, to stop the anarchy that usually follows historical shifts.

Doughty-Wylie had also heard the accounts of Gertrude Bell's exploits and the stories of her travels to Asia Minor and to Persia. She reminded him of his uncle, Charles Doughty, whose famous travels were related in *Arabia Deserta*. He also knew her from her earlier books. *The Desert and the Sown*, published some months earlier (1907), or *Safar Nameh: Persian Pictures*, published in 1894 after her first visit to Persia when she was only twenty-six. But nothing she had written up to this first encounter with Doughty-Wylie could equal the works of Charles Doughty or Sir Wilfred S. Blunt. She had not been able to do it 'Doughty's way' – to live with the people, and to tell their tales. The fact that she was a woman had made it impossible,[5] she explained to Dick. But one day, she hoped, with age as her shield, she would leave for the East and write the book of her life. For the time being, she explained, she could only 'ride through the country with a compass in hand, for the map's sake and for nothing else'.[6] She would accept and respect the customs and norms she would find along the way without disguising herself. She would tell tales of the Bedouin, and of the desert's order. And she would let the Bedouin saying: *adat-hu* (it is his custom), become her motto, and her guide while searching for the real story, the one that was yet to be written.

In their first encounter, Gertrude had also explained to Doughty-Wylie that *The Thousand and One Churches*, the book on churches of the Roman Empire, still in print then, was just a description of her archaeological mission to Binbirkilisse in Eastern Turkey with Professor William Ramsey in 1905. 'Why a thousand and one?' Doughty-Wylie had then asked. 'Just a Turkish habit', she explained, of quoting 'a thousand and one' (*bin bir*) when referring to an unknown number. She herself had counted forty-eight ruins of churches at Maden Shehir and Binbirkilisse, while studying the types of basilicas, the cruciform churches and octagonal chambers typical of these constructions. The book's main purpose, she also explained, was to stress Asia Minor's influence on Byzantium and consequently on all Western art.[7]

The book she valued the most however, was her translation of the poems of Shams-al-Din Muhammad Hafiz, the celebrated Persian poet. *The Teachings of Hafiz* had been published in 1897 when Gertrude was only twenty-nine years old. In this book she had focused on the treasures of eastern languages. Together with his poetry, Gertrude Bell had wanted to decipher the mystery of Hafiz's life. 'A mystic, a libertine, a good Muslim or a sceptic' – as defined by one of the greatest experts on Persia, Professor E. G. Browne – or all these by 'turns',[8] Hafiz still remained, for her as for others, a riddle.[9]

2. Gertrude Bell and Fattuh, her loyal Arab servant,
camping in Asia Minor in 1907.

In her translations of Hafiz's *diwan* Gertrude Bell had not just attempted to unravel the secrets of a recently acquired language – Farsi – but she had also tried to use her own words to reflect the verses' hidden meanings. Familiar with Sufism, Gertrude Bell could, already, seize the full meaning of the precept *al-mujaza qantarat al-haqiqa* (the 'phenomenal as a bridge to the real'[10]) and reflect it in her translations while emulating the perfection of the diwan's internal structure.[11] She also knew that in some verses, Hafiz referred to the concrete pleasures of life and not to their symbolism. Inebriation with wine did not always refer to elation with God,[12] and 'if the world was no more than the tangible reflection of its Creator, the reflection in itself was also worthy to be admired',[13] she explained in the book's preface.

In other passages, however, the allegorical spoke more strongly: in them, 'wine' referred to the spirit of God poured out for his disciples. The 'tavern' was the place of worship; the 'tavern keeper' was the *murshid* (religious guide); the Prophet was the cypress or the sacred tree, the head of the Sufi order; and the 'True Beloved', the spirit of truth, of beauty, was God himself. All these themes had been exposed in Bell's translations of one of Hafiz's most famous poems:

> Arise, oh cup-bearer, rise! and bring
> To lips that are thirsting the bowl they praise
> . . . . . .
> Hear the tavern-keeper who counsels you:
> With wine, with red wine, your prayer carpet, dye!

In another poem she explained, the rose was the symbol of beauty and the nightingale the poet, the only one who understood the rose's secret language:

> The nightingale with drops of his heart's blood
> Had nourished the red rose, then came a wind,
> And catching at the boughs in envious mood,
> A hundred thorns about his heart entwined . . .

Extracts of Hafiz's verses still had great impact on her. One particular passage seemed very relevant when she recalled Doughty-Wylie's visit to Rounton:

> Light of mine eyes and harvest of my heart,
> And mine at least in changeless memory!
> Ah, when he found it easy to depart,
> He left the harder pilgrimage to me!

She wondered whether her version of these poems would satisfy the purists and pass the test of time,[14] or would it 'vanish like snow upon the desert's dusty face'?[15] In fact, it did not matter much, she realised, after having matured in her understanding of life and men. It was the text that counted, the logic of its structure and the magic of its meaning that were important, not the critic's need to prove his mastery over the text. She didn't know then that, years later, Professor Browne himself would praise her translations of Hafiz as 'the finest and most truly poetical renderings of any Persian poet ever produced in the English language'.[16]

The mystic images of Hafiz's verses followed her in the desert, blending with other memories of past times in the East, their apparent meanings shifting in some cases.

> The days of absence and the bitter nights
> Of separation, all are at the end!
> Where is the influence of the star that blights
> My hope? The omen answers: At the end!'

What was 'the omen' in Hafiz's poetry? she would wonder, and what was 'the end' that the omen referred to? Gertrude herself was connected mainly to the beauty of Hafiz's poetic messages, not to their religious implications. A staunch atheist, she would dismiss the search for God, or the truth, as exposed in Hafiz's verses. She believed, however, in moments of truth; defined moments that carried a significance of their own, as during the ceremony of the fire at the Church of the Holy Sepulchre in Jerusalem, which she witnessed in the spring of 1900. 'Suddenly a man came out from the darkness, running with a torch held high over his head', she wrote then in a letter home, describing the Greeks and Armenians pushing to get closer to the torch. 'And then it happened . . . the fire leapt to the roof . . . and people were washing their faces in the fire.'[17] The memory of that moment and the emotions it had aroused connected her back to the memory of Doughty-Wylie's visit to Rounton. From then on Doughty-Wylie became Dick in her letters.

Some days after the visit to Rounton, Dick wrote to her from his bachelor's residence at 29 Half Moon Street, the officers' club near Hyde Park. 'I am so glad you took me to Rounton. I so much enjoyed the people, the place, the garden, the woods . . . everything . . . and I am glad you told me things and found you could talk to me . . . I've always – ever since those Turkey days – wanted to be a friend of yours'.[18] He was then waiting for his wife to join him 'till we see the hows and whys and wheres . . .'. And yet he asked her to write back to him: 'While I am alone, let's be alone.'[19]

They would only meet in 'thoughts and fancies', he then explained, asking her to keep the small book she had given him at Rounton in which 'all was written'. Pondering about the moment in which their hands met on the book's cover and the emotions it aroused, Dick begged Gertrude to go on with her life 'being wise and splendid', avoiding encouraging her.

He would always be her friend, he promised then, while dismissing all other possible meanings to what had happened that evening in Rounton. 'We might have been man and woman as God made us and been happy . . .' but that would not have changed the situation they were in. They would have had to part again and 'there [would be] the afterwards sometimes to be afraid of . . .' he explained. Dick's memories of that night at Rounton were also punctuated with tormented images. These were images of a 'shadowy woman . . . hostile and alarming, that swept across my bed like a hawk . . . The woman meant attack', he explained, 'and I wanted the light.' Who were the ghosts? Gertrude wondered when pondering about the hidden meanings of these images. Were they the shadows of a 'physical desire emanating from a room only a few doors away'? she asked herself, echoing Dick's own interpretation.

If his desires or, as he then called them, 'the vehicle of the fire of the mind' could not be appeased, Dick explained some time later, he would take refuge in solitude. He saw solitude 'on every hill, in every forest', and had welcomed it while transmitting to Gertrude some of his thoughts and his longings for it. 'And you, too, know the goddess well, for no one but a worshipper could have written what you did about the hush of dawn in the garden . . .'.[20]

Gertrude shared Dick's need to be alone. She herself had chosen solitude when she decided to 'cut the threads' linking her with the world, 'leaving just one thread uncut' – the one running through the diary of her desert journey. 'The world must get along without me for a bit', she explained to her closest friend, Valentine Chirol, the well-known correspondent of *The Times*, now in Delhi. 'Domnul' ('gentleman' in Romanian; an allusion to his gentlemanly manners), as she called him since Bucharest days, had become her confidant and intellectual counterpart. She would find refuge 'in the long days of camel riding and the long evenings of winter camping', wondering whether she would still be able to 'carry it through the next day'. But when the light of the early mornings penetrated her heart, she would 'bear pain without crying out . . .'.[21]

And this journey to Ha'il, this cutting of threads, this refuge in silence became a voyage into her inner self.

CHAPTER 2

'She Had Known Ruptures,
She Had Known the Whole'

Gertrude was forty-five at the time of this journey. Tired of facing 'back-wards and forwards along the floor of hell', she was in search of peace of mind. She would find it in the desert and connect more easily to the memories of her earlier days. There she brought to mind the carefree life of her twenties, when everything seemed to be within reach. She recalled the parties, the dances, the ballrooms lit by the glitter of chandeliers, the Ascot races, the theatre and other social events of London's season. She remembered the political circles, the cultural reunions at the Bells' residence at Sloane Street, the debates and the controversies of optimistic rationalism in a *fin-de-siècle* atmosphere of apprehensiveness. She recollected her first encounter with Valentine Chirol in Bucharest in December 1888 when she was a guest of the Lascelles. 'Domnul' would soon become her closest friend; he was then the correspondent of *The Times* in East Europe and opened doors for her to the most exclusive social circles in Europe. Gertrude would attend the events of '*la crème de la crème*', as her cousin Florence Lascelles used to describe the European fashionable elite. She would also get acquainted with the serious world of European diplomacy, as her uncle, the ambassador Sir Frank Lascelles, called it while teaching her how to avoid the political minefields she would find in her way.

Bucharest at the turn of the century was a centre of frantic political activity disguised in a vaudevillian atmosphere of balls, receptions and musical events. But the veneer of conviviality barely covered the unrest simmering underneath. Gertrude easily grasped Europe's artificially maintained peace, but she also knew that the conditions for war had not yet matured and that there was still some time to travel, to write, to discover and to describe new worlds.

Gertrude's political flair and intellectual maturity contrasted even then with her juvenile enthusiasm, sense of humour, and outspoken curiosity. The mastery of the *pas de patineur*, a variant of the *pas de quatre*, seemed to her at the time just as important as other social and intellectual activities. She visited art galleries and churches in Italy in 1894, and listened to Bruckner and Wagner in Germany in 1897, again as a guest of the Lascelles. In December 1897 she left for a round-the-world trip with her brother Maurice. Her cheerful and yet authoritative manner, enlivened by a daring straightforwardness, sharp insight and occasional intensity, attracted many new acquaintances, among them Charles Hardinge, later Lord Hardinge of Penshurst, one of Domnul's friends.

In those days, she still remembered they were all concerned with the decline of Britain's position in Europe. Britain's naval supremacy, which had made its worldwide commercial dominance possible, had been questioned by the naval rearmament of France, Russia and Italy. It was mainly the French and Russian naval alliance, contracted in 1892, that had endangered Britain's control of the Mediterranean and threatened the sea route to India. But the side effect of Britain's economic and strategic dependence on India was India's growing influence on England's daily life.

The colourfulness of the overseas territories, their fauna and flora and their ethnic objects, had changed the decor of official buildings and private homes to the point that even the queen's private surroundings were decorated with giant palm baskets, tiger skins, and elephant ivories.[1] But much of the image of Britain's 'imperial extravaganza' – diffused by the India exhibit that had taken place in Earl's Court in 1895 – vanished with Queen Victoria's death on 22 January 1901.

Gertrude attended the queen's funeral on 2 February: 'It was wonderfully fine and simple', she reported then to Domnul.

> The blaze of colours in the midst of the black crowd. The splendid heralds and the low gun carriages, all red and gold, with the flag and embroideries and the crown and the orbs lying on it . . . extraordinarily martial and royal . . . And the crowd of kings and kings to be . . . a long procession of gorgeous uniforms.[2]

And when it was over, 'the people dispersed, very quietly'.

Attracted to India, as were other members of the upper classes and aristocracy, and to the excessively romantic idea of the empire, Gertrude left for the subcontinent to attend the *durbar*, the traditional Indian ceremony organised after Queen Victoria's death by Lord Curzon, India's viceroy. It was an attempt to strike a note of continuity with the durbar of 1878 that had followed Queen Victoria's coronation as Empress of India, and signal a natural transfer of power and authority to Victoria's son, King Edward VII. This was a round-the-world journey with Hugo, her half-brother, with whom she had a very different relationship to the one she had with Maurice, her full-brother. Maurice, rather introvert and quiet, seemed to accept without much debate Gertrude's authority. With Hugo, her relationship was different. In 1902, Gertrude was thirty-four, very certain in her rationalism, and somewhat scornful of Hugo's religious beliefs. Impatient and arrogant at times, Gertrude failed to take advantage of what was meant to be a journey of reunion, after one of her long absences from home, to draw closer to Hugo. Having tacitly agreed to disagree on conflicting issues, particularly philosophy and religion, Gertrude and Hugo expressed the contrasting views and influences prevalent in their environment at the time, influences that often led members of the same family to adopt diametrically opposed philosophical views and lifestyles. Their trip to India left different imprints on both of them. A land of exotic gardens and marbled courtyards, coloured bazaars and numerous amenities, India remained a colonial reverie.[3]

Arriving in Bombay in December 1902 after visiting Jaipur and Fatterpore Sikri, Gertrude tried to communicate with the people in Hindustani. Only by speaking their language, she believed, could she capture the tones and subtones of people's intentions and designs. An intellectual exercise at first, it seemed insufficient to let her cross cultural borders, however. Nonetheless, Gertrude would describe the contrasts between the two cultures with wit and humour: 'It's disconcerting to find that an Indian, when he wishes to ascribe ideal movement to a woman, calls her "elephant gaited"... an eye like a gazelle, a waist like a lion, and a gait like an elephant',[4] she explained to Florence in a letter written on the train from Alwar to Delhi. After discovering other tips for 'good elephantship', she finally reached the camp where the durbar was to take place. There she found 'a town of tents stretching for miles with streets, wide roads, telegraphs, running water and hospitals . . .',[5] their modernity contrasting with the traditional ways of a population still riding 'every sort of animal'.

Lord Curzon, known for his love for theatrical displays, had retained the magnificence of the ancient ceremony. Believing that India's inhabitants were sensitive to pomp and circumstance and would more easily accept British rule if the sumptuousness of their predecessors, the Persian-speaking moghuls, was preserved, the British indulged in luxury and extravagance. The viceroy's surroundings in Delhi were therefore even more elaborate and luxurious than those of the British monarch in London.[6] But it was precisely the lavishness of the ceremony that made Gertrude aware of the inherent contradictions of the British presence in India. Her descriptions of the durbar illustrated the contradictions of the entire imperial adventure: it 'began with a procession of veterans . . . cheered by the public; followed by twenty or thirty gurkas . . . some bent double with years'. They were followed by 'the soldiers and the native cavalry and then the cadet corps – all sons of Rajas'. Behind them, on elephants, the 'Viceroy and Lady Curzon, followed by the Connaughts representing King Edward', and then 'a troop of some hundred rajas, . . . a glittering mass of gold and jewels' preceding a group of elephants with 'tassels of jewels hanging from their ears'.[7]

Punjabis, Sikhs, Tamils, Baluchis, and Nepalis, all dressed in their traditional garments and adorned with centuries-old ornaments, marched in the streets of Delhi. The show was a 'gorgeous fantasy'[8] in her view, and a symbol of Britain's misconceived attitude toward the East. The combination of imported modernity and borrowed tradition was meant to convey to the peoples of India not just the image of communion with the British Crown but also the intention of unity and shared identity. It was an exercise that would try to conceal, momentarily at least, Britain's de facto attempt to make the subcontinent yield to its political aims.

Gertrude felt, however, the lack of spontaneity and enthusiasm of the participants. In her eyes the durbar was no more than a political extravaganza that proved to be an expensive burden for the rajas themselves.[9] For her, the durbar suggested divisiveness more than unity. 'A magnificent alienation, an industrious oblivion and an impressionist set up',[10] the durbar also set the scene for power games and status quarrels as when 'the Nizam of Hyderabad entered the horseshoe through the entrance reserved to the Viceroy and the Duke of Connaught, to the despair of the authorities and the amusement of the public':[11] a faux pas that seemed to imply the precariousness of hundred years of supremacy.

India's quest for unity – one of the motifs and justifications for Britain's presence on the subcontinent – seemed to Gertrude a far-reaching goal. 'India doesn't exist at all,' Gertrude summed up in her report: 'Jaipur, Mysore, Hyderabad, yes – but India . . . there is no country of that name outside the geographical books'. 'It was a jigsaw of 602 states ranging in size from Kashmir and Hyderabad to tiny holdings of a few acres'[12] that were ruled by the British in the name of progress. Artificially united, to comply with Britain's imperialist designs, India seemed then to illustrate that 'unify and rule' could be, in fact, as much of a strategy as 'divide and conquer'. The success or failure of Britain's presence in India could not be measured by the amount of 'Britishness' instilled in the local elite, Gertrude thought, as the whole adventure seemed to her too ephemeral and too costly. In a letter to her family she explained why: '. . . They send the princes to colleges, to Oxford, and they bring them back to marry purdah wives and to rule over Hindu subjects with whom, if education is of any value at all, they have completely lost touch.'[13] Britain's rule over the sub-continent could not be justified by the amount of progress it brought nor by the sense of unity it was meant to instil in such a diversified population. Moreover, Lord Curzon's refusal to appoint Indians to the vice-regal council and advance them to senior posts in the administration only led to a growing opposition to the British Raj.[14]

Gertrude Bell understood the problems created by Lord Curzon's rigid policy and its effect on Britain's growing unpopularity among the population. Although sensing some of the problems ahead, Gertrude understood how 'Britain's colonial arrogance and vision of supremacy induced peoples to be ruled by consent.'[15] But together with politics, this visit to India had been an adventure on a personal level as well, providing Gertrude with the chance to meet again with Valentine Chirol, then *The Times*' correspondent in Delhi.

Gertrude's visit to India left an imprint on her that would follow her to other places and situations. These impressions remained vivid after her return to England. Once at home, Gertrude had to face the changes occurring in English society. Her own family was an example of the new classes that had risen to the upper layers of England's society: liberal in their economic and social outlook, they were nevertheless conventional and 'good mannered' in the traditional sense of the word, and attracted to the aristocracy's lifestyle.

Affected by the aristocracy's charm, the rising elites emulated its *savoir-vivre*; the garden parties, hunting expeditions and other pleasures of country life had been quickly adopted as the natural corollary of social ascent. The glittering events of London's season also provided the perfect setting for social mingling and, in the countryside, the new aristocracy of money – industrialists, financial magnates, railway executives – rubbed shoulders with the aristocracy of birth in social gatherings, in municipal councils, and on the directorial boards of regional projects.

Gertrude was well aware of the underlying contradictions, however. The memory of her family's objection to her proposed marriage to Henry Cadogan was still keen, as was the sense conveyed at the time, that marriage into the aristocracy was an upward move only when underpinned by financial security. Gertrude had met Henry Cadogan in Persia in spring 1892, during her visit to the Lascelles, then serving in Teheran.[16] She was twenty-four. The son of the Hon. Frederick Cadogan, Henry seemed then tailored for her, having shared the same social upbringing and the same cultural background. It was with him that she strolled along the rivulets cascading down the slopes of the Damavend that 'gleamed brown, snow white and grey, touches of sun on the valley and low creeping lines of soft cloud coming gradually across the lower hills'.[17] Her parents' objection to her marriage to a poor diplomat was for her a first sign of the changes that would alter their lives, when economic upheavals would lead to loss of fortunes and prestige. A dutiful daughter, torn between her desire to please her parents, and her impulse to break with conventions and to open up to less constraining rules, Gertrude started then, perhaps unconsciously, to search for places where these contradictions were less pronounced.

She had already discovered that the ephemeral glamour of London's social circles annoyed her after a while. Too broad-minded to comply with the unwritten rules of the countryside and too independent to live by the social codes of the capital, Gertrude also considered the possibility of getting back to Oxford. But again, the new perspectives she had acquired on her journeys to the East and her impulse to travel and to defy social codes, prevented Gertrude from considering Oxford as a viable option. Even Oxford – and the study of Hindustani and Tibetan languages appeared, already then, as a less attractive possibility. Too creative, flamboyant, and original in her judgement of men and ideas to conform to the traditional setting of academic scholarship and too perceptive to ignore the compromises required to live in the hierarchical, often intolerant society of academe, Gertrude rejected the idea. More amused by the snobbery of the younger Oxford dons than annoyed by the stiffness of the older ones, she nevertheless felt that few of them really understood the world beyond university. Apparently, Gertrude knew already that she needed more growing room than the stifling society of Oxford could provide, and she realised that her inclination to study archaeology and history would be fulfilled outside its walls.[18] Even her old passion, mountain climbing, didn't seem to satisfy her any more. After climbing the perpendicular ragged peaks of the Engelhorn in 1901 and the Finsteraarhorn in 1902 and measuring up with the frozen ravines and ridges of the Matterhorn in a 'very disquieting dawn' in August 1904,[19] Gertrude still felt that she wanted to be part of a larger adventure with which her own family was directly and indirectly connected. In spite of their liberalism at home, the Bells would profit from Britain's gains abroad, which were linked, more often than not, with an aggressive foreign policy.[20]

However, still seeking for consent and approval at the time, Gertrude was not yet prepared to sever her ties with England and her family. In fact, even when engaging in long periods of hectic travelling, she would carry with her a sense of desolation that sometimes replaced the curiosity that had driven her to far places at first. The freedom her father's financial support gave her had kept her, ironically, in a position of dependence. But there was little she could do about it at a time when dependence on a man, be he a father or a husband, was not only accepted but also expected, and marriage was still considered the most important achievement in a woman's life.

Marriage had always been Gertrude's sisters' main aspiration. The Bells had greeted the engagement, in 1903, of their daughter Molly to Charles Trevelyan, a member of the local Northumberland gentry with great satisfaction.[21] Apparently, her parents' attitude brought Gertrude much pain even if overtly she had to demonstrate excitement and solidarity. She couldn't help comparing the message forwarded by her parents years earlier – the one that had ended her relationship with Henry Cadogan – with their approval of Molly's marriage to Charles Trevelyan. Their pleasure had to do not only with the Trevelyans' social position but with Charles' financial ability to give Molly the kind of life she had always led.[22]

But even more than financial or social considerations, it was the Trevelyans' position in local politics that had attracted the Bells. The Trevelyans' family story was intertwined with the history of the area, providing the Bells with an instant link to the historical and political destiny of north-east England. This legitimacy, this indisputable right to become a part of the region's annals, were goods that could not be purchased, only acquired through marriage or by endless participation in patriotic endeavours. This reverence for the keepers of prestige by those ascending to power, like the Bells, was presented in terms of political solidarity and common interest in the welfare of the area.

In addition to these political considerations, Charles Trevelyan had all the qualities a young girl like Molly could hope for in a husband: 'wealth, intelligence, good looks and good manners'.[23] He was already a politician then, having run as a Liberal candidate at Richmondshire in the 1901 elections and again as a Liberal candidate for Northumberland in 1903. Molly had met him in 1902 at the local railway station 'looking very beautiful in a panama and a rough blue suit'.[24]

Their romance would flourish some months later when he showed Molly the lands surrounding Wallington, the Trevelyan's estate, comparing the peacefulness around the lake to the inner calm he felt at Molly's side. Seated under a fig tree in the midst of barley fields near Redcar woods they would watch the sky 'growing dark, the stars coming out and the line of furnaces growing red against the sky'. These were the furnaces of Middlesbrough, the industrial city on Teesside to where the Bells had transferred their firm from Port Clarence at Cleveland Hills. After dinner, Charles and Molly would read 'Macaulay's marginal notes on a copy of Romeo and Juliet'. The book had been found at Wallington's library, since the famous historian T. B. Macaulay was Charles Trevelyan's great-uncle, the brother of his grandmother Hannah. When back in London, Charles Trevelyan would write to Molly almost daily. Not letting Florence Bell enter their intimacy, Charles would always write a 'public letter' especially drafted for Florence's eyes.[25]

All believed that Charles Trevelyan had a great future ahead of him. The eldest of the 'Trevies', as the Trevelyan brothers were then known, Charles seemed the most promising of the three. Heir to a baronetcy and to Wallington, the estate that was a source of pride for the family, Charles stood out as the bearer of the family's political mission.[26] A politician by personal choice as well as by familial design, he was expected to continue his grandfather's public endeavours. Sir Charles Trevelyan had initiated reforms in education and finance in India and was co-author of the Northcote–Trevelyan Report, the regulation that opened the civil service to retainers of merit and not just those equipped with connections and patronage. Charles' father, George Otto Trevelyan, a member of Parliament in the 1860s and the chief secretary of Ireland during the Gladstone administration, saw to it that Charles and his brothers were brought up in an atmosphere of intellectual openness and political liberalism. However, Charles' political expectations differentiated him from his two brothers, as neither Robert, an unfulfilled poet, nor George, an accomplished but rather melancholic historian, felt compelled, as Charles did, to stage their lives in accordance with the Trevelyans' double mission – as patricians and Whigs.

Elevated by Molly's engagement to Charles to an equal footing with the Trevelyans, the Bells became more closely connected to the network of socially prominent families in England, which included the Wedgwoods, Butlers, Russells, Thorntons, Haldanes, Dixons and Huxleys. Not all sharing the same ideas or identifying with the Trevelyans in their perception of their role in society, they seemed, however, to find great interest in these gatherings.

Family gatherings were festive occasions, in which a favourite entertainment was the 'game of the great uncles', whose purpose was to reveal shared ancestors to the youngest cousins.[27] There was even 'The Monthly Cousin', a typewritten and hand-written periodical that appeared regularly from 1897 to 1907. Elsa and Molly edited it and the 'cousins', including Gertrude, contributed to it occasionally.[28] Becoming even more connected to the interrelated world of the 'old families', the Bells now enjoyed not just the prestige bestowed upon them by their wealth and entrepreneurial achievements, but also a kind of transcendental eminence that had been carried nonchalantly by the Trevelyans for generations. The historical heritage that would be annexed to the Bell coat of arms seemed to fit the political legacy of Sir Isaac Lowthian Bell, a Liberal MP for Hartlepool in the 1870s.

Gertrude was attracted to the Trevelyans for their historical interest, but she did not seem to be as impressed as the other members of her family by the Trevelyans' social position. Her feelings for the region and its history were connected with the pride she felt in the Bells' own record of accomplishments. Her writings suggest that Gertrude's feelings about the Bells' roots in Durham and Northumberland were no less deep than the Trevelyans'. She had felt this special connection to the region when living in Red Barns at Redcar, one of the family's main residences. As a child she would walk 'along the sands to the end of Redcar' and dig, with her brothers and sisters, castles in the sand.[29] Redcar's colourful images had left imprints on her that even the melancholic wilderness of Northumberland's coast could not erase. She did not need the Trevelyans to connect with the history of the region. An irretrievable link to earlier civilisations and to the history of the Roman ruins scattered along the coast reinforced her sense of a direct historical connection with northern England. That was mainly felt through her attitude to local politics and her sense of belonging to the classes that, rooted in Britain's countryside, considered themselves entitled to carry Britain's message to new worlds.

Gertrude viewed Wallington, the Trevelyans' mansion also known as 'the quintessential Whig house',[30] more as a centre of political and intellectual activity than as an emblem of prestige. A symbol of the Trevelyans' political message – liberal, intellectually driven and aristocratic[31] – Wallington was host to the social and cultural circles of the day. Debates usually started indoors, among shelves furnished with history books and walls decorated with pre-Raphaelite paintings; conversation continued, weather permitting, on strolls through the garden or long walks in the countryside. Hunting and riding were other open-air activities shared by the Trevelyans' guests. These pastimes were a symbol of status, as much so as the composition of the guest lists for the assorted parties at which issues of national and regional importance were discussed.

Molly's wedding in January 1904 to Charles Trevelyan was celebrated by the employees at the Trevelyan estate in Warwickshire and at Wallington, and the workers at Clarence Ironworks, the Bells' enterprise in Middlesbrough. After the religious ceremony at the Holy Trinity Church, the wedding reception held at the Trevelyan's London residence, 8 Grosvenor Crescent, near Hyde Park Corner, became an illustration of the family's connections with the political circles in the capital. The Bells' townhouse at 95 Sloane Street, beautifully decorated for the occasion, with 'festoons of foliage draped along the walls and lovely flowers of varying hues lending added brightness to the scene', also became a scene of display of social and political connections. The usually quiet Sloane Street was 'busy with dashing equipages [laying] carpets across the way'.[32] The guests represented the exclusive inner circles of London, including family members of William Ewart Gladstone, the first Liberal prime minister and a close friend of the bride's grandfather, Sir Isaac Lowthian Bell, whose political activities in the 1870s and 1880s had overlapped with Gladstone's terms in office. Also attending the festivities were members of the Bells' extended family, among them Edward Grey and Louis Mallet, Sir Edward's secretary, who years later would become Britain's ambassador to Constantinople.

The wedding gifts matched the exclusivity of the guestlist. Among them were Chinese pottery; sterling silver trays; silver bowls, silver candlesticks, enamel boxes, silver snuff boxes,[33] and matching hand-woven pillow covers, personalised with *ton-sur-ton* initials. Among the crystal glasses, and Limoges services were two books: *The Life of Gladstone*, a present from the Gladstones, and William Blake's *Grave*, a present from Gertrude and Maurice Bell. There was something symbolic in the gift – a beautifully illustrated book on the mysteries of life and death by one of Britain's most celebrated poets and painters – being handed to Charles and Molly conjointly by Gertrude and Maurice, the children of Hugh Bell's first marriage.[34] Gertrude had read Blake's poems to Molly, Elsa and Hugo when they were young children. They specially loved the happy ones 'The Little Boy Lost' and 'The Little Boy Found' and even 'Why was Cupid a

Boy'. Gertrude and Maurice, however, certainly had a preference for the less cheerful ones, like 'Long John Brown and Little Mary Bell' or even 'The Chimney Sweeper' that starts with an eloquent line: 'When my mother died I was very young . . .'.[35]

Financial arrangements had also been made at the time of their engagement. Sir George Trevelyan would give to Charles £600 a year for election expenses and £300 to cover his political activities, while Sir Hugh Bell would give £500 a year to cover part of Molly's personal expenses.[36] After the wedding, Charles Trevelyan, by then a MP, bought a house at Cambo, a model village in the Trevelyans' estate, where he and Molly would reside when Parliament was not in session. When in London, the young couple would stay at the Trevelyans' house at 11 North Street, near Westminster.[37]

Well suited, glamorous, promising and socially compatible, Charles and Molly embodied Florence's dreams. Gertrude was more perceptive, however. Molly's marriage had been a turning point for her, at a time when she was already considered 'unmarriageable'. Not just too old (for those days' standards), but she also lacked the feminine sexuality and the coquettish side of her sisters. Gertrude clearly appeared then to be not at ease with feminine women, perhaps because she herself would have liked to have more of those qualities. She was also aware of the importance of the Bells' fortune for the Trevelyans. 'The Trevelyans do not make marriage mistakes', George Trevelyan once explained to his cousin Bertrand Russell. 'They wait until they are thirty and then marry a girl with sense and money.' [38] Although Charles and Molly's marriage seemed to be based on true love, this inadvertent revelation not only pointed to the broader considerations behind interclass marriages but also showed how the gilding of a coat of arms became imperative to the country's gentry like the Trevelyans at the time. Ironically, the Bells' fortune had already begun to suffer, albeit indirectly, from fluctuations in the iron and steel market caused by the technological leaps of England's main competitors, Germany, Belgium and the USA.

At his presidential address to the Iron and Steel Institute in 1907,[39] Hugh Bell explained to a crowded audience the reasons for Britain's difficulties. Among others he pointed to the conditions that had placed Britain at the top of the world's iron industry: the connections between steam transport and iron trade, the increasing accessibility of remote mines of coal and ore and the expanding iron industry in Britain itself, coupled with an advanced financial system.[40] All those had lost much of their importance, however. Already in the 1890s, the USA had had challenged Britain's position as the leading producer of iron in quantities, equalling the joint output of Germany, Belgium and France.[41] The advance of technical education in Europe, as Hugh Bell then explained, sponsored by entrepreneurs such as Krupp and Bresseneur of Germany, Le Creuset of France, and John Cockerell of Belgium, had raised the productivity of these countries, striking a definitive blow at Britain's competitive ability.

In Britain, 'workshops rather than colleges [functioned] as technical schools',[42] Hugh Bell continued in his 1907 address. Much of the spirit that had led his father, Sir Isaac Lowthian Bell, to publish two textbooks that became classics in the field – *Chemical Phenomena of Iron Smelting* and *Principles of the Manufacture of Iron and Steel* had faded away. 'What would the twenty-first century keep in hold?' Hugh Bell asked then at the end of his speech, outlining a futuristic image of the post-steam age:

> How in a hundred years will the great swiftly-gliding ship of those days be propelled? . . . With no machinery on board, with barely any crew, [the ship would] speed on her way, drawn by the electric force generated at [the] Niagara and transmitted over the Atlantic by wireless telegraph.[43]

Hugh Bell's address had ended with a note of optimism in spite of the financial and technological difficulties still ahead. A great believer in Britain's future and in his own ability to promote it, Hugh Bell relied, perhaps too naively, on his fortune and connections to push forward his political ambitions.

As a member of the board of directors of the North-Eastern Railways, founded by Sir Isaac, Hugh Bell shared with Sir Walter Trevelyan, the Earl of Carlisle, Sir Edward Grey and other members of the north-eastern elite, an important position in regional politics. He was then influential enough to arrange for the train to stop in the backyard of the family mansion, as was the custom among the country's aristocracy.[44] This external sign of social status spelled more than just participation in the control of the area's economy. It meant an informal mandate to promote the population's welfare and to represent its interests in London. A Liberal by vocation, as were the Trevelyans, Hugh Bell wanted to carve his way onto the political scene. He would run for political office as a Unionist candidate years later.[45]

Hugh Bell had raised his children to patriotic endeavours. Maurice as a schoolboy read popular magazines such as *Boy's Own Paper*, *Chums*, *Pluck and the Union Jack* and *Young England*.[46] Years later he departed as a young officer to South Africa, to fight the Boers, the descendants of the Dutch settlers in South Africa that rebelled against Britain.[47] Spending most of his time as a country gentleman or as an officer in the army, Maurice didn't seem to have been very involved in the Bells' firm in Middlesbrough, despite the family's tradition.[48]

Middlesbrough's rapid transition from a modest urban borough in the 1850s to an overpopulated centre for the production of ore and pig iron with 'its furnaces lightening the sky at night',[49] had been depicted by Florence Bell in her book *At the Works* (1907), dedicated to Charles Booth, a forerunner of social scientific inquiry who had devoted his life to the study of poverty in London. Florence, as other members of the families of the leading ironmasters, had volunteered to improve the living conditions of the workers and their families. Newspapers and magazines such as *The Middlesbrough Chronicle* and *The Literary Pilot*, *The Weekly Exchange* and *The Weekly Gazette* covered local and cultural events. But Florence's approach had more to do with a kind of social paternalism than with a real programme of political improvement.[50]

In the twilight hours and at night, Middlesbrough appeared, with its 'pillars of cloud by day, [and] pillars of fire by night'[51] as the visions of Blake's 'dark Satanic mills', and other images drawn from the heartless realities of England's Industrial Revolution. Middlesbrough was then an unhealthy town where filth from trains, factory chimneys and houses added to the noise 'from the carts and carriages and horses on the cobblestones'.[52] When in England from her frequent trips abroad, Gertrude used to join Florence in her visits to Middlesbrough. As a member of the proprietor's family – and, as such, feeling, in some way, responsible for the workers' welfare – Gertrude attempted to improve their living conditions by trying to set them standards of self-discipline and physical endurance she had adopted, believing these were the right ones not just for herself but also for others, notwithstanding their position in society. Largely this was due to the Victorian values she had absorbed in her formative years, values that were also part of a collective world vision, but it was also partly due to her character.

However, Gertrude (like other upper-class factory and coolery owners holding Liberal views) minimised social inequities by expressing her empathy for the working classes, while underscoring shared responsibility (of owners and workers alike) in the productive process. This moral bond would, so the owners believed, permit a dialogue between the classes to take place without radically affecting the class divisions themselves.[53] In spite of her visits to Middlesbrough, Gertrude was not a great believer in the possibility of bridging social gaps. However, her encounter with the hard reality of north-east England after her return from India, her discovery of poverty, of the danger surrounding people's daily lives, made her realise partially at least, how heterogeneous English society really was.

When returning to a changing homeland after her visits to the East, Gertrude seemed constantly disappointed with the dull and pale reality of England's industrial countryside. This was not the England of her childhood either, whose images she had carried with her on her journeys abroad. Too clever to cover up with philanthropic messages the unbridgeable gaps created by hasty industrial development, Gertrude could not find her heart in the darkness and dust of the iron furnaces.

Florence's concern with the lot of the underprivileged seemed an intellectual exercise rather than an authentic attempt to cut across social barriers and sympathise with the predicament of the lower classes. Although offering a vivid snapshot of living conditions in England's industrial towns and of Victorian women's plight, Florence's book conveyed a message that was typical of an upper-class observer.[54] For her, welfare depended on the good management of family finances, not on sweeping or radical changes. The daily life of working-class women was almost unbearable, as described later by other authors. Cooking for men working on different shifts, washing infinite laundry and stitching the quilts to be later sold in London's markets, Middlesbrough women could barely raise their families.[55] In public speeches or in their writings Florence and Gertrude typically overlooked these difficulties. Believing that no real conflict of interest existed between master and worker because both sides would gain from increased productivity, Florence clearly misunderstood the complexity of the situation.

Although Gertrude subscribed along general lines to these viewpoints, she was becoming too detached from England's social problems and even, in some ways, from her family's daily life to take a more militant position. She loved her family and England as she would write sometime later. 'But I feel rather detached from you . . .'.[56]

The north of England that she longed for in her trips abroad was not now the same one she had left behind. But she had changed too. Although searching for new answers when away from home, Gertrude wasn't yet ready for real changes when back to familial surroundings. Too attached to the advantages of her position to fully re-examine her life, Gertrude was unable to identify with the predicaments of others. Perhaps this was linked to her feeling – shared by other privileged women in late Victorian England – that she belonged in a category by herself. The destiny of the lower classes, men and women alike, seemed unconnected to her own. Like that of other upper-class women, Gertrude's sense of inherited superiority was combined with the benefits of an effortless existence, and the prospect of an unworried future guaranteed not just by the monthly allowance received from her father but also by the money (£5,000) inherited from the grandfather, Sir Isaac Lowthian at his death in 1904. This sum, when added to the estimated worth of the Bells' estate (£768,676), financially assured her future.[57] Her increased wealth diminished even further her sense of shared interests with the lower social classes. The freedom of opinion and movement she enjoyed distinguished her from other women and permitted her to break away from the restrictions of society.[58]

Gertrude, like other upper-class women, took part in debates that changed politics on regional and national levels. These debates generally took place in their own mansions, or those of their relatives or friends: mansions that became an organic part of the country's history. Although public office, professions, full university degrees were still closed to them, and their rights to property were more limited than those of their brothers, this privileged class of women enjoyed a freedom of conduct that was not accepted in all corners of society at the time. This sense of individual liberty helped them develop an identity based on their personal ability to circumvent social restrictions[59] and become the exception that proves the rule. In fact, upper-class women in late Victorian England managed to be subjected only to the codes and customs prevalent in their immediate social environment.

There were, however, variations in these cases and a large part of them identified with the struggle of women for political rights. Gertrude, for her part, decided to take advantage of the amount of independence she could enjoy personally and did not feel to be a part of the collective strife for suffrage and other rights. Although inspired by the women whose accomplishments she certainly admired, Gertrude did not feel the urge to contact them and develop personal relationships. Perhaps emulated unconsciously, these women were the forerunners of a trend that was just beginning to gather momentum; Gertrude apparently admired them, but did not place herself in the same category.

The only woman that Gertrude perhaps identified with was Lady Anne Blunt, whom she visited during a stay in Cairo in 1906. Lady Blunt's famous crossing of the Great Nefud[60] and visit to Ha'il in the late 1880s had enticed Gertrude's curiosity. Together with her other exploits, Gertrude certainly admired Lady Blunt's linguistic skills, demonstrated in Blunt's translation of the mu'allaqat (*The Moallakat*, 1904), the pre-Islamic poems hung in the Ka'ba.

Gertrude also knew of other women achievers by reputation and by their deeds, for example, there was Isabella Bird, a world traveller and the first woman to become a fellow of the Royal Geographical Society, of which Gertrude also became a member in 1914. Gertrude had also heard about Lady Charlotte Guest, who operated earlier in the nineteenth century in the world of Gertrude's father, running one of the largest iron and steel mills in England.[61] These were women who had successfully flouted convention in both their personal lives and in their professional accomplishments, and found a way to circumvent the restrictions of British society.

Gertrude Bell's position as an anti-suffragist seemed contradictory to her way of life, because she wasn't just apathetic or vaguely opposed to suffrage for women, but clearly against it. Gertrude seemed to have adopted in this subject, as in some others, the conservative views of Lord Cromer and Lord Curzon, in spite of her Liberal upbringing. She was, in fact, contradicting the positions of other upper- and middle-class women from Liberal families who joined the different branches of the women's movement and those who became the movement's backbone, 'to their husbands' great shock'.[62] The reason for Gertrude's position is not quite clear. It might have been, at the beginning at least, due to her desire to please her parents, as they were against general suffrage. With the years, however, her interest in the issue decreased in proportion to her increasing interest in the Middle East. Suffrage for women seemed to have become less relevant, as she got involved in 'the great scheme of things', namely the upper classes' role in Britain and their imperialistic mission abroad. Needless to say, she felt superior or rather non-attached to women's collective destiny and common struggle for equality in society.

More than any other point of debate at the time, the issue of suffrage had become a very personal stand, cutting across class and party affiliation and Gertrude Bell was no exception. Even if the conservatives were seen as opposed to the extension of suffrage and the more progressive seemed to be more sympathetic to it, there were important exceptions in both camps. Arthur Balfour among the Conservatives, supported suffrage and Herbert H. Asquith among the Liberals opposed it. Also Winston Churchill, as a young Liberal candidate, was opposed to women's suffrage 'as contrary to natural law'.[63] So divided was British society on the issue, that even Beatrice Webb, the progressive social thinker, had signed a petition against the measure in the late 1880s.[64] Many changed their views as perceptions evolved, but suffrage remained a debateable issue until the end of the First World War.

Sir Edward Grey, a Liberal MP and a friend of the Bells, explained that he had withdrawn his support from the bill on woman suffrage in 1905[65] because he believed that a sudden rise of the electorate from seven to fifteen million with the addition of the female voters was as unpredictable in its immediate results as it was threatening in its long-term implications.[66]

Because of the confusion over the true meaning of women's rights,[67] a large part of the British public viewed suffrage as an excess that threatened to reverse social order as a whole. The movement's sometimes confused goals and the aggressive stance of its militants provoked mixed reactions even to some of its more modest proposals. The implications of equality between the sexes in daily life and in codes of conduct were debated with the same ardour as the question of suffrage itself. Even styles of courtship had become a topic: 'Was it right for girls to flirt? What about courtesies in public transportation? Must a man give up his seat to a woman on a trolley? And what should be the norms in colleges and other educational institutions?'[68] Gertrude Bell asked in one of her letters to Lord Cromer, even if she herself had to confront inequalities when studying at Oxford.[69] In spite of these obstacles, or perhaps because of them, Gertrude Bell drew the conclusions she had about her personal experience, mainly her ability to compete with her male colleagues on a basis of knowledge, intellectual skills and physical fitness.

In her view, women should compete with men without taking advantage of artificially created privileges. This is perhaps why Gertrude Bell opposed separate institutions such as Bedford College at London University, where girls were educated separately by female teachers. In her opinion, the unbalanced views so created could be dangerous in the long run. 'It is rather serious', she commented in a letter to Lord Cromer, 'for history shows that all the most distinguished men have been those who have clever mothers . . . and if all the clever and intellectual young women are to remain unmarried – it appears to me that the coming generations will only have as mothers the intellectual refuse.'[70] By ignoring the possibility that women could be educated and then get married, Gertrude Bell showed little concern for women in general and for women of the lower classes in particular. Since she was also used to privilege in regard to education and did not have to make any effort to get into the right institutions, she underestimated the amount of effort required to raise lower- and middle-class women to the point where they could take advantage of modern education and participate in the debates and decisions of their time.

Refusing to consider women as a class per se, Gertrude Bell viewed the gaps between women of different social classes as more unbridgeable, in some cases, than the inequities between the sexes. And being an athletic record breaker herself, she underestimated the limitations resulting from physical differences between men and women. All in all, she believed in personal achievements, in physical and intellectual excellence, as the tools with which to circumvent gender divisions. While accusing the women of being personally responsible for their low achievements, Gertrude Bell underestimated the environmental factors that limited them.[71]

In fact, she was out of touch with the realities of her time, and did not attribute enough importance to the fact that she enjoyed advantages given only to a few. With the self-confidence, if not the blindness, of a wealthy and educated young woman, she purposely forgot that her career would have been impossible without the privileges of fortune, and the preferential connections that opened her way to the outside world. Although not part of the 'old-boys network' that helped her male colleagues cultivate connections and use their personal abilities to straddle class lines, Gertrude did not have much to complain about. And yet, her lack of humility and her reluctance to ever apologise show that she lacked the self-criticism that could have helped her adopt more balanced views on this as on other issues. The demonstrations, the headlines, and the passionate debates on women's rights increased Gertrude's opposition to the movement. Nevertheless, she valued her private conversations with one of the leaders of the movement. There, in the intimacy of lowered voices, Gertrude could listen to their arguments more patiently.

The one woman Gertrude most liked to talk about this issue with was Elizabeth Robins, the American actress, whom the Bells called Lisa. Lisa was Florence's best friend[72] and also a close friend of Gertrude's. With her clear eyes and clarity of mind, Lisa seemed far more persuasive than the most elaborate of arguments formulated by other suffragists. Perhaps it was Lisa's more direct, American upbringing, or the control she, as an actress, had over her voice that allowed the dialogue to take place. Whatever the case, Gertrude's conversations with Lisa affected her profoundly. But, strangely enough, the conversations always stopped whenever Florence entered the room, as if there was something inappropriate in this intellectual complicity between her best friend and her stepdaughter. Unwilling even to consider women's rights as a topic of conversation, Florence was as rigid on this point as she was in her approach to rules of behaviour and personal manners. 'I do not see you in the suffrage debate', Florence used to say, dismissing Lisa's attempts to win her over to the cause.[73]

The split within the movement between the constitutionalist suffragists, led by Millicent Garrett Fawcett, the head of the National Union of Women's Suffrage Societies (NUWSS), who believed in a steady and progressive promotion of the cause, and the more aggressive suffragettes from the Women's Social and Political Union (WSPU),[74] led by Emmeline Pankhurst and her daughters Christabel and Sylvia, further diminished the movement's appeal in Florence's eyes. It was mainly the violence of the suffragettes with their militant lobbying, window breaking and hunger strikes that put her off. The women's cause remained a taboo subject, rarely mentioned in the many letters that passed between Lisa and Florence over the years. Both women avoided the subject, thus evading the possibility of finding themselves in a deadlock. Apparently, their different backgrounds reinforced their positions. For Lisa, there was a direct connection between liberal views on all other social issues and the question of suffrage. And as an American, she was less tolerant of class divisions. More than once, Lisa had wondered why the suffragists, who campaigned by constitutional means to remove sex discrimination from the existing franchise, could not get more support from the Liberal Party. Gertrude had to explain to her that the Liberals were apprehensive about the measure, fearing that the extension of voting rights to property-owning women would, in the end, serve the Conservatives.

Gertrude Bell wasn't just against the extension of suffrage to women on the same basis as men at the time; she was, in fact, vehemently 'anti'. The 'Antis', as they were contemptuously called by the suffragists, also opposed adult suffrage, namely the institution of democratic franchise for both sexes,[75] according equal voting rights for equally qualified men and women. The issues were, in fact, interrelated, since women's suffrage would also affect other sectors' claims in the wider movement for electoral reform.

As the president of the northern England section of the National League for Opposing Woman Suffrage (NLOWS, launched in 1908), Gertrude Bell played a very active role in the campaign against the suffragist movement, organising meetings and demonstrations and in 1912 even preventing a debate on the issue organised by the Church Suffrage League at Middlesbrough by using her influence with the Archbishop of York.[76]

The 'Antis' position was anchored on three main arguments: the danger of having uneducated voters make political decisions, the importance of having only financially independent voters take part in the political process (a measure that allowed only heads of households to vote, excluding married women from the process, but including property-owning widows and spinsters) and, more important, the view that the extension of suffrage to women was against the 'natural order' of society.[77] Gertrude, as other 'antis', also nurtured the notion of 'Separate Spheres' regarding the political sphere as a men's domain and communal welfare (education, health) as a women's domain,[78] believing that women's duties lay first of all in their obligations toward their families, and not in political activities.[79] But that was a most controversial position taken by a woman whose life would focus on politics and other activities that were considered men's domain

In her moments of introspection, however, Gertrude remembered the delegations, the petitions, the debates. More particularly, she recalled the delegation that went to 10 Downing Street on a windy morning in December 1908 when suffragists shouting 'Votes for women' clashed with policemen in Trafalgar Square.[80] The Countess of Jersey, Lady Priestley and Violet Markham were among the members of the delegation that had gone to Downing Street to pledge anti-suffrage causes to Prime Minister Herbert Asquith. Representing the NLOWS – of which Gertrude was a very active member also in the capital – the delegation wished to explain the concerns of the 'Antis' about the possible consequences of the measure. They didn't need to employ much effort to convince the prime minister, as Asquith himself believed that women were 'politically unstable, inexperienced and irrational'.[81]

The escalation of this stage of the campaign culminated on 18 November 1910, 'The Black Friday', in which women's demonstrations in Parliament Square were violently suppressed by the police. Winston Churchill, then home secretary, was accused by the suffragettes of having instructed the police to use physical force.[82] His opinions on the subject crossed camps and lines and when asked his opinion he once answered that he refused to be 'henpecked on a question of such grave importance'.[83]

In spite of her prominent position in the 'Anti' movement, Gertrude Bell was not part of the December 1908 delegation to Downing Street. She certainly regretted later having missed the opportunity to meet again with Lord Curzon, now Earl Curzon of Kedleston. As inflexible during his debates on internal policies as he had been as viceroy, Curzon opened the discussion with the women by praising Britain's traditional institutions. Outspoken and articulate as always, he dismissed the idea of a referendum on suffrage, claiming that such a measure could affect the whole constitutional system in Britain. Encouraged by Curzon's tough position, the anti-suffragists rejected the possibility of letting 'unmarried women' (especially those entitled to become part of the electorate by virtue of their participation in the labour market) decide the country's political fate. The anti-suffragists wanted women to participate only in issues of welfare, hygiene and education, generally the responsibility of regional councils, town municipalities and other local political institutions.[84] Suffragists, from their side, viewed women's political participation on a national level as indispensable, together with their appointments in local councils, school boards, charities and other local and regional activities.

This opinion was not shared, however, by Sir Hugh Bell, who was one of the leading figures in the Men's Committee for Opposing Female Suffrage launched in December 1908 by public figures such as Austen Chamberlain, Lord Cromer, and Rudyard Kipling.[85] Kipling's poem 'The Female of the Species', published in *The Anti-Suffrage Review*, hinted at a correspondence between anti-suffragism and imperialism, which, in fact, was not always the case.[86] It wasn't, however, just pure coincidence that Lord Curzon subscribed to both.

Over time, the suffrage question became so central that even Florence felt compelled to take a more active position in the debate. She was convinced, however, that the women's plight was a direct consequence of their personal lack of skills and faulty attitudes. 'Babies often die from their mother's lack of knowledge', she claimed, 'and not just because their father hasn't provided for them'.[87]

Comparing working-class women's lack of preparation with the skills of her own daughters, Florence pointed to Elsa's and Molly's *savoir-faire* as the main sources of stability for their families. She described the arrival of Elsa and Molly on Christmas Day, 'radiant in their pregnancy, only to find Gertrude rushing to find drawings for her book'.[88] For Florence, neither Gertrude's books and articles, nor her other accomplishments could ever compare with Molly's and Elsa's realisation as wives and mothers. 'I do not like unmarried women whose minds run in unpleasant directions',[89] Florence wrote to Lisa some time later, forgetting that Lisa herself was one of them.

Florence's feelings and attitudes on suffrage, however, did not match her otherwise intellectual openness. As a playwright, a lover of theatre in general, and an admirer of Ibsen in particular, Florence Bell was counted among the intellectual elite of her time. And yet, her positions on women's issues hardly reflected the messages pervading Ibsen's plays. Ibsen had in fact taken London by storm. The theatrical productions of *A Doll's House*, *Hedda Gabler* and *The Master Builder* had stirred further interest in women's causes and in the problems of the institution of marriage. *A Doll's*

House, staged in London in 1890, showed the conversion of a housewife, Nora, into one of the first feminists on stage. It was not just a play about the injustices of modern society, where laws made by men judge women who are, by society's very rules, condemned to endure coldness and unfairness in a marriage built on shaky foundations. It was also a play about the crumbling of authority and the revelation of hidden destructive powers in otherwise socially acceptable relationships.

Gertrude Bell did not like the play. 'It is extremely good in some places and extremely bad in others, ludicrously and crushingly bad',[90] she told her father at the time, proving again her outspoken and exaggerated self-confidence, as well as a marked tendency to be overly critical. And yet, she had found the play interesting and original in some aspects as it had, for her too, opened a first breach into repressed feelings. She was then in her early thirties, an age when life's 'certainties' normally suffer a first blow.

Hedda Gabler, produced in 1891 with Lisa (or Elizabeth Robins to the general public) in the starring role,[91] became another landmark in the history of London's theatre. For the first time, a drama performed on the stage spoke clearly about the demeaning effects of women's economic subordination to men and the outcomes of a situation in which freedom spilled over into the realm of creativity. *Hedda Gabler*, perhaps more than Ibsen's other plays, focused not just on social conventions and conflicting class aspirations but also on the torment of men and women caught in the drama of distorted human relations.[92] It reflected a cold and hard reality that emerged from beneath nice manners and attitudes. Lisa's portrayal of Hedda Gabler captivated audiences and attracted Florence in particular. While conquering the Bells with her personal magnetism, Lisa came to represent different things to each woman in the family. To Gertrude, she was a friend on an equal footing. To Molly and Elsa, she was a family member and a dear presence. But for Florence, she represented freedom and the way it challenged the stiffness of her own manners.

Together, Lisa and Florence anonymously co-authored *Alan's Wife*, first staged in 1893. The play dramatised the tragic death of a miner and its effect on his pregnant wife. The birth of a deformed child, killed by its mother in an act of pity, her subsequent conviction and sentencing to death, were intended to draw attention to the plight of the lower classes and the inconsistencies of England's judicial system.[93] The unfavourable critical reactions to the play cemented Lisa and Florence's relationship, and the secrecy surrounding their collaboration bestowed upon their friendship a hitherto unknown intimacy.

Gertrude enjoyed Lisa's long stays at Rounton and considered her, as did all the Bells, a member of the family. There was something in Lisa, a mixture of candour and strength that appealed to Gertrude immediately upon meeting her. For her part, Lisa admired Gertrude's courage and intellectual skills. Seeing Gertrude as a 'law-lover and a law breaker', Lisa also became, in some instances, Gertrude's confidante. Both women had recollections of personal unhappiness from their earlier years; their understanding of life's injustices could not be shared with others.[94] Lisa's husband, George Parks, a discouraged actor at the Boston Theatre Company, had committed suicide by leaping into the Charles River, leaving Lisa as powerless in face of the absurdities of life as Gertrude had become after Henry Cadogan's death. Strong enough to defy pressures and conventions, they were drawn to each other in spite of Gertrude's long absences from home. This shared experience could not be created through intellectual effort but by the sense of freedom of mind that both appreciated so deeply.

Although their opposing stands on women' issues mattered to Lisa, she did not let these differences spoil her friendships with Florence and Gertrude. Lisa's membership of the executive committee of the WSPU and Gertrude's belonging to the NLOWS[95] did not affect their underlying complicity. Neither did their different stands on the 1912 strikes alter their friendship:[96] 'The strike has cost the Bells Bros £26,000 and the men £58,000 in [unpaid] wages . . . Hugh Bell looked tired . . .',[97] Molly noted then. But while the arguments about the reasons for the strike had brought a temporary halt in the correspondence between Lisa and Florence, they did not seem to interfere in the relations between Gertrude and Lisa. It was the intellectual respect, mutual admiration and silent complicity that maintained their friendship from souring during a period of great social and personal tension. Both women knew that suffrage was just one of the issues heralding a long series of changes in Britain's society and that the consequences were still difficult to foresee. However, their awareness of the real issues underlying politics coloured their respective stands with nuances that distinguished their lives from those of the other women in the Bell family. It was also Lisa's and Gertrude's choice to remain single that sealed their friendship.

Although Gertrude's sisters, Elsa and Molly, had less interest in privileges outside the walls of marriage, Molly supported the constitutionalists. Lisa, for her part, wanted privilege for others, while she herself enjoyed the advantages of glamour and success in an adopted country, a combination that placed her life in a category of its own. Only Florence's position on the broader aspects of women's rights was tinged with ambiguity. On one hand, she was aware of the reality of women's position in society, on the other hand, there were manners and traditions she wanted to keep. Her book *The Minor Moralist*,[98] published some years earlier, still reflected her philosophy and way of life. For Florence, there were ways to live in a world in which real problems were only hinted at. She accepted the ambiguities that were part of women's lives, and she found that manners were the only certainties to live by.

Sometimes, however, more open feelings would emerge from beneath her strictness of manners. On the day of Elsa's marriage to Commander Herbert Richmond of the Royal Navy in July 1907, Florence wrote to her eldest daughter:

> There is not a person in the world who cares for you more than I do. I don't think you have up to now (since Molly married) made the difference in anybody's life as you have made in mine. You are truly my own child, the child that we have had together. How amused we have been and how we have understood each other then.[99]

This sense of unconditional belonging that linked Florence to Hugo, Elsa and Molly did not include Gertrude and Maurice, pushing Gertrude, so it seems, to the need to distinguish herself from the 'triumphant image of mother-wife'[100] embodied by her two half-sisters.

Gertrude's way out was to excel, to travel, to write. 'Gertrude is writing, busily',[101] reported Florence to Lisa, hinting perhaps at her own frustrated aspirations. In spite of her many published books and staged plays, Florence carried within herself a sense of frustration that grew with the years. Forced to abandon a promising musical career for the sake of convention, she did not attain, through her writing, the degree of professional success found in Gertrude's and Lisa's works. Not always getting as much encouragement from Hugh Bell as she had expected and needed, Florence turned to Lisa as a source of inspiration and professional accomplishment.

Envying Gertrude's intellectual ability, persistence, and, most of all, freedom, Florence revealed in some intimate passages a rivalry with Gertrude that was not always apparent on the surface. 'Travelled to London by car only to arrive there and see Gertrude entertaining guests',[102] she wrote to Lisa some years later, hinting at Gertrude's excessive independence and lack of attentiveness. Although they clearly cared for each other and shared occasional moments of togetherness and intellectual exchange, Florence and Gertrude needed to maintain some distance. Two strong personalities, relatively close in age and yet distant in focus and purpose, Florence and

Gertrude needed to live away from each other, to follow different paths. Both needed the ocean – or the desert – between them.

*   *   *

Years later, on her way to Ha'il, in her search for the 'Empty Quarter' of Dick's writings, Gertrude tried to understand this complex relationship. She remembered her first encounter with Florence at the age of six, when Hugh Bell brought his future bride to meet the children from his first marriage. Gertrude remembered how she was attracted then to Florence's strong personality, elegant outfits and personal charm. There was something compelling about Florence, Gertrude had already discerned then – an air of distance, yet an ease of speaking and playing, as if she were moving on a stage or in the salons of Europe. This aptitude for the refined and the cosmopolitan had, however, diminished over the years with the daily care of a family of five children. Occasionally, a vivacious radiance illuminated Florence's face, bringing back the image of the younger woman, once enthusiastically drawn to art, music and literature. The years spent in the countryside had, however, erased her childlike enthusiasm. It was only when writing for the theatre or staging plays for family gatherings that Florence's inner fire rekindled. That was why Gertrude's freedom and her outpourings of creativity were perceived by Florence as defiance. And Gertrude's taste for solitude was seen by Florence, as by others, as a luxury reserved for only a few. To Florence, who was too conditioned by the social rules she herself had helped establish, Gertrude's lifestyle was a pretext, a flight. To Lisa, however, Gertrude's life was an encounter with her own drives and aspirations, as was Gertrude's way of circumventing convention and ambiguities, and her attempt to overcome the loneliness that had become part of their lives.

On her way to the Rub' al-Khali, the Empty Quarter, which in fact she never reached, Gertrude remembered moments of loneliness at family gatherings, a loneliness she found harder to endure than the solitude in the desert. There, she used to say, solitude was a feast. 'Lavish and copious', as Dick once described it. In the desert, Gertrude understood better the ambiguities she had lived with and left behind. And the ambiguities she had found in the East, in Hafiz's poems: ambiguities that juggled with images, words, and thoughts. She compared them with the ambiguities she confronted in the West, material, crude and rational. She had known them all; the ambiguities of *Alan's Wife*, or those that no suffrage could yet bridge.

CHAPTER 3

'The Shadow of a Stone'

In her imagined search of the England that was gone, Gertrude remembered the holidays spent at home, the good and more difficult moments, the clashes with her sisters and with Florence. 'I don't like your kitchen-maid gown', Gertrude had once remarked, reducing Molly to tears as she ran up the stairs. Florence ran after Molly, consoling and persuading her that 'no one else', meaning Gertrude, looked as 'nice as she did in a blue velvet gown'.

Gertrude had regretted her rudeness and run up to Molly's room to appease her. Why, she then wondered, did she have to hurt Molly every time she came home to Rounton for Christmas? What was it in these family gatherings that brought suppressed conflicts to the surface, erupting in open quarrels? And why was Molly always the main target for Gertrude's sarcastic remarks? 'Every remark I make has been met with a direct snub though she had been charming to everyone else', Molly complained at the time. [1] Maybe it was the way that Florence looked at Molly that provoked Gertrude's reaction. And why then there was so much pain and regret on Gertrude's part? Perhaps it was Gertrude's complex relationships with her sisters and with Florence that underlay the uncertainties that took the form of her famously imperious and haughty manner. It was, perhaps, a way to disguise vulnerability and, by emulating men and their achievements, a way to protect herself from her inability (or unwillingness) to compete with women in what were then considered feminine activities, goals and gains.

Still, there were good moments – after-dinner charades, recitations and plays composed and directed by Florence, even the spontaneous staging by the members of the family of Gertrude's adventures in distant lands. Maurice dressed then as Fattuh, her loyal servant in the desert, Molly disguised as 'a camel with a brown paper bag for its head and a cushion for its hump', and other members of the family came on the scene as chiefs of the desert.

Hugo played the thief, debating with the governor of Baghdad, while 'smoking the vacuum cleaner and refusing to give Gertrude back her stolen goods'.[2] Elsa was the suffragette complaining to the home secretary, Winston Churchill, about the police's rudeness toward her fellow suffragists who demonstrated on Parliament Square on that 'Black Friday', some weeks earlier. There were also guests, from among the area's important families.

There were other games evoking laughter, like the one called 'rabbiting'. It was a local custom to say 'white rabbit' on the first day of each month (and in some cases on Mondays) to bring good luck. On New Year's Eve, they would go to their parents carrying wishing candles. At midnight, while lighting their candles with the 'Devil's match' and counting the clock's strokes, they would say 'white rabbit', hoping to get their presents. These common memories of the games they had played together helped the family to overcome occasional clashes and underlying resentments.[3]

These were moments of togetherness, when minor – and perhaps not so minor – differences were forgotten. These were beautifully reported insights into the ambiguities of family life, whose patterns were, apparently, too clearly defined. These moments of emotional nonchalance did not endure, however. With time, Christmas at home made Gertrude feel lonely and misplaced when confronted by her sisters' personal happiness. Gertrude was still searching for her own, and time was running out fast. Gertrude's hair had already turned grey, and even though she kept herself fit and slim, she knew that she showed her age. She was an 'overdressed forty-three', as Molly had once described her.[4] Gertrude was aware of it. Although she often wore a low gown for tea and a velvet dress for dinner, Gertrude knew that such elegant outfits were more than what was required in the country at the time. But she could not help it. Her taste for fashion – outdated and somewhat theatrical – had not changed. Possibly it was her way of evoking continuity in the face of the changes surrounding her. It was perhaps reassuring for her to cling to artefacts like gowns and dresses, however out of style they might be, when her own world was changing too fast.

Christmas of 1910 was perhaps the last one that corresponded to the Bells' 'age of innocence'. After that holiday at home, Gertrude left for the East again. She had wanted to check the shifts in a world that still seemed intact on its surface. After packing a few things, among them her fur coat and her diaries, she left, this time leaving Molly and Florence 'feeling dreadfully flat and sad after her departure'.[5] She had tried during this visit to allay

the tensions, trying not to provoke the reactions that her adventures sometimes evoked, and attempting to conform to Florence's conventions. She
was well aware that her perceived freedom was a warning, a reminder to
others, mainly to Florence, that she could still enjoy the challenge of mystery and excitement. However, her taste for travel was just a seemingly easy
release from the limits of her home, an attempt to escape demands that
would have been impossible for her to accomplish. This attempt to reach
for new sensations in foreign and exotic lands was also a search for the
emotional space made only possible by physical distance.

The romantic vision of the East with the desert camp-bed under a star-
studded sky or the scent of the scarlet blossoming pomegranates in Eastern
orchards was, in fact, an illusion. Beneath it all was an attempt to travel
emotional distances in order to avoid the introspection that would make
her face her deepest fears. Molly and Elsa were too happy with their lives to
understand or to feel threatened by Gertrude's freedom. But Lisa understood all too well, since she herself had searched for freedom in foreign
lands, and for the good omen that might have come with it.

Gertrude's departure after that Christmas had left Florence sad. It was
perhaps the feeling that her own omen was linked to England's decline and,
inescapably, to the reversal in the Bells' fortunes. Gertrude could try to
escape it, Florence could not. Florence certainly felt that Gertrude's leaving
was an escape from what had haunted her at home, a rehearsal for the big
departure, for the 'final cutting of strings'. And although forewarned by
Gertrude's low spirits she couldn't but envy her. Gertrude's hopes were
pinned on prospects that were as shifting as the desert's sands, and yet Florence could not help feeling envious of Gertrude's search for chimerical
castles.

Gertrude's target in spring 1911 was Ukhaydir, the Sassanian palace
south-west of Baghdad. To get there, she had to cross the Syrian Desert by
'post-road and a camel back'. She had anticipated the pleasures ahead: 'The
cold and the frosty moonlit mornings, and the tales told, the songs sung,
and the long slow swing of the camel'.[6] Once in Damascus, she saw some
of the changes brought about by the Young Turks' revolution. 'The country
is changing slowly', Gertrude reported then. 'The army is paid, the police is
paid, and there is a general consensus of opinion that Syria has never been
so well policed before'.[7] Order also reigned in Baghdad: 'The roads were
safe, the desert was quiet, and everyone trembled at the name of Nazim
Pasha, the Turkish governor'. But Nazim had also committed excesses in
the name of progress, she explained later to her father. 'He had pulled down

thousands of houses in order to widen the streets and none could get compensation'. And as the road construction remained unfinished, all the money and heartache it caused had been squandered.[8] In fact, the reforms and modernising project initiated by the Young Turks in 1908 did not bring the expected results. The constitutional reforms introduced by the Young Turks after the deposition of Sultan Abdul Hamid and the reinstitution (in July 1908) of the 1876 constitution,[9] were meant to signal to the European Powers that far-reaching reforms were being introduced in the Asiatic provinces and in the Balkans, in order to prevent the Powers' interference in favour of the empire's subject peoples. However, the sense of unity that the reforms had meant to create or the impression of greater representation in the parliament in Istanbul, were aims difficult to reach. 'Every vilayet [was] a one man show',[10] and the scepticism of the inhabitants in the provinces toward the *Dustur* (the constitution) and the alleged advantages to be derived from it, were still largely felt.[11]

In the desert, no changes had occurred that altered in any way the unwritten social codes preserved for centuries.[12] The 'Anaza, the Shammar, the Dulaym, and the Jeraif would continue to behave as the Bedouin tribes at the top of a social hierarchy that had been in place for generations,[13] Gertrude had noted in her diaries. Also in the rural areas, the *fallahin* resisted reforms, conscription and taxes. The peasants working in the sultan's private lands – the sanniya – wanted to go on receiving the three-fifths of their land revenues after the 1908 coup as they did before. In other areas, as in the Muntafiq, the peasants 'pocketed all they made. If asked for his *aghnam* (sheep tax), the peasant would point the rifle at the tax collector and say, "Here is my aghnam"'.[14]

At the end the regime deteriorated into a military oligarchy, and the population's low expectations dwindled as the time passed.[15] And yet, there were some hopes. As in Baghdad, where Sir William Willcocks, the British irrigation expert was planning the irrigation scheme that would change the geography of Lower Mesopotamia forever.[16]

Sir William Willcocks, 'the dear old madman', had suffered at the hands of Nazim. But Willcocks had somehow managed to go further with the Hindiyya's dam project, as the first reconstruction work in an ambitious and costly scheme that would regulate the waters of the Tigris and the Euphrates. He had managed to advance his plans 'all the while quoting the Bible'. 'Have you got a picture of Sir William now?' Gertrude asked in one of her letters at the time. 'He is a twentieth-century Don Quixote – erratic, elusive, maddening, and entirely loveable . . . A streak of genius – a good slab of unreasonableness . . . the whole making as gallant a soul as ever you met'.[17]

Britain's interest in Mesopotamia was then linked to the benefits it could bring to India. Mesopotamia was meant to become an outlet to India's surplus population. In this greater scheme – in which Mesopotamia would serve as a corridor, granary and shelter – a railway network linking the Persian Gulf to Alexandretta seemed paramount. However, sections of the line, the Baghdad railway running from Baghdad to the Mediterranean and the Persian Gulf, were in the hands of a German company from 1903. The control of it would permit the Germans to undermine Britain's predominance in the Middle East.[18] South of Baghdad, the tensions were high. Quarrels between impoverished *fallahin*, tribal shaykhs and administrative authorities had become a daily fact.[19]

Reaching Hilla, Gertrude rejoiced in a re-encounter with an old friend – Hajji Namuh Beg, the town's *qaimaqam* (governor). 'He loves me more than a sister, he says, because I am a man',[20] a remark that told Gertrude more about gender relations than all the suffragist fights that she would not endorse. From Qasr-i-Shirin where she searched for more Sassanian castles, she went to Hawran, 'Urfa, Birejik, and finally to Carchemish, where she arrived in March 1911. There she found Reginald Campbell Thompson, the assistant of David G. Hogarth, Oxford's best-known archaeologist and curator of the Ashmolean Museum, and 'a young man called Lawrence . . . who is going to make a traveller'.[21] Carchemish, the leading city of the Hittites in northern Syria (seventy miles north-east of Aleppo), lay in a lawless region among Kurdish tribes and was strategically located at a juncture controlling the upper Euphrates. It had been magnificent in the past, 'when its sculptures were gay with colour and sunlight glistened on its enamelled walls . . . when plumed horses rattled their chariots along its streets and the great lords with long, embroidered robes and girdles of black and gold passed in and out the carved gates of its palaces'.[22] Centuries later, Carchemish was 'a great mound rising a steep hundred feet out of the river, a ruin set in a windswept, treeless land'.[23] Lawrence and Thompson, at the time of their encounter with Gertrude, were excavating ancient Hittite sites and studying the civilisation that had occupied the geographical space between the Semites and the Greeks. Carchemish, which is mentioned in the Old Testament,[24] was located near the colourful village of Jerabulus, which is in some sources identified with the site.[25] It was in Jerabulus that Lawrence and Thompson lived during the excavation seasons, among the Jerabis, settled Arab tribesmen. Their aim was to precede the Germans, whose archaeological team was expected to come to the desert as soon as the Baghdad Railway was extended far enough. The beauty of the Hittite buildings and the royal city, with its towers and portals guarded by lion statues, had attracted Lawrence during his studies at Oxford, and Hogarth had helped him join the British expedition to the site.[26] Lawrence liked the surroundings, the plain on which two villages of the same name were situated. He used to cross the short distance between the two villages on his way to the ruins of Al-Qal'a (The Citadel) situated at the northern extremity of the plain. He followed the colonnaded street leading to the citadel mound watching over the Euphrates, his imagination certainly stimulated by the vision of the forum of a Roman Syrian city that might have existed there.[27]

Gertrude Bell was more experienced than Lawrence and Thompson, and professional enough to spot immediately the technical flaws of the excavation. Pits had been dug randomly without any idea of what was to be found in the lower strata. When she pointed this out, Lawrence and Thompson tried to divert her attention by flooding her with a display of effected erudition.

Lawrence reported these strategies:

> She was taken (in five minutes) over Byzantine, Crusades, Roman Hittite and French architecture (my part), and over Greek folklore, Assyrian architecture and Mesopotamian ethnology (by Thompson), prehistoric pottery and telephoto lenses, Bronze Age metal technique, Meredith, Anatole France, and the Octobrists (by me), the Young Turk movement, the construct state in Arabic, the price of riding camels, Assyrian burial customs, German methods of excavation, and the Baghdad railway (by Thompson). This was a kind of hors d'oeuvre and when it was over (she was getting more respectful), we each settled down to seven or eight subjects and questioned her about them.[28]

If they had convinced her, or rather had managed to exhaust her, the fact is that she left Carchemish without writing the critical report for the *Journal of the Archaeological Society* with which she had threatened them. At the end of the initial four-month exploratory season (that had started in February 1911), Lawrence was able to expose a great deal of ceramics and pottery and a large relief of a fertility goddess, 'the lady', as she was thereafter called by them. Although the findings seemed insufficient to convince the British Museum to continue supporting the diggings, a sudden donation permitted five more excavation seasons conducted by Lawrence and by Leonard Woolley, already a well-known authority in the field.

Clashes with the local Turkish authorities and with members of a German construction company building a river bridge over the Euphrates did not stop them. After the stay at Carchemish, Lawrence's life would take a different turn. It was there that he had met Dahum, the Bedouin boy who became his travel companion. Like Gertrude before him, Lawrence could not confine himself to the study of the Middle East at Oxford. 'I don't think anyone who had tested the East as I have would give it up halfway, for a seat at high table and a chair in the Bodlean', Lawrence explained some months later.[29] He too became addicted to the East's mythic image, an addiction that amounted, as time passed, to a real obsession.

Gertrude's summer of 1911 was spent in England, where she installed a new water garden. She found some serenity in the green spaces outlined by hedges abloom with colour and harmony in the geometrical designs of paths dividing the lawn, leading to a large central circle around a basin. Lime, apricot and chestnut trees reflected their shapes in the water. Climbers and ramblers in green and silver completed the picture. Gertrude liked evenings in the garden, when roses were fragrant, and trees filtered the dwindling light. During the day, it seemed a different garden. Elsa, Molly, and their cousin Florence, now married to Cecil Spring Rice of the Foreign Office (known affectionately as 'Springy'), used to bring their children, filling the garden with joy and laughter. Gertrude documented their visits, taking pictures and recording anecdotes, as if gathering strength for her next adventure.

Amurath to Amurath had just been published and was receiving mixed reviews, but that did not bother Gertrude. She knew what to expect from reviewers. Like every other professional, they needed to exert mastery over something, in this case a text, to show off their expertise. Besides, some of their comments were mere differences of opinion, she explained later.[30]

The same garden seemed different to her two years later. It was as if the melancholy of England's autumn had added to her sense of entrapment and as if life itself was intruding to dash Gertrude's hopes. Even her presence during the autumn of 1913 at an anti-suffrage meeting in Middlesbrough, a clear act of political participation, was also tinted by aloofness. There were few attractions for her in northern England. Strolling in the garden on gloomy windy mornings she would remember her first encounter with Dick in Turkey and the way in which their relationship evolved as the years went by.

Gertrude could still see Dick as she had met him in Konya, the heart of mystical Turkey in 1907. He stood then silent and dignified, the darkness of his Royal Welch Fusiliers uniform contrasting with the brightness of the dome tiled with a 'blue, bluer than heaven or the sea, and adorned inside with rich and sombre Persian enamel'.[31] In the garden surrounding Jalal-al-Din-al-Rumi's tomb there were 'fountains and flowers set round with the monastic cells of the order'. Rows of tombs of the master's disciples with the sculpted bust of the deceased contrasted in their static silence with the dances of the dervishes during the *mawlid*, the ceremony commemorating the master's birth. The dancers turned, their right arm pointing up and their left arm down, as if liberating themselves from their own weight to reach heaven. Their movements suggested an easy passage from *dunniya* to *akhira*, from this world to the other. And then, as if caught again by gravity, they returned to their initial position and started their silent whirling all over again.

Gallant and fearless, duty-bound, courageous and loyal, was the image Gertrude had kept of Dick. Loyal to ideas, to conventions, to his soldiers, and to his wife. Hesitant to spell out his wishes, and yet resolute, years later, Dick wrote to her: 'In my mind there was a little feeling, natural to first opening of doors that I wasn't properly appreciated, properly under-stood. But I was . . . Now I feel as if we had come closer – and I want to hold it'.[32] Gertrude remembered the manifested rationality in some pas-sages and the signs of suppressed embarrassment in others, when the conversation tilted toward more personal issues. Letters had followed, some written at the Naval Military Club, which conveyed much more by what they omitted than by what they actually said.

'Why aren't you here to talk to me of Turkey?',[33] Dick asked some years later. Gertrude knew then that it was not just Turkey he had in mind, but Abyssinia, Somalia, Albania, and all the other places, rearranging them-selves in the pre-war map. He needed her, he said then, her intellectual openness, her clear opinions, her intimate knowledge of the East and her attraction to the dangers of Britain's imperial adventure.

For him, danger was an escape, an evasion from a wrenching situation that had no resolution. He saluted danger with indifference, as well as soli-tude, as 'we [are] all born alone, die alone, really live alone'. Doughty-Wylie tried to convince Gertrude that she could cope with 'the Goddess', as he called solitude, more easily than his wife could. She had the courage and the character, he claimed. Gertrude, however, wanted to come out into the open with their affair and stop fearing the ghosts Dick mentioned again.[34] Before leaving for Eastern Europe as a member of the Balkans Boundary Commission, Dick tried again to convince her not to expect much from an occasional moment, which should be seized and treasured, but forgotten later. Gertrude, however, seemed helplessly in love, or what she thought was love. She was in fact a victim of emotions, contradictory impulses and irrational attitudes.

The commission's task as defined by Sir Edward Grey was not easy, however. The 1912 military victory of the Balkan League states over the Turks had created a disequilibrium that could not be contained for long. The Montenegrins, Bulgarians, Serbs and Greeks were jubilant in their victories, but the Great Powers, taken by surprise, felt their interests endangered in this outburst of Balkan nationalism.[35]

This crescendo of national feelings in the Balkans had been partly an outcome of Turkey's own policies, of the Young Turks' cultural assertiveness and political centralisation, and their attempts to recruit more soldiers from among their Christian subjects. Together with territorial disputes, cultural claims were also prevalent. The Serbs and the Bulgarians wanted to keep the Cyrillic alphabet, the Romanians the Latin, and the Greeks their Greek characters. The Bulgarians even wanted to be recognised as a separate region-state, still referring to the March 1878 San Stefano agreement and the 'Grand Bulgaria' it created, illusory gains that had been dissipated by the Congress of Berlin some months later. Austria feared Bulgarian expansion and Britain wanted to prevent Russia's possible access to the Mediterranean.

The main problem was Serbia, however. The central power in the Balkans, Serbia epitomised the conflict between Pan-Slavism and Pan-Germanism, becoming a bone of contention between members of the Triple Alliance (Germany, Austria-Hungary and Italy) and of the Triple Entente (France, Russia and Britain). Serbia's assertive Pan-Slavism also meant the disruption of pan-Germanic influence extending from Berlin to Baghdad. Macedonia, with its Bulgarian-speaking Slavs, remained a point of discord. Fearing that Serbia and Greece wanted Macedonia for themselves, Bulgaria launched an attack on the Serbs and the Greeks in June 1913. As a result of the Second Balkan War, Turkey regained Adrianople (Edirne), keeping the area around it and Constantinople (Istanbul) as the empire's last strongholds on European soil. Macedonia went then to Serbia.

The stratagem of creating an independent but ill-defined Albanian state, to prevent Serbia from encroaching on the Adriatic Sea, was backed by Austria and endorsed by Britain. Doughty-Wylie would defend Britain's interests in the commission created by Grey at the London Conference in May 1913: 'The Albanians don't want any of those damned international idiots in their country – ditto Greeks, Austrians, Italians and Rumanians',[36] Dick explained in a letter to Gertrude.

Greece and Serbia wanted to annex Albania in order to expand their territories while Italy and Austria wanted it as a buffer against Serbia. Germany, on the other hand, considered an independent Albania as a hindrance to the interests of the Triple Alliance, Dick went on.[37] Dick wondered whether it would be possible to overcome so many prejudices, keep Christians and Muslims 'from cutting their throats'[38] and still emerge with some positive solutions.[39]

While remembering the cries of 'Hellenism or Death' of the Greek soldiers advancing northward toward Koritza, in south-east Albania, and the Albanians advancing eastward toward Monastir, in Macedonia,[40] Dick wondered whether there was an alternative to a territorial compromise: 'Wallachia [should] be attached to Greece and Aggrocantes [should be] given to Albania', he believed.[41] He didn't know, however, whether his suggestions would be accepted by the politicians. Dick also asked himself what criteria should be used for delineating borders. How could one know whether a village belonged to one territory or another? The language spoken in the families? he wondered. 'That we cannot do. We have made efforts and [we have] been dissuaded'.[42] Language by itself could not define new nations, he thought, asking, however 'what should be the key?'[43] He realised that he did not have the right to deal with so many people's lives 'and [still] I do it and would do it again'.[44] 'The Muslims were fleeing, and there would be so many people killed . . . only fewer if they take my scheme than if they don't'.[45]

He didn't care so much for the frontier itself, he once explained, but for 'peace and good government'.[46] But when confronted again with the unmeasurable religious jealousies, he realised that one was linked to the other. 'Neither the Serbs, nor the Bulgarians, nor the Greeks could overrule the others'.[47] In Adana, Dick recalled, the Turks fought the Christians, and the Bulgars, Greeks and Serbs had chased the Muslims from Salonika and Macedonia.[48] 'And the Great Powers – les Grandes Puissances or les Grandes Impuissances', as the members of the commission used to call them, 'could not do a thing but contradict one another'.[49] They all wanted chunks of Albanian territory. The Greeks pressured from the south and the Serbs from the north, while Austria-Hungary wanted an expanded Albania to serve as a buffer against the Serbs. Russia pressured for a small Albania in order to comply with Serbia's and Bulgaria's interests in the Balkans.

'Who would deal with the Bektashi dervishes (the main Sufi order in the Balkans), the Cretan patriots, and the Macedonian peasants?'[50] Dick believed that the Greeks would, but only as a temporary settlement.[51] At that point a more lasting solution seemed to him to be an Austrian–Italian occupation of Albania. But that, in Dick's view, would mean the end of the Triple Alliance as Germany's position within and outside the alliance would be weakened.[52] Again what should be the key? Dick asked himself. 'Religion, nationalism, politics, when there were so many lives at stake? Lives should be lived', he concluded, 'not spoiled in vain'.

Life and 'serenity at dawn', that should be the key, he wrote, 'The best of all things and the most immortal one'.[53] And solitude . . . 'where floats the essence'.[54] Feeling, perhaps, that their relationship could be broken by distance as much as by the relentless conventions of English society, Dick asked Gertrude what had suddenly happened at that night at Rounton that stopped the magic moment, 'Did I say too much? Or was it that you thought that the time had passed?'[55] 'If I had been your man for you in the bodies we live in, would it change us?'[56]

In this interlude of mutual intimidation, he wondered what Gertrude would have made of a direct invitation to disregard conventions and bring their relationship from their imaginary world to the real one. For him there was no division between feelings and sex, as he saw purity and poetry in both. He was 'an ordinary man and a follower of delights', he explained, 'but I know so well that that way might be misery for you'. For him, Gertrude was the one that still needed to get in touch with herself, to overcome her reluctance to commit, or at least to get rid of the puritanical strain that prevented her from living, fully, a many-sided life. He had loved other women, he confessed:

> as much as a man like me does love them – well and badly, little and much – as the blood took me, or the time, or the invitation . . . But that is all now behind me. . . . For though I have friends, . . . even a wife, they are far removed from our garden.[57]

But Dick himself was incoherent, vacillating between conflicting demands and promises. Assertive at times, and lacking assurance at others, Dick was clearly sending double messages. In the real world, he explained to Gertrude, they would only be friends. 'You shall walk in my garden – even ghostwise and imperfect in this life, and I will walk in yours, ghostwise and still more imperfectly'.[58] The uncertainties evoked by these messages only increased Gertrude's confusion.

It was not just for his wife that they could not be together, Dick explained, but because he didn't like 'lives at close quarters'. Even with Gertrude, he would not have enjoyed it. 'That is, not always, only when [we] wanted to'.[59] In their secret garden, however, he went on, they would enjoy closeness and freedom, because they were equals. This reciprocity would make their love different, even if incompatible with life itself. Real life was 'restricted, bound in chains, and difficult to bear', he explained. Oscillating between expressions of idealised love and physical desire, Dick proved again that he was at odds with the image of a free, and yet bonding, relationship. Gertrude wondered again whether Dick would be able to break the chains, to make decisions, even if knowing deep in her heart that he had erected an emotional wall that protected him from real intimacy. He would again seek refuge in thoughts: 'I have often looked out to the world, felt alone, turned to dreams and philosophy and the worship of a quiet death'.[60]

They would never be lovers in the full physical meaning of the word and yet he asked if she would still be his friend. Without answering his question, Gertrude left. In the desert, she believed, 'where things do not weigh more than they ought to weigh', time would be measured differently. She would have time to think it over. Feeling that her erotic impulses had long been buried under the intellectual ones, she entered a long period of introspection. Dick promised to follow her in his thoughts:

> I wish I had a map [but] I can follow you by memory fairly well. A little south of Ma'an and from there to Ha'il, surely a colossal trek. For your palaces, your road, your Baghdad, your Persia, I do not feel so nervous; but from Ha'il to Ma'an – mashallah![61]

In his eyes she was 'a rolling stone . . . if not in body, then in mind. And, after all, it was the mind that mattered', he still wanted to believe.

She was 'free as a cloud, and [he was] in prison', he explained. He lived in his own heart seeing the 'fences round it growing thicker with content'. If she were a bird, he still asked, would she come and sing in his garden? 'For in my garden I am always alone . . . and so are you, and so are we all'.[62] He would miss her, he said, asking her to come back before he would have to leave for another mission.[63] Pushing aside his worries, Dick adopted a more pragmatic or even patronising, attitude: 'Keep well. Be happy. Get an easy camel, and take something to eat. And when it snows, God sends you find a valley. And don't get taken for a witch for writing down the "beled" [country]'.[64] 'Don't forget to write me', he entreated. Gertrude wrote, but Dick burned her letters. 'One might get killed', he explained later, and his wife would still be alive.

*   *   *

In a letter to Valentine Chirol, now a freelance journalist in Delhi, Gertrude had opened her heart: 'O Domnul, if you knew the way I have paced backwards and forwards along the floor of hell for the last few months, you would think me in the right to try for any way out'.[65] And yet, for the moment, it would only be 'the road and the dawn, the sun, the wind and the rain . . . the campfire under the stars, and sleep and the road again'.[66]

The conflict in which she found herself was mostly her fault, she recognised now, even though it had been an 'irretrievable misfortune' for both of them. She needed some time out, as time would 'deaden even the keenest things'. Disappointed to the verge of despair, she had arrived at a point where she expected to be physically exhausted in order to forget the dramatic changes in her personal fortune. Feeling perhaps too old already to engage in a sexual adventure, Gertrude wouldn't try to come to terms with deep buried fears. Although leaving in a search for new definitions, she would take with her the symbols of her world – clothes and cutlery – proving perhaps that in her search for new worlds, she would not quietly leave behind the old one. 'The [old] world would have to get along without me for a while', she explained to Domnul.

In her next letter to Chirol, Gertrude included a commemorative stamp, marking Bulgaria's takeover of Adrianople. Turkey had lost its last bastion in Europe, except for Constantinople. How ironic it was to send the stamp from Damascus, 'the heart of Asiatic Turkey', while still feeling so close to Dick in the Balkans. The crumbling of the Ottoman Empire would change their lives; Dick was mapping the empire's European domains, and Gertrude, although she didn't yet know it, would try to do the same in Asian ones.

But in the meantime, Ha'il was the real challenge. From the days at Delhi and her encounter there with Lieutenant Colonel Percy Cox, she was trying to get in touch with Ibn Rashid, the ruler of Ha'il.[67] Percy Cox arranged an invitation for Gertrude to visit Ibn Rashid's principality after decades during which no Western traveller had been allowed to enter the city-fortress. The journey would not be easy. At first Gertrude thought to start her journey from the Gulf, but the inevitable clash with unfriendly tribes was a risk. She would instead reach the city of Ha'il by leaving from Damascus and travelling straight into the desert, taking the route east of the Hauran Mountains and then turning south-east. Without taking the road to the Jawf where the camels would have good food, she would go to

Qasr al-Burqa and Jiza. And beyond Bin Ba'ir it would be the Nefud, 'made of nothing but real sandstone and red-gold sand'. There would be long days of travel with no source of water whatsoever, but she wasn't afraid of them.

The plan was set. She would follow the Hijaz Railway and pick up her mail at the railroad station. Occasionally, she would send a telegram home. She would telegraph from desert posts in Arabic, and the message would be translated into English in Damascus. Before leaving, Gertrude met with Ibn Rashid's agent, 'a curious figure – young, very tall and slight – wrapped in a gold embroidered cloak, his head crowned with an immense gold bound camel's hair rope which shadowed his crafty, narrow face'. He handed her an invitation from the emir, with whom she had been in touch for some time. After a while, he got up. 'Finally, we ate together – that bread and salt might be between us',[68] Gertrude reported before her departure to the Najd.

They marched 'between broken hills, the beauty of the landscape arresting [their] gaze at every turn', she reported then. 'The low ground [was] covered with green plants and even some little flowers – white, purple, and yellow', the green looking startlingly brilliant. The hills were 'rusty red with a dropping of coal black stones . . .'.[69] After some days of travel, Gertrude's caravan reached a valley, 'where black tents had been pitched on the clear sand'. These tents belonged to the Huwaytat, the Bani Sakhr, and the Bani 'Atiyya tribes.[70] The Abu Tayy, members of the Huwaytat, were camping somewhere to the south-east. 'As night came', she wrote in the diary she would keep for Dick, 'the tribesmen sat on rugs spread upon the clean, soft sand to listen to the tales of the Huwaytat and the exploits of 'Awda Abu Tayy, the most famous raider of the desert'. As they sat in the dark, the *nagas* – the mother camels – 'would come home with their calves and crouch down in the sand outside the open tent', Gertrude explained to her family:

> Then Muhammad, one of the tribesmen, would get up, draw his robes around him and go out, bringing back a wooden bowl full of camel's milk. When you have drunk the milk of the naga over the camp fire of Abu Tayi, you are baptised of the desert – and there is no salvation for you[71]

In the morning, they watered the camels, filled the water skins, and continued their march south-east. The November rains – 'the ones that really mattered' – had been plentiful that year. The *khabras* (rain pools) were full of water, and in the midst of the desert, 'the sand had broken into strange shapes, contoured by the wind'.

By the time she reached Tuwaiya, thirty miles west of Ha'il, spring had almost arrived. 'Thorny bushes were all grey-green, contrasting with the red gold of the sand'. 'In spite of the desolation and the emptiness, it is beautiful, or is it beautiful because of the emptiness?' she asked Dick in her letter. The camels paced slowly, 'eating as they went', and she felt the calm of the moment. At times, when a cold wind blew, they would smell the aroma of the desert plants. 'The wind smells of amber', [72] observed one of Gertrude's servants and 'the thorns [were] covered with white green drops of rain . . . looking as separate jewels'.[73] Rain had fallen during the night, the sand smelled fresh and was easier to walk on. But as the storm continued, the caravan had to stop. The men pitched the tents while Gertrude sat down and read *Hamlet*, 'to bring the world back into perspective'.[74]

She would wonder then what exactly was she trying to accomplish 'To figure out early palaces? Would it be worth the trouble?' Oscillating between the two conflicting sides of herself – the intellectual and the emotional – Gertrude tried to find the connected vessels to balance both. And yet, pondering the effect of both sides on her, she wondered, what would she achieve at the end of the journey? She had had problems with the Ottoman officials at Jiza, suffered the contempt of the British officials in Damascus, and the lack of support of the authorities at home.[75] She would perhaps wonder, while feeling alone and lonely, whether solitude itself was the ultimate goal and the journey just a pretext.

Most of the time, however, she would cling to the official reasons. Her desires to learn about the situation in Arabia, map the tribes around the railway, trace the route of wells and note the ruins. She would avoid searching for other deeper, personal, buried reasons. She had been planning the journey to Arabia for quite a while, collecting material and confidential documents published only for internal use in government circles. Among them was a document issued in June 1907 by the General Staff of the War Office.[76] It had been forwarded to her by Valentine Chirol, whose book, *The Middle Eastern Question*, served as one of its sources. It described the situation in Arabia before the Young Turks' ascent to power in 1908, and the Wahhabis' desire to conquer the littoral of the Persian Gulf and win over the tribes on the coast from Britain's influence.

Gertrude learned from this secret document about the existence of a political conspiracy aiming at the expulsion of the Turkish garrisons from the Arabian Peninsula. The writer of the document wondered, however, whether the Arabs were able to stand up to the Ottomans. Only their involvement in an European war could force the Ottomans to withdraw from Arabia,[77] the official writer concluded. More information about the Arabs' desire to gain independence from the Ottoman Turks floated around. Among it were rumours that Sayyid Talib, the son of the *naqib* (head of the notables) of Basra, was planning a reunion of Arab chiefs in Kuwait. In her report to Chirol, she explained however, that the jealousies between Mubarak of Kuwait, Ibn Sa'ud of the Najd, the Shaykh of Muhammara, and the shaykhs of the Muntafiq and the 'Anaza were too strong to permit such a gathering.[78] Split and locally focused interests would not allow a general Arab rebellion against the Turks to materialise, she then believed.

Her ideas would change with time and with the deepening of her knowledge of the area. On her way to Ha'il, Gertrude realised that the tension between the specific, the precise and the vague and ambiguous remained a constant in the East. Even Islam, in the weightless reality of the desert, seemed to be in a constant quest for redefinition. This dualism could also be found in the conflict between Ha'il and Riyadh and their battle to conquer Arabia and redefine Islam.

The rejection of the elaborate and the superfluous had been the life purpose of Muhammad 'Abd al-Wahhab, the guide and preacher of the Wahhabiya, the Islamic doctrine adopted by the reigning dynasty of Riyadh. The quest for the message at its purest, the direct connection to the Prophet's teaching, and the belief in the Divine Oneness – as described in his book, *Kitab al-Tawhid*, – by which only God is the keeper of spiritual authority. A follower of Ibn Taymiya, Muhammad Ibn 'Abd al-Wahhab called for a return to the foundations of Islam and a rejection of all innovations (*bid'a*) expressed in the worship of saints and rituals. The pact (*mithaq*) concluded in 1744 with Muhammad Ibn Sa'ud, the ruler of Dera'ya, opened the way for the Saudi–Wahhabi expansion to the Hijaz and Mesopotamia. His fervent followers, the *muwahiddun* considered *jihad* (holy war) as a primordial duty aiming at the imposition of the shari'a on non-believers and innovators. For them, all efforts to interpret Islam were restricted to the Qur'an, the Sunna (the Prophet's sayings and deeds) and Sirat al-Salaf (the caliphs' lifestyle and conduct).

In 1801 the Wahhabis attacked Najaf and Karbala, the Shi'i sanctuaries in southern Iraq in a protest against the 'cult of tombs', namely the Shi'is' veneration for the burial places of 'Ali and Husayn. In 1803 they conquered Mecca, covering the Ka'ba with a red *kiswa* (silk cloth). They failed, however, to capture Baghdad and Damascus, long-distance targets with less receptive populations, and suffered a heavy defeat when Ibrahim Pasha's Egyptian troops destroyed Dera'ya.

The return to power of the Saudi emirs in 1824 to Riyadh, south of the old capital, and the expansion to the coast of the Persian Gulf did not prevent rivalries from developing, making possible the rise of new leaders. Among them was 'Abd Allah Ibn Rashid, who had been appointed governor of Jabal Shammar in 1834, and founded Ha'il's ruling dynasty. The tension that developed between Riyadh and Ha'il spilled over into questions of governance and style. The ornamental forms in · Ha'il contrasted sharply with the austerity reigning in Riyadh.

It was a different Islam from the one Gertrude had found in the towns of Syria or the plains of Mesopotamia. And it was different from the mystical Islam that she had found in Persia and rediscovered in her travels to Kurdistan, Turkey and India. She felt it even more clearly when she reached Ha'il, 'with its towers and gardens, its low mud walls, and its palm trees, all made so memorable in Charles Doughty's *Travels in Arabia Deserta*'.[79] Two slaves were sent out to meet Gertrude and to assure her that Ibrahim, the emir's *wakil* (agent), would be glad to see her. The emir himself – a boy of sixteen – was away raiding the Rawala, a northern division of the 'Anaza. While riding around the walls of the city-fortress, searching for the gate, Gertrude wondered whether the Shammar had still retained their power. The rest of the story is well known.

Gertrude was lodged in the emir's summer palace, and her tents were pitched in the courtyard where Persian *hajjis* spent the night on their way to Mecca. Following a wide empty street, she reached a large hall, its walls decorated with verses of the Qur'an. She was then led to the *roshan*, the city's reception room, furnished with carpets and cushions, their colours echoing the tones of the desert.

She was greeted by two women and an old widow called Lu-lu-ah, followed by a younger woman, 'gaily clad in red and purple cotton underrobes, an Egyptian gold embroidered scarf . . . strings and strings of rough pearls with a few emeralds and rubies round her neck . . . This was Turkiyya, a Circassian slave'.[80] Turkiyya belonged to Muhammad Ibn Rashid, the emir's uncle, and was 'a chatterbox of the first order'. She amused Gertrude while showing her around: the *kosh* – the open court with sweet lemon, quince, apple trees and pink almond flowers – and the small rooms that lodged Muhammad's other women. 'Turkiyya talked much of Istanbul: the tramvai . . . the arabanat, the food. But in Ha'il, *al hamdulillah* – the meat was good, and the dates – *ya hatra al Stambul*!! If only were the dates of Ha'il there!'. Back at the roshan, Gertrude waited for Ibrahim, who had taken the role of the regent in the emir's absence. Announced by a slave, Ibrahim entered 'wearing on his head a purple and red *kuffa*'. He was 'wrapped in a gold and embroidered abba and carried a silver mounted sword . . . his face was long and thin with a scanty beard . . . and kohl blackened eyes'.[81]

They talked of the Blunts, of Charles Doughty, and of the affairs of the desert: the 'Atayba, who did not want to pay tribute to the Sa'uds nor to the Rashids, and the 'rights' of the Shammar to rule over all, given their centuries-long presence in the area. Ibrahim told Gertrude that the *ulama* opposed her presence in Ha'il, and he asked her not to leave her quarters unless invited to do so. She had to spend some days and nights waiting in her rooms for an invitation to the palace, but none came. She then decided to send a message to Ibrahim, and was finally invited to the *qasr*.

Gertrude left her quarters at night. The streets were dark and empty, with occasional 'black figures of women creeping along the wall'.[82] Arriving at the qasr, she was escorted to the roshan, 'a very spacious and lofty room . . . the roof supported by great stone columns covered with jir-square capitals. Round the wall, carpets and cushions . . . the floor of white beaten bare stone as if it were polished'. Ibrahim sat before a fire burning in a marble fireplace, surrounded by the *qadi*, the shaykhs and court companions, the slaves, the chiefs of public service, the *rajaj*, the men-at-arms, the riders and the *ghazzu*.[83] 'Exactly as described in *Arabia Deserta*', Gertrude noted then. She had enquired about the history of the Shammar and the Banu Rashid, and impressed her hosts with her erudition. After coffee and tea were served, slave boys brought in 'censors with burning ads, and swung them three times before each of the guests as a sign that the meeting was over'.[84]

Gertrude was worried, however. The money she was supposed to receive in exchange for the letter of credit given to her by Rashid's agent in Damascus had been retained. It had been handed to the emir's treasurer and could be reimbursed only with the emir's permission. 'It was like a story in the *Arabian Nights* – but I didn't find it particularly enjoyable to be one of the *dramatis personae*', Gertrude reported later. While she waited, Gertrude ventured out at night to see the women at the qasr dressed in Indian brocades and jewels, surrounded by eunuchs and children. 'There was nothing but me myself which did not belong to medieval Asia . . . We sat on the floor and drank tea . . . as I say, the Arabian nights, passim'.[85]

After eleven days of imprisonment in a charged and suspicious atmosphere, Gertrude went to the men's tent and spoke her mind 'without any Oriental paraphrase'. She then rose, leaving the men sitting – 'a thing which is only done by great sheikhs'. Her courage won her the regent's respect. He sent Sayyid, the eunuch, 'with £200 in a bag and full permission to go where I liked . . . I replied with great dignity that I didn't intend to leave without seeing the Qasr and the town by daylight'.[86] Gertrude was shown the city and allowed to photograph what she wanted and to do whatever she pleased before leaving the town. After an affectionate farewell with Turkiyya, they parted forever, 'except in remembrance'. With the people of the town gathered around her, Gertrude threw copper coins in the air to be picked up by them. 'With this . . . my strange visit to Ha'il ended, in a sort of apotheosis'.[87] Once safely outside its walls, Gertrude was able to review in her mind the escape schemes she had planned if things had gone wrong. She thought of Fatima, the emir's grandmother, and of her power in court, And of the fear reigning at Ha'il, where murder was like 'the spilling of milk'. None of the shaykhs or princes felt his head 'sitting steadily upon his shoulders'. She left Ha'il with a sinister impression: of the rule of women and eunuchs, the deadly strife of succession and the jealousies preventing the unification of the desert.

Gertrude wanted to go south and then to Medina, but the tribes were in rebellion. Ibn Sa'ud had driven the Turkish troops from the roads when he reconquered al-Hasa on the littoral. 'He will certainly turn against Ha'il now', she wrote. 'If Ibn Sa'ud combines with the Ruwala and the 'Anaiza, they will have Ibn Rashid between the hammer and the anvil' she concluded.[88] She tried to avoid the rebellious tribes by using the game she used to play with Maurice when they were little: 'by trying to wander all over the house, up and down the staircases, without being seen by the housemaids', as she had noted in her diaries of January 1914. But there, in the desert, the rules were different. It was difficult to hide or to play. There was only dust, silence, and the pad of the camels on the soft grit.

*   *   *

Gertrude would never reach the Rub' al-Khali, as insurgent tribes were in her way. She would only dream about the unreal Empty Quarter, the one invoked by Dick in his nights of solitude with its 'devils of sand, wonders, discontent and weariness of life . . . the ones of the soul – not of the desert'. Only there, in his spiritual refuge, where solitude made dreams more palpable, would he become himself 'a sand devil, a thornbush . . . a quiet breeze under the clouds'. There, 'when you were breeze, I would be rain . . . and you, the sandstorm blotting over me, the shadow of a stone'. But this refuge 'in some hushed desert of ourselves',[89] would never come to pass.

Dick was back in England. Albania and the Balkans were behind him, even if the issue had not yet been resolved. Italy was now leading the way for control over Albania, leaving Greece, Serbia, and Austria-Hungary behind. The annexation of Albania, together with other territorial gains, had become Italy's main condition for joining the Central Powers then preparing for war. The prospect of an independent Albania seemed even more remote, and Doughty-Wylie prepared to go to other parts of the world to try to save, at least there, the interests of the Crown. While waiting in Suffolk to be sent on his next mission, he wrote to Gertrude. 'It's nearly dawn here – or it would be if it wasn't winter. It's deep snow . . . and too cold to go out. But I know it's rosy heaven in the desert'.[90]

He still imagined her – 'strong and Arab-like'. He wished to sit at her bedside and wake her to the 'desire of life in the morning'.[91] He was proud of Gertrude, particularly of her reports to *The Times* about the talks and quarrels over a united Arabia. He could see her sitting among the Arab chiefs and warning them of 'the frayed edges and the holes in the weaving' of desert politics.[92] 'You, queen of me – and Arabia'.[93] There was tension and responsiveness in their love, he once wrote, and there was equality. In Albania, he had wanted her by his side to help him and share the 'long peace of companionship and equal mind'. 'I never had it', he mused. 'Only with you I would have it and I love and thank you for it'.[94]

He wanted to keep their friendship. The knowledge of it made him humble, he wrote. Claiming that he was 'old and tired and full of a hundred faults',[95] Dick unravelled the conundrum he himself had created. 'Are you in love with me the man, or with love itself?' he once asked. 'Surely not with me. But love, the Great God, you love him. And to him I turn my prayers, that you may love my unworthy self'. He had known lesser feelings, but this was the true one, Dick assured her, and he would wait for the day they would meet again.[96] 'When I get older and half crippled . . . and possibly fat . . . may I still sit at the fire and be happy in your mind . . . as you will be in your body?'[97] 'It was not the fatigue of age', he explained, as much as resignation. 'Something eludes me always',[98] and he could not find 'the magic word that would unlock your heart and mine . . .'.[99]

There were the chains, he once said, the prison he lived in.[100] They would never reach the ecstasy.[101] 'Still, there was so much left. And all there is – we will take'. To her questions, he answered: 'Let it be for a moment – and perhaps in many thoughts, in many hours, in many lives, I will answer it'.[102] He did not know when would they meet again. He was waiting in England to be transferred to Africa, 'where there would be things to try for, to climb over, to get round, to win, more probably to lose. But of them I scarcely think'.[103] He deplored only the fact that he would not see her when she returned from Arabia. And yet, he had to go.

He had some thoughts about changing his life, about getting a permanent position in the diplomatic service – 'at least to ask'. He would not fight for the position, however. 'For it was all written – in the book': the little book she had given him at Rounton. If he left, would he burn the book, as he had burned her letters? 'I burnt the letters because I thought I ought to. Now I am sorry', he confessed. 'Even if you can write me thousands of others, still they were from you to me – and I burnt them, poor martyrs, in the fire!' He promised at the end not to burn the book but to leave it in his safe at the bank. 'Alone it shall come out and talk to me'.

Dick left then for Abyssinia. A dispute had broken out with the Italians over Lake Tana, and a conflict was about to erupt. He had even mentioned it in one of his reports to Lord Cromer, whom he would meet again on his way to Africa.

'Bless you, my dear', Dick wrote in his last letter. 'Do not march too many days running, do not let them know you have money with you – only the power to give it later – and wire to me, British Minister, Addis Ababa, your safe arrival: "safe Baghdad." How immensely happy I shall be to see it'.[104]

CHAPTER 4

'I Will Dedicate This Year to You'

Baghdad was many days away. Long days of riding and long nights of solitude and anxiety on her way from Hayaniya to the wells of Loqa.
Exhausted physically and mentally, Gertrude longed for peace and calm,
and the rest that would come after, as she later wrote to Dick. She certainly
wondered whether the marriage of minds was closer than that of bodies
and why the so longed-for – and yet unachievable – sensation of intimacy
prevented them from getting together. In Baghdad, she hoped to find his
letters.

In the meantime she would write about 'things that she could not tell
[her] family or friends, not even Domnul'. She would write to him about
'the irregular pulse of the mind and the excitement that followed it'. She
had sensed it in Ha'il, she recalled, and in the streets of the bazaars where
the force of law was felt less. She had sensed it in the desert where 'fear was
a way of life'. Near Loqa, the Shi'i tribes were dangerous, she explained.
'Yuzbahuna', she had heard her camel drivers whisper as they talked of the
ghazzu. 'They will slay us'. 'Al khawf qarib', they would say. Fear was near.

Paralysed at the view of the empty tents of the 'Amara after the ghazzu
had left, she listened to the sound of wind blowing through the abandoned
village. The view of 'corpses left on the sand to be eaten by the dogs' made
her cry, 'out of weariness and delusion as much as horror'. 'Oh, Dick, don't
let it be known . . . my reputation as a traveller would never survive such
revelations',[1] she pleaded. Time, the sense of place, the notion of danger
and the conquest of one's own fear. All seemed useless and vain.

She reported to Dick how the *rafiq* (guide) had reassured her: '*La
tifkikeri*' – don't be anxious. 'We are here to protect you'. She remembered
the rafiq's kindness and the way he helped her later in the journey. When
they stopped, he brought her a gift – a gazelle found near an empty tent.
The gazelle leant on Gertrude's lap and fell asleep, 'it lay curled round like a

Mycenaean ivory – with one absurd pointed horn stretched out over its ear'. The night would be long and frightening. 'There was no one around wholly free from apprehension, but the little gazelle asleep upon my knee'. Danger was still ahead, however. 'The (ghazzu) might slay us during the night [if they do it] . . . *nasib* – so be it', Gertrude wrote and fell asleep. But 'in the middle of the night, a strange moon rose and shone into the open tent, monstrous, deformed and red on the misty horizon',[2] threatening men and animals.

In the early hours of the next day, they would perceive the golden dome of Najaf glittering at distance. 'There was light . . . perhaps salvation . . .',[3] Gertrude still wanted to believe. The caravan could not camp inside the walls, she explained to Dick, nor even around them, because of the grave-yards. These were the graveyards of the Shi'i pilgrims, buried as near as possible to Imam 'Ali's tomb so he would intercede on their behalf on the resurrection day.[4] Gertrude saw how the transfer of corpses – *naql al-jana'iz* – proceeded. The bodies lay in 'long narrow wooden boxes' on the backs of mules,[5] waiting for their turn. Witnessing the ritual brought Gertrude back to the feeling that Najaf was a world apart, a 'world within a city'.[6] They camped in the *sabkha*, 'the salt grove where the palms grew'. It was a hot day and sand flies zoomed around, preventing Gertrude from writing her letter. She felt weak and tired. The adventure was over and, in the end, she concluded, 'there was always . . . nothing. Dust and ashes on one's hand . . . and dead bones that look as if they would never rise again'.[7] She wanted to write about Ha'il, to tell Dick the story, but she wasn't able to do it. She could only add some remarks on the edges of the pages already written while asking him to lend her the journal some day for her to write the full story of 'Arabia Infelix'. Although finding some support in the closeness that had developed in this exchange of letters, Gertrude was devastated by the thought of their impending separation.

When she reached Baghdad on March 24, 1914, her feelings changed, however. 'Safe Baghdad!', she telegraphed two days later.[8] In Baghdad she had found his letters, sent weeks and even months earlier from England and Africa. She would read them then and try to decipher the veiled messages, the hidden appeals, the eloquence of half-pronounced words.

A feast after seventy days in the desert, Baghdad had 'the pulse of life'. The railway and the new irrigation system projected a sense of progress. Modern locomotives had been imported in pieces and reconstructed on the spot. German technicians responsible for the German section of the railway handled the mission with accuracy. In the Hindiyya dam, the waters of the

Euphrates 'flew gaily down the Hilla branch'. And the Habbaniyya dam, when completed, 'would allow the draining of the swamps and the laying of the last piece of railway connecting Baghdad to the rest of the world'. Gertrude could compare the progress made in the last few years with what she had found there in her earlier visits. The inauguration in 1913 of the new barrage on the Hindiyya canal, planned by Sir William Willcocks, would prevent the floods of the Euphrates menacing Karbala with the drought that followed in nearby areas,[9] Gertrude explained.

Two English firms, Jackson and Pearson, were then competing for the concession that would turn the Habbaniyya Lake into a great reservoir. Its waters would then feed the rice fields, Gertrude recounted. The Tigris was yet untouched, but when the Tigris became again 'what it once was – mother of the cornfields, of date gardens and of villages . . .', then Iraq would turn into 'the garden which it is said to have been . . .'.[10]

Although this was an outcome of the efforts of the British in their attempt to retain control over Mesopotamia, the Germans were about to win the competition over the population's hearts. The planned Berlin–Baghdad railway would stretch from the Mediterranean to Gaza, 'Aqaba, Basra, reaching the Persian oil fields. Britain's planned railway across the Sinai would open the way to Taba, the little bay near 'Aqaba. The Baghdad railway project, initiated as a concession to a German company in 1899, was meant to open the Middle East to German economic penetration and damage Britain's hegemony in the Gulf area and the Middle East.[11] In fact, only a small section of the railway had been constructed at the time, representing more an irritating factor than a real threat and Britain had already managed to circumvent some of it by placing two directors on the railway board to preserve British interests.

In Baghdad, Gertrude recalled the good moments of the journey, 'the little pleasures of the desert, [her] canvas washtub and how it served to water the camels', and the warm reception she got from her old friends, the Naqib of Baghdad and 'Abd al-Qadir al-Qudayri, 'the man who held Baghdad in the palm of his hand'. Baghdad [seemed] then 'like a fairy city shimmering through the heat haze'.[12] In Baghdad, Gertrude left the rafiqs and prepared to cross the Syrian Desert on her own. Just her, Fattuh, her 'negro' camel, and two other servants. It was risky, she knew. Fattuh, her Armenian servant, was a 'man of the city and no less a stranger to the desert than [she was]'; he couldn't serve as her mouthpiece and 'explain, to avoid the dangers'. But she liked the [idea of] speaking for herself, 'to run [her] own show, and to be alone'.

'It was almost like having the desert to myself – *khala*, empty', she explained to Dick. She was alone with her thoughts, and the memories of that evening at Rounton. In twenty more days she would reach Damascus and stroll through vineyards and orchards, and describe 'the rushing water and the deep green corn, the grey shade of olive trees, and the rustle of chestnut leaves',[13] and the effect these had on 'eyes weary with deserts . . .'.

In Damascus, she found a message waiting for her, an invitation to visit Istanbul from Sir Louis Mallet, Britain's ambassador to the Ottoman Empire. She decided to go. She took the French boat that left from Beirut. In Istanbul, she revealed to Mallet 'the veiled secrets of the desert'. She told him the story of Arabia, of the Banu Rashid, of Ha'il, of the intrigues, the murders, and the 'Anazas' victory over the Shammar. She told Mallet of Ibn Sa'ud's raid on al-Hasa and the Porte's loss of control over the desert. She explained to Mallet that a Turkish garrison could not keep the border intact and save Ha'il for the Banu Rashid.[14] 'It is over – Ibn Sa'ud will have the desert', Gertrude concluded; she had a sense for politics.

On the train to London, Gertrude reread some of Dick's letters. He felt old, he wrote, 'older than his age, poor and unknown', 'and when one feels old, there is the shadow of death and a sense of the futility of life itself'. And yet, 'there was a wonder in ageing', he still believed, 'to sit on the hill top and watch the others climbing up through the thorns – and see the tops of all the hills . . . while the wind blows out of the clouds and the sun shines'. At the top of the hill, Dick hoped, he would find calm, confidence, and serenity'.[15] 'Serenity in death', he once explained, 'was the right way . . . the other way [was] torture, like hugging a thorn when it hurts so much'.

Dick answered her questions about fidelity, about the courage to choose and to sever chains. He believed only in 'the fidelity of the mind', he explained. When he mentioned fidelity of the mind, he meant not other women, but his wife. She wouldn't enter their garden,[16] 'but she has her place in the world and the right to be in it . . . and she is my wife . . .'.[17] They would never live in the garden – 'only know it was there' and they would never dare 'the altogether plunge . . . where mind and body see the new together'.[18]

Dick left for Cairo to see Field Marshal Horatio Herbert Kitchener (commander of Britain's imperial armies and the British agent in Egypt) in order 'to hear from the Great K' about Britain's interest in controlling the sources of the Nile and developing agriculture in the fertile plain between the Blue Nile in Abyssinia and the White Nile in East Sudan. Dick also planned to go to Khartoum and meet General Reginald Wingate, the new *sirdar* (commander-in-chief) of the Egyptian army and governor general of Sudan, and then continue to Abyssinia, 'always with your ghost upon me'. Dick would not wait for her return. But he hoped to hear from her in Cairo. Would she write? he asked.[19]

In his dreams he could see her 'by the Belqa castles, measuring, photographing, writing, working like ten men, tired, hungry and sleepy'. And yet, sometimes, he wanted 'to feel [her] lonely, missing [him] and love'. Dick would only write when he was by himself, and tell Gertrude that he would never be her lover. 'I read that beautiful and passionate book and know it'.[20] He would read the little book she gave him at Rounton for the last time, and leave it at his bank before he went. 'One might be killed', he reminded her. He would go, but he would write, he then promised, 'sometimes just a line, a thought, a wish'.

Gertrude did not fully grasp Dick's devotion to his wife, perhaps because, unconsciously, she did not want to shake off her own illusions. In some ways, this unconsummated love affair suited her, as it did not mean a surrender of her independence and intellectual pursuit, implying at the end a need to settle down and compromise. It was easier to entertain the thought of a distant, unobtainable love, than relinquish freedom and cope with the daily requirements of a steady and, with time, a less appealing relationship.

It was also easier for her to create idealised images of distant lovers, distant lands and distant families. Doughty-Wylie too, lived in the realm of fantasy, cherishing the image of an unrealisable happier life with Gertrude, than he apparently had with Judith. Why couldn't he leave her? Dominated by a rich and intelligent wife, and caught in what seemed to be a sexless marriage, Doughty-Wylie would search for some peace of mind in other missions and far away countries.[21]

*   *   *

Dick's letters from Abyssinia reached Gertrude in London. The first letter was posted at the end of April 1914. He had received the Ha'il journal sent from Baghdad, but he did not want to talk about it; he would only write and explain his next moves. He was far away, negotiating the location of a dam on Lake Tana with Abyssinia's rulers. The lake was one of the main sources of the Blue Nile, 'the river which was a life line for the Sudan and for Egypt'.

The Abyssinians believed that whoever ruled Tana, their sacred lake, would rule the country, which had remained an independent kingdom from Biblical times. Doughty-Wylie would have to reassure them that ruling Abyssinia was not Britain's purpose. What he wanted was to recover Eritrea (which the Ethiopians considered as Abyssinia's natural littoral) from the Italians. And yet Doughty-Wylie wanted to avoid a full-scale war between Italy and Ethiopia, as had happened in 1895. Clashing interests, among them Americans, Germans, French and British were making his mission a very difficult one. F. A. Thesiger, Britain's consul in Addis Ababa, had taken a hard line, while Doughty-Wylie thought that Britain would gain much more by negotiating the option to build a dam, a telegraph and a railway system than by declaring an open conflict.

But times were changing. 'A young man – Ras Mikhail – had risen to power after Emperor Menellak's death, and been crowned king of the Tigre', Dick explained in his letter to Gertrude.[22] He still believed that he would be able to convince Ras Mikha'il to sign an agreement with Britain that would prevent the dismemberment of Abyssinia, by letting the Italians have Eritrea. He had obtained Kitchener's and Wingate's approval for his plan. If the agreement were accepted, he would be appointed Britain's consul in Ethiopia in Thesiger's place. If he failed, he would have to leave, and 'see at the end of the day, England lose control over the waters of Tsana and the Nile surrendered to the Italians'.[23]

Conveying the sense that his principles were as strong as the solution he proposed were adaptable to the problems on the ground, Doughty-Wylie clearly misjudged others. Once his mission was accomplished, Doughty-Wylie wanted to come back to England to take part in the war that was about to break out in Europe. He wanted to be active again, he explained, and to 'command men in combat and in peace'. Understanding the causes of the war, the fury in the Balkans, the conflicts between religions, and the growing national feelings, he recognised now that his efforts had been in vain.

Much had happened in Europe since he had left for Ethiopia. In England Doughty-Wylie was brought back to the debates that had impaired the relations between the powers. In high circles there were those who remembered how the July 1911 dispatch of the *Panther*, the German gunboat, to Agadir as a reaction to France's invasion of Fez in May, had speeded up the events. The violation by Germany of the previous arrangement between it and France (that neither would annex Morocco) and most of all 'the display of naked force'[24] in the Mediterranean, had placed Germany at the top of Britain's list of enemies. France, Russia and Belgium would now fill the column of Britain's allies.[25]

What Churchill's future moves would be and how they would affect him, Dick didn't yet know. However, he would find out sooner than he expected. Churchill's appointment as first lord of the Admiralty in September 1911 had led him to endorse the 'close blockade strategy' that asked to 'seek out, hunt down and destroy'[26] any vessel that would challenge Britain's naval supremacy in the Mediterranean and the North Sea. Doughty-Wylie knew that Churchill's hawkish positions had met with cynical remarks from the assistant director of war operations at the Admiralty, Captain Herbert Richmond, the husband of Gertrude's sister Elsa. Doughty-Wylie followed these moves very closely. Churchill's resignation in February 1914 over the question of an increased naval budget when the Home Rule crisis was at its peak[27] did not lessen the tension, as the need to retain naval supremacy in 'decisive waters' – the Straits of Gibraltar, the eastern Mediterranean and the North Sea[28] – had become even more pressing. Britain's insularity and dependence on merchant shipping and on the navy for its safety, were at the basis of the belief that a blow to Britain's naval supremacy would mean the dismemberment of the empire, and the loss of control over the colonies. Europe would then pass 'into the iron grip of the Teuton and of all that the Teutonic system meant'.[29] From a more Middle Eastern focused viewpoint, the tension between the Entente Powers and Germany had been rekindled by Turkey's approaches to Germany. Underlying this tension was the need to keep Turkey neutral in order to maintain the straits open to Russia's trade.[30] Their interest was also to prevent a military threat to the Suez Canal, also needed in times of war for the passage of Indian troops to France. This could only be achieved by avoiding an open conflict with the Caliph of Islam.[31] Turkey's tilting toward Germany was also connected to the fact that Germany had not seized parts of Ottoman territory, while France had appropriated Algeria and Tunisia, and Britain was present in Egypt and Cyprus.[32] By the same token, the growing influence of the Triple Alliance (Italy, Austria and Germany) in the Mediterranean reinforced Britain's need to safeguard the north and west coast of France.[33] Believing in Britain's strategic advantages, Churchill was caught by surprise as the events unfolded.[34]

Planning to get back to Europe, Dick explained that he would like 'to do things', 'to straighten up the arrears of years; to settle questions without end . . . some small, some big'.[35] But now it was too late. 'Menelaus has attacked Flandres defying Britain's ultimatum', Dick explained to Gertrude in a hurried letter in August. The allusion, apparently, was to Menelaus, King of Sparta, who attacked Troy to recover his wife, Helen, from her abductor, Paris. What he meant to say was that Germany had attacked Belgium while aiming at Paris, the heart of France. Britain would have to decide whether to declare war on Germany, by aligning herself on the terms of the Entente Cordiale of 1904.[36] Dick would have to relinquish his former dreams to serve in the Middle East[37] and deal – 'oh, irony! – with Najd politics', having her, 'the wife of his heart', help him spot the intricacies and subtleties of desert politics.[38]

Gertrude had followed the debates preceding the outbreak of the First World War and had obtained the notes exchanged between Serbia and Austria-Hungary following the assassination in June 1914 of the Austrian archduke Franz Ferdinand in Sarajevo.[39] These notes related to Austria-Hungary's annexation of Bosnia-Herzegovina in 1908, the shattered equilibrium in the Balkans, Russian's claims to concessions over the Straits, and the bitterness that resulted from Germany's pressure on Russia to comply with the annexation.[40] The agitation against Austrian rule that culminated in June 1914 had precipitated the events. Austria-Hungary had declared war on Serbia on 28 July, Russia mobilised her troops against Austria-Hungary, and Germany had declared war on Russia and France.

On 4 August 1914, Britain declared war on Germany; a British expeditionary force crossed the Channel, reached France, and opened the Western Front. It was not only armies that were at war now; the whole imperial system was in conflict: Germany and Austria-Hungary were at war against the British Empire, it would not take long for the Ottoman Empire to align itself with Germany and Austria-Hungary, a move expected for some time. The Dardanelles had been closed and Turkish troops mobilised. Indian Expeditionary Force 'D' had sailed from Bombay in October 1914, and was preparing to land at Basra to secure the Persian Gulf for the government of India, to prevent German eastward penetration, to protect the shaykhs of Kuwait and Muhammara from the Turks and to assure for the Admiralty the 25,000 tons of oil exported monthly from oil fields in south Persia.[41]

There were also rumours regarding a planned advance of Turkish troops to Suez through the Sinai. Dick wasn't convinced it would be a wise move to confront the Turks in the desert. 'Both Napoleon and Alexander had tried to cross the desert and failed' he pondered. And still, 'there was the canal to be protected from the Germans'.[42] He asked himself whether the Arabs would align themselves with the Turks in the name of Islam and whether Britain would bolster the Arabs, placing the Sharif of Mecca in charge of the Holy Places and taking Baghdad and Basra for India.[43]

The announcement by Percy Cox on 5 November 1914, that the landing of the British at Basra was just a move 'to protect commerce and old friends' (the shaykhs of Kuwait and Muhammara) was a wise step, Dick believed. So, too, was Britain's assurance that the Holy Places in Najaf and Karbala would be protected. And yet Dick asked himself whether the Arabs would accept the presence of the British troops and whether the British would advance northward, to Baghdad. He was against it. In his view, the British should stop at Qurna, at the junction of the two rivers.[44] Would the plans of the India Office, to have Mesopotamia's wheat appease the famine in India and help Britain maintain Indian troops on the land, or would it increase the resistance in Mesopotamia and, in the end, incite India's Muslims against Britain? he asked himself.

All was still uncertain. To flee these uncertainties, Doughty-Wylie would again become Dick in his intimate letters, 'take up the pen and fly' to Gertrude. 'Tonight, I shall make love to you', he wrote once while apprehending the 'hundred edges' that would suddenly rise and tear them apart.[45] In his view the importance she gave to sex and chastity were highly exaggerated.[46] Only love was important: 'First, one must love beyond all caring and be loved ... and then ... the Gods must smile – and Venus cover us'. But 'love could float away, crystal clear and unattainable', and escape them, as the world was escaping, too.[47]

The Germans would occupy Paris and the Italians would occupy Eritrea, and at the end of it, 'there will be only two powers in the world – the Kaiser and Islam'.[48] Abyssinia would escape the British too 'and refuse to sell, at a splendid price, the only thing Britain wanted from her – Tana waters'. An agent of Britain's imperial designs, Doughty-Wylie underestimated the lake's importance as a symbol of independence in a country that had maintained its political autonomy from Biblical times. Tired and disappointed, Doughty-Wylie gave up. Thesiger would come back to Abyssinia and Dick would leave for Europe. He felt then very old, 'looking back at the lovely world for the last turning'.[49] 'The war had changed the course of life and death' and, while imagining Gertrude still young and full of life, he wondered whether they would be able 'to welcome death with a smile . . .'.

*　　*　　*

War had changed the course of life in England as well. 'Isn't it incredible?' Florence had asked Lisa in August, after being appointed president of the Yorkshire branch of the British Red Cross. 'There was a time when we were going calmly about our business, thinking that the writing of books was the only thing that mattered'.[50]

Yorkshire was now preparing to assist the troops on the front, if the need arose. The city hall had been turned into a convalescent home, also serving as a school. Men trained, while women organised health services. Boy scouts delivered the mail and prepared the equipment for the evacuation of the wounded from the front lines. Back home, Gertrude helped to design a camp-bed like the ones she had used on her travels abroad. It consisted of a wooden structure fastened with canvas, on which lay a straw mattress.

The younger men in the family had been mobilised. Elsa's husband, Captain Herbert Richmond, directed the war operations at the Admiralty while continuing to criticise Churchill's moves as impulsive and non-professional.[51] Maurice was sent to the front with his battalion, and Gertrude herself would soon leave for Boulogne Seine et Oise, near Paris, to locate Britain's missing and wounded soldiers. Doughty-Wylie's wife, Judith, had established a private hospital in France, a local branch of the British Red Cross, and offered its services and facilities to the Allies.

On the last day of the year, Gertrude wrote to Dick again.

> I will dedicate this year to you and all the years that come after it . . . Would you accept my meagre gift? Would you fill my cup – this shallow cup that has grown so deep to hold your love and mine? . . . In the midst of all the waste and the misery, the anxiety and the lives laid down, would you understand the importance of life?[52]

Feeling the proximity of death around her, Gertrude wanted to let Dick feel that life was a supreme value.

The year closed in an apparent military deadlock. The stalemate on the Eastern Front confirmed earlier predictions. Britain and France had lost more than a million soldiers. British soldiers were stuck in the mud and 'wade waist deep through rain-soaked clay'.[53] The cavalry was unable to move – and 'frostbite made the soldiers' feet and legs so tender that the lightest touch was agony', Gertrude reported.

The most unfortunate were the Indian soldiers brought to Europe to fight beside the British troops. They were physically small, suffered from the weather and 'fell like flies in the trenches'. In October 1914, in the attack on Neuve Chapelle, 500 of them were killed. They should have been sent to Egypt, Gertrude thought, or to Mesopotamia, where they would be better suited to the climate, but she wondered whether they would agree to fight Muslims. Gertrude had visited the Indian soldiers in their camps at Christmas and saw 'the Sikhs, the Gurkhas, and the Yats sitting cross-legged, playing cards'. Their cooks were preparing Hindu and Muslim dishes and the smell of lamb and spices filled the air. 'It was like stepping into the East again',[54] Gertrude commented with Dick. This was the only good memory she kept from Christmas 1914. In all, it had been a 'Christmas of mud, slime, and vermin'.[55] She was worn out. And then, to her surprise, she received a message from Judith, Dick's wife. Judith needed a surgeon for her hospital, and asked Gertrude to locate one. 'I put on my hat and ran to the head of the Commission and found a surgeon doctor for her',[56] she wrote to Dick.

An encounter with Judith was hard for her to bear. From Judith, she learned that Thesiger was returning to Ethiopia and that Dick would be back to England soon. His plan to reach an agreement with the Ethiopians over the Lake Tana had failed. He resigned, letting Thesiger take over again. His plan was to engage in Kitchener's new armies, which were training to attack in the spring. When Gertrude realised that Dick could be sent to the front if he returned to Europe, where all was 'deadlock, and vain courage', she asked him not to come. But, if back, would he wire her at the Hotel Maurice, Boulogne, or at her office, 36 bis rue Victor Hugo? she pleaded. If he did, she would take a leave of absence and meet him in London. 'It is worse, so much worse than if I were your wife . . . I must stand aloof and trust the chance . . . But it shall not be quite chance, you will not let it be all chance, will you?',[57] she pleaded, urging him to come to Paris.

The war had had a wrenching effect upon Gertrude, but her reactions seemed to reflect more than just anguish under wartime conditions. Gertrude was exhausted physically and mentally after months and months spent counting the losses. Death was around her at every step, she wrote to him again, at the office, in the faceless files, or in the battlefields with the crowds of wounded.

Overwhelmed by the scenes of destruction, Gertrude asked Dick whether she could come to see him in London. 'In Boulogne', she pleaded, 'among all those curious eyes, we would not even have a place to talk'.

Dick seemed clearly more detached and his letters more evasive. Entangled in his own problems, Dick let his indecisiveness pervade his now shorter letters. While waiting for his answer in her hotel room, Gertrude perceived the moon 'shining through shifting clouds onto the wet street',[58] and she wrote to him again: 'I won't hinder you in any way . . . wouldn't you say I mustn't come?'[59] Dick wrote back saying that he would come to France to see Judith, but he would not meet with Gertrude. Nor did he want her to come to London. 'Don't come even if I am alone. I shall have a hundred of things to do and people to see. We shall see but a little of each other and under bad conditions: of hurry, business and interruption. It will be hard and things would seem wrong, unnatural, intolerable'.[60]

There was much to say, he wrote to her – but she would have to understand them herself, 'to talk with my lips and my silence'. She had to think of the aftermath, and the consequences, 'of those things that keep running down this pencil, shouting to be written but which I won't write . . .'. If still afraid of the 'devils' – the images of their sexual desires – 'don't come'.[61] Frustrated by Gertrude's unwillingness to engage in an experience of physical intimacy and unsatisfied with a mere union of minds, Dick was getting tired of Gertrude's inhibitions, fears and inexperience in love's physical expression. It wasn't just her puritanical strain or perhaps her inexplicable embarrassment with her body. The fact was that Gertrude's vibrant, but suppressed erotic nature, had driven both of them to very frustrating situations. In these moments, Gertrude certainly felt more emotional than sexual deprivation, while Dick, 'an earthly man', as he had once defined himself, became even more exasperated with Gertrude's constant indecision.

Feeling perhaps the uniqueness of the moment or moved by an inexplicable sense of urgency, Gertrude flew to London to stay with Dick for a day or two. They would meet in a hurry, 'there was no time, no time for anything',[62] They had planned a visit to Kew Gardens, but time slipped away, leaving both of them frustrated and apprehensive of what the future held in stock. Gertrude regretted her indecisiveness when she was back in Boulogne. Sad and disappointed, also because she had spoiled the few intimate moments they had together, she tried to explain that she feared the 'unknown', as she called the act of love itself. Dick should be the one to free her from the 'ghosts'. In the meantime, she would wait 'until you give me the only name I ask for'.[63] Dick did not answer this very specific demand. Disappointed at the word not spoken and tormented by doubts, regrets and desires, Gertrude could not rest:

> I can't sleep, I can't sleep . . . You and you and you are between me and any rest – but out of your arms there is no rest. Life you called me – fire. I flame and live and I am consumed . . . Is it I who must breathe courage into you, my soldier? Before all the world – claim me and take me and hold me forever and ever. That's the only way it can be done.[64]

Unwilling to face the fact that Dick did not have the strength or the will to leave his wife, Gertrude planned to live with him openly when the war was over. 'I will give you tears and laughter and silence, speech, fondness on twilight rest. All the day between shall be made light for you, and the night – a glory', 'And the world would forgive . . .'. But if what he had in mind was just 'a moment, a night, a week, and then separation', 'then have that hour and I will have it and meet the bill'.

And if you die – wait for me. I am not afraid of that other crossing . . . if there is nothingness, then there is nothingness . . . I have said goodbye to the world I knew. I shall never write again, nor travel again, nor touch my flowers, nor work in the garden – it has all bloomed in vain for me since August 1913 . . .

August was when he had come to Rounton.

While feeling that life, or perhaps death, were intruding to dash her hopes, Gertrude begged: 'Dick, take care. Take care to live'.[65] But even at that crucial moment, Gertrude was unable to confront the reason for her fear of physical intimacy. One explanation may lie in the fact that she feared the moment in which, so she perhaps believed, she might lose control over her body and her feelings. That possibility for someone whose whole life had been defined by discipline and self-restraint, was perhaps more frightening than all the other possible reasons brought together.

'Having spoken what was in [her] heart, [she] would now write of kings, principalities, and powers'. Britain's policy makers were still wondering what would be the best way to end the deadlock in France. Churchill came up with a new strategic approach, to break through the Dardanelles, the slim water passage linking the Sea of Marmara to the Aegean. If successful, this move would break the Turkish defences, possibly forcing Turkey out of the war and would open the way for British and French battleships through the narrows connecting them with the Russian ships in the Black Sea. Churchill's idea had not yet won the cabinet's approval, however.[66]

The year had opened with the sinking of a British battleship by a German submarine. On both fronts, the deadlock continued. The Allies' prospects appeared slim. Britain searched for a military breakthrough, as Kitchener's new armies prepared for the spring offensive. While the 'Westerners' believed that the war should be won in France the 'Easterners' believed that the key for a victory could be found in Asia Minor, the Balkans or the Baltic.[67]

But more than anything else, Kitchener, now war minister, was focused on attacking the Turkish posts at the Dardanelles. A naval attack on the straits would distract Turkey's attention from the Eastern Front and perhaps help resolve the stalemate on the Western Front. It would also serve to release the wheat trapped in the Black Sea, helping to solve, temporarily at least, the problem of food supply to the Indian army. The operation was based on the idea that the Turkish garrisons at Gallipoli would evacuate their positions without the British troops having to go ashore. Churchill believed that the attack on Gallipoli would be the best way to defend Egypt. Kitchener also believed that the evacuation of the Turkish troops from Gallipoli would spread panic in the Turkish army, cutting it in two, leading to Turkey's surrender in Europe and, possibly, to a reversal of power in Constantinople.

The importance of Constantinople was enormous.[68] A victory in the Dardanelles could lead Turkey to leave the Central Powers, and help persuade Greece, Bulgaria and Romania to enter the war on the side of the Triple Entente. It would also mean territorial gains for other nations directly or indirectly involved in the operation.[69] But above all, a naval victory in the Dardanelles would give Britain control of the Sea of Marmara, providing a link to the Russian navy on the Black Sea, opening the straits to its fleet,[70] and, finally give Britain access to the Danube. That all meant Russian and British armies' penetration, if victorious, to the very heart of Austria-Hungary. As Rupert Brooke, the young poet wrote when preparing to take part in the campaign to conquer Constantinople:

> It's too wonderful for belief.
> If . . . shall we [then become] a turning point in history?[71]

But all these considerations were at that point, doubtful hopes or terrible 'Ifs'.[72]

Lord Hardinge, India's viceroy, was even hopeful that a victory in the Dardanelles would reinforce Britain's position in India, enhance its influences on the Muslim populations in Persia and Afghanistan and permit certain territorial gains. Among them were Alexandretta, the natural outlet for northern Syria and northern Mesopotamia,[73] and the Euphrates Valley (stretching from 'Urfa to Baghdad and then to Basra), thus preventing Russia from gaining access to the warm waters of the Persian Gulf. Basra would then become a part of the British Empire. There were even some thoughts about Turkey's reaction against German influence on the Turkish army, if defeated. In parallel to the British scheme, the Turks were advancing their plan regarding an attack on Egypt by crossing the Sinai Desert and the Suez Canal with the help of the Germans. By that they expected to incite a popular uprising in Cairo and bring about the expulsion of the British from Egypt.

In a letter to Doughty-Wylie, written days after their furtive encounter in London, Gertrude expressed her opinion on the situation: 'If Russia takes Constantinople, Germany would have Asia Minor and other substantial gains'; otherwise 'there will be another war in twenty years, and another . . . a cycle of them'. But there was fear in the air, and fear paralysed nations as much as men. 'Fear [also] paralyses you, Dick, and that's a thing you scarcely know'.[74] Fear paralysed her too, something she still refused to fully admit.

She wanted to share with him her ideas on the Palestinian question, referring to a memorandum she had prepared for Herbert Samuel, the president of the Board of Trade, an influential political figure and a personal friend. The idea was to create a state for the Jews under Britain's aegis, which would serve as a buffer between the British in Egypt and the French in Syria. As tempting as it could seem at first sight, the idea of settling Jews among Muslims presented unforeseen difficulties, she admitted. 'I wish I could talk of it to you, Dick'.[75]

Jerusalem, she explained, was the third most holy city to Muslims. 'You could not turn out Islam but with the sword – and the sword we cannot use'. Gertrude believed that British Eastern policy should be guided primarily by its concern for its Muslim subjects. Therefore, Gertrude suggested the creation of 'Palestine Prima' under the guarantee of the powers. The Jews would settle in the area north of Jerusalem, including the port and railway of Haifa, and the Arabs would keep the rest. 'It's a great plot I am weaving'.[76]

But moods, plans, and plots such as Gertrude's changed when, on 19 February 1915, the British naval bombardment of the Dardanelles began. Eight British battleships and four French bombarded Kum Kale and Cape Helles. It was a short naval attack. The warships returned since bad weather prevented a longer action. Some days later Royal Marines landed in Gallipoli, destroying forts and ousting the Turkish and German gunners from the coast. A number of them had hidden, however, among the ruins of destroyed villages.[77]

After the naval bombardment, Doughty-Wylie wrote to Gertrude. He too wanted to talk about kings and politics and 'the rest of the emotions of the last days'. Jamal Pasha, the Turkish general, had given up the attack on Egypt and was moving his troops in the direction of Mesopotamia. 'Would the Arabs go with the Turks?' he asked, 'or would the Turks abandon the fight and return to Anatolia and sit there?'[78] His guess was that the Turks would fight neither for the Arab provinces nor for their leading role in Islam; but this was just a guess. A new Middle East was emerging. Ibn Saʿud had won the desert, and Dick's friend, Captain W. H. I. Shakespear, sent to advise Ibn Saʿud on his moves and to negotiate an accord with the Wahhabis, fell in the battle with Ibn Rashid. Britain would have to adjust to these new developments and rethink its policies.

Gertrude answered on 10 March, telling Dick that Judith had come to see her: 'We talked of nothing . . . but I am torn with regret and with desires'. She had found wild daffodils in the market. 'Their calm little faces watch me and ask me how shall I endure another spring . . . and they mock at me because I turned away from life'.[79] And yet she wondered, 'What will it be when I reach it? Will it be momentary glory and ecstasy past all believing?' She did not regret their closeness. 'What was given is given, there is no taking back . . . I wish I had given more . . . except that more of it is my hand for you to take'.[80]

A few days later, her regret grew deeper as she might have felt that the moment had passed:

> If I had given more, should I have held you closer – drawn you back more surely? . . . And suppose the other way had happened. The thing you feared and I half feared. *That* must have brought you back. If I had it now – I would magnify the Lord and fear nothing . . . 'A bond would have come into being', as a poet said. This is the strongest instinct of mankind – to love and be loved and thereby to carry our life . . . I don't want to die . . . I want life from you . . . And the price? Let's laugh at it together.[81]

The 'living bond' – perhaps a child – she wanted from Dick was now no more than a regret. Her desires were now confined to memories. And yet there was urgency in the historical moment. The naval attack on the Dardanelles that continued for almost a month did not bring the expected results. The Dardanelles and the Bosphorus forts were still under Turkish control. Churchill's belief that battleships could destroy Turkish artillery without the use of troops was illusory. While 80,000 troops were assembling at Lemnos under General Ian Hamilton, another naval attack was planned. On 18 March, sixteen battleships renewed Britain's attack on the Dardanelles. At the end of the day, 600 men had been killed and sunk battleships had been left near the shores. Britain had to revise positions regarding the landing of troops. On the larger strategic level there were no signs of the Ottoman Empire's fall. Greece, Bulgaria and Italy still remained neutral. On 20 March a secret agreement was signed between Britain and Russia, by which

Russia would take control of Constantinople and the Bosphorus, and Britain would focus on the Middle East and Persia. On 26 March Turkey's appeals to Germany to send military aid were answered, and General Liman von Sanders arrived in Gallipoli to take control of the Turkish Fifth Army. Doughty-Wylie had written to Gertrude as he was preparing to leave with the Mediterranean Expeditionary Force that would take part in the landing at Gallipoli planned for the end of April. 'I will leave to Malta and . . . it will be as God pleases'.[82] 'Dick, take care to live', Gertrude pleaded in return.

As his day of departure drew nearer, her requests became even more specific.

Dick, I have had a few resplendent hours. I could die and not be pitied. But you – you have not had what you wanted. Live to have it . . . I have swung of my own self into the rhythm which you beat out on my shoulder. I am in tune with that measure . . . part of it . . . [but] the choice is yours.[83]

and again a few days later:

I am so wrapped in glory. Glory and longing and the thought of what will be – whatever way you choose to give it to me. For a day long as a lifetime or for a lifetime short as a day . . . I am yours.[84]

Alternating between exuberance and melancholy, passing from one feeling to another with great speed, Gertrude conveyed mixed messages. Things weren't clear for her either. She had been asked by the War Office to return to London to help map areas of the Middle East that had not been charted previously by anyone but her. Gertrude refused to go for more than a single day. 'I don't at all want to go to London. It's closed to me now . . . those days too near . . . I would hate going back'.[85] 'I want to stay here and step out of people's memory a little – until I slip out of it altogether . . . one way or another'. Finally, she accepted the assignment, for four or six weeks, 'to pull the things straight' and then to return to Boulogne, where 'I would be freer to live or die as I might want'.[86] If Dick had returned in the meantime, he would find her in London, and if she were to join him, she would leave from there. 'What will become of me if you don't come back?'[87] she asked.

There was a way out, she explained, but she didn't yet dare to take it. She wanted him back and she warned him 'Don't be missing . . . There is no one to make enquiries and I might be led astray'.[88] Her sister Molly had just given birth to twins. 'This should be her answer to the weariness of war and not the other way around', she pleaded, 'To live, not to die'.[89] 'I am chained now [but] I don't want to die . . . I want life from you'.[90] While wondering what would she have made of it had he accepted her suggestion, it seemed clear now that they were both incapable of meeting each other on their own terms. He was holding back while she still wanted to believe in a life together. But time was running out.

So were the chances of a breakthrough in the stalemate at the Western Front. On 10 March the British tried to break through the German lines at Neuve Chapelle and capture Aubers but failed.[91] In the attack thousands of British and Indian soldiers lost their lives trying to get through to the German trench lines. It was the first important defeat of Kitchener's New Armies, which for long months had embodied the hopes and expectations of the British and their allies. 'The Cameronians lost all their officers. All. It is horrible and yet splendid . . . But is it worth the cost?', Gertrude asked some days later, understanding that the 'splendour' of heroism, as promoted by imperial Britain, also meant the lives of those who wouldn't profit from the empire's gains.[92]

In her letter of 15 March to Doughty-Wylie, Gertrude enclosed a letter dated 10 February 1915, written by her close friend Domnul aboard the *Northbrook*, a Royal Navy vessel anchored in the port at Basra. The engraved letterhead, 'Viceroy's Camp, India', was a palpable illustration of Britain's presence in the Persian Gulf. Indian Expeditionary Force D (IEF D) had landed at Fao on 7 November 1914. The British had occupied Basra and reached Qurna at the confluence of the Tigris and the Euphrates. 'From our outposts on the Tigris just beyond Qurna, I have had a glimpse of the Turkish camp. The water has been rising rapidly in both rivers during the last few weeks and operations will be difficult if not impossible', Domnul informed her, not yet knowing that the price that Britain would have to pay to get Mesopotamia would be even higher.[93]

Nor had the prospects of Britain's more marked presence in the Middle East improved. The British had expected the Arabs to rise up against the Turks and eventually join the Allies. But nothing of the sort had happened yet. Neither Shaykh Mubarak of Kuwait nor the Shaykh of Muhammara, with whom Britain had special agreements, made any move in this direction, and Ibn Sa'ud, 'who has just taken a bad knock from your friends at Ha'il, does not seem inclined to burn his boats'.[94] In fact, the struggle for supremacy in the Hijaz went on in spite of the Wahhabis early victory over the Shammar and developed in the context of a continuous political turmoil until the First World War made possible the penetration of foreign powers and the formation of new alliances and political configurations.

The big surprise was Mesopotamia's Shi'is' response to the sultan's call for a jihad against the Allies. Britain was afraid of the effect it could have, not only on Indian Muslims, but also on Afghanistan, the buffer state between India and Russia, 'Asia's other power'. A united Muslim front against Britain, which would also enliven the pro-German sentiments of the Muslims in Persia, could cause the Allies great trouble in Central Asia. 'Pan-Islamism is not yet a force fully ripe for explosion', Chirol explained in his letter '. . . (but in a few years) [it] will become a very serious danger'.[95]

In effect, pan-Islamism was a force to be reckoned with. In spite of the Young Turks' mistakes, 'the Nizam of Hayderabad and the Shaykh of Kuwait – to take two instances pretty far apart – have been afraid to insist upon the omission of the Sultan's name from the Khutba',[96] proving at that juncture the sultan's lasting prestige as the caliph of all Muslims and not just as the temporary ruler of his subjects.

What would happen once the war was over remained a moot question. One of Britain's main concerns were Abadan's oil fields, south of Muham-mara, whose economic and strategic importance was growing. The same was true of Britain's permanent presence in the Persian Gulf. The need to retain Basra in order to prevent Germany from extending the Berlin–Baghdad railway southward also meant stopping Germany's access to the Persian Gulf and the Indian Ocean. '[But] if we mean to retain Basra, we shall have, sooner or later, to go to Baghdad',[97] explained Chirol, a remark illustrating the debate taking place as early as February 1915 on Britain's presence in Mesopotamia.

The British had not made up their minds regarding a possible advance toward Baghdad, however. An agreement had been negotiated with the notables of Basra, by which 'special measures of administrative control' would be established in the vilayets of Basra and Baghdad in order to pre-serve Britain's interests in the area. Its terms were loose, however, and the British were indecisive about how to implement it. Turkish garrisons were stationed at Nasiriyya, north of Basra, their presence tactically accepted. The chaos and political vacuum that could result from Turkey's total loss of control could endanger Britain's position in the whole area, a position that had been prepared by the agreements signed separately with the shaykhs of Kuwait and Muhammara (in 1899, 1907 and 1914). These agreements would open the way to other agreements: the one with Sharif Husayn of Mecca and, the British wanted to believe, with Ibn Sa'ud. How these agree-ments could comply with the interests of Britain's allies, mainly France, was still to be seen. Among others, the question of Palestine emerged as the most complex one.

In April 1915, Mark Sykes, the former British traveller and now MP, came up with the idea of assigning Palestine's holy places (Jerusalem and Bethlehem) to Russia, opposing the Foreign Office's suggestion to hand over Jerusalem, Bethlehem and Nazareth to the United States. Kitchener, on his part, wanted the Syrian towns of Aleppo and Alexandretta to be included in the territories under British influence. Haifa would then become a British port and the terminal of Mosul's pipeline. Herbert Samuel wanted Palestine to become a Jewish national home under Britain's protection.[98] From the viewpoint of those focusing on the repercussion of these developments on the Middle East there were other considerations, however, some of which preceded the contradictory tendencies that prevented more conclusive policies. Their effects were still felt, however, looming behind other, older and newer ideas, that emerged as events unfolded. First of all, there was the declared need to ensure that the Holy Cities (Mecca and Medina for the Sunnis and Najaf and Karbala for the Shi'is) remained in Muslim lands; secondly there was Britain's need to secure control over the land route to India and the Suez Canal, and to find a way to preserve a British presence in Egypt, in spite of the provisional nature of the protectorate (declared in December 1914). There were, as well, the claims of Russia (over Constantinople and the Straits) and of France (over 'Great Syria' including the coast, i.e. Lebanon and Palestine) that had not been addressed yet. But above all, there was the burning question of Palestine, dealt with by the interdepartmental Bunsen Committee (April–June 1915) and the various possible solutions it raised (kept secret until 1939). It all depended, however, on Turkey's fate and the division of her territories either by partition or by negotiation between the Powers regarding informal spheres of influence allocated to each of them.[99] But none of these plans could materialise without a victory in Gallipoli and Britain's access to the Dardanelles.

From the general headquarters of the Mediterranean Expeditionary Force, whose soldiers were preparing to land at Gallipoli, Doughty-Wylie wrote to Gertrude. He had read once more the letter containing 'the ultimatum'. 'My dear, I have read it but of that I cannot write'.[100] Neither could he tell her what was going on. The censor 'cramped his style', he confessed, but someday they would talk freely about the 'show', the term they used for the military campaign. As for what had happened between the two of them in London, he reassured her: 'It was right in London and the sober part of one does not regret . . . The drunk part regrets and remembers, until he goes to sleep. No . . . that isn't a bad thing to break any fool law, as long as it is a law'.[101]

Italy had joined the war on the side of the Entente. 'Italy is finally bought – the bargain signed. A big price but little of it out of our pockets . . . [Italy would get] all of Southern Anatolia and something in Africa. I don't know what. I hope it's not Abyssinia'.[102] It was not Abyssinia, at least not this time.[103] Italy's gains would come from Austria-Hungary and Turkey if the Central Powers were defeated in the war. From Austria-Hungary, Italy would get Trentino, South Tyrol, Trieste, Gorizia and Gradisca, the Istrian Peninsula, Northern Dalmatia, and islands on the Dalmatian coast. From Turkey, it would receive a 'sphere of influence' in Anatolia and some colonial territory in North Africa.[104] But a victory at the Dardanelles should come first.

On 19 April, Gertrude wrote to Dick, 'Don't you realise that after these months of being alone with one another – at least in letters – we could never go back to the old rules?' 'No . . . it wasn't an ultimatum', she explained,

> I will never bargain with you . . . I love you so that if you had rather that I dropped out and left the world free for you – I will do that too . . . Only it must be a complete dropping out, you understand . . . Therefore, you must choose for me . . . remembering only that you can't have it both ways.

Gertrude had told her sister Elsa their story. 'She observed, after many hours of talk, that it would be a very interesting end to my remarkable career . . .'. Although Gertrude could keep their secret, she didn't want to. 'I can't live a pretence and you couldn't wish it', she concluded.[105]

Germany had issued a stamp bearing the legend *Gott strafe England* (God punish England) but the war was not yet over. Pan-Islamism could still become the force the Germans expected. 'It is well known in the bazaars that German guns pronounce the "Allahu Akbar" when they fire and that Hajji Wilhelm has given his daughter to the Sultan to be his wife', Dick commented sarcastically. On 20 April, Doughty-Wylie wrote to Gertrude from the headquarters of the Mediterranean Expeditionary Force: 'Today I pack up all your letters, dear queen of words, and leave them addressed to you . . .', 'Tomorrow if the weather moderates, I am embarking on the collier . . . "the wreck ship" or the wooden horse of Troy which we are going to run on the beach and disembark by an ingenuous arrangement . . .'. It was a daring operation, to get to the coast in boats, 'If we fail, it is political disaster, not only here but also in India and Egypt. If we win – a surprising success from which England gains but little'.[106]

General Sir Ian Hamilton, famous for his courage, would command the operation. Five separate beaches at Cape Helles were designated as destinations for the landing troops and code-named S, V, W, X and Y. Two thousand two hundred troops were hidden aboard a collier named *River Clyde*, prepared for the landing. Colonel Doughty-Wylie, who should have been aboard the H.M.S. *Queen*, had asked to be on the *River Clyde*, to be among the first to land. His knowledge of Turkish would help in the attack, he claimed. Watching the beach from the deck of the *River Clyde*, Doughty-Wylie reread Gertrude's last letter: 'I long for the rest, of letting myself go down the flood and out into the great sea . . . if you die – wait for me . . . I am not afraid of that other crossing . . . I will come to you'.[107]

'My dear Gertrude', he answered on the night of 21 April. He had written 'a very stupid letter . . . not liking to go without a word.' He had made arrangements in case he was killed, to carry for Judith's wellbeing. To Gertrude he wanted to write 'the free things of the spirit', and begged her

> don't do what you talked of, it's horrible to me to think of it . . . it is unworthy of so free and brave a spirit . . . You, to die, for whom the world holds so much, for whom there is always the pure delight of capability and power well used . . . don't do it . . . Time is nothing – we join up again . . . *'ave valeque'* . . . I shall write to you again by the first post which I hope may go from Gallipoli.[108]

Gertrude's letter to Dick, written some days later, crossed his in the mail: 'I am sick with hope – why do people talk of hope as if it were a blessed thing? It's hateful, exhausting, deadening. I want fulfilment'.[109] Later on the same day, Gertrude added more words to her previous message:

> Rupert Brooke has died at Lemnos. Did you realise that they were his little verses I quoted to you the night you left? And the couplet I began to quote to you [when] you got up very hastily? I will tell it to you now for I am not the least afraid of the omen, and it is so fine:
>
> > I thought when love for you died
> > I should die
> > It's dead – alone, most strangely,
> > I live on . . .
> > and Rupert Brooke, who died at
> > Lemnos will live again in us.[110]

While these words were being written, the last arrangements for the landing of the 29th Division, formed by the Munster and Dublin Fusiliers and the Hampshire Regiment, had been made. An armada of 200 ships and 30,000 troops were heading to Gallipoli's southern beaches and to Gaba Tepe on the Aegean coast.[111] The landing started four days later, on 25 April. The operation nearly failed at first, due to Turkish gunfire from the ruins of the village. Protected by the darkness of the night's first hours, Doughty-Wylie left the boat and returned hours later with important information. On the morning of 26 April, he took command of the attack on V beach and captured the old castle at Sidd al-Bahr.

> All he carried was a small cane, and from a band he wore round his arm, the men gathered he was a staff officer. He walked about in the open under a continuous fire, talking to the men, cheering them up, and rallying them together. Then, when all was ready for the bayonet charge, he placed himself in front of them all, and armed simply with his cane, led them in a great charge up the hill. . . . As he entered the old fort on Hill 141 ahead of his men, Doughty-Wylie fell to rise no more.[112]

3. Memorial window in Theberton Church, Suffolk,
showing Lt Col 'Dick' Doughty-Wylie VC as a modern St George,
by kind permission of Lynda Clarke and the PCC of St Peter's Church,
Theberton, Suffolk.

He was shot by the Turks next to Major Grimshaw of the Dublins. The death of 'gallant Captain Unwin and the boy Drewry'[113] was reported to the authorities with the description of how he had walked 'fearlessly to his death'. It was his attraction to the empowering sense of danger that rescued him, at the end, from the indecisiveness that had marked his life.

Next morning, a red stain of blood spread in the blue Aegean Sea. 'A horrible sight to see' reported a naval aviator flying over Sidd al-Bahr.[114] 'Doughty-Wylie was buried at midnight where he fell', reported one of his men, 'and the River Clyde's carpenter made a simple wooden cross for his grave'.[115]

Hearing the first news about the landing, Gertrude hurried to write:

> My dear, today at last we have the account of your splendid achievement . . . Please, send me even the briefest word whenever you can – so that I may know it's well with you. It's dreadfully hard to bear. I feel to have been so broken by the emotion of this week that I cannot write.[116]

Gertrude never finished the letter. The news of Doughty-Wylie's death reached her the day after. Devastated, she would return to Hafiz's line 'And the wind of Death had swept [her] hopes away'.

The Times published a eulogy on 4 May: 'A typical officer of the old army which had always held him in high esteem, Colonel Doughty-Wylie was an ardent sportsman, good rider and good shot, who hunted big game as well as small, but always retained the literary interests of a Winchester scholar'.[117]

Colonel Charles Hotham Montagu Doughty-Wylie was awarded the Victoria Cross (VC) posthumously. His bravery, and the bravery of his fellow officers of the Lancashire Fusiliers at Gallipoli, were remembered in 'Six V.C.s before breakfast', a motto that reflected the myths of heroism at the time.

The conquest of the fort at Hill 141 did not produce the long-awaited breakthrough in the war. General Mustapha Kemal, the commander of the Turkish forces at Gallipoli, and General Liman von Sanders contained the advance of British forces to the interior of the peninsula. The unexpected bravery of the Turkish troops turned Gallipoli into a symbol of their resistance to the Allies, and forced the British and French to search for other offensives to win the war.

To Dick and Gertrude, Gallipoli was the line, crossing their parallel lives.

In November, Judith Doughty-Wylie, dressed in black, landed at Gallipoli to visit the grave of her husband. He had been buried at the fort itself, so she was told, after it was taken and while his men were still saluting him. She had a reception from the French, and on that day, so the legend goes, 'the enemy fired neither bullet nor shell'.[118]

*   *   *

Colonel Doughty-Wylie was buried as he had always desired: 'in as simple a manner as possible'. His meagre estate, valued at £4,683, was left in its entirety to his brother Henry Montagu Doughty of the Royal Navy. Doughty-Wylie's wife, Judith, 'already well provided',[119] was given only a small share of his possessions. It consisted mainly of guns and other military devices that would also be transferred to Henry later. Judith did not need or want any part of it. All she wanted was permission from the British government to wear the Star of Ethiopia, a decoration bestowed upon her by the Ethiopian government for her help in saving the life of an Ethiopian princess when she had served as a nurse in the Anglo-Ethiopian Hospital at Addis Ababa. Judith wanted to wear the decoration, in spite of the tension between the two countries, as it had 'never been awarded to any woman, Abyssinian or European'.[120] Wearing the Star of Ethiopia was her way to share the life and deeds of her husband, and a symbol of continuity and identification with his own accomplishments. She wore already the Turkish Order of Mejidiye, the Companion of the Order of St Michael and St George, awarded to Dick for having saved the lives of Armenians during the 1909 attack on Christians, and the Companion of the Bath (CB) that he had received in 1913 for his services as head of the Commission for Albania's Southern Frontier. It was a way to share his official life after his death, as she had done when he was alive. They remained a good team, even posthumously. And the friendship, mutual respect, and loyalty that had characterised their marriage for so many years would continue to guide her life after his death.

Loyalty to their ideals, and in a way, to each other – that was the keystone of their marriage. As for his silences, withdrawn behaviour, she had learned to accept them without interfering. He was in his private garden, he once answered. She never asked again. She felt the barriers of words and silences and his need to seek refuge behind these walls. She would wait patiently for him to come back into the real world. There were no children to keep them together, but invisible chains. Bonds or burdens? Both, she knew it. And this was the way it was. Their marriage had had its good and bad moments. She knew that in her rivalry with other women who occasionally attracted Dick's attention, she might lose.

But she had her moments and the memories of a shared past and common goals. And she had had Dick's presence, affection, and companionship. She wouldn't ask for more.

* * *

They had married in June 1904. Lilian Omara, as Judith was then known, was the eldest daughter of the late John Wylie of West Clyffe Hall, Hampshire, and the widow of Lieutenant Charles Henry Adams Wylie of the Indian Medical Service. Both husbands had taken on her maiden name.

Two years after their marriage, Captain Doughty-Wylie was appointed vice-consul at Mersina and Konya, Turkey, where he served until 1909. These were their best years together. She remembered their search for a house in Konya and her first acquaintance with the *bakshish* system – the little bribes distributed all along the way that made daily life in the East more manageable[121] – and her efforts to get used to the local people, to their customs. Judith had followed Dick in his visits to crafts schools and to American missions. There she had heard about the missionaries' influence on the local clergy and the community's reactions. But at Christmastime, all Christians gathered together to celebrate the season and Judith used to take an active part in preparing the festivities. She dressed dolls and made up bags of sweets to be distributed to the children, ordering toys from England's best stores for the children of the Baghdad railway employees. Their little faces, shining with the lights of the huge Christmas tree set up in Judith and Dick's living room, compensated for the children they never had. It never occurred to her then that their presence in eastern countries, as the works of the missionaries themselves, could awake Muslim suspicions.

She had also felt the pressures of historical events and the way they transformed their own lives. She remembered the Young Turks and their calls for liberal reforms, the formation of the Committee for Union and Progress (CUP), and Dick's comment about their poor coordination. The governor of Konya had refused to recognise the committee in Smyrna, only acknowledging the committees of Istanbul and Salonika. 'It is a curious situation', she remembered Dick saying. 'The real masters are men whose very names are not known'.[122] In the best 'orientalist' tradition, Dick believed in the possible benefits of an open autocracy, worried as he was by the gap between the CUP's proclaimed ideals and the people's ability to seize them. Judith herself had heard the inhabitants of Konya claiming that 'liberty is good. We won't pay taxes . . . and elections will be amusing'.[123] They couldn't really understand, then, how democracy would come about.

She had watched these ambiguities with amusement. She remembered the flags and slogans and the dignitary who had come once to dinner carrying two flags, one inscribed with the CUP's motto 'Liberty and Progress' and the other, the sultan's flag, with 'Al-Umma' embroidered on it. The sultan would buy off the deputies who opposed him, Dick commented then, drawing from his personal fortune, some £30 million invested in European banks.

Judith also recalled Turkey's war with Bulgaria and the reactions it provoked. Dick feared jihad: 'Religion divides', he once said. 'Whether it be Christian or Muhammadan, they bring a sword, and there is no powerful motive to unite them except patriotism, and the peace and prosperity which goes with it'.[124] Believing, as early as 1907, in the possible advantages of modern nationalism for Eastern peoples, Dick was, already then, ahead of his time.

In spite of minor tensions, Dick and Judith's years in Turkey remained the happiest ones in her memory. They shared leisure times, wild-duck hunts, pony rides and an admiration for Arabian horses. They used to spend their evenings at home, exchanging ideas about the events of the day or quoting from books they read. She remembered Dick's comments after reading *The Age of Justinian and Theodora*. Holmes' portrayal of the Byzantine court was a parody of their own times, he commented then. She also remembered the visit of Professor Ramsay, the renowned archaeologist, who was heading to Binbirkilisse to write a book on Byzantine churches, together with his collaborator, Miss Gertrude Bell. At the time Judith and Dick had plans to return to England and live quietly at the Fordly Hall farm she had bought.

But then, all of a sudden things changed. As did their plans. The Balkan war broke out and Dick left for Albania. Their separation did not affect their sentiments for each other, she still believed, and it was with great pride that she greeted him when he returned to England with the Companion of the Bath.

Although she spent with him part of his tenure as Britain's consul in Addis Ababa, Judith felt a growing gap between them. Was it the war? The tensions, the fear? Or was it just the geographical distance between them? Or were there other motives she could hardly guess? Judith knew no more after packing Dick's private belongings, collected after his fall at Gallipoli. His diaries did not say much more about him than her own recollections, but she found some consolation in reading them. There were a few little notes that would bring back the flavours and scents of those past years. There were also some documents that reminded her of Dick's mission: a petition by the inhabitants of Premetis and Frassaris in southern Albania asking to be annexed to Greece,[125] and a private print of Sir Valentine Chirol's official paper, of restricted circulation, entitled 'Serbia and the Serbs'. Judith could not but ask herself how this selected brochure could have reached Dick in Addis Ababa. Among other papers, Judith had also found a reminder of Miss Bell's appeal to join her in an anti-suffrage activity.

It was, however, an entry in Dick's diary of May 1908 that left her somewhat puzzled: 'A horrible bad dinner . . . I really must leave alone'.[126]

PART II

ARRIVAL

CHAPTER 5

'On the Edge of Important Things'

The British troops retreated from Gallipoli in January 1916. From the Middle East, her perpetual shelter, Gertrude wrote to Florence, 'We are all out now, leaving only our dead to keep watch there'. All that remained at that moment of the attempt to get through the Dardanelles were the tales of the survivors. They decried 'the folly, the vain courage, and the muddle of it all'.[1] The campaign had achieved none of its goals, only causing Italy to join in on the side of the Entente, becoming later a contender for the spoils of the empire. Gertrude was in Egypt, serving as a member of an embryonic intelligence agency established in January 1916 by an inter-departmental committee headed by Arthur Hirtzel, the India Office under-secretary and by Lancelot Oliphant of the Foreign Office. Its declared aim was to coordinate and centralise the collection and distribution of information on the Middle East to the Foreign, India and War offices during the war.

One of the agency's main tasks, as set out by a naval intelligence dispatch in December 1915, was to collect information about the movements of the Germans and in the Middle East, the Persian Gulf, and the Arabian Peninsula.[2] This was needed, in view of the necessity of securing the route to India by protecting the Suez Canal and the supply of oil from the oil fields and refineries of Abadan required by the Navy.

The agency, later called the Arab Bureau, was subordinated to the political and military intelligence branches in Cairo, led by Colonel Gilbert Clayton, an acquaintance of Gertrude's from her earlier visits to the area. Clayton, a representative of the Sudan Agency in Cairo, worked, at first, under the orders of General Archibald Murray, commander of the British Expeditionary Forces (BEF) stationed in Isma'iliya[3] on the Suez Canal until early 1916, before becoming responsible for the Arab Bureau. The bureau, also attached to the intelligence department of the Admiralty, was located at the Savoy Hotel not too far from the general headquarters of intelligence in Cairo.

The Savoy Hotel was a fine example of a blend of Eastern and Western architecture with a display of oriental luxury. It had been invaded by 'staff officers with suede boots, fly whisks and swagger sticks' when the war broke out.[4] It was at the Savoy that Professor D. G. Hogarth, the bureau's director, assembled over 300 volumes on Middle East topography, ethnography, history and theology.[5] It was the best pool of academic expertise available at the time and placed at the service of the Crown. Among the people were travellers and archaeologists and experts on the culture, history and traditions of the area, including T. E. Lawrence, Gertrude's acquaintance from Carchemish and other experts on the area, who were joined later by army officers. The bureau's members had been attached to different units: D. G. Hogarth and Gertrude Bell to the Admiralty Intelligence, Gilbert Clayton and Kinahan Cornwallis to the Sudan, T. E. Lawrence to the War Office. Ronald Storrs, the residency's oriental secretary, described the bureau's members in a rather humorous way:

> Do you know
> The Arab Bureau?'
> Asked Hogarth; and answered:
> 'Clayton stability
> Symes versatility
> Cornwallis is practical
> Dawnay syntactical . . .
> Lawrence licentiate to dream and to dare
> And Yours Very Faithfully . . . bon a tout faire.[6]

However, this amusing description concealed the collective and personal ambition underlying the work of the bureau. The members' sense of superiority and their ambiguous understanding of their mission reflected, in a thousand little ways, the inflexible manner in which they tried to impose their will and imagination on how the area's political future would be shaped. Awarded temporary military ranks, the bureau's civilian members would later become known as Lieutenant Commander D. G. Hogarth, Lieutenant Colonel. T. E. Lawrence, Major C. L. Woolley, and Captain R. C. Thompson. They were all linked by high ideals in spite of very personal views on how to turn those ideals and their own knowledge into political gains. One of the bureau's tasks was to compile geographical guides and political handbooks based on locally obtained information. Gertrude Bell's earlier acquaintance with the principal tribes and confederations of the Syrian Desert and Central Arabia made her uniquely suited for the collection of information in northern Sinai and the Persian Gulf. She updated old maps and records, which later helped the Allies in their military movements. Aided in part by her efforts, the bureau began to issue the *Arab Bulletin* in February 1916, a classified publication that eventually became a valuable source of information on the politics of the area during the war.

Gradually, the Arab Bureau evolved into an axis of political activity and propaganda, and a place visited by all those involved in political activities in the Middle East. Attracted by its casual atmosphere, London's politicians found the ambience in Cairo far more appealing than the constricted and dull atmosphere of Britain's other intelligence offices around the world.

One of the most frequent visitors to the Arab Bureau was Mark Sykes, the controversial Tory baronet and MP, who was behind the idea of establishing the bureau and who, in earlier years, had competed with Bell for the title of the most knowledgeable traveller in the Middle East. Sykes was now acting as a liaison officer between the war and foreign ministers on issues connected to the Middle East. Outspoken and opinionated, he would appear at the bureau's office unexpectedly, develop new ideas on the history and politics of the Middle East, and infuse its members with a spirit of adventure that seemed to many to be too daring and too risky. Lawrence described Sykes, years later, in *The Seven Pillars of Wisdom*: 'He [Sykes] would take an aspect of the truth . . . inflate it, twist it and model it'. A gifted caricaturist, Sykes 'would sketch out in a few dashes a new world all out of scale'. Sykes' efforts 'to turn native minds into his own paths of idealism often ended in his snatching at a pencil and dashing off a whole series of caricatures',[7] as Hogarth himself recognised. Sykes' sketches underscored the seemingly unbridgeable cultural differences between the British and the local leaders. He portrayed the arrogance of the former and the bewilderment of the latter in the face of what Britain considered to be a 'civilisatory mission'. However, he lacked the discipline of a solid academic foundation and the persistence to pursue and bring his ideas to fruition. That may have been one of the causes of his misunderstanding of the Middle East and its peoples.[8] Sykes considered the bureau a semi-autonomous body in spite of its formal subordination to Britain's high commissioner in Egypt, Sir Henry McMahon. The lack of clarity regarding the bureau's immediate objectives was seen by Sykes as an advantage. In his view, this ambiguity allowed room to manoeuvre and could help establish unofficial contacts with the area's chief leaders.[9] However, this same vagueness about the bureau's purposes became a source of friction between the bureau and other policy-shaping bodies. Each of them, the India Office, the Admiralty, the War Office, the government of India, and even the Residency in Egypt, jealously safeguarded its interests,[10] largely differing in their policies. The government of India at Delhi and the British Residency of Cairo had different views regarding Mesopotamia, given that the Persian Gulf still remained under Delhi's influence. Lord Hardinge, the viceroy of India, openly opposed Cairo's tilt toward the Sharif of Mecca, as he believed that the sharif lacked the authority to deal with Britain in the name of other Arab leaders. Ibn Sa'ud, and even Ibn Rashid, seemed to him better choices. But Ibn Sa'ud was as yet too cautious to align himself with Britain and Ibn Rashid was openly pro-Turkish.

The need to reconcile the divergent views and policies and some of the conflicting positions prompted Lord Hardinge to summon Gertrude Bell to India. Taking Valentine Chirol's advice, he offered Gertrude Bell the role of mediator between Cairo and Delhi. She was transferred to Basra, and appointed editor of the *Gazeteer of Arabia*. From Basra she reported to the government of India on the activities and manoeuvres of the Arab Bureau and the Force Military 'D'.

She was lodged in a big house near the headquarters, but after a lunch with Sir Percy Lake, the military commander of Basra and the Tigris area, and other generals, she was moved to a 'splendid great veranda with a cool room behind it', where she sat among her maps and books while trying to sort out the information on the tribes she had found in the files of the Intelligence Department. On her way to the office, she traversed palm orchards, 'jumping over small irrigation channels or tightrope dancing across a single palm trunk . . .'.[11]

The chief political officer of the occupied territories and the Persian Gulf area was Sir Percy Z. Cox, whom Gertrude had met in 1909 in England. Cox and Captain Arnold Talbot Wilson, his deputy, the former political officer in Muhammara, were responsible for Britain's contacts with the shaykhs of Muhammara and Kuwait. Henry R. C. Dobbs, another member of Cox's staff, reached Basra after serving in the political department of the India Office. Among Dobbs' main tasks were the creation of a new revenue department and the inspection of land records and *waqf* (pious foundation) revenues in order to delineate Britain's taxation policy. A periodical, *The Basra Times*, was published in three languages (English, Arabic and Persian) and informed the population about Britain's administrative policy.

Because of Basra's strategic position, Cox and his superiors at the India office in London regarded with suspicion the contact between the Sharif of

Mecca and Sir Henry McMahon regarding the Arabs' possible gains in exchange for their uprising against the Turks. Delhi also suspected that the sharif's defiance of the sultan's role as *khalifah* (caliph), the supreme leader of all Muslims, would lead to unwanted reactions from among India's Muslims, an opinion shared by Hogarth himself.[12] All this made Gertrude Bell's mediating mission more difficult. Still lacking a clear personal opinion on the divergences between Delhi and Cairo, she would gradually adopt Cox's views, mainly regarding the embryonic stage of the movements of national revival within the borders of the empire which, in his view, did not yet offer a real alternative to Istanbul's position and influence.

Basra seemed to epitomise the different positions regarding Britain's strategic and political aims. A major asset in Britain's strategic scheme, Basra was also a gateway to Mesopotamia. Basra's occupation, initially an end in itself, became thereafter a starting point in Britain's advance toward Baghdad.

*   *   *

'Basra is not an easy place to live in', Gertrude discovered then: 'It is a singular experience to be living always in a Turkish bath . . . and [to] wash in a solution of Tigris mud'.[13] But there were also little treats, such as the 'tea *à la* Venice', served daily on the deck of Cox's boat, anchored in the blue waters of a little creek surrounded by a palm garden. In the spring, Basra 'had its bursts of glory . . . Palm gardens deep in luxuriant grass and corn, blossoming pomegranates' and ripening fruits reminded Gertrude of very different springs at home: 'Very soon the wild daffodils by the little pond will come out and nod their heads to the east wind. It is three years since I saw them'.[14]

As daily exercise, Gertrude would ride in the early mornings to 'the great sea', as she called the desert. She would often reconsider her mission in Basra: 'What am I doing here? . . . Really nothing . . . though I work at it like a nigger all day long'.[15] On other occasions, she would wonder about the possible impact of Britain's adventure in the Middle East: 'We are now on the edge of important things and we hold our breath in'. In her vision, so typical of British officials' abroad, the population would have little to say, accepting passively what the West had in store for them. That wasn't the case, however, as she would discover pretty soon. The British military authorities in Basra did not have an answer regarding their chances to win in the larger game. Neither did Cox: 'He does his job, a gigantic job – and thinks no more about it'.[16]

Things changed after T. E. Lawrence's visit to Basra in the spring of 1916. At her office, from which they could see the river's curving course, Gertrude and Lawrence had great talks and 'made vast schemes for the government of the universe'.[17] A quote that pointed, if one subtracts the humour underlying it, to their ambition and to a subjective vision of the historical moments. Lawrence had been sent by his superiors in Cairo to appraise the first results of Delhi's administration in Basra. Among others, he learned that a Shiʻi public waqf had been created and that its revenues were being remitted to the mujtahids in Karbala. This measure was intended to enhance Britain's prestige among its Shiʻi subjects also in other parts of the world.[18] Was it meant to promote equality among the religious factions, or was it a mere stratagem to bring both sects to act in Britain's favour? Lawrence asked in one of his reports to Cairo.[19] For him this measure was only valuable if it helped to win over the Arabs in their entirety to Britain's side, without straining Britain's relations with the Sharif Husayn of Mecca, the leading Sunni authority, and bearer of the banner of Arabism against the Turks.[20]

After long debates, Lawrence finally persuaded Gertrude of the merit of his ideas. 'We treated Mesopotamia as if it were an isolated unit – instead of which it is, part of Arabia', Gertrude commented later, when finally convinced that Mesopotamian politics should be 'indissolubly connected' to the great and far-reaching Arab question. For that reason, Gertrude argued, Britain's policy in Mesopotamia should be shaped in London, not in Cairo or Delhi, so as to become part of a wide scheme framing Britain's relations with the Arabs.[21] On a more immediate level Gertrude was referring to the need to integrate the policies of the India and Foreign Offices regarding the Middle East in general. Mesopotamia was a case apart given its strategic and economic importance, and the government of India's special interest in Basra and the Persian Gulf. That meant, in fact, Gertrude's adoption of Lawrence's views while serving as an envoy of India's viceroy.

On a broader level it also meant her acceptance of a policy that would lead to the creation of an independent state in the Arab territories to be liberated from Turkey with Britain's help. She underestimated the Arabs' free will, their assessment of their needs and their own definition of progress.

*   *   *

In the spring of 1916, Kut's fall seemed inevitable. 'Nothing happens and nothing seems likely to happen ... it's a desperate business', Gertrude reported home. The only solution for the siege at Kut al- 'Amara , to which the British troops had withdrawn after their defeat at Ctesiphon, forty miles south-east of Baghdad, seemed to be Lawrence's offer, (strongly condemned by Cox) to bribe the Turks with £1 million for the release of the besieged troops. Following General Khalil Pasha's refusal, 17,600 British soldiers were led into captivity. 'They marched slowly, wading through blood and tears that need never have been shed',[22] wrote Gertrude in April 1916. This was part of the price they had to pay for Britain's 'muddling through' Arabian politics, as Gertrude herself would recognise later. The four-month siege had demoralised the British troops in Basra and forced the military authorities to reconsider the possibility of an advance toward Baghdad.

Lawrence's mission to Basra poisoned the relations between Cairo and Delhi even further, when, in a report, he set forth his criticism of the campaign's mismanagement. 'We dared not to show it [the report] to the C in C, but had to water it down', confessed one of the officers at the time, 'I have regretted ever since that I never kept a copy of the original; it was Lawrence at his best'.[23]

New initiatives were needed to narrow the gap between Cairo and Delhi. Sir Percy Cox's efforts to gain the support of Ibn Sa'ud and other Arab leaders in the Persian Gulf area and the Arabian Peninsula became a high priority, when the first whispers of the sharif's unsuccessful operations in the Hijaz reached Cairo. The sharif's 6,000 fighters that rebelled against the Turks in June 1916 were having great difficulty in keeping the rebellion alive. Unprepared and poorly motivated, the sharif's forces seemed to have lost their initial enthusiasm. Lawrence, wearing at the time the rank of captain, was sent to the Hijaz to serve as liaison officer between the sharif's forces and the Arab Bureau. Meanwhile, Major Kinahan Cornwallis, the acting director of the bureau at the time, published a *fatwa* (religious edict) that had been issued by the leading ulamas in Egypt in support of the sharif of Mecca. Food, money and weapons were then shipped to the Hijaz, to appease the tension that reigned in Mecca and Medina, and in the tribal areas around the cities.[24] The difficulties in the Hijaz increased Britain's need to secure their foothold in Mesopotamia. However, launching a second advance northward required some preliminary arrangements, and tighter control over the tribal areas around Kut, Nasiriyya, Samawa and the Hammar Lake.[25]

Among the members of Cox's staff, in the political department of the IEF 'D', to which she had now been officially attached at Sir Percy Cox's request, Gertrude Bell was charged with the task of reporting on tribal movements in the areas up the Tigris and the Euphrates. She left Basra, taking the train to Qurna, a village on the eastern marshes of the Tigris. A van was attached to the train, furnished with no more than a camp-bed, a chair and a lantern. Gertrude mused,

> If I ever come back to this country and travel to Baghdad by the Basra Express, I shall remember, while I eat my luxurious meal in the dining car, how first I travelled along the line in a guard's van and dined on tinned tongue, tinned butter, and tinned pear by the light of the stationmaster's lantern.[26]

Falling asleep while the train crossed the desert, she awakened just as 'the dawn crept in at my windowless window'.[27] At the bazaar of Khamisiyya she met the shaykhs and tribal chiefs who came to this desert town market to sell their camels and exchange goods. She remembered some of them from her trip to Ha'il.[28] Based on her conversations with the shaykhs of the Bani Lam and the 'Uzayriyya who came to the market from Shatt al-Hay and the marshes of the Tigris, Gertrude wrote the memoranda that would help the British plan their advance to the Muntafiq.

During this visit Gertrude discovered the marshes and 'a whole world under the water . . . villages built on floating piles of reed mats anchored to palm trees, linked only by boat'. A dense forest of reeds extended infinitely and among the reeds the *mashufs*, and anchored little canoes. As she watched the river 'bending and winding and curving back on itself, a fleet of white sails rising out of the heart of the thorny waste appeared now on one side of you, now on the other'. At the edge of 'the submerged fields of rice, the mounds of straw and garnered fields of grain',[29] stood the mud tower of a landowner's house and his reed-built *mudhif* (guest house) 'a huge tunnel made of evenly arched reed bundles and woven reed mats'.[30] Gertrude listened to tales of the Sa'dun's arrival in Mesopotamia from Mecca in the fourteenth century, of how they became powerful landowners and the effective rulers in southern Mesopotamia. In the spring they would leave the marshes and go to the desert with their camel herds, 'as real Bedu, nomads of the open wilderness'.[31]

These contacts, and Gertrude's other efforts to create a favourable atmosphere toward Britain, helped in planning the advance of British troops northward. She evaluated the tribes' forces, appraised changes in mood and explained to the military authorities the rules of 'the politics of the desert'. The alliances, easily made and unmade, were in earnest, at least while they lasted.[32]

*   *   *

In September 1916, Sir Percy Cox received a long-anticipated message from Ibn Saʻud. Its contents, however, did not match Cox's expectations. Not only was Ibn Saʻud offended by Cairo's choice of the sharif as the representative of the Arabs, he was also hurt by the sharif's pretensions to claim higher status over all other Arab leaders in the Hijaz and the Gulf area. Cox tried to dispel Ibn Saʻud's doubts about his importance and status by inviting him to a durbar in Kuwait in November. There, Ibn Saʻud would be honoured with the K.C.I.E. (Knight Commander of the Order of the India Empire) in the presence of the emir of Kuwait, the Shaykh of Muhammara, and the Bedouin chiefs of al-Hasa and southern Mesopotamia. Ibn Saʻud took full advantage of the occasion and, in an unexpected speech, pointed out to his Arab peers the benefits of aligning with Britain. With 'the processional arrival of Ibn Faraʼun's 700 camels, each bearing his well-known brand, the gathering ended in an apotheotic mood',[33] Gertrude reported some days later.

Carried away by Ibn Saʻud's majestic demeanour, Gertrude fell under the spell of her idealised vision:[34]

> . . . the strongly marked aquiline profile, full-fleshed nostrils, prominent lips and long, narrow chin accentuated by a pointed beard. His hands are fine with slender fingers . . . and in spite of his great height and breadth of shoulders, he conveys the impression, common enough in the desert, of an undefinable lassitude.

Relying largely on his enormous personal magnetism, Ibn Saʻud had managed to draw 'the loose mesh of tribal organisation into a centralised administration', she argued then.

When some days later Ibn Saʻud came to meet Percy Cox in Basra, 'this was already an encounter between partners' Gertrude claimed, obviously carried away by her excessively romantic interpretation of British–Arab relations at the time. The visit had its purposes: 'In the course of a few hours, the latest machinery of offence and defence was paraded before him'. Amazed at the sight of airplanes, railways and motorcars, Ibn Saʻud was also shown an X-ray of his own hand. 'He looked at it all with wonder and with the interest of a man who seeks to learn'.[35]

Ibn Saʻud was more pragmatic, however. Only after being reassured that the Najd would not be included in the borders of the territory claimed by the sharif, he agreed to exert economic and military pressure on his rival Ibn Rashid, still aligned then with the Ottomans. In exchange, Ibn Saʻud

would receive a monthly subsidy of £5,000, 3,000 rifles, and an extra one-
off allowance of £20,000.[36] The deal suited both sides. Ibn Sa'ud had
improved his financial and political position, while guaranteeing security in
the desert south-east of Baghdad, its tribes, and the Shi'i centres in Najaf
and Karbala.[37]

The way to Baghdad was now open. Counting also on the neutrality of
the 'Anaza, who controlled the desert north-west of Baghdad, the British
began their march to the city. British forces under the command of General
Stanley Maude entered Kut in February 1917, and on 11 March, they
marched into Baghdad. 'That's the end of the German dream of dominat-
ing the Near East', Gertrude reported then from Basra.[38] The Berlin–
Baghdad axis had ceased to exist, at least for the moment.

*   *   *

Some days after their entry into the town, General Maude issued a procla-
mation to the people of Baghdad, promising that Britain would not impose
alien institutions on them, only 'institutions that are in consonance with
[your] sacred laws and ideals'. In a clear display of ambiguity toward the
liberating character of Britain's mission and its long-lasting effects, Gertrude wrote then: 'It is an open question whether we don't do these people
more harm than good . . . One feels still more despairing about it now that
our civilisation has broken down so completely'.[39]

Her ambiguity, stemmed, on one hand, from her sense of belonging to
the moment itself and, on the other, from her knowledge of the area, and
her perspicacity in evaluating the complexity of the enterprise. She was also
doubting Britain's right to interfere and change the course of lives. A country of divisions, Iraq could not be united but by the Iraqis themselves.

*   *   *

In July 1917, 'Aqaba was conquered by Faysal's troops, in their way to
Damascus, the birthplace of Arab nationalism.

To rule over Damascus was to rule over the Arab nation as a whole. Syria
covered at the time the territories spreading west to Lebanon, and south-
west to Palestine. 'I must write of Syria as I knew it', Gertrude opened her
'Syrian Report', written in June 1917.[40] Syria was 'a place of religious
diversities, of communities revolving around their axes, of contradictions
and absoluteness . . .', but, above all, it was a lovely country, as she
described it:

grey limestone rocks, grey-green olive groves, upland vineyards haunted by little foxes . . . a land where hyacinths, anemones and cyclamens flourished in valleys . . . a land of strong men and beautiful women, of contrasts and extremes . . . of Christians, Moslems, Jews, Druzes, Circassians . . . of Bedu, peasants and merchants . . . and Jerusalem, equally sacred to all.[41]

It was also a land of rifts and ambitions. Gertrude was against the Balfour Declaration of 2 November 1917, which recognised a Jewish national home in Palestine. 'It is a poor land, incapable of great development, with a solid two-thirds of its population [made up of] Muhammadan Arabs who look upon the Jews with contempt. They will "ficher themselves pas mal of Zionist ambitions"'.[42] In her view, the Arabs would never accept an artificial and ill-fated scheme. And at the end of the war, the Arabs' ambition would clash with Britain's ambitions, too.

The questions again, were many: would Syria then go to the Arabs? Would Palestine go to the Jews? Or would the secret agreements between France and Britain seal the fate of them all? Britain wanted to retain Basra and allow Baghdad to become an autonomous area, with a separate Shi'i enclave in Najaf and Karbala. Or, as Lawrence had put it, Britain would control the area between the lines of 'Aqaba–Kuwait and Haifa–Tikrit and allow France to control the area between the lines of Haifa–Tikrit and the southern edge of Kurdistan.[43] All those questions added to the confusion created by the incongruities in Britain's promises to France, to the Arabs and to the Jews, which were revealed by the Bolshcviks' disclosure in 1918 of the Sykes–Picot agreement. McMahon's correspondence with Sharif Husayn and the Balfour Declaration also added to the confusion.[44] It would be argued later that these incompatible promises seemed at the time less conflicting.[45]

Gertrude's arrival in Baghdad in 15 April 1917, equipped with a special permission obtained by Sir Percy Cox from General Maude (to help Cox mediate between the commander-in-chief and the Arab population) was followed by a period of great stress. The precarious conditions in the camp were especially difficult. 'Coming to luncheon at the canteen on a grilling day, she had one look at the bully beef, which appeared on the menu day in and day out, burst into tears and left the room'.[46] A frugal meal on the floor of her bedroom was the only luxury she could afford. Over time, the situation improved, however. A small house near the secretariat, surrounded by a rose garden, was hired from Musa Chalabi, an old friend. A gazelle, brought as a gift, strolled in the garden, eating fruit and leaves and, occasionally, Gertrude's papers.

Gertrude had much to do in Baghdad: talks with visiting tribal shaykhs, interviews with local notables, and tea parties with women of the various factions of Baghdad society. In some ways, it was easier for Gertrude to communicate with Middle Eastern women than with European ones. Perhaps that was because she felt more protected by the clear racial and cultural barriers and an obvious dominant position of authority and 'masculine' prestige when dealing with Middle Eastern women. The same wasn't true, however, when it came to English 'wives', as she called the spouses of her male colleagues who had made femininity their main occupation in life. On the whole, this period seemed at first to be a time of stability, of acceptance by the population of the British and the changes ahead. It didn't take long for the events to prove the contrary. Gertrude compiled a confidential file, writing portraits of Baghdad's leading political figures to let the British know better the men with whom they would have to deal in the future.

Gertrude became known as 'Kokusa', the feminine for 'Kokus', as the local population pronounced the name 'Cox'. '[There is] a Kokus', she explained, 'just as once upon a time [there was] a Chosroes or a Pharaoh. I am currently described as "Kokusa", i.e., a female Chosroes . . .'.[47] It was through and with Cox that she perceived the magnitude of her too idealised mission. Gertrude definitely enjoyed the fact that she was exercising power and positioning herself in a highly ranked official role. She had, in her own earlier words, become 'a person'.

Among the many visitors who daily came to Gertrude's office at the secretariat was a man of the Najd in search of his clan, as the old tribes had split up.

> He had searched among the Banu Tamimi of the Persian frontier, among those of Jabal Hawran, and on the Tigris. At last, he came to Baghdad. There he discovered his fellow tribesmen by identifying a common mark found behind their camels' right ears. He was, however, much surprised to find that in Baghdad, his fellow tribesmen were Shi'is [whereas] – down in the Najd, they were all Sunnis.[48]

Gertrude had heard stories about the conversion of the nomad Sunni tribes from the Hijaz who had settled on the banks of Mesopotamia's two rivers. Gertrude had also heard about Suq al-Shuyukh,[49] the Sa'duns' capital in the Muntafiq, which had been divided into two rival factions: the Hadhr, protected by the Sa'dun, and the Najada, still connected to the Mutayrat, the Nawashi, and the Hasawyya in Najd.[50] At Suq al-Shuyukh, Gertrude also heard tales of Ibn Khamis, the leader of the Najada, who had moved part of the community to the far side of the marshes and established the town of Khamisiyya, the market town at the edge of the desert she had visited prior to Baghdad's conquest by the British troops.

In June, waters rushing from the mountains to the rivers inundated Suq al-Shuyukh. Gertrude described the abundance that was the gift of the waters: 'Dates, pomegranates, figs, nectarines and grapes growing all in the same ground, elbowing each other'.[51] She told of the prosperity at Suq with its products – dates, wool, sheep, and cattle – sent regularly to Basra's markets, prosperity that resulted from the new irrigation system covering the entire area between Suq al-Shuyukh and Khamisiyya. The rapid expansion of these two cities, as well as of Zubayr and Nasiriyya, was also a result of the hasty settlement of the tribes in the area and the breaking of tribal confederations some decades earlier.

In spite of this abundance, there were signs of unrest. Tribesmen refused to pay the *mallākiya* (property taxes) to the landlords,[52] and Gertrude wondered whether the British would support the Sa'dun or the fallahin.[53] Protecting the Sa'dun would mean creating a situation of perpetual trouble, whereas supporting the fallahin would mean interfering in the traditional social order of the Muntafiq. The British should opt for a middle course, she suggested, allow the landlord to retain his land but make him refrain from interfering in its management. In case of trouble, the British could always use the *shabana*, the mounted police created by Dobbs and commanded by Thamir Beg al-Sa'dun, brother of the famous 'Ajaimi al-Sa'dun, the most powerful tribal chief in the area.

The conflict between the Sa'dun and the fallahin was not the most pressing problem for the British, however; control of the cities of Najaf and Karbala was more urgent. Najaf was, for the Shi'is, a main religious centre. For the British, it was a place of veiled and mysterious myths and legends. Gertrude still remembered her first glimpse of Najaf's golden dome from a distance. Seen from across the desert, on her way back from Ha'il, 'the dome seemed to be floating in the air. At a closer distance, its beauty shone in midst of surrounding poverty'.[54]

Najaf was a market town for the desert tribes, a graveyard for pious Shi'is from as far away as Persia and India, and a centre of religious learning. Its community of mujtahids, ulama, and their mass of students was led by Sayyid Kazim Yazdi Tabataba'i: 'No government could succeed without his approval, but it was idle folly to expect his active support',[55] reported one of Gertrude's friends, Captain Frank Balfour, the political officer for the middle Euphrates, later transferred to the Sudan. The extension of Britain's authority to Najaf and Karbala depended on the approval of the ulama and of the *kelidar*, the guardian of the keys to the shrines.

Najaf's population was divided into two tribal factions, the Zugurt and the Shumurt, whereas the Kammuna Zada led Karbala.[56] The British had established some contacts with the urban leaders, but the tribes and the ulama remained hostile to the British presence. Mirza Muhammad Taqi al-Shirazi, the son of Najaf's leading *'alim*, was the main instigator of resistance against the British and the one responsible for the political unrest fomenting below the surface. An artificial calm had been maintained during the spring of 1917, interrupted only by the summer duties of the fallahin: the cleaning of canals and sowing of *shitwi* (winter crops).

In January 1918, Gertrude returned to the tribal areas in the company of Frank Balfour. 'Water ran in the canals and barley sprang in new fields',[57] Gertrude reported, after travelling in a boat pushed by two tribesmen. Commercial boats navigated the Hindiyya, delivering new supplies of wheat and barley to the markets. The shipments relieved the shortages of food in Najaf and Karbala, helping to stifle possible disturbances in the two cities. Najaf's rebellion some months earlier marked the first sign of local armed resistance against the British. The siege that followed was suspended in March 1918 and Captain Balfour then received a sword of honour from Najaf's ulama and notables.[58]

The situation north of Baghdad was not much better. By December 1917, British troops had reached the Kurdish city of Khaniqin[59] and Major Soane, the area's administrator reintroduced the idea of an autonomous Kurdistan, a constant topic on the British agenda after the war. At the same time, General Allenby, the commander-in-chief of the Egyptian Expeditionary Force, advanced toward Jerusalem, conquering the town in December 1917 after having defeated the Turks in Gaza. That was the last event in a rather eventful year. Gertrude reported these in her letters, adding much of her own feelings and personal moods to her descriptions. She would have liked to see Jerusalem and Bethlehem at Christmastime – the first Christmas under Christian rule.

Gertrude longed for the grey hills of Judea, feeling that her personal destiny was tied now to the Middle East. 'My England is gone', she wrote some months later to Valentine Chirol. 'Not much is left [there] for me . . . very few acquaintances which one called friendships seem to stand the test of absence. I don't miss them and can scarcely realise how one could pick them up again'.[60] These earlier feelings were reinforced by the changes brought to the area by the end of the war. The war had changed both the

Middle East and the personal fate of those embroiled in it, as this was the area most affected by the crumbling of the world's old order.

Four empires had been dismembered. Germany, Turkey, Austria-Hungary and Russia would now see their territories disputed by the victors while a series of contradictory engagements would prevent an easy and orderly transition to new arrangements.[61] President Woodrow Wilson's Fourteen Points and the Anglo-French Declaration, both issued in November 1918, raised hopes among the populations concerned regarding their rights to self-determination and stirred controversy as to their feasibility at the same time. Baghdad's population exulted, however: 'The Franco-British declaration had thrown the town into a torment. It doesn't happen often that people are told that their future as a state is in their hands', wrote Gertrude in November 1918. In her view, the Baghdadians wanted Sir Percy Cox as high commissioner, '[but] beyond that, all is divergence'.[62] It was a mistaken assumption based on her wishful thinking. When Percy Cox left Baghdad in September 1918 for Teheran, Gertrude Bell's name was suggested, as a second choice, to fill the post of high commissioner. It was 'as much a "female's job," as a man's job, concerned with handling people individually',[63] she commented when making her case in a letter home. More and more voices, however, were heard in favour of an Arab administration, headed by an Arab emir.

Immersed in political activities, Gertrude felt at times 'as the Creator in the middle of the week . . . He too must have wondered what it was going to be like, as I do'.[64] It was clearly an intentionally exaggerated opinion of what the British had set up to accomplish and a statement that implied the population's passive role in the process, in spite of the mischievousness underlying Gertrude's words. But again, with all her sense of humour, Gertrude was certainly thrilled by her suddenly acquired power. Still opposed then to the idea of an Arab administration in Mesopotamia, Gertrude Bell considered the idea of bringing an Arab emir to Iraq as a potential source of trouble. 'I wish they [would] drop the idea of an Arab Emir. It is tiring to set up a court here'.[65] She also believed that only the British could bring the country together. 'They realise that an Arab emir is impossible because, though they like the idea in theory, in practice they could never agree as to the individual . . .'.[66]

Gertrude would, however, change her mind some months later and adopt the idea of having an Arab emir crowned as ruler of Mesopotamia. Erratic, Gertrude was once defined by Lawrence as too devoted to the dominant idea at the time and to the individual behind it.[67] Other historians would see her frequent changes of mind and mood as a strength and as an 'ability to adapt to new circumstances'.[68] Either moody or versatile, Gertrude understood more quickly than others that the local population wanted to manage their own affairs even if less efficiently than the British.

Gertrude expounded her ideas on the subject in a memorandum entitled *Self-Determination in Mesopotamia*, published in February 1919.[69] She had seen the anxiety that prevailed before the Anglo-French Declaration was made public and the calm resignation that followed it. The declaration, while opening up the possibility of national emancipation under Arab rule, also drove a wedge between different elements of the population.

Baghdad, Ba'quba, Najaf and Kazimayn emerged as major centres of nationalist activity, generated partly by agents of the Sharif of Mecca. In the tribal areas, important tribal leaders still supported the idea of having the country administered by the British. This was also because the British (Dobbs and Gertrude as the ones leading support for these views), reinforced the position and authority of the tribal shaykhs, seeing them as the country's backbone.[70]

In the Shi'i towns of Najaf, Karbala, and Kazimayn, agitation against the British was led by the sons of leading religious figures, among them Sayyid Isma'il al-Sadr, the scion of the famous Sadr family. In Baghdad, Ja'far Abu-Timman, a young member of a Shi'i family of merchants, led the movement, which had already spread to bazaars and coffee shops. On the other hand, the Jews, Christians, Circassians and other minorities, alarmed by the prospect of an Arab government, threatened to leave the country as soon as an Arab government was installed.

At that point, however, the debate focused on who should be appointed ruler of Iraq: Among the suggestions were one of the sharif's sons, the son of the Sultan of Egypt, a member of a family of notables from Mosul, a member of the Naqib Zada family of Baghdad, or even the Shaykh of Muhammara, supported by the Shi'i shaykhs of Basra.

In this stormy atmosphere, filled with petitions and counterpetitions over the possibility of having an Arab emir either under or without British protection, Gertrude went to visit the naqib, asking for support and guidance before leaving for the Peace Conference at Paris. The naqib's house, opposite the *takiyya* (sanctuary) of the Qadiriyya mystic order of which he was head, was humble. The white colour of the sofas and walls in the visitors' room contrasted with the orange and yellow colours of the cypress trees predominant in the courtyard. Seated behind a small table covered with a white cloth, the old naqib expressed his apprehension about France's designs over Syria and Percy Cox's transfer to Persia at a time when he was so needed in Iraq.[71]

The contradictory opinions in the streets and Gertrude's own debates with Colonel A. T. Wilson (who was replacing Percy Cox as civil commissioner of Mesopotamia) about Iraq's political future and the idea of an Arab prince as ruler of Mesopotamia were the cause of her strained relationship with Wilson.[72] Their first serious disagreement dated from September 1918, over the possibility of bringing the vilayets of Basra and Baghdad together under a single administration. Gertrude opposed Wilson's suggestion, referring to the cultural and economic differences between the two provinces.

She wanted to believe, however, that it was her increasing popularity and active participation in politics (exceeding the normal authority of an oriental secretary) that triggered Wilson's opposition to her ideas. She was partly right. Independent and outspoken, Gertrude was often perceived by her male colleagues as a threat.

But there were also more substantial differences in the way they referred to the events that would shape Mesopotamia's future. The blunders created by the Sharif–McMahon correspondence, the Sykes–Picot agreement and the question of the Mosul vilayet and its possible annexation to Iraq reinforced Wilson's opinion that the British had to stay in the country for many years to come. Wilson, misunderstanding the new political climate following the armistice, opposed the 1918 Declaration and the promises of local autonomy to the population.[73] Wilson's idea of a plebiscite that would assess the population's willingness to retain Britain's presence in Iraq also seemed to Gertrude to stand against the atmosphere in Baghdad in those days. The same was true of his views of Iraq's internal administrative divisions with its local and municipal councils.

From the Hotel Majestic, not too far from the quarters of the Foreign Office delegation, Gertrude reported to her father: 'Our Eastern affairs are complex beyond all words . . .'.[74] The contradictions between the different pre-war agreements were now emerging, causing a great stir and provoking endless debates.[75] And yet, the atmosphere at the conference was exciting.

Gertrude participated in the social events, the whispered conversations, and the striking of deals at luncheons, teas, and dinner parties. At the conference, she met Lawrence in the company of Emir Faysal. Tall and charismatic, the emir was also 'hot-tempered, and restless in movement'. At a soirée at the house of Wickham Steed, the editor of *The Times*, Gertrude met the emir again. Lawrence stole the show, however, with the way he 'induced a sort of "cards on the table" atmosphere',[76] trying to win over French journalists of *Le Temps*, *Le Debat* and *Le Matin* to their case. Together with Valentine Chirol, who was also present at the conference, they debated the idea of creating three Arab political entities – Syria, Mesopotamia, and the Hijaz – instead of the unified Arab state promised during the war to the sharif.

But more than anything, Britain's inclination to let France rule over Syria left Gertrude worried, since the decision, if taken, would certainly affect Britain's image in Iraq. Seeing Faysal disappointed by the United States' support of France's claims, Gertrude approached A. J. Balfour, asking him to inform Lloyd George, the prime minister and head of the British delegation to the conference, of Faysal's apprehensions. Balfour called Ian Malcolm, one of the British delegates, and asked him to take note of Gertrude's complaints. Malcolm removed his 'exquisite notebook from an exquisite and impeccable pocket', leaving Gertrude with the feeling that 'Ian's notebook was the epitome of all culs de sac'.[77]

The outcome of the conference affected Gertrude profoundly, feeling that the post-war arrangements dashed the Arabs' hopes. 'Before the war our hearts were so light when we travelled, now they are so heavy that a camel couldn't carry us', she complained later to Fattuh, her loyal servant during the expedition to Ha'il. 'My lady, no . . . a camel couldn't carry you', Fattuh answered,[78] referring, certainly, not just to the area's destiny, but also to Gertrude's perceptions of her role in its remaking.

And yet, Gertrude still believed that the Middle East was getting to 'the edge of important things'.

CHAPTER 6

'Father, Think!'

Back in Baghdad from Paris, Gertrude was entangled in the debates and continued to believe that this polished game and web of deadlocks had spilled over into the debates on Britain's future in Iraq. She assembled her thoughts and impressions some months later in a 1919 memorandum, 'Syria in October',[1] which dealt with the conference's main issue: the Arabs' ability to govern themselves.

She started her document with imaginary quotations from a fictitious conversation held at a meeting of the Eastern Commission:

1st statesman: 'The country will be very badly governed.'
2nd statesman: 'Why should it be badly governed?'
3rd statesman: 'It ought to be badly governed.'[2]

To counterbalance the scepticism regarding Faysal's administration in Syria, Gertrude Bell described the impressions she had retained from her visit to Damascus in October of that year: 'Tramways have run, streets have been lighted, people have bought and sold . . . and a normal world has been maintained'.[3]

In her view, things had greatly improved since the time of the Turks, and Gertrude believed in the possibility of a Syrian independent state under Faysal's rule. In her view, an Arab autonomous government could also do as much for Iraq as it had done for Syria. Although disagreeing with Bell, Wilson summarised the debate on the issue in the preface of Bell's document. Without detracting from its value, Wilson refused to endorse the memorandum's main assumption. In his view, the idea of an independent Iraq with Baghdad as its capital would be resisted by the Kurds in the north and the Shi'is in the south. The Kurds would not agree to be ruled by Arabs, and the Shi'is would never accept a Sunni domination, he claimed.[4] Neither would the tribes accept the authority of the Sunni effendis.

Pressures from within and pressures from Iraq's neighbours would lead in the end, so he believed, to the return of the Turks.[5]

Wilson also believed that the only way to prepare the population for direct participation in the political process was to create divisional and municipal councils. In his opinion, this more representative system would make it easier for the British to withdraw their forces as it would diffuse power and diminish resistance to Britain's direct and indirect interference in Iraqi affairs. He also favoured the creation of a fringe of autonomous Kurdish states that were supposed to serve as buffers between Mesopotamia and its northern neighbours, Turkey, Persia, and Syria. It would be easier, in his view, to deal with the Kurds than with the Arabs, in so far as the oil fields known to exist in the vicinity of Kirkuk and Sulaymaniyya were concerned.[6]

Wilson's scheme of dividing Iraq's territory into five provinces (Baghdad, Basra, Euphrates, an Arab province of Mosul, and an autonomous province in Mosul's Kurdish areas) was meant to reflect the diversity of Iraq's population and its different needs. However, the way it had been structured did not give the population the impression of greater freedom or control over their affairs, since the POs (British political officers) and not the Arabs would control the administration in the provinces. The Arabs would only serve as advisers and the local and municipal council's members would be appointed, not elected.

Needless to say, Wilson's ideas were greeted with shrill discontent in nationalist circles,[7] also because they felt that the state should exert control over the councils, not the other way around. Support for Wilson's idea wasn't great in London either. A larger number of officers and officials would increase, not reduce, Britain's expenditures in the country,[8] and entail a heavier burden for the taxpayer.[9]

Wilson's opponents, mainly Iraqi nationalists, wanted to see an independent Iraqi state with Baghdad as its capital and councils elected by the population, not appointed by the British.[10] They also considered Wilson's ideas about efficient administration and gradual evolution toward national institutions, an impediment to real independence. Gradually Gertrude was won over by the nationalists' ideas, abandoning her initial inclination to see Wilson's scheme as better suited to Iraq's specific needs.

She was now fully convinced that Wilson's referendum, organised in February 1919 to prove the nationalists wrong, could hardly reflect the population's real wishes. Even the more specific questions regarding the extension of Britain's presence in the country, the choice of an Arab emir to rule over Iraq and the inclusion of the Mosul vilayet with its mixed Arab and Kurdish populations in Iraq's territory, would not produce credible answers.

She had already expressed some of these views in *Self-Determination in Mesopotamia*, written before her departure to Paris[11] in which she had also explained the limitations and possible fictitious results of elections still to be conducted according to the old Turkish system of secondary electors and its 'behind-the-scenes' manipulations.[12] A legislative assembly so elected could not mean a step forward to independence, nor to political partnership. In fact, the Sunnis would want to control the country through the emir and the Shi'is through their majority in the assembly.[13]

Gertrude was partly right. The process was more complex than Wilson thought it would be. Delays, conflicting interests, and different agendas emerged. Tribal shaykhs, merchants, mujtahids, all held different opinions regarding the continuation of Britain's presence or regarding Iraq's independence under an Arab emir.[14]

Because of the complexities of the process, Wilson was facing more and more problems in Iraq and at home: 'I am not loved in the India office, . . . and shall not be loved [there] before long', Wilson confessed in September 1919,[15] while describing in other documents his own version of the different cause for his failure.[16] Wilson's problems in London and in Iraq (with the military authorities and his subordinates, among them Bell and Garbett, the assistant secretary) were also a result of his inability to understand the connection between Britain's presence in the country and the different manifestations of Iraqi nationalism.[17]

Wilson's difficulties became even more serious with the temporary capture, in December 1919, of Dayr al-Zur on the Syrian eastern frontier, by a mixed Arab-Turkish force. It meant a more active interference in Iraq by the Arab government in Damascus. In effect, money started pouring from Dayr al-Zur to tribes in the northern Euphrates.[18] Pressured by the more extreme nationalists, mainly by Yasin al-Hashimi – whom Gertrude had met in October during her visit to Damascus – Faysal was adopting a more assertive position regarding Iraq's future.

A strong and charismatic personality, Yasin was the chief of staff of the Arab forces in Faysal's government and president of the Military Advisory Council. Together with his fellow members of the 'Ahd, the ex-Ottoman officers that formed the pre-war Arab nationalist society, Yasin was very active in promoting the idea of an independent Arab state, uniting Iraq to Syria, guided for a limited period of time by the same mandatory power,

Britain. 'Dressed in khaki with khaki helmets to which the Arab kerchief, but in khaki, bound with a rope of gold and fine headdress', the 'Ahd members were led by Taha al-Hashimi (Yasin's brother), Mawlud Mukhlis, Jamil al-Midf'ai, 'Ali Jawdat al-Ayyubi, Nuri al-Sa'id, Ja'far al-'Askari and Hamdi al-Pachachi. Highly ranked, their modern uniform contrasted with the traditional Arab dress worn 'by the crowd of negro eunuchs brought from the Mecca palaces'.[19]

'I don't trust him a yard',[20] Gertrude commented after meeting Yasin in Damascus. The mistrust was mutual. Acknowledging, perhaps tactically, that Iraq was still unprepared for an administration based on representative institutions, Yasin also favoured the creation of *majalis* (local councils) that would be responsible for the administration in the provinces with the help of British advisers. He also recognised the need to maintain Britain's presence in Iraq for ten years or more.[21] But again, these might have been tactical positions that changed once he felt more secure politically.

Although suspicious of one another regarding politics, Gertrude Bell and Yasin al-Hashimi seemed to understand each other on a personal level. They had common memories of Gallipoli (where Yasin had served as chief of staff of the Turkish Army Corps) even if they would have found themselves on opposite sides at the time. Gertrude's encounter with Yasin and other members of the 'Ahd, now part of Faysal's entourage, reinforced her opposition to Wilson's scheme. Disregarding questions of hierarchy, Gertrude complained directly to Sir Arthur Hirtzel of the India Office.[22] Trying to moderate between the two, Hirtzel explained to Gertrude that Wilson was not against an Arab government in Iraq, but wanted to develop and consolidate the municipal and divisional councils as a first step to independence.[23] Hirtzel was against the idea of forcing alien institutions on peoples of the East and stressed the importance of letting them adopt a political system consistent with their own traditions. But above all, he explained, the British had also to consider the costs of maintaining British forces in Mesopotamia.[24]

Not fully convinced by Hirtzel's explanations, and because they ran against what she herself believed, Gertrude already planned to write directly to Edwin Montagu, the secretary of state for India, to forward her views 'on the sort of government we ought to set up here'. Opinionated, straightforward, and too pushy for some, Gertrude proved yet again that once her mind was set, she would not move an inch. At least not until new ideas caught her attention, making her defend them as staunchly as she had done with the previous ones, reinforcing the impression that she was even more erratic and mercurial. She then sent to Montagu the first draft of a constitution and delineated the measures that, in her view, should be followed. 'The rest is – as we say – *'ala Allah*, on God'.[25]

Gertrude tried to obtain more answers to her questions by touring the provinces. In Najaf the atmosphere was 'so thick with the dust of ages that you can't see through it . . . nor can they'. The mujtahids (religious Shi'i leaders) in the Holy Cities would not talk to an unveiled woman, and even the women would not see her. 'If they were allowed to see me they would veil before me as if I were a man . . . . So you see . . . I appear to be too female for one sex and too male for the other',[26] Gertrude commented ironically. She enjoyed this supra-gender status which gave her a man's power and authority, while at the same time, she was a woman. In her search for excellence, she tried to send a signal that she could compete with her male colleagues and also beat them. This could be attributed to the fact that from early childhood she had to compete with her siblings in order to get the attention she would have received (unconditionally) from a mother.

In Kazimayn, 'at the end of narrow crooked streets', she found Sayyid Hasan al-Sadr's house. She was the first woman ever to be received by a mujtahid. The house was old, its windows opening into an interior court, which was a pool of silence. Sayyid Hasan's son, Sayyid Muhammad al-Sadr, 'black robed, black bearded and on his head a huge dark blue turban of the mujtahid class', received her in the balcony: 'Sayyid Hasan sat inside, an imposing figure, with a white beard reaching halfway down his chest'. Using the language of a learned man, he spoke about the Sadr family in all its branches, Persian, Syrian, and Mesopotamian and of the collections of Arabic books in Cairo, London, Paris, and Rome'.[27]

Gertrude wanted to speak about Syria, and Faysal's coronation as King of Syria. 'Over the whole [of] Syria, to the sea?', asked Sayyid Hasan. 'No', Gertrude answered, 'the French will stay in Beyrouth . . .'. 'Then, it's no good',[28] Sayyid Hasan concluded, concerned with Faysal's fate and the possible effect France's presence in Syria could have on Iraqi politics. It was an indication that Iraq's Shi'is were no less worried than the Sunnis about the possibility of success or failure of the Arab movement, personified at the time by Faysal and his rule over Syria.

Gertrude then travelled to the marshes, at the convergence of the Tigris and the Euphrates, where she found the semi-nomadic *ma'dan* (or *al-ma'di*) sailing their boats 'among floating villages and forests of reeds'.[29] In wintertime, villages on islands rise from the low waters. In summer, melting snows of the mountains in Persia and Turkey inundated the area. The ma'dan would then take their buffalos to pasture on the banks of the flooded rivers.[30]

On her way back to Baghdad, Gertrude visited the town of Shamiyya, near Najaf. She had been invited to the mudhif of 'Ibad al-Husayn, the principal shaykh of the district. The mudhif, made of arched reeds, was a 'perfectly regular, exquisitely constructed yellow tunnel, fifty yards long'. In the middle, coffee was brewing on a log fire 'against the walls a row of brocade covered cushions; the whole lighted by the fire and a couple of small lamps, and the end of the mudhif, fading away into a golden gloom. Glorious'. Shamiyya was located in the rice country, 'its reed villages . . . banked up with rice straw. The great golden heaps of rice [laying] on the harvest floors . . . Did I say glorious before?'.[31] In a letter home, she recounted how, at the Hor (Hawr) canal, she

> rowed out by passageways through the reeds to the open water. There were thousands of ducks and other water birds . . . [On] the water, covered with the dying leaves of a small water lily, buffalos were peacefully browsing, standing belly deep in the Hor . . . . of all the incongruous diets for a buffalo, water lilies are the most preposterous.[32]

Some time later, Gertrude heard that 'Ibad al-Husayn, her host in Shamiyya, had resigned, together with other members of the recently appointed council of the Shamiyya division. The reason was the lack of clarity about Iraq's political future and the events in Syria. The dispute over Dayr al-Zur, the *mutasarriflig* (administrative unit) that had become a bone of contention between Faysal's Arab government in Damascus and the British authorities in Iraq, had led the council members to their decision.[33] The clashes with the nationalists at Dayr al-Zur and the growing anti-British campaign conducted by the members of the 'Ahd had also led the Shi'i towns of Karbala and Najaf and the Shi'i rural areas, to align themselves with the Sunni nationalists.

'I think we are on the edge of a pretty considerable Arab nationalist demonstration with which I am a good deal in sympathy', Gertrude wrote then, worried, however, by Britain's possible withdrawal. 'If Mesopotamia goes, Persia goes inevitably, and then . . . India'.[34] And that was not a possibility the British wanted to face.

Gertrude's views on Iraq's future also adjusted to the events. After seeing Faysal crumbling under financial debts and yet determined not to accept the only European help offered, namely that of France, and, having witnessed the troubles in Egypt, a country 'turned into a second Ireland largely by our own stupidity', she realised that in Iraq the British would be better off if they did not try to 'squeeze the Arabs into our mould'.[35] In her opinion, the lesson to be learned from the insurgency in Egypt some months earlier (March 1919) was that it could become violent and difficult to contain. It had been an illusion that tolerance, as the British understood it, could prevent insurgency. In effect, the resentment and dissatisfaction simmering underneath erupted into anti-British demonstrations, as the resistance to the protectorate persisted.[36]

Gertrude would stay in Baghdad, in spite of her clashes with Wilson, to 'try to preach wisdom' to both sides, as she saw it. Appointing herself to the role of mediator, she also tried to restrain the young Baghdadi nationalists, 'whose chief fault is that they are ready to take on the creation of the world tomorrow without winking . . . and don't realise for a moment that even the Creator himself made a poor job of it'.[37] She invited both sides to her weekly garden parties and, under the dim lights of old Baghdadi lanterns, she let them engage in dialogues, hoping to find a way to bridge their positions.

But her chances grew slighter, she mused to Florence. At the end of March 1920 Gertrude took the train to Basra to meet her father who was coming for a short visit. She wondered at the progress made in just three years: 'It's a Basra I scarcely know . . . all the roads widened and straightened . . . public taxies running . . .'.[38] But, the country was facing difficult times. The frequent demonstrations in the streets of Baghdad refuelled the agitation against Britain's presence in Iraq.

Gertrude's relations with Wilson had also reached a point of no return. Their clashes had become more frequent as Gertrude engaged in new attempts to reach some understanding with the nationalists.

Exasperated with Gertrude's defiant attitude and the ease with which she managed to advance her opinion in London and Delhi, Wilson seemed also irritated with the presence of Gertrude's father in Baghdad. 'A funny dogmatic old gentleman who is as certain of his own opinion as his daughter is of hers';[39] Sir Hugh Bell was also resented because of his blind support for Gertrude's views. Back home, Hugh Bell, or 'al Walid – the Father', as Gertrude's Iraqi friends now called him, had been put in charge of 'putting a word in' with the authorities to promote Gertrude's personal opinions.

'A. T. has been given a KCIE (Knight Commander of the Indian Empire), he well deserves it . . .', Gertrude commented later with Florence. 'I wish that in giving him a knighthood they could also endow him with the manners knights are traditionally credited with'.[40] Despite signs of an inevitable breakdown, Wilson refused to engage in a more conciliatory policy toward the nationalists.

A constitutional committee was set up under Sir Edgar Bonham-Carter in March 1920, aiming at better solutions for the political impasse. While giving Britain a mandate to stay in the country, an Arab government would function according to a provisional constitution. Elections for a legislative assembly would follow and the president of the council of state (formed by six Arab and six British members) would become head of the state. This plan, however, left the population underrepresented and practically subordinated to the British.[41]

The elections for a legislative assembly wouldn't solve the problems, either. In towns and cities, the Turkish system of indirect elections remained, whereas in tribal areas, the representatives would be appointed by the shaykhs. It was clear, however, that the real keepers of authority were the council's British members, as they held executive powers while the Arab members acted merely as advisers.[42]

The debates on the division of power reached an impasse after Britain's 'acceptance' in San Remo of the mandate in May 1920. It had become clear that the population would not be consulted and that the decision had been taken in order to comply with British interests. Messengers sent by the members of the 'Ahd reached the Shi'i towns of Najaf, Karbala, and Kazimayn, and mobilised some of the leading mujtahids against the mandate. Gertrude's saw their union more as a political than as a religious alliance.[43] 'There are a lot of semi-political and semi religious speeches', Gertrude explained,[44] referring to the Shi'i religious motifs used by the Sharifians in their messages.[45]

Some aspects of the historic moment eluded her, however, as Sunnis and Shi'is had started attending religious meetings together. During the month of Ramadan, which began on 19 May 1920, services known as *mawlids*, celebrating the birth of the Prophet, were held in every Sunni and Shi'i mosque in turn, in the presence of members of both sects. Sunni mawlid prayers, were followed by a *ta'ziya*, the Shi'i ritual condolence on the martyrdom of Husayn Ibn 'Ali and then by political speeches and recitations of Habib al-'Ubaydi's patriotic poetry, attesting to the communion of interests enhanced by the desire to expel the British from Iraq.[46]

Outside the mosques, the anti-British agitation took a more political stance. Members of the Haras al-Istiqlal (Guards of Independence), a secret Shi'i nationalist society led by Muhammad al-Sadr, pushed for unity between both sects, while the Sunni 'Ahd members spread a more secular message based on the Sunni–Shi'i joint national agenda. Meanwhile, the deadlock in Dayr al-Zur, the tribal uprising spreading from Tel 'Afar to the surrounding villages west of Mosul, the armed clash with Jamil al-Midfa'i's Syrian troops, and the rumours about the arrival of Amir 'Abdallah at Dayr al-Zur increased the tension in the capital.[47]

The pressure further corroded the already strained relationship between Gertrude Bell and A. T. Wilson. An open confrontation around a piece of information (a draft of the constitution authored by Yasin al-Hashimi that had been attached to Gertrude's Syria report) led to the incident. She had forwarded it to an Arab friend in an attempt to encourage the moderate nationalists, as she referred to them. 'A. T. was in a black rage that morning . . . He told me my indiscretions were intolerable and that I should never see another paper in the office'.[48] Disregarding Wilson's warnings, Gertrude went on with her work, only to find the usual documents on her desk next morning and Wilson 'more pleasant than ever'. To what this constant defiance of authority could be attributed remains an open question. The fact is that Gertrude displayed it with the assurance of someone that had strong support in London's corridors of power. Stronger, one should say, than Wilson himself.

Their clashes stemmed not just from Gertrude's unintentionally committed 'little indiscretions', as she herself described her manipulations, but from their growing disagreement on whether to install one of the sharif's sons on the Iraqi throne, thus allowing the Arabs to run the country themselves. Both positions could be considered acts of colonial arrogance that differed only in accordance to the degree in which they were exercised.

In a nutshell, their positions differed mainly over the amount of advice Britain should give to Iraqis. Wilson, a representative of the Indian school, seemed to underestimate the strength of nationalism in general and the way it manifested itself in Iraq; he believed that Britain should rule Iraq with a firm hand or leave altogether. He also believed that efficiency and good governance were substitutes for self-rule.[49] By the same token, he felt in the need to give expression to cultural differences and particularisms by opting for different systems of governance, adapting administrative methods to the different provinces. Already in 1918 he thought that Mesopotamia should become a protectorate 'under which all classes and races [would] be given forthwith maximum liberty . . .'.[50] In his view, Iraq should be divided into administrative provinces that would be ruled in accordance with the needs and beliefs of the dominant groups, underestimating the power of nationalism (as it expressed itself at the time) as a unifying force, and as a justification for centralism. He also felt that the Kurds and the Shi'is would never accept the Sunnis as rulers of Iraq and feared a return of the Turks in such a case.[51] Gertrude Bell, influenced by Lawrence, believed in the power of Arab nationalism, of which Iraqi nationalism was part and parcel and not just a local manifestation. She also believed in the need for Britain's guidance as she did not see, erroneously, any major contradictions between Arab nationalism and Britain's imperialistic designs. But she started to realise, already then, that the Iraqis preferred self-governance even if it should come in place of a more efficient administration led by the British. Lawrence identified even more with the Arab nationalists' views and claimed that Britain should let the Arabs conduct their own affairs in the way they saw it fit. The main lines of this debate spilled over into different issues during the years to come, centring also on timetables and the scope of the mandate itself.

In the early months of 1920, the debate between Gertrude and Wilson had already become a subject of open gossip in London's official circles. Wilson's refusal to change his position regarding the mandate and the amount of authority to be bestowed upon Iraqis rekindled the activities of the 'Ahd's envoys in the Shi'i tribal areas and in the Holy Cities. Different versions of events give various immediate reasons for the rebellion that erupted some weeks later. Some documents claim that it was ignited by the arrest of the *alim*, Mirza Muhammad Rida, on 24 June, and, shortly after, that of Hajj Mukhif, the most influential man in the Daghara canal area.[52] Other sources refer to the arrest of Sha'lan albu Chon of the Zawalim over unpaid taxes. In any case, Wilson's rigidity, coupled with the agitation in the Shi'i tribal areas, enticed the spread of a rebellion from Rumaytha to the entire middle Euphrates.[53] Wilson's urgent invitations sent to the Iraqi (CUP-appointed) former parliamentary representatives to discuss elections for the Constituent Assembly and the provisional government could not appease the anger caused by his previous intransigence. Sayyid Muhammad al-Sadr of Kazimayn and Yusuf al-Suwaydi of the 'Ahd travelled to London to gain support for the idea of an independent Iraq. At the same time other petitions made the rounds in London's corridors of power. Among them was a petition forwarded by Basra's magnates, asking the British to give Basra special treatment under Britain's mandate.[54]

By July 1920, the rebellion had reached Diwaniyya and the Muntafiq, and the Baghdad nationalists began to realise that they had lost control of the tribal areas.[55] The tribes were not only motivated by nationalist slogans and religious fatwas calling for the establishment of an Islamic state; they were also fully enjoying the rebellion, looking forward to a period of lawlessness when they would not be compelled to pay taxes.[56] 'The troops we have got are not good', Wilson complained at the end of July.[57] 'The 37th Lancers ran like hares between Rumaytha and Diwaniya . . . the regiments from India who have never fired a musketry course . . . are not material with which to fight the Arab on their own ground . . .'.[58] On 12 August the tribes marched on Qal'at Sikkr and then on Nasiriyya.[59] In September all railways and bridges from Samawa to Hilla were burned.[60] And as the rebellion spread northward, Kirkuk, Kifri, and Mosul were cut off from Baghdad.[61]

Colonel Leachman, now PO of Dulaym/Ramadi, had been killed near Mosul after a confrontation with Shaykh Dhari of the Zawba' (Zubu'), a subsection of the famous Shammar tribe. In her eulogy, Gertrude described her friend: 'Lean and active, his face full of weather . . .';[62] Leachman was another British officer who had paid with his life for Britain's political failures, renowned for his notorious haughtiness and his own illusions of being an indispensable factor in a shaping moment in the Middle East. Gertrude's eulogy points again to the discrepancies in perceptions regarding this and other historic episodes.

The loss of lives and political opportunities was due, in Gertrude's view, to the fact that '[Iraq] could not be reduced to any system, . . . The Turks did not govern at all and we have tried to govern too much',[63] she concluded. The rebellion had cost hundreds of British lives, thousands of Arab lives, and £50 million. It was then too early to relate to the rebellion as a historical turning point. For the British at that time, it was just a tribal uprising that went out of control. However, the implications of the revolt obliged them to reconsider their whole policy in Iraq, turning the rebellion in a national myth.[64]

It didn't take long, however, for the first cracks in the Sunni–Shi'i alliance to emerge.[65] The 'United Islamic front has, I may say, fallen into discredit', Gertrude wrote on 30 August. 'The Sunnis never lose an occasion for pointing out that it's all the fault of the Shi'ahs and I take considerable pleasure in replying that the whole thing began from the Mesopotamians in Syria who were all Sunnis'.[66]

Would Britain stay in the country and for how long? And would Britain's departure leave the country in a state of chaos? Gertrude asked herself.[67] Having refused to send in her resignation when asked by Wilson to do so, 'I shall only go if I am ordered',[68] Gertrude asserted, while she continued to manipulate behind the scenes. She also tried to run Iraq's affairs almost like a private business, sending confidential papers to her father, among them a copy of the country's budget.[69] Another sign of presumption was the freedom she took when passing more direct information to London, circumventing, time and again, her superiors in Baghdad. All that would certainly have exasperated the Iraqi nationalists even more, were they better informed on how things really worked inside the administration at the time.

Along with the agitation in Iraq against the mandate, Britain's newspapers continued to raise questions about the benefits and disadvantages of direct British rule over the country. And this was at a time when a number of Iraqi leading personalities seemed to understand that an Arab government under Britain's protection was the best choice at that moment. Or perhaps that was what Gertrude wanted to believe.[70] Wilson had attempted to 'Indianize Mesopotamia', *The Times* explained in June 1920 when the rebellion was still brewing.[71] T. E. Lawrence, known then as Colonel Lawrence, joined in the press campaign, writing from All Souls' College, Oxford. The first article, entitled 'Ferment for Freedom', was published in the *Daily Herald* on 9 August 1920, when things were getting even more serious.[72] Considered the most influential authority on Middle Eastern affairs (and a celebrity after the Covent Garden screening of Lowell Thomas' filmed report of the Arab revolt), Lawrence's words had an enormous impact. Referring to the high costs of Britain's presence in Mesopotamia (£30 million a year) to provide for the presence of troops, Royal Air Force (RAF) squadrons and jobs for 450 British advisers who, in his opinion, could easily be replaced by Arab officials, Lawrence explained to the British public the intensity of national feelings among the Arabs:

> They have reached the stage out of which we, in the West, seem to have passed – the stage in a people's development when nationalism matters tremendously . . . They seek to be governed after their own fashion. We in Mesopotamia and the French in Syria are trying to impose an alien government upon them, and the attempt is bound to fail.[73]

Nationalism, Lawrence maintained, united Sunnis and Shi'is in Iraq and Muslims and Copts in Egypt, and any European attempt to divide and rule would necessarily backfire. Lawrence was also convinced that the European era in Asia was over. The Bolshevik revolution was, in his opinion, 'an Asiatic revolution' and therefore 'exportable' to the East, as its ideas were 'far more explosive things than troops or weapons'.[74]

In another article, published on 8 August in the *Observer*, Lawrence praised Faysal's Arab army and called for its expansion.[75] In his press campaign, Lawrence also defended the Iraqi nationalists' views regarding the need to develop secondary and higher education in Iraq. Arabic should also be the official language in schools and in the administration. A priori, Gertrude agreed with him. She also viewed universities as indispensable for the creation of cadres and politicians, while also improving primary and technical schools to raise the average level of the population. Otherwise the Arabs would think that the British were trying to prevent their progress, she explained to her father.[76] The main problem, however, again was money. 'Where is the money supposed to come from? The government? . . . The government hasn't a penny'.[77] She also disagreed with Lawrence on the use of Arabic in the administration:

> When he says we have forced the English language on the country, it's not only a lie, but he also knows it is. Every official work is done in Arabic – schools, law courts, hospitals – no other language is used. It's the first time that that has happened since the fall of the Abbasids.[78]

As for the large Iraqi national army the nationalists wanted to see established: 'Where are your divisions to come from?' she asked her Iraqi friends.[79] At the time they only had officers, no soldiers, she teased the Sherifians. It would take five years to conscript 20,000 peasants. In the meantime they would need the Assyrian levies and the British forces to keep order,[80] she maintained. This argument was dismissed by the Sherifians who regarded the army as a tool with which to forge the Iraqi nation, and a means to establish their own position in the army and the country.

Wilson also attacked Lawrence's views regarding Iraq's independence, claiming that Mesopotamia as a single unit had never been included in the Arab state McMahon had promised to Sharif Husayn.[81] While quoting from McMahon's second note to the sharif (24 October 1915), referring to the special status of the vilayets of Baghdad and Basra as an outcome of Britain's interests in the Gulf area, Wilson tried to bring opinions back to a 'pre-1920' state of mind. It was too late, however. His already tarnished prestige could not stand up to Lawrence's influence and to the effects of the rebellion on Britain's public opinion. Britain had to reconsider her policy in Iraq,[82] abandon Wilson's idea to 'evacuate or rule' and find another formula that would permit the continuation of British presence behind an Arab facade.

Wilson's two memoranda – describing the rebellion as just a result of sherifian anti-British propaganda – failed to win support in official circles.[83] The British themselves understood the impact of national feelings and the need to lose their control over Iraq. But at this point, Wilson's opinions were already considered political nostalgia. Need we look farther for the origins of the revolt?', an article in *The Times* asked. In fact, hundreds of excessively paid British officials reinforced anti-British feelings, leading observers to the conclusion that the rebellion was in fact a reaction to the India-like administration imposed on the country by Wilson.[84]

Anonymous articles put forward the same arguments that had previously appeared in T. E. Lawrence's articles in *The Times* (22 July 1920) and the *Observer* (8 August 1920), reinforcing the impression that these had also been written by him. Gertrude Bell in another typical outburst of defiance for authority wrote very opinionated letters to Edwin Montagu, the secretary of state for India, Arthur Hirtzel, the under-secretary, and to Herbert Asquith, the former prime minister, leading Montagu to ask her, vehemently, to stop circumventing the civil commissioner.

Wilson's time in Iraq had passed, though. It wasn't long before he was asked to leave the country, thus allowing Lawrence's friends in London's political circles to savour their victory. At farewell teas and dinner parties organised in Baghdad for the retiring civil commissioner, Wilson tried to disguise his emotion. The night before he left, he came to visit Gertrude. 'I said I felt discouraged that we had not made a better job of our relations', Gertrude wrote after the encounter, 'He said he had come to apologise . . . I stopped him and said it was my fault as much as his'. Nonetheless, she wanted to see him withdrawing from Middle Eastern politics altogether. In her opinion, the new kind of relations between Asia and Europe called for men of 'less mental power and greater human understanding'.[85]

Wilson's departure allowed an intermediary approach – a compromise between Wilson's theory of tight control and Lawrence's vision of total independence – to emerge. The solution would be to bring Sir Percy Cox back as high commissioner, to form a council of Arab ministers assisted by British advisers. Gertrude Bell opted for Cox's middle-of-the-road solution and embarked on her mission to support it wholeheartedly. But again, it was just a facade of Arab sovereignty, because the British would continue to control the country's affairs, albeit indirectly.[86] The next step would be to organise elections for a constituent assembly even if the large majority of the rural population *'se fichaient pas mal'* (could not care less) about its results,[87] accustomed as they were to Ottoman-style 'on paper' rigged elections.

On 17 October 1920, Sir Percy F. Cox arrived in Baghdad to take his place as high commissioner. Notables, important qadis, the mayor of the town, heads of departments, and other British officers assembled at the railway station. A seventeen-gun salute was fired and the band played 'God save the King'. 'And he stood there in his white and gold lace uniform with his air of fine and simple dignity', Gertrude reported, 'never had an arrival been more momentous and never was there anyone on whom more conflicting emotions were centred: hopes and doubts and fears'. 'As the low sun picked out his tall, white figure from the muted surroundings', Gertrude made her curtsy: 'It was all I could do not to cry', she reported then, showing again how emotionally charged her approach to Iraqi politics was. A famous Baghdadi orator read an address in Arabic; Sir Percy replied, also in Arabic, that he had come to set up an Arab administration under Britain's guidance.[88] Taking on the 'role of a moon in orbit around her planet, Sir Percy', Gertrude would help Cox establish an Arab government that would permit the British to present themselves in a different light.[89] Guidance or supervision? the Baghdadis asked themselves while trying to find the English equivalent of the Arabic term *nidara*. Gertrude explained some time later that supervision was the correct translation, despite the hope of the nationalists for a much looser control. It would be, in effect, a less blatant form of control but yet required Iraq's subjection to the British. Lady Cox, looking, after the dusty, ten-hour journey, 'as if she had just emerged from the finest bandbox', invited all the dignitaries to the Residency for tea, concluding the debate, for an afternoon, on an agreeable note.

Gates adorned with flags, palm branches, and triumphal arches erected in the gardens greeted the guests, as Gertrude described the setting, explaining also the expectations floating in the air. 'Complete independence', insisted the nationalists, but what did that mean? Gertrude asked them. 'Complete independence is a beautiful maiden, 14 years old . . . her hair fondling her waist', explained Ja'far al-'Askari to Gertrude in one of their discussions. 'Khatun, she does not exist', he still argued. 'Complete independence', Gertrude replied, 'is what we ultimately wished to give'. 'My lady, complete independence is never given – always taken', Ja'far then concluded,[90] making his aim very clear. How to help the Iraqis take on new responsibilities became the key issue in Gertrude's further dialogues with the nationalists.

A provisional council headed by the naqib of Baghdad, the venerable 'Abd al-Rahman al-Kaylani, would be appointed in November 1920 to serve as an interim administrative body. Sayyid Talib, the eldest son of the naqib of Basra (who headed the committee charged with revising Turkish electoral law) filled the post of minister of the interior in the provisional council.[91]

The council members represented the different communities that formed Iraq's population; British advisers were attached to each ministry. Among the advisers, St J. Philby acted as adviser to the Ministry of Interior; Sir Edgar Bonham-Carter, as adviser to the Ministry of Justice; and Lionel Smith as adviser to the Ministry of Education.[92]

Lionel Smith was an old acquaintance of the Bells, and Gertrude found herself organising dinner parties for him to meet local figures whose ideas about secondary education and its importance were more compliant with Britain's policy on the subject.[93] Hikmat Sulayman, whose family connections with Turkey's elite set him in a different position, was a frequent guest. Gertrude's friendship with the naqib had also turned the elections to the Provisional Council into almost a 'family affair', as even her father had made a point of personally cabling the naqib to congratulate him on his appointment. This direct intervention by the Bells in Iraqi politics, apart from its rather peculiar aspects, is also an indication of the exaggerated rights taken by those involved in the imperial adventure, to influence the running of the country's affairs. The Provisional Council would organise the framework for the administration in the provinces and appoint Arab Sunni officials in administrative posts all over the country.[94] The drawing up of an electoral law and of guidelines for the formation of an Iraqi army were also important items on the council's agenda.

Gertrude would set up a scheme of tribal representation to the Constituent Assembly: twenty members representing the largest tribes and ten representing the smaller tribes would be grouped together along the lines of the ten new divisions.[95] She selected the tribal representatives in such a way as to permit the Shi'i tribes to collaborate with the new administration.[96] It was, however, a Sunni-dominated council and Gertrude was very much in favour of it as the alternative, in her mind, would be a Shi'i theocracy.

But then again, in this new configuration the Mosul vilayet was to be retained and annexed to Iraq 'in order to adjust the demographic balance between Shi'is and Sunnis' she explained.[97] The Kurds and the Turkmen, the majority of whom were Sunni, would then contribute to keep the balance in Sunnis' favour. The Shi'is were clearly disappointed. The Sherifians, once their allies, would now profit from the gains of their joint struggle against the British.[98]

As the fissures in the Sunni–Shi'i front became more evident, Gertrude came to the conclusion that the Shi'i dilemma was in fact a choice between being 'echt Arabisch, or echt Shiistisch',[99] hinting at the fact that the Shi'i tribesmen were yet to be won over to the idea of Arab nationalism. She was wrong in her definition, however, as the Shi'is in Iraq saw themselves as exponents of Arab traditions, culture and language, in no less a measure than their Sunni counterparts, who positioned themselves as the leaders of the movement. For some tribal leaders, however, the idea of an Islamic government, with Najaf and Karbala as religious and economic centres, was still much more appealing than the prospect of a Sunni-led government in Baghdad with modern, Western-style institutions.

The question still remaining was, who would be placed at the head of the new government? Faysal's name had been raised again when the rebellion was at its peak.[100] Banished from Syria by the French, after his army's defeat by General Gouraud's forces in the battle of Maysalun (27 July 1920), Faysal was searching for another throne. Gertrude, captivated by the idea of having him crowned as King of Iraq, renewed her efforts in this direction. Faysal's appointment was in effect a foregone conclusion, even if not yet an official decision. He was freer, however, than before to consider this option, after Abdallah's stepping down from his candidacy and his acceptance, through Lawrence's interference, of Trans-Jordan as a second choice.[101] Another possible candidate was Sayyid Talib of Basra. Gertrude started abandoning this idea gradually not just because of his anti-British record, as a Basra nationalist, but also because of his too-independent position.[102] In addition to problems in Iraq's domestic arena, Gertrude and her colleagues had to cope with difficulties imposed from home. Pressure from London political circles to cut back on Britain's expenditures abroad reduced the British forces in Mesopotamia from two divisions to one, now deployed along the Nasiriyya–Qurna line. 'You can't withdraw troops to Basra and carry out the mandate', Gertrude explained to Asquith in December 1920. 'No government in this country, whether ours or an Arab administration, can carry on without force behind it'.[103] But London would not listen.

In January 1921, the situation went from bad to worse. 'We have reached, I fear, the end of the chapter', Gertrude complained to her father.[104] The nationalists accused the naqib and the council members of being too traditional in their support of religious leaders, land owners and tribal shaykhs,[105] whereas the British still pondered the costs of retaining their forces in Iraq to support the new government. Winston Churchill, now head of the Colonial Office, had cabled Sir Percy Cox, explaining that the British government could not burden the British public with more taxes. The reduction of Britain's forces to one division and one brigade meant maintaining order with only police forces and Indian units, a doubtful task.[106] Churchill also considered a withdrawal of British troops from Mosul. Gertrude was very much opposed to the idea: 'As soon as we withdraw from Mosul, the Turks will take over', Gertrude warned Cox, without concealing her feelings about Churchill's orders. In her view, a partial withdrawal of British troops to Basra (an idea that regained momentum in the fall of 1920) would mean, for Britain, the loss of control over the country. A local conscripted army was needed, Gertrude now believed, in spite of the costs involved. In another typical change of mood, she now pleaded: 'Father, think! If we had begun establishing native institutions two years ago, by now we should have gotten an Arab government and an Arab army'.[107] In an extremely confidential letter to her father, she displayed again not just her disregard for established norms and political channels but also her characteristic belief that her knowledge of the country gave her the right to reshape it.[108] She felt that way even if she was aligning herself this time against imperial policies, because she was able to sense, better perhaps than her male colleagues, the rhythm and the intensity of national feelings taking root in the country.

CHAPTER 7

'To Make Kings, to Invent Kingdoms'

Even when fulfilling the post of managing director of the Anglo-Persian Oil Company (APOC), A. T. Wilson continued to follow the events in Iraq and to offer his own interpretations to friends. 'Cox doesn't seem to be making much headway in Mesopotamia with his precious government',[1] Wilson wrote in January 1921 to Frank Balfour, the former political officer for the Euphrates and military governor to Baghdad. The idea of a Council of State headed by the Iraqis seemed to him illusory at best. He still clung to his old idea that Britain had to abandon the mandate altogether if no British troops could be kept there to support the new Iraqi government.[2] Balfour, now in the Sudan, was also a close friend of Gertrude's and thoroughly familiar with the approaches of both sides.

The possibility of withdrawing British troops to Basra – a re-emerging idea – wouldn't be effective at all, Gertrude believed, because Basra, Iraq's only port, would be constantly pressured by Baghdad to get rid of the British troops and become part of an independent Iraq. Given the pressures and the alternatives, Winston Churchill, now secretary of state for the colonies, summoned a conference in Cairo to help convince the British public that an annual disbursement of £5 million per year to keep the troops in Mesopotamia (as Iraq was still officially called) would be a justifiable expenditure. The conference was organised by the new Middle East department created to administer the territories under mandate, and would relate mainly to the reduction of military expenditure, the selection of Iraq's new ruler and on the refugee problem, the location of bases and the financial arrangements related to the military and civil assets to be transferred to the Iraqis.[3] The department, headed by Sir John Shuckburgh of the India Office, included among its members Colonel T. E. Lawrence, Major

Hubert Young (from the Foreign Office), R. W. Bullard (former consul in Basra and governor of Baghdad) and Colonel Richard Meinertzhagen, former chief political officer for Palestine.[4] Churchill would use the department to neutralise the India Office and France's influence on the Foreign Office.

In spite of the congenial atmosphere at the conference, Gertrude was surprised to discover that Britain's plans for Mesopotamia had not been entirely disclosed to the British authorities in Baghdad, and had already been decided upon in London at the meetings of the new department. Some of the topics had also been discussed by Churchill and Lawrence 'over dinner', at the Ship Restaurant in the Whitehall, so the rumours went.

Yet, the debates at the Cairo Conference were no less formal. A new treaty would be negotiated with Iraq's future government and change the patterns of colonial rule putting an end to Britain's direct control. Britain would still control Iraq's foreign relations, however, and intervene in financial and judicial matters.[5] Britain's indirect control over the country would only be possible through the use of an air force, much cheaper to maintain than land troops. Air Marshal Hugh Trenchard's air defence scheme (a network of air bases, RAF battalions and auxiliary troops) was then adopted.[6]

As for a Kurdish autonomous state in the Mosul area, no clear decision had been made. Although Churchill declared that the Kurds should not be subjected to the Arabs if they didn't want to be, a final decision on Mosul's fate, its attachment to Baghdad or its return to Turkey, or yet its existence as an autonomous entity, would be postponed until a peaceful agreement had been negotiated with Turkey. As the administration of Kirkuk and Sulaymaniyya was too costly, some (among them Wilson) believed that Iraq could do without Mosul, an idea Gertrude dismissed totally.

The atmosphere in Cairo was optimistic. All the major figures directly or indirectly connected with Middle East policies were there: Winston Churchill, Sir Herbert Samuel (now the high commissioner for Palestine), Colonel T. E. Lawrence, Lieutenant Colonel Sir Walter Congrave (commander-in-chief in Egypt and Palestine), General Sir Edmund Ironside (commander-in-chief in Persia), Sir Percy Cox, Colonel Kinahan Cornwallis and Gertrude Bell. The Sherifians were represented by Ja'far al-'Askari, Nuri al-Sa'id, and 'Auni 'Abd al-Hadi.

In Cairo, Gertrude certainly realised that Britain's moment in the Middle East was the sum of other private adventures, sometimes as improvised as her own. Churchill's 'Forty Thieves', filled with a sense of responsibility toward history, and yet bemused by their role in its making, seemed to

4. Gertrude Bell and T.E. Lawrence 'the uncrowned potentates of Arabia'.
Cairo, March 1921.

5. Winston Churchill, Gertrude Bell and T. E. Lawrence
on a visit to the Pyramids during the Cairo Conference, 1921.

ignore the reactions their presence was evoking in the Middle East in general and in Cairo in particular. Mounted on camels, on a sunny March afternoon, Bell and Lawrence rode to the Pyramids – a symbol of continuity – only to witness Churchill fall off his camel, as if to demonstrate their lack of preparedness in standing up to the notions of time in the East.

'It has been one of the longest fortnights I ever lived . . . we live in a marble and bronze hotel, very expensive and luxurious: horrible place: makes me Bolshevik', wrote Lawrence to his mother from the Conference.[7] 'We are a very happy family: agreed at everything important and the trifles are laughed at'.[8] But this was not exactly the case. The conference had also served as a forum for different views to surface, some more covert than others.

When things became tough, a bottle of wine was brought to the lobby to ease the tension. On other occasions, Churchill would sit down 'with his easel to paint the Sphinx, the Pyramids or a dam on the Nile, undisturbed by the passing cars carrying "a bas Churchill" stickers'.[9] The debates were also affected by contacts made in the corridors of the conference hall and the information exchanged informally among participants. F. Seymour Cocks's book *The Secret Treaties and Understandings*, published in 1918 by the Union of Democratic Control (UDC), was circulated among the conference members, explaining the Liberals' anti-war position.[10] The UDC's leader, E. D. Morel used it, to attack Lloyd George's war politics and the secret commitments at its base. It was meant to generate a rapprochement between the UDC and Labour while alienating the Liberals. Its preface, written by Charles P. Trevelyan, reminded Gertrude of the atmosphere at Wallington and the debates that had preceded the war.

In spite of Wilson's opposition to the conference, to its main aims and to Churchill's fondness for Lawrence 'whose advice on Mesopotamia and Palestine isn't worth much', Lawrence and Gertrude Bell seemed amused by his presence. He was no less amused when witnessing Gertrude's well-known intolerance toward other women in action again. She picked on Rosita Forbes, a well-known Middle East reporter and writer: 'It was very amusing to watch their attitude to each other – cats',[11] Wilson noted.

He was having a difficult time, given the increasing competition for oil concessions in the territories liberated from Turkish rule. Standard Oil, Shell and Anglo-Persian were accusing one another of fomenting unrest in Mesopotamia,[12] revealing conflicts among the shareholders and the countries backing them. Tense, as he was not yet sure how it would all work out for him, Faysal, now appointed as the official candidate for Iraq's throne, asked Colonel Kinahan Cornwallis, then an official at the Egypt Ministry of Finance, to escort him to Iraq and help him negotiate with the British the terms of the treaty and his position in the country. An expert in tribal politics[13] and a personal friend from the Arab Bureau's days, Cornwallis would help pave Faysal's way among Iraq's tribes.

In order to prevent possible antagonism from the nationalists, Cox suggested that Cornwallis be appointed a member of his own staff first and then be transferred to Faysal's service, on condition that 'the latter makes good',[14] that is to say, if Faysal managed to gain the population's support. Once arrangements regarding his salary and period of service were made, Cornwallis sailed for Basra aboard the *Northbrook*, and Gertrude Bell was chosen to introduce him to the country's affairs and to explain 'how the wind blows throughout Iraq'.[15]

Faysal's main rival to the role of Iraq's leader was still Sayyid Talib of Basra after his elder brother 'Abdallah fell from favour after the Dayr al-Zur episode. In spite of Sir St John Philby's (the adviser to the Ministry of Interior) support, Gertrude's opinion of Sayyid Talib diminished in proportion to his decreasing usefulness, as he started to be considered by the British as 'too capable, energetic and intriguing a character to be left at loose ends'.[16]

When Sayyid Talib had become too articulate, complaining about Britain's intervention in Iraq's affairs, he became, in Gertrude's words, 'a nuisance'. His speech, at a dinner, regarding the naqib's possible appeal to Islam, was depicted by Gertrude as an 'incitement to rebellion . . . not far from a declaration of Jihad'.[17] Sayyid Talib's deportation to Fao after having been invited to a tea with Lady Cox, left no doubt about the British intentions to get rid of him. But Gertrude shrewdly went to bid farewell to Mme Talib, before her departure to rejoin her husband in Ceylon, to where he had been expatriated. Sayyid Talib's deportation, Abdallah's acceptance of Trans-Jordan as an alternative throne, the return of the Sherifians to Iraq and the dropping of other candidates (the Naqib of Baghdad and the Shaykh of Muhammara) helped create the atmosphere for Faysal's appointment by the British as the official candidate for Iraq's throne. It was also the Hashemites' reputation of tolerance toward the Shi'is and Faysal's role in the Arab revolt that appeared to boost his popularity, possibly enhancing his chances of being accepted by the population.

Faysal's arrival in Basra in June 1921 had been preceded by a petition signed by the town's notables asking that Basra be kept as a separate area, with a separate legislative council, army, police force and taxes department. 'I said *No*', Gertrude wrote then to her father. 'Until HMG [His Majesty's government] gives its decision on the matter, I must exercise my private opinion',[18] she affirmed. After having received a rather lukewarm reception from the Shi'i tribes, Faysal's fate improved slightly as he advanced northwards.

'Already the whole town is flying the Sherifian flag', Gertrude had reported from Baghdad some days prior to his arrival, telling her family about the anticipation Faysal's arrival had generated.[19] Was the red triangle over the black and green stripes of the Sharifian flag a mistake? 'Father, for Heaven's sake, tell me whether the flag is heraldically right. You might telegraph',[20] she pleaded, proving again the exaggerated hold she had on Iraqi affairs. Gertrude suggested a new flag:

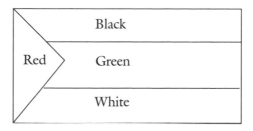

Thinking that the flag's basic design was good: 'White for the Fatimids, green for the 'Ummayads, black for the 'Abbasids, and the red triangle set across the three bands for Islam', Gertrude believed it was necessary to differentiate it for Iraq by putting a golden star on the black stripe or on the triangle.[21] She asked her father again for better suggestions.

The flags in the streets announced Faysal's arrival in Baghdad. On 29 June 1921, a crowd gathered at the train station to greet the newcomer. Gertrude reported,

> Faysal stood at the carriage door, looking splendid in full Arab dress, saluting the guard of honour . . . Sir Percy and Sir Aylmer (the Commander-in-Chief of the British military forces in Mesopotamia) went up to him as he got out and gave him a ceremonious greeting and all the people clapped . . . I espied Mr. Cornwallis stepping out of the carriage looking rather gloomy, so I went to receive him.[22]

Faysal noticed Gertrude amid the crowd and advanced to shake her hand. The question afloat was how would the naqib and his council receive him. The tension dissipated only a week later when the naqib gave a dinner party in Faysal's honour. It was an official welcome to the new ruler.

Among the English guests at the reception were Sir Percy and his staff and General Sir Aylmer Haldane, and two of his staff. All the rest were the ministers and notables of Baghdad.

> The streets were crowded with people as we drove up. The Naqib's family received us at the door and we climbed up two flights of stairs onto a roof overlooking the mosque, a sort of wide balcony. It was carpeted and lighted; the mosque door opposite was hung with lamps and the minarets ringed with them . . . A burning wind blew on us while we drank coffee and talked, till the clapping of hands in the street announced the arrival of Feisal. The Naqib got up and, helped by his personal physician, walked across the whole of the carpeted space and reached the head of the stairs just as Feisal's white-robed figure appeared. They embraced formally on both cheeks and walked back hand in hand to the end of the balcony where we were all standing up. Feisal sat down between the Naqib and Sir Percy and, after a few minutes, dinner was announced . . . The ordered dignity, the real solid magnificence, the tension of spirit which one felt all round, and with it all, the burning heat of the night. For, after all, to the best of our ability, we were making history.[23]

The stressful task of 'king making', as she saw it, was not yet over, however. Gertrude spent long hours with Cornwallis in the Residency's vaulted room, studying tribes and discussing the formation of Faysal's first cabinet.[24] What would Faysal's policy be? she asked herself now, just as she had before his arrival. Would he opt for what she saw as a 'milder' kind of nationalism, one that was not too 'anti-British'? Or would he opt for a 'jihad', as she called a fierce anti-British campaign. By separating the moderates from the extremists, Gertrude adopted the imperialist tradition of driving a wedge between both camps. 'Can we get enough of the breath of life into him without it?',[25] Gertrude wondered, obviously underestimating Faysal's own political agenda and the fact that he wouldn't comply with Britain's designs to let him rule nominally only.

Faysal was an enigma to the British. Was he a weak figure, or was he a subtle politician, ready to listen and able to appeal to the country's disparate groups?[26] How would he react to the divergences of opinion among the British themselves and the nationalists? Faysal would prove, as time passed, that he knew, perhaps better than others, how to juggle all the elements at the same time.

A plebiscite was meant to legitimise Faysal's ascension to the throne, as Britain had to justify his appointment to the League of Nations. 'I do not want to impose myself on the people of Iraq',[27] he declared, while meetings in the Ja'fariyya and Husayniyya Shi'i schools reinforced the Shi'i mujtahids' anti-British and anti-monarchic protests.[28] The pressure was relieved only by the divisions inside the Shi'i camp itself, where tribal rivalries and personal jealousies drove a wedge between the parties. In the towns of Najaf and Karbala, pro-Arab and pro-Turk sections, headed by Sayyid Muhammad al-Sadr and Shaykh Mahdi al-Khalisi, organised meetings both in favour of, and against, Faysal and the new council of state. But even those in favour of Faysal made their support dependent on a guarantee from the British regarding a Shi'i majority in parliament and a better definition of the Shi'is future political role.[29]

Faysal's difficulties were too numerous. In part those had already been predicted by Wilson before he left,[30] and there were others. In the northern provinces where pro-Turkish sentiments were still strong, fatwas issued against the Hashemites 'who dared to rise against the Sultan' were coupled with demands for the return of Mosul vilayet to Turkey.[31] Seeking approval in Iraq's main towns Faysal approached 'Izzat Pasha, a Turkmen leader who wasn't very keen at having Faysal, or the Arabs, ruling Iraq. 'If he has ['Izzat Pasha], Faysal has got Kirkuk', Gertrude commented then. Among the groups that still had to be won over to this position, were the Christians.

A reception organised in the Armenian church in Baghdad 'was one of the prettiest of all the Baghdad functions', Gertrude reported in August 1921. 'The courtyard in front of the Armenian Church was hung with carpets and covered with awnings'.

> . . . There are a few palm trees in the court, bearing now their heavy bunches of dates. The great fronds with their hanging crown of fruits looked like huge Corinthian capitals carrying the awning roof. Feisal, who catches at beauty, was delighted. He called me up onto his dais, to sit on one side of him, with the Armenian bishop on the other. . .[32]

Other functions were no less impressive. In the Residency's court, 'roofed over with an awning and its gallery hung with flags and streamers of the Arab colours, Jewish rabbis in turbans and twisted shawls sat together with Christian and Moslem notables and black cloaked ulama'. Iced lemonade, coffee, cakes, and ice creams were served while Jewish children sang their songs. 'The Rolls of Law in three gold cylinders were then brought in and kissed by the Grand Rabbi and by Feisal who was presented with a small gold model of the Tables of Law and a beautifully bound Talmud',[33] Gertrude wrote. Faysal managed, momentarily, to appease tensions. The speech he delivered at the reception delighted both Jews and Christians, but aroused apprehensions among the Shi'is, who complained that Faysal treated Jews, Christians and Muslims on an equal footing.[34]

Gertrude reported on Faysal's tours to other parts of the country in her monthly intelligence reports. His visit to Dulaym Liwa was one of her most vivid accounts, and had special political significance as it portrayed Faysal's welcome by Fahad Beg, the paramount shaykh of the 'Anaza, a supporter of the British, and by 'Ali Sulayman of the Dulaym, a supporter of Sayyid Talib, the Naqib of Basra:

> Suddenly in the clear light of the early morning the wilderness was peopled with mounted tribesmen. 'The Amir?' they shouted as we passed. 'Is the Amir coming?' 'He is near, he is near', we answered, and at the news men scrambled into their saddles and waved their white cleeves to their comrades behind them, bidding them [to] hasten. The great tribe of the Dulaym, half nomad, half cultivators, had turned out in force to acclaim Feisal, king of tents and flocks and of lands where the slow waters of Euphrates roll down the long canals to quicken their sown fields,

Gertrude reported then in 'The Fealty of the Tribes' in a display of descriptive skills that surpassed many of her previous reports. She was becoming inspired by the converging images of traditional and modern Iraq.

Faysal and his entourage arrived at Falluja 'sweeping out of the desert clouds raised in the wild escort of tribal horses that galloped by his ear'. Dressed in his white *'abaya*, 'girt with a gold belt holding a gold dagger, white headdress bound with a silver rope and fine black mantle', Faysal entered the big tent [that] was 'carpet-strewn and set with diwans, . . .' 'It is 700 years since an Arab king walked among his Mesopotamian subjects, a longer interval even here where we reckon history by millenniums', Gertrude described in a historically minded note.

> At the black tent of Fahad Beg Faysal spoke to five or six hundred men wrapped in brown mantles, . . . a chieftain of tribesmen in the sonorous language of the desert, with command and injunction and question to which his audience gave deep-tongued answer. So it has been in such gatherings since the earliest days of Arab civilisation . . . I never saw him look so splendid.

She continued in her report of Faysal's historic tour 'He spoke the great tongue of the desert which I have never heard him use before: sonorous, magnificent – no language like it . . .'.

'I have my rights over you as your lord'. Faysal said '. . . I will settle your differences'. And then, '30 or more shaykhs or the Dulaym strode up to [Faysal] and laid their hand in his hand in token of personal fealty'. Then Fahad Beg of the 'Anaza, and 'Ali Sulayman of the Dulaym, stood up on either side of him and said, 'We swear allegiance to you because you are acceptable to the British government'.

'No one can doubt what my relations are to the British, but we must settle our affairs between ourselves'. Faysal answered while searching for Gertrude's approval. Holding her two hands 'clasped together as a symbol of the union of the Arab and British governments',[35] Gertrude smiled, as the moment was an attempt to bridge the differences all knew still existed. 'And then the meal was brought in. Eight men staggered under each rice dish, each of which was crowned by a sheep roasted whole, while serving men circulated glasses of water mixed with sour curds, *shinirah*, one of the best drinks invented by man . . .'.[36] Late in the afternoon there was another assembly. From Falluja to Al-Qaim, the townships sent their mayors, qadis, and leading men to declare their allegiance to the emir.

> They gathered in a palm garden, Faysal sitting on a platform with softly coloured Persian rugs hung on the wall behind him. The evening sun sent slanting rays through the palm fronds, touching the white turbans and long robes of the qadhis, the brown cloaks of the villagers, the red kerchief and the silver handles of the daggers at the belts. The peaceful beauty of the hour held us . . .[37]

In his attempt to consolidate his position, Faysal had to learn how to neutralise other foci of power, and how to cultivate the loyalty of different elements in the population. He meant 'to be a real king not a creature of a foreign power',[38] Gertrude explained, proving that she herself understood, at times, that Faysal had to speak for the people, not for Britain. At dusk Faysal prayed, turning to Mecca 'We sat silent, but I think that in spirit we prayed with him . . .'.[39]

Imbued with a sense of responsibility towards 'a people who trusted us'. Gertrude worked hard, receiving delegations of notables from all parts of the country. Among them was the Mutasarrif of Karbala, who came to tell her about politics in Najaf, Karbala and in the Shi'i tribal areas. Tired, she would fall asleep, 'his voice seemed to retire fainter and fainter into a dim distance'. While the preparations for the referendum continued to take up most of her time, she would travel with Faysal to Ctesiphon, the most famous of the later Persian palaces. At this historic site, dating from the third century,

> The Garbetts, Fakhri Jamil, and Mr. Cornwallis were treated to a breakfast of eggs, tongue, sardines, and melons . . . After breakfast . . . I took him into the high windows to the south, whence we could see the Tigris, and told him the story of the Arab conquest as Tabari records it, the folding of the river and the rest of that magnificent tale. It was the tale of his own people.[40]

The importance of Ctesiphon lay in its two-fold significance. It was in Ctesiphon that the British had suffered a military setback in 1915 that had prevented them from advancing toward Baghdad. Ctesiphon was also the Sassanid winter capital that fell to the Arabs in 637 and became as much a symbol of Arab supremacy over the Persians as the battle of Qadisiyya in 651. Gertrude laid out before Faysal and his entourage the history of ancient Mesopotamia: the story of Abraham's Ur in Chaldean times, the city-states of Sumeria, the irrigation systems, the political and social organisations that developed out of the need to master the waters of the two rivers, the trade, the cuneiform writing, and the Sumerian calendar (comprising twelve months in a year and twenty-four hours in a day) that laid the ground for all calendars in later civilisations. Gertrude reminded them of Baghdad's glory under the 'Abbasids and the thread linking these times to modern Iraq. She would also remind Faysal's entourage of Al-Tabari, the great historian born in Tabaristan (d. 923) who wrote *The History of Prophets and Kings* (*Ta'rikh al-rusul wa al-muluk*) an account of the world's creation until his times. It was in this historic context that Faysal would have to perform.

How would the traditional society adapt to modern times, Gertrude wondered, while reporting to her family the naqib's attempt to explain to a Shammari shaykh at one of the council's meetings, the principles of democracy (*al-damakratiya* in Arabic), and Faysal's future role as king of a constitutional democratic state. 'Are you a Damakrati?' asked the naqib. After learning from the naqib about equalities in a democratic society, the Shammari shaykh answered. 'Wallahi, no!' 'I'm not a Makrati!'[41]

The attempt to teach democracy to a tribal population was a difficult mission at best. At this stage, Gertrude would tour the country trying to explain what all that meant and assess each group's wishes and designs. But no group had a clearer idea of who they were and what they wanted to achieve than the Kurds.

The British first encountered the Kurdish tribes after conquering Baghdad in 1917, as they were marching northward toward Mosul. 'Physically the Mosul vilayet presents certain contrasts to that of Baghdad', Gertrude explained in a later report.[42] 'On the left bank of an undulating plain, broken only by the mass of Jabal Sinjar, rise the Kurdish mountains ... extremely steep and sheer, their separate ranges forming narrow and isolated valleys between which the roads must either climb different passes or follow exiguous gorges'.[43] Mosul was more diverse than other parts of Iraq. Arab tribesmen of the Shammar or Tayy tribes in the Tigris valley and Jezira desert, the Kurds in the mountains east and north of Mosul and the Yazidis in Jabal Sinjar. 'Besides the Yazidis and Christians, Turcomen Arab and Kurd stand in close juxtaposition . . .'.

Britain had maintained close contacts with the Baban of Sulaymaniyya and the Badr Khans of northern Kurdistan, the Talabanis, and other tribal and religious leaders. At the end of the First World War, Shaykh Mahmud, Agha of the Barzinji, a descendant of Kakha Ahmed, the venerated leader of the Qadiriyya, emerged as the local leader. Once the first contacts with Shaykh Mahmud were established, Wilson issued, in December 1918, an invitation to all Kurdish chiefs of the area stretching from the Great Zab to the Diyala to join efforts under Shaykh Mahmud and create a semi-autonomous Kurdish enclave under Britain's aegis.

Personal rivalries stood in their way, however. What they needed was a 'Kurdish Faysal', Gertrude wrote in 1921, 'Someone who could form a nucleus for the Kurdish movement'.[44] It was a difficult task. Kifri and Kirkuk chiefs had refused to be annexed to Sulaymaniyya and become Shaykh Mahmud's subjects. The unrest that followed and the subsequent bombing of Sulaymaniyya by the RAF brought this first chapter in the modern story of the Kurds' strife for autonomy to its sad conclusion.

The situation remained unsolved until August 1920, when the Treaty of Sèvres recognised the rights of Turkey's Kurds to create an autonomous state, extending to Mosul's Kurds the prerogative to join in the experiment. These resolutions stirred the spirits of Mosul's population, reinforcing their refusal to take part in the plebiscite supporting Faysal. Gertrude Bell had understood the Kurds' dilemma but was becoming more and more convinced of Mosul's importance to Iraq as a possible reservoir of oil and a demographic stabiliser against a Shi'i majority. Mosul's attachment to Iraq was not yet assured, however. 'Our prospects are again very black', Gertrude wrote in February 1921.[45] That was because the Turks were pressuring for a revision of the Treaty of Sèvres, whose terms had caused great resentment in Turkey. Mustapha Kemal, Turkey's new leader, also refused to recognise Kurdistan's and Armenia's rights to independence and considered Mosul an integral part of Turkey.

The situation reinforced the decision of Sulaymaniyya's notables to form an autonomous Kurdish enclave administered directly by Sir Percy Cox. 'We hope it will eventually drop in to Iraq but it is no good trying to force matters. The population is wholly Kurdish and they say they don't want to be part of an Arab state',[46] Gertrude concluded at the time. In the summer of 1921 delegates from the Kurdish nationalist society in Istanbul, headed by Amin 'Ali Beg Badr Khan, arrived in Baghdad to ask the British to support a Kurdish autonomous state federated with Iraq.[47]

*Madbata*s (petitions) against Faysal and the referendum were distributed in Altun Küprü, Tauq, Malha, Shuwan, and other Kurdish areas. The populations in those towns and villages wanted Kurdish autonomy but were reluctant to be included in Sulaymaniyya's administrative sphere. Mosul's fate remained unclear for years to come.

* * *

Faysal's coronation on 23 August 1921 as King of Iraq was well orchestrated. The procession of RAF officers, headed by Sir Percy Cox, Sir Aylmar Haldane and Colonel Kinahan Cornwallis, all dressed up in white uniforms decorated with ribbons and stars entered the *serai*, where a two-and-a-half-foot high dais had been erected. They were accompanied by Sayyid Mahmud (the naqib's eldest son) and Sayyid Husayn Afnan (secretary of the Council of Ministers). When Faysal, in his military uniform, entered the room filled with Arab and English officers, ministers and delegates from all over the country, the audience rose to their feet. Gertrude, standing in the front row, wore her Commander of the British Empire (CBE) star and three war ribbons. As Faysal, very tense, caught Gertrude's eye, she gave him a tiny salute. When Sayyid Husayn announced Faysal's election by ninety-six per cent of the electorate, the audience stood up again. 'The national flag was broken on the flagstaff and the band played "God Save the King" . . . they have no national anthem yet',[48] Gertrude reported in August 1921.

Faysal's administration began with the institution of administrative councils (*majalis idara*) in the smallest administrative divisions: *liwas* and *qadas*. Municipal councils were created in the towns. The army was nationalised by the establishment of a scale of equity between its Sharifian and non-Sharifian officers, the first divisions taking over Hilla, Kut, and Falluja from the British troops.[49]

Despite these auspicious initiatives, Faysal's first steps in his new country were not easy. 'People in the provinces complain bitterly of the Istiqlal (independence)' Gertrude reported in 7 February 1921.[50] His difficulties reminded Gertrude of Husayn, the Prophet's grandson, who had been invited from Mecca to become the caliph but was greeted with indifference and a lack of support.[51] These analogies came to Gertrude's mind during the Muharram procession when Shi'is mourned Husayn's death. Watching

6. King Faysal I, after his coronation on 23 August 1921.

the passing cortège from the roof of the Persian consul's home, she thought again about Husayn and his followers and how they died of thirst and the wounds inflicted on them by Mu'awiyya's soldiers.

Lighted torches, drums and beating of breasts, distinguished the Muharram procession from any other. Drum players were followed by men riding ornamented horses and by banner bearers

> And then a black-robed company spread out in two rows across the court, swinging chains, [around their chests] with which they beat their backs . . . They swung them very skillfully, with a little jerk at the top of the swing so that the chains barely touched the skin, but the effect was wonderful – the black figures in the glaring torch light, swinging rhythmically from side to side with the swing of the chains, and the drums marking the time. Next came the breast-beaters, . . . beating their breasts in unison to a different rhythm of drums. Each procession surged through the courtyards, swung their chains, beat their breasts and surged out into the street. And so it went interminably.[52]

The tenth day of Muharram, the 'Ashura, was the final day of the period mourning the anniversary of Husayn's death. Gertrude drove to Kazimayn to see the ceremonies, knowing that she would not be allowed to watch the Muharram play performed in the mosque's courtyard. The procession preceding the play alluded to the burning of tents and the cutting off of heads, by Mu'awiyya's soldiers: 'These were the feda'i of Husayn . . . their heads shaved, their scalp cut with a sword and their blood running down their face and on their white cotton robe'.[53]

These symbols of martyrdom, so deeply ingrained in Shi'i collective memory, pervaded their daily rituals. How would all this affect the country's future? Gertrude wondered. Faysal would try to bring the Sunnis and Shi'is together, help them overcome their differences and build the nation's foundations. Arabs sharing the same language, the same roots and the same feelings toward the nascent Iraqi nation as their Sunni counterpart, Iraq's Shi'i would make Gertrude's definition of their dilemma as 'Echt Arabisch or Echt Shiistisch',[54] seem anachronistic. With time Iraq's Shi'is would demonstrate that they could cling to both categories without damaging either.[55]

*   *   *

Imagining Faysal sitting on the porch of Kazimayn's mosque watching the play, Gertrude could almost feel the burden falling on his frail shoulders. Faysal, Gertrude well knew, was feeling lonely. He was paying the price they all were paying for taking part in Britain's overseas adventure. They were not just far from close friends and family, but they also had to cope with the rupture of friendships after years spent abroad. In May 1921 Gertrude wrote to Frank Balfour, who had been transferred to the Sudan: 'Oh, dear, I do miss you so much, there are few people I love more than you'.[56] Balfour was to marry and so escape what Wilson once called 'the dreadful fate of bachelordom for life',[57] which seemed to be the fate of many British officers abroad. Some months later, Wilson himself would try to escape it by marrying a young widow of a RAF pilot killed during the war.

One night, some weeks after the coronation, Faysal called Gertrude. Sinking into melancholic thoughts as he foresaw the difficulties ahead, Faysal anticipated the confrontation with the British on one hand, and with the extreme nationalists on the other. Faysal and Gertrude sat on the balcony overlooking the river, where 'a late moon rose behind us and shone softly on the water while the guffas loaded with melons floated down, each with its twinkling yellow light'.[58] Uncertain of what the future held in store, Faysal still hesitated to bring his wife and children to Iraq. 'I sometimes think how curious it all is', Gertrude wrote in September 1921.

> People whose upbringing and associations and traditions are all so entirely different, yet when one is with them, one doesn't notice the difference nor do they. Think of Faysal, brought up at Mecca, in a palace full of eunuchs, educated at Constantinople, Commander in Chief, King, exile, and then King again . . . sitting down to tell me what he makes of life as if I were a sister. And I feel like a sister, that's the oddest part.[59]

Until his wife could join him, Faysal asked Gertrude to help him in the palace and draw up lists of guests to be invited to dinner parties. He had to get acquainted with the country's elite.

Gertrude and Cornwallis were the king's closest counsellors among the British. 'Perhaps the king does hold my hand more, though he embraces Mr. Cornwallis oftener – we compare notes',[60] she reported then. Gertrude really believed at this stage, that by guiding the king, she and Cornwallis 'guided' the destinies of the Arab world.[61] Faysal was more independent in his views than Gertrude realised then, and the Arab world would bestow upon the British in the years to come more surprises than she could ever have imagined.

At that stage, however, Gertrude and Cornwallis believed that they could also dispose of political figures that disagreed with their personal viewpoints. 'Cornwallis dropped in and we had a long and very amusing talk . . . we freely cursed all the people we didn't like and discussed what we should do to them', Gertrude joked.[62] It was clearly a private expression of typical British aloofness when referring to local leaders in their imperial domain. That held true also on other occasions even if, in Gertrude's case, the underlying motives were mixed. The irony, and sense of humour with which she described the differences of status that derived from the role she was playing shows that she took it at times, with a grain of salt. This twinkle, when analysing complex situations, distinguished her from her male colleagues, despite the fact that belonging to their group provided her with the characteristics that would define her. Gertrude and Cornwallis were aware of the nationalists' growing influence.

Among the members of the 'Ahd and the Young Men's Society of Mosul, expelled from Syria by the French authorities in March 1921, was also Yasin al-Hashimi[63] who seemed to have changed positions from the time he met Gertrude in Damascus. He was less diplomatic in his assertions after he came back to Iraq. Yasin resented the British presence and expressed it openly.

Although still immersed in her vision of her role 'of making kings and inventing kingdoms', as she once defined her mission, Gertrude began to wonder whether her role would end once Faysal stood firmly on his own feet. She had renewed her correspondence with Lord Hardinge of Penshurst, now Britain's ambassador to France. 'Do you remember that it was you who set me off on this road?', she asked Hardinge in August 1921. 'There is nothing I could rather have taken a hand in than the thing we are doing now'.[64] Hardinge proudly felt responsible for 'the tremendous change in your life and outlook occasioned by that visit you paid to me at Delhi . . . and the splendid use you have made of the opening that presented itself'.[65] They exchanged ideas on the rapid 'change of colours in the political kaleidoscope' in the Middle East as well as in Europe. And they concentrated on the still unsettled questions: the fate of Mosul vilayet and the Dardanelles. 'If Mosul goes, Baghdad goes', explained Gertrude to Hardinge then. But 'Iraq [can not] afford it', she then concluded.

To her surprise, Gertrude discovered that Lord Hardinge had never believed that Britain's war operations were limited to Basra and that he had always thought that the British would settle in Baghdad. Regarding Mosul, he believed that Iraq would have to manage without it, as Turkey would

7. From second left to right at the front row, Kenahan Cornwallis, Sassun Effendi Hayskal, Gertrude Bell. Standing behind Gertrude Bell, Bernard Bourdillon among British and Arab dignitaries. Baghdad in 1923.

have to do without the Dardanelles. He warned her of the dangers of 'conflicts in water tight compartments', namely the repercussions of the post-
war stalemate in Europe on the Middle East. This line in Hardinge's letter
reminded Gertrude of her own personal confinement. 'I almost forgot that
there is a world outside Iraq', she revealed in her answer.[66] She had put so
much energy into her work in Iraq, that very little of it was left for other
issues in her life. But when her job was completed, she would start thinking
about Europe and about going home. 'You are not to talk of going home –
your home is here', said Faysal when he heard of her plans, 'You may say
you are going to see your father'.[67]

'I can't tell you', Gertrude explained to her father, 'how delightful our
relations are, an affectionate confidence which I don't think could well be
shaken. The King usually addresses me with "oh, my sister," which makes
me feel like someone in the Arabian nights . . . He is of course an excep-
tional beguiler, everyone falls under the charm'.[68] Again, captivated by the
romantic vision of the East and the more than affectionate friendship with
the king, Gertrude decided to stay and accept the offered official position of
Sir Percy Cox's oriental secretary. In fact, she thought, she had practically
fulfilled the functions of an oriental secretary from the moment she had
landed in Basra. The mapping of tribes, the interviews, the network of relations with the local population from magnates to peasants, the writing of
reports sent to London and Delhi in the name of A. T. Wilson or Sir Percy
– all were the functions of an oriental secretary, even if she had not been
officially appointed. It was the challenge of new times, and the recognition
of the population's affection. *Khatun*, they called her, the lady of the court,
the one who keeps an open ear, who carves people's way to the authorities.
Sometimes she was even called *Umm al-Mu'minin* (Mother of the Faith-
ful), and that was for her a much greater award than any title or decoration
bestowed upon her by the British Crown.

*   *   *

The leading figures in Faysal's first cabinet were Ja'far al-'Askari, minister of
defence; his brother-in-law Nuri al-Sa'id, chief of staff of the newly created
Iraqi army; and Naji al-Suwaydi, later succeeded as minister of interior by
his brother Tawfiq al-Suwaydi. Two among Faysal's followers originated
from Syria: Rustum Haydar, a Shi'i from Ba'lbek who became chief of the
Royal Diwan and Sati' al-Husri from Aleppo, who served in the Ottoman
educational system and became Iraq's director of education. The Sherifians

provided Faysal the support he lacked from other sections of Iraq's population. The higher classes (the *sada*) felt threatened by the young officers from more modest origins.[69] Of all the challenges facing the British and the new Iraqi government, the Kurdish problem seemed, at the end of 1921, the most acute. It was the first serious problem faced by Faysal and his cabinet.[70]

The Turks were pressing on the Kurdish areas from the north, and an abortive Turkish attack on Rawanduz in the autumn of 1921 had raised concerns about the possibility of the Turks' return. The British did not want to confront the Turks, on the assumption that a peace treaty with Turkey was imminent. And yet the Turkish menace continued to cast a shadow across Mosul.

Gertrude's visit to Kurdistan in autumn 1921, together with Faysal and Ja'far al-'Askari was another example of the way she perceived her mission. And yet, she described the area in her usual style:

> It was sunset when we got to Sulaimaniyya. We went straight up to Major Goldsmith's house, an enchanting Persian house with a garden full of yellowing pomegranate trees and rows of late-flowering cosmos . . . At the centre of the house, there was an open diwan with wooden columns looking at the garden, where we had tea.

She had been lodged in a 'long Persian room with latticed windows onto the garden, with white walls and Persian niched recesses, wooden ceilings and big fireplaces in which a wood fire was burning'.[71] Sulaymaniyya was located about 2,500 feet above sea level 'and felt deliciously late autumnal'.

No British troops were stationed in Sulaymaniyya. 'We are running Sulaimaniyya as a purely Kurdish province, directly under the High Commission and detached from Iraq, with whom it won't have anything to do. The Levies are Kurds, all the officials are Kurds and all the work is done in Kurdish'. The city's council consisted of one British *mutasarrif* (governor) – Major Goldsmith himself – three Kurdish officials, and four representatives of the town of Sulaymaniyya, one from each of the four districts. Peasants cultivated their vineyards and tobacco plantations and brought the produce to a lively and picturesque bazaar, peopled by Kurds with huge, 'twisted turbans and baggy trousers held up by yards and yards of knotted cotton belt and short felt jackets'. The townsmen added 'bright coloured or brocaded silk robes under the jacket and a silver handled dagger stuck into the belt'. There was no need to carry arms, Gertrude explained, 'though a cartridge belt or two looks well when you are swaggering round the town'.[72]

'Independent Sulaimaniyya – won't even say Kurdistan – is what they are out for with us to help and advise'.[73] But there was no money coming from the British to help the Kurds, 'and we must now be careful to make it absolutely clear that we haven't a penny to spend in furthering Kurdish independence . . . If we encourage them, we shall only have to abandon them in their hour of need, which would be the worst thing possible', Gertrude concluded. It wasn't just Britain's fault, Gertrude believed, as the Kurds themselves could not decide on a leader – 'not two Kurds agree when it comes to practice', Gertrude said of them[74] – and there was little hope of seeing an autonomous Kurdish state established in Mosul, which, according to the Sykes–Picot Agreement, was included in the area under France's influence.

Gertrude did not consider too seriously the letters and messages from Kurdish leaders to Faysal calling for an autonomous Kurdistan with Faysal as their king: 'a sort of Austria-Hungary, absit omen!', she then observed. Faysal wanted to know Britain's policy on the Kurdish question, 'a thing that H.M.G . . . doesn't know'.[75] During this visit to the northern districts, Gertrude also stopped at the Ba'quba gardens. It was a hot day:

> The dates were late in ripening and are still hanging in great golden crowns on the palms; below them the pomegranate bushes are weighed down with the immense rosy globes of their fruit and the orange trees laden with the pale green and yellow of ripening oranges . . . There was also a big stretch of vineyard where the last of the grapes were hanging on the vines – gigantic bunches of white grapes each sheltered from the sun by a little roof of liquo-rice stalks'.[76]

In Ba'quba, she met with Assyrian refugees. Fifty thousand Assyrian and Armenian refugees who had fled from the Turks during the war waited at Ba'quba, a camp north of Baghdad, to be repatriated to Urmiya in Turkey or be collectively settled in Mosul.[77] Gertrude had begun to realise the magnitude of the problem of Assyrian refugees during her October 1920 encounter with Surma Khanum, the sister of the late Assyrian patriarch and the aunt of his young successor. In fact, the Assyrians were feared by the local population, who saw them as uninvited foreigners that came to the country through the intervention of foreign powers.[78] Gertrude's Bell's description of Surma Khanum, however, reveals her admiration for Middle Eastern women who defied rules and conventions and took a stand in their attempts to protect their communities. 'A very handsome, capable, nut brown woman, with white hair and complexion of a russet apple, she ran the whole community as in her brother's day'.[79] The meeting with Surma

Khanum would prepare Gertrude for her meeting with 'Adla Khanum, the outstanding leader of the Jaf Kurds at Halabja. 'The feature of Halabja is 'Adlah Khanum', Gertrude reported in November 1921.[80] The great lady was the widow of Othman Jaf Beg, head of the Jaf tribe in Halabja, and the mother of Ahmad Beg. Originally from the Ardalan leading family, she continued to rule the Jaf after her husband's death, as it had been ruled in his time, Gertrude explained. Understanding the temporary advantages of siding with Britain, 'Adlah handled local politics by 'intriguing more than you think anyone could'.[81]

'Adlah Khanum behaved 'as great Kurdish ladies behave'. Gertrude wrote, feeling that 'we must be birds of a feather . . . She is a striking figure in her gorgeous Kurdish clothes with jet black curls (dyed, I take it) falling down her painted cheeks from under her huge headdress'. Gertrude held the conversation in Persian, in the course of which 'I managed to tell her how well Iraq was doing under Faysal and to assure her that all we wished was that our two children – Iraq and Kurdistan –should live in peace and friendship with one another'.[82] It was, one could argue again, a self-appointed position.

On her visit to Mosul's Kurdish areas in the autumn of 1921, Gertrude rediscovered the power of the mystical orders and the magic of the language connecting her to the reminiscences of her earlier Persian days. In Awroman, a spiritual centre of the Naqshabandiyya, the mystical order founded in the fourteenth century by Baha' al-Din Naqshaband, Gertrude recalled Hafiz's magic world. She had stopped at Shaykh Hisan al-Din's garden, where 'a tank with a creeping water refreshed the visitors after a long ride over the foothills, and along the irrigation channels that ranged aside rows of mulberry trees . . . A tree trunk portico framed the glimpse of plain and distant mountains and a rush of water flanked by steep stone stairways led down to the next flowery terrace'.[83]

As they sat on the carpets of the diwan, Shaykh Hisan al-Din came in to greet his visitors. He was 'the merriest, jolliest old man you ever beheld; with large shining eyes, a large hooky nose, a beaming smile and a huge white turban'. All around the room sat the begs and the shaykhs, 'these in their gay reds and blues and those in their sober browns and whites and blacks'. The place had been previously called Bagh-i Kun – the Old Garden – until Hisan al-Din's father came to the village and established a *takkiyya* (sanctuary) and started to preach the *tariqa*, 'the way' – to the people of Awroman. People would come to the garden, kiss the shaykh's hand, and learn from him the principles of pious behaviour as explained in the sacred books, as well as the tales and stories transmitted orally from generation to generation.[84]

In the village of Biara, Gertrude found another Sufi shrine – the tomb of Shaykh 'Umar, another famous Naqshabandi preacher, who still attracted new members to the takiyya decades after his death.

On this visit to the Kurdish areas, Gertrude understood better the social network created by the mystical orders, where complex links between people also had political meanings. She realised the power of mystical Islam and the differences between the Naqshabandiyya, whose members were called Sufis, and the Qadiriyya, whose members were called dervishes, perhaps suggesting explanations for the rivalry between the Talabanis and the Barzinjis, two leading families in Iraq's Kurdistan, connected as they were to different religious orders. After this visit she certainly understood better the tension surrounding the reappointment of a trustee to the Qadiriyya waqf in Baghdad, as it referred not just to religious but also to financial and political matters.[85] Once back in Baghdad, she would ask her friend, the naqib, the head of the order in the town, for more details.

*   *   *

The beginning of 1922 found Gertrude in a gloomy mood. The memories of the trails in the snow-covered mountains, which could only be crossed by man and donkey, were still fresh. And yet she had to concentrate on her daily work. She went to dine with her friends the Bourdillons, enveloped in her fur coat, 'feeling miserable and lonely'. She seemed to be suffering already the first spells of a depression that would afflict her whenever things became too difficult to bear. There were already some symptoms of new states of mind that she didn't seem to have developed earlier. She did not follow the Bourdillons to the ball organised by the Residency, as she no longer danced. Her loneliness somewhat dissipated in the morning when her old friend Hajji Naji came to visit, bringing a basket of fruits from his garden. This was followed by a visit from the Shaykh of the Dulaym. Their breakfast was a feast. It had been prepared by Marie, Gertrude's French maid, and was sprinkled with the shaykh's laughter while tackling a poached egg with a silver spoon. The stream of visitors that filled the house 'as the day wore on' comforted Gertrude for a while. 'I am happy I have got the love and confidence of a whole nation', she wrote some time later. 'It may not be the intimate happiness which I have missed but it is a very wonderful and absorbing thing – almost too absorbing perhaps'.[86] This was perhaps the primary reason for her depression. She felt too attached to events and people that could, she now realised, do without her. It also stemmed from the lack of a real emotional commitment that could not fill the void of the one she missed.

The weeks that followed were marked by elections for the municipal councils, and for the Constituent Assembly. Many of Bell's acquaintances were appointed to new administrative posts, and even Hajji Naji had been elected mayor of Karrada. On the whole, the British viewed the election outcome as satisfactory, resulting in part from the work of British agents on the ground and in part from the natural tendency of populations to align themselves with those in power. Even in Kirkuk, the town that still resisted being attached either to Baghdad or Sulaymaniyya, a pro-British candidate had won the election, in defiance of Turkish appeals for pan-Islamic solidarity.[87]

Matters weren't so simple, however. In Baghdad three new political parties were active against the treaty: Hizb al-Watani, Hizb al-Nahda and Hizb al-Hurr led respectively by Ja'far Abu Timman, Sayyid Muhammad al-Sadr and Sayyid Muhammad al-Gaylani, the naqib's eldest son. Anti-treaty activities spread out also to the Shi'i countryside. A conference summoned in April 1922 as a protest against a menacing raid by the Wahhabis became a demonstration against the treaty.[88] Clashes between the Iraqis and the British continued as the debate over the treaty (its essence, the nature of the subsidiary agreements with their judicial, financial and military complications) intensified.[89] Newly formed political parties were compelled to submit their platforms to the high commissioner, whose approval depended on their compatibility with Britain's policy.[90] This measure sowed greater discord between Faysal and the British, as the king declared his right to call for the formation of new political parties and the submission of their platforms for approval to the Ministry of Interior, as in Turkish times.

Faysal was more at ease cutting deals with Cornwallis, now adviser to the Ministry of Interior, than with Percy Cox. He also sought Gertrude's advice, as she played the role of intermediary between the king and the high commissioner.

Iraq's relations with the British were not the only cause of political unrest. Crises also arose out of friction between Iraq's different communities. The first internal crisis after Faysal's ascent to the throne was precipitated by a Shi'i campaign against the Baha'is, a religion founded by Baha' Allah, a Persian Islamic reformer who had fled to Mesopotamia in the 1860s. The Shi'is wanted to close Baha' Allah's house in Baghdad, which served as a centre for his followers both inside and outside the country. The resulting crisis created new points of conflict between the British and Faysal.

The next confrontation, which took place a few weeks later, in March 1922, was caused by Faysal's dismissal of five ministers. Claiming that he had lost confidence in their ability to conduct the country's affairs, in view of the tension initially created by the attack of Ibn Sa'ud's Ikhwan on Iraq's tribesmen, the king forced Naji Suwaydi and 'Abd al-Latif Mandel to resign. The subsequent departure of Sassun Effendi, who resigned in solidarity with his colleagues, added to the tension that was eased only when Ibn Sa'ud's telegram to Percy Cox reached the capital after a week or so. 'The telegram was sent to Bahrein by camel and telegraphed from there to Baghdad', Gertrude noted, describing, in a single witty remark, the environment in which they acted.[91]

In spite of these confrontations, Gertrude still saw in Faysal Britain's greatest hope, for he seemed to have an intuitive understanding of both sides. 'It is almost impossible to believe that while he had been born in Mecca and educated in Constantinople and I in England and educated in Oxford, there is no difference whatsoever in our points of view', Gertrude wrote in February 1922, forgetting, at times, moments of disagreement.[92] She would come to the palace and listen to his complaints. She felt guilty for Britain's elusive policies[93] as she noted Faysal's face, 'narrow and eager between the folds of his white kerchief . . . [and] his shining eyes deepened by sorrow and disappointment and yet no reproach in them'. She departed 'loving and respecting him more than I can say'.[94] On one occasion, Gertrude took Faysal to Karrada to see the apricots blossoming and on another helped him plant 300 trees given to him by Hajji Naji for his newly acquired dairy farm.

In fact, the spring and early summer of 1922 seemed to have changed her mood. Her friendship with Cornwallis spilled over from the political level into more private moments. On Sundays, they would drive out of Baghdad and take long walks through gardens and wheat fields. A sudden rain, 'making the world feel leaden and heavy', would bring them back to Gertrude's house for tea. Over silver trays covered with fruit and cakes (a symbol of their own world brought into the adopted reality in which they lived), they continued their discussions on Iraq's daily affairs, indulging from time to time in personal confidences. Sometimes they would drive to Mahmudiyya, halfway to Hilla, to see the Yusufiyya Canal: 'It was an enchanting ride, the soil covered with short thick grass starred with tiny purple geraniums and golden marigolds'. 'When a sudden rain surprised them, they would cross the marshes 'ankle deep, knee deep in mud and water and reeds'. The next day, a miracle occurred: 'the clouds melted away, the sun shone out, the mud dried up and it was the most glorious weather conceivable'. Reaching the bridge where the Mahmudiyya canal split from Yusufiyya, they would recount the history flowing in the old canal's waters: 'It was the Babylonean Nahr Malke, Julian sailed down it to Ctesiphon and the Abbasids redug it'.[95] Following the beat of Iraq's history, Gertrude took Cornwallis to Suq al-'Ukadh, a bazaar dating from the Jahiliyya times, and introduced him to the mysteries of Arab classical poetry. Among the displays of hand-woven carpets, copper trays and coloured tiles, Iraqi poets gathered and read from their poetry, as they had done in the Prophet's time.

Drawn together by their mission, as they saw it, and their concern for Iraq's political future, Gertrude and Cornwallis spent most of their leisure time in the summer of 1922 discussing the terms of the treaty. The possibility that the treaty would not automatically abrogate the mandate intensified the debate between the nationalists. The king himself took on a more extremist position, having even declared himself in favour of a time-framed mandate instead of a long-term treaty. A quarrel between greater and minor shaykhs in the Hilla division lit the spark leading to another crisis, which took on a more nationalistic character.

Gertrude went to see Faysal once more, asking him to leave the British advisers involved in the affair in place. She also asked him to dismiss a newspaper report on the case in order to prevent the resignation of Major Yetts from his post. 'I would resign too . . .', she complained when facing the king's refusal. 'I preferred to go before the snow image which I had created . . . melted before my eyes'. This and other similar scenes ended on a dramatic note: when, on leaving, she attempted to kiss his hand, the king warmly embraced her. 'We parted on rather unsatisfactory terms of close sentimental union and political divergence'.[96]

And again, this display of emotions interfered with her vision of men and situations: 'I am still *sous le coup* of this interview', she confessed later to her father. 'Faysal is one of the most loveable of human beings, but he is amazingly lacking in strength . . . He has hitched his wagon to the stars, but with such a long rope that he gets entangled in every thicket'.[97] This was, of course, her opinion. But the fact was that Faysal's role wasn't easy. Seeing himself as a mediator between the different groups of the population, Faysal had to proceed carefully. He felt that if he infringed upon the feelings that he had carefully cultivated, he could damage his own position.[98]

Gertrude Bell did not fully understand Faysal's refusal to play along with Britain's dictates, believing that his policy would immerse the country in disorder.

'Oh, darling', she asked her father, 'can they save themselves from chaos? Their one cry is "Help us"! And one sits there, in their eyes an epitome of human knowledge and feeling oneself so very far from filling the bill!'.[99] In that she was certainly wrong. Even the most moderate did not see the British as indispensable let alone as the sole retainers of truth on earth. As for the chaos that was predicted to follow Britain's departure, it was, so most thought, exaggerated in order to provide the British with an alibi to stay. The main question was whether the Iraqis would ratify the treaty without rejecting the mandate altogether, as such a step would have repercussions in Syria and Lebanon and further implications in Palestine.

These political difficulties did not prevent Gertrude and Cornwallis from having a good time together, enlivening Gertrude's illusions. The summer of 1922 was at its peak, and they often swam in the river, 'My dressing room is under the fig trees where I can eat ripe figs while I dry my hair'. The king bathed too, and after a while a palace servant roasted huge fish on a bonfire of palm fronds. After dinner 'we lay on carpets and cushions – like ancient Greeks and ate by the light of a little moon, after which we remained for a long time under the tamarisk bushes; I don't know what the others talked about but the king told me his family history; . . . whom his daughters should marry and how he would educate his son. It didn't seem at all fantastic in that setting of crescent moon and quiet river and sheltering tamarisks . . .'.[100]

But summer pleasures could not efface the problems stirring the country's political scene. Meetings in Shi'i and Sunni mosques in Kazimayn and Baghdad were led by Yasin al-Hashimi, Shaykh Muhammad ibn Mahdi al-Khalisi, and Shaykh Muhammad al-Sadr.[101] The continuous debate on the real meaning of the term 'mandate' tended now to a comparison with the word 'protection' (*himayya*), as the protectorate in Egypt was often referred to, acquiring the same negative connotation.[102] This was because the idea of a protectorate (with its Arab facade and Arab ministers), a less binding form than a mandate, which was supposed to pave the country's way to self-government more quickly and surely, proved to be more a question of form than of substance,[103] mainly because both systems subordinated the country to Britain's interests at the end of the day, placing similar obstacles before the country's full independence. Wilson had suggested a protectorate years earlier as an alternative to the Anglo-French declaration and its message of self-determination, but now it was too late to reconsider it. Again, the case of Egypt provided incontrovertible proof that it could not appease the nationalists' claims.[104] In fact, the nationalists did not want a protectorate but clearly favoured the abrogation of the mandate. They wanted a different arrangement, one that would augur a free and independent Iraq linked to Britain by a less restraining treaty of alliance.[105] They also wanted to manage their own affairs without having the British decide whether they were or were not performing accordingly to British standards of 'good governance'.[106]

The game was tricky, however. If there was chaos and unrest as a result of a withdrawal of British troops to Basra and Faysal's departure, a return of the Turks to the country seemed, to Gertrude, unavoidable. The dream of an independent Iraq would then vanish, she believed. But things were not as simple as she thought. Faysal openly opposed the mandate, wanting to prove that he was able to negotiate a treaty with Britain from a position of parity and free choice. The king, like the nationalists, rejected Britain's argument that the mandate was a consequence of Britain's commitments toward the League of Nations and the United States. Gertrude believed that the Iraqi nationalists should take advantage of British public opinion that Iraq was a costly burden and not a strategic or economic necessity,[107] and put more pressure on Britain for the abrogation of the mandate.

The debate had spilled over into the tribal areas, where officers appointed to administrative posts in Hilla and Nasiriyya promoted tribes that had aligned themselves with the government, supporting them in their long-standing disputes over land and water rights, taxes, and remittances. 'Ancient and perilous tribal jealousies were ignited into a flame by the breath of injustice', Gertrude explained to Sir Percy Loraine, the resident in Teheran, in August 1922. 'We who had lived through 1920 know how fast disorder spreads from small focus . . . and the question is – have we the time?'[108]

Anti-British demonstrations had reached their apex that summer. In July 1922 a fatwa issued by Shaykh Mahdi al-Khalisi prohibited the burial in Muslim cemeteries of those favouring the continuation of the mandate. In August anti-mandate petitions calling for the dismissal of British officials from their advisory posts in the Shi'i areas of the Euphrates circulated in the south. Faysal wrote a letter to Percy Cox asking the high commissioner to give him a free hand to deal with the situation.

On 23 August, the anniversary of Faysal's ascent to the throne, a crowd gathered in the palace courtyard and in inflamed anti-British speeches called for the suspension of negotiations for the treaty with Britain. When Gertrude and Percy Cox walked up the stairs, a cry was heard: 'Down with the Mandate!', proving that their position in the country had clearly deteriorated. The demonstration, organised by the nationalist parties, was directed from the palace balcony by a number of white-robed leaders, among them Fahmi Mudarris, the palace chamberlain. Not having clearly understood the words that provoked the enthusiastic reaction from the crowd outside the palace, Cox and Gertrude proceeded to the audience room, where the king, rather nervously, tried to appease the guests. The king himself was saved from the confrontation with Sir Percy (after having refused to take measures against the protesters) by a 'timely' attack of appendicitis the next day. 'Five doctors, two English and three Arab, were debating whether an immediate operation was necessary; at 8 they decided it was and at 11 it was successfully performed'.[109] 'For once, Providence has behaved as a gentleman', Gertrude wrote then, revealing her true opinion this time, 'Since the King could not summon up courage to come out into the open, his illness was beyond words, fortunate'.[110] She was displaying again a position more attuned to Britain's interest, by adopting one of the main principles of Britain's imperial doctrine, which was, again, to distinguish between moderate and extremist nationalists and play one against the other. The king's absence gave Sir Percy Cox the opportunity to take control over the country's affairs, arrest the more radical nationalists, shut their newspapers and arrange for the signature of the treaty.[111] The treaty was finally signed on 13 October 1922, mandating a twenty-year engagement between Iraq and Britain. A proviso stipulated that the treaty was to be approved by a Constituent Assembly, yet to be elected, which was also in charge of passing the Organic Law which laid down the foundations of the new Constitution.

The treaty left the nationalists and the king only partially satisfied. On one hand, it put an end to the mandate but on the other, it retained Britain's indirect control of Iraq's affairs.[112] Faysal understood, however, that he would have to work with the British at least for the time being. Iraq had strong neighbours and, given its weak structure, it needed Britain's protection in order to handle threats from outside and inside the country.

But that wasn't the end of the battle either for Faysal or for the nationalists or the British. The debates in the bazaar now centred on the treaty's ratification, because Britain's presence in Iraq was formally dependent upon the population's acceptance of its interference in Iraq's affairs, even if indirectly. A new plebiscite would be needed to ratify the treaty,[113] but many problems, brewing at the same time, made it all more complicated: the question of Mosul, with its potential oil reserves and Turkey's pressures to get the vilayet back; the confrontations with the Shi'i ulama and their opposition to the whole process; and the pressures in London for Britain to leave Iraq altogether.

The elections were only held in July 1923, as the confusion resulting from an indirect electoral system delayed the process. The Constituent Assembly would only meet some months later. The process of creating a modern nation was exhausting, as Gertrude would complain again to her family, as if it was her private enterprise. Events would prove again how ambivalent her perception was of a rather complex, controversial, perhaps impossible and yet fascinating, mission.

CHAPTER 8

'A Tower of Strength and Wisdom'

'Are national governments created as easily as universes?' Gertrude had asked Sir Percy Loraine in March 1923. 'Would the Creator confidently pronounce them to be good?'[1] She was referring not only to the Arab government in Baghdad but also to an embryonic autonomous Kurdistan, with a Kurdish administration and Kurdish national symbols. 'Now that the Treaty of Sévres is dead and the dreams of an independent Kurdistan [are] dashed, Iraq should come to terms with its own Kurds on a basis of decentralisation',[2] Gertrude suggested in April, after attempts to create an autonomous Kurdish state – either as a unified state or as scattered principalities linked to Britain – had failed. The reason for this failure lay not only in the apparent inability of the Kurds to close ranks and overcome long-standing personal and tribal feuds, but mainly in Britain's policy, Gertrude believed. Britain's 'Kurdish opportunism',[3] as Gertrude called it now – backing or withdrawing support from different Kurdish leaders according to strategic interests or transitory moods – was the culprit. Britain's Kurdish policy had to change after the creation of Iraq as a modern state, she believed. Gertrude was unsure whether it could work, but she believed that Britain's Kurdish policy needed to be revised.[4] She was against the idea of bringing Shaykh Mahmud back to Sulaymaniyya in order to resist possible Turkish advances on Kurdish districts[5] after their attacks on Rawanduz and Sulaymaniyya. At the same time, she was toying with the idea of setting 'some other national ideal to work, as the Arab national ideal is no goal for Kurds',[6] she predicted in 1922.

However, the idea was more complex than she thought at that moment, and Gertrude herself would change her opinion on the matter, while trying to find the best way to incorporate the Kurds in the new state. Gertrude had in mind a plan in which Tawfiq al-Wahbi, a highly educated Kurdish officer in the Iraqi army, would play a major role in setting clearer goals for

Iraq's Kurds. An ardent Kurdish nationalist, Tawfiq al-Wahbi would select ten other Kurdish officers to spread his doctrine in Kurdistan. Among other things, the plan called for a Kurdish administration in Sulaymaniyya, headed by a Kurdish *hukumdar* (governor), with regular relations with the Iraqi government in Baghdad. In practice, this meant the establishment of an autonomous Kurdish administration under the aegis of the Iraqi throne. Other Kurdish districts would then join in, creating a Kurdish administrative zone linked to Baghdad. The only exceptions would be Kirkuk and Arbil, with their assertive Turkmen communities. It was far reaching, she admitted, 'but why not try?' Gertrude asked.[7] Among the potential candidates for the post of hukumdar of Sulaymaniyya was Hamdi Beg Baban, a member of the well-known Kurdish family and of Independent Kurdistan, a pro-British Kurdish nationalist league.

However, Turkey's military pressure and growing influence among the Dizai, Zibar and other Kurdish tribes[8] finally persuaded the British to abandon the idea of an autonomous Kurdish area linked to Baghdad under British protection. Shaykh Mahmud became again the only alternative. Brought back from his exile in Kuwait, he met, in Gertrude's office, with Major Noel, the British officer closely associated with him during his first term as governor of Sulaymaniyya. Their re-encounter after years of separation was described with typical hyperbole. 'Sheikh Mahmud fell on the neck of Major Noel, this Eton mad-man and enchanting adventurer',[9] believing that with Noel's help his reign was assured. Shaykh Mahmud's arrival at the railhead near Kifri on his way back to Sulaymaniyya was depicted in no less emotional tones by Major C. J. Edmonds, the political officer in the northern districts:

> Hundreds of horsemen from local tribes who had assembled for his *istiqbal* [reception] invaded the station shouting and waving banners. They fell upon the sheikh and dragged him away in triumph before an official deputation from Sulaimaniyya could get in a word of the speeches of welcome they had prepared to deliver.[10]

Once reinstalled, Shaykh Mahmud worked to extend his control to the adjacent areas of Arbil, Kirkuk and Kifri. In Kirkuk, however, the Turkman population was still reluctant to join Sulaymaniyya, which would mean their submission to a Kurdish government. Kirkuk's local administration continued to be conducted in Turkish by local officials, and even though it was formally connected with Baghdad, 'the Iraqi flag wasn't flown over the Serai'.[11] Edmonds suggested installing an *'idara makhsusa* (a special regime) in Kirkuk and Arbil and only as a second stage in the process, allowing it to federate with Sulaymaniyya.[12]

Other obstacles lay in the road to unity. From Kifri, near the railhead in Kirkuk division, Gertrude reported on the Shaykh Mahmud's nepotism, 'Every agha who wasn't Sheikh Mahmud's relative was an enemy', and it was impossible to 'cook elections' to the Constituent Assembly. That meant that the British had to comply, at least temporarily, with the idea of a Kurdish local autonomy in Sulaymaniyya under Shaykh Mahmud.[13]

In November 1922, Shaykh Mahmud proclaimed himself King of Kurdistan, amid huge demonstrations. Festive parades greeted other Kurdish leaders who had come to visit, among them the famous Simko, Agha of the Shikak, who had fought the Russians, the Turks, and the Armenians during the First World War and who had murdered Mar Sham'un, the temporal and spiritual leader of the Assyrians.[14] Shaykh Mahmud appointed a cabinet of nine, a commander-in-chief, and an inspector general, realising the population's desire to be administrated by Kurdish officials. The elation and cultural revival that these changes brought about were reflected in the number of newspapers published in Sulaymaniyya at the time: *Peskewtin* (Progress), *Rozh-i-Kurdistan* (Sun of Kurdistan), and *Bang-i-Kurdistan* (The Call of Kurdistan), to mention only a few. Sulaymaniyya became a literary centre during this period, 'temporarily eclipsing even Cairo and Istanbul'[15] as one of the reports of the time exaggeratedly described. The dialect spoken in Sulaymaniyya – Sorani – was in prominent use, edging out the Kirmanji and Gurani dialects (spoken in the north and south-east, respectively) as the possible official language[16] to be used in the cultural reunification of Kurdistan.

Feeling threatened by this cultural revival and its possible political implications, the British once more perceived Shaykh Mahmud's increasing influence as a menace. How the Kurdish situation would resolve itself, Gertrude did not know yet. But she would leave for a while and deal with it after her return from England.

*   *   *

Before her departure, Gertrude sent one last letter to Sir Percy Loraine. This was 'the hastiest of letters, little more than a greeting'. She hoped to be back in Iraq soon, she said, but she was not sure.[17] Percy Cox had left and Henry Dobbs was to be appointed to fill in the role of high commissioner. Although on good terms with Dobbs, whom she knew from their earlier service together in Basra, Gertrude did not feel as indispensable as she had in Cox's time. But there was still much to accomplish, and she hoped to be part of it. She perceived some changes already in April 1922 when she had met her father at Jiza and toured with him in Haifa, Beyrouth, Ba'lbek and Jerusalem. It wasn't just Iraq that was changing, she then discovered, but the whole Middle East. Everything there seemed so fluid: there were even rumours that Syria wanted to rejoin Turkey, forfeiting its claims to independence from France. But these were just rumours and if they came to pass, would mean a setback for France and, by implication, for Britain as well. If Syria went, Palestine would follow in her footsteps and 'Transjordan would succumb at once',[18] Gertrude pondered in May 1922. The scheme devised at the Cairo Conference would then crumble like a sand castle. Were all their plans and efforts about to come to 'naught – *fadi* – meaningless, empty'?

When Gertrude returned to England some months later, after almost three years of absence, she had, in a way, come full circle. Her trip was an occasion for introspection, a chance to re-evaluate her role in the Middle East – and a search for comfort, support, and relief. 'I do not want to see anyone but the family', Gertrude wrote to Molly on New Year's Eve before her departure for England. She was lonely and discouraged with her lot in Iraq. 'There are very great drawbacks in living so much alone – it must seem an almost incomprehensible way of life to you in the middle of your children'.

She had had her compensations, though, mainly her relations 'with things and people'. But this was not always enough. And now she knew that she did not want to guide policies or make final decisions. 'It's a bigger task than I am capable of undertaking', she confessed, but she was glad that she had helped to 'pave the way, to induce a mental atmosphere on either side'. She realised by now that it was not European efficiency that mattered, nor the ninety per cent of the population that preferred Britain's rule, or so she thought, but the remaining ten per cent: 'They, and not we, will command all when time comes'.[19]

But, at the same time, Gertrude still felt that Britain was 'inventing the right way to deal with the East . . . it's like the interest and difficulty of climbing a new mountain with the path all to be found'. That meant, in her own words, finding a way to accommodate the ten per cent that mattered. There was great challenge in it and a personal price to pay as well: 'You see the results of my detached existence!', she wrote to Molly, 'I have written a letter all about things and nothing about people',[20] she concluded then.

People could not be invented, only discovered and understood in their strengths and weakness. People were sometimes like nations, she felt, strong and weak at the same time, Britain was weak in spite of its apparent strength, she explained to Molly.

'We are all living on nothing or on credit, there being nothing else to live on till Europe is settled', Gertrude commented after her return to England.[21] Britain had experienced several years of industrial unrest, including union crises in the mining industries and the difficulties in setting up post-war arrangements in Europe. One crisis, in the autumn of 1922, following the victory of the Kemalists against the Greeks in Smyrna, had been precipitated by Mustapha Kemal's intention to cross the Dardanelles and attack the territories assigned to Greece at the Paris Peace Conference. Britain's reinforcement of its land forces at Chanak, on the Asiatic shores of the Dardanelles, culminated in a crisis that brought about the fall of Lloyd George's coalition government, as conservatives became alarmed by the possibility that the country was heading to war.

Strength and weakness, two sides of the same coin, were reflected also in Britain's politics. Gertrude felt the changes that had occurred among her inner circle of family and friends. The Trevelyans, the Russells, Oswald Mosley and his wife, Cynthia (Curzon's daughter), seemed to question again their political affiliation. Members of the upper classes, some of them landed and entitled, now counted themselves among the members of the Labour Party. Former members of the Liberal Unionist Party, successors to the Whigs (the democratic leaders of the nineteenth century and aristocrats who saw themselves as champions of civil and religious freedom), adhered now to the Labour Party, apparently 'shorter on talent' than the Liberal or Conservative parties.[22] In search of greater opportunities to participate in the political process, they became disappointed by the lack of political energy displayed by the Labour Party as well.

Visiting England during the Chanak crisis and the fall of the coalition government, Gertrude, as 'a good Liberal', wanted to see Lloyd George back in power, but not in a coalition with the Conservatives.[23] She preferred him to Herbert Henry Asquith, whose support for Iraq would be more difficult to obtain. Stanley Baldwin's rise to power as the head of the Conservative Party had left the Labour Party stagnant, needing time to prepare for an offensive. Baldwin was then at the height of his popularity; an ironmaster and a member of the entrepreneurial classes, like the Bells, he was elected over Curzon (now Marquess Curzon of Kedleston), 'a grandee with fine houses and many titles', and appointed a cabinet with fewer 'landed' ministers than expected.[24]

Charles Trevelyan, now a Labour Party member, was extremely disappointed 'by the unruliness of Labour members'.[25] He wanted Labour to be more assertive in its fight to get back to a position of power. Charles was eager to play a more determining political role at that historic crossroads, feeling that he was predestined to carry on the Trevelyan tradition. Gertrude visited Charles and her sister Molly at Cambo, their country home in Northumberland, where they still lived in between political seasons. Sitting in the main room at Wallington, the family's residence, she felt overwhelmed once again by a sense that Molly was already a part of England's history 'as it played itself out like an unfolding Whiggish drama. Molly was working at the time on a tapestry representing the Trevelyan coat of arms: a horse rising from the waves. It portrayed the first Trevelyan, the knight that traversed the distance across the sea from Saint Michael's Mount to the Cornish coast, while King Arthur's other knights drowned.[26] 'It wasn't a time to pull back', Charles explained, referring as well to the point in history where they found themselves, when England's society was changing and Europe seemed unable to rise from the myths of 'vanished supremacies'.[27]

Gertrude enjoyed her long talks with Charles and Molly, and she grew closer to Molly as time passed. Although Molly's manner was somewhat authoritarian (a quality she, seemingly, had inherited from Florence), she was quick, bright, and funny. She updated Gertrude on the latest episodes in the Bell family and indulged in gossip about the Bells, the Trevelyans, and their extended family. Linked by marriage with Britain's land-owning elites, the Trevelyans moved now not just in the world of public affairs and finance but in the world of art and learning. They were also connected with the Wilberforces, whose cousin Octavia had now officially become Elizabeth Robins' life companion.

Octavia Wilberforce was aspiring to become one of the first women doctors when she first met Lisa. 'That would be a worthwhile life', Lisa commented at the time, and she offered moral support to Octavia during her studies at the London School of Medicine for Women.[28] Their relationship became quite close as time passed, as they both were mutually committed to women's rights movements, living 'a woman-centred life'.[29] Lisa's history of heterosexual liaisons with strong men, among them the critic William Archer, seems to indicate that her friendship with Octavia was platonic. Lisa's beauty and talent had also attracted George Bernard Shaw, who, certainly in retaliation for her unresponsiveness to him, referred to her as a 'puritan spinster' and an 'insecure foreigner trying to find a niche in English society'. The fact that an American-born actress was actively involved in the social issues of England was a concern that had also been raised by Florence. 'My commitment is where I live', Lisa replied then to Florence, 'I must, if I can, give something in return . . . The nationality limit to obligation is a superstition', Lisa argued, concluding, 'You are Irish-French, but you serve most where you live most – but we need not agree on this point'.[30]

Gertrude could not have agreed more. She too was torn between her possible return to England and her deep commitment to Iraq, where she spent most of her time. Intellectually drawn to Lisa, Gertrude liked her optimistic outlook on the future – 'new ideas, new purposes and above all new power of enjoying life'.[31]

Molly kept Gertrude updated with the latest literary events and the newest plays written by Lisa and Florence. Their general theme of women's emancipation had not changed, but now was presented in a new guise. They wrote stories of women developing strength of character and independence through personal suffering and life experience. Florence had placed her stories in social settings that allowed her to criticise the working classes and their belief that women had to obey their husbands. Florence's ideas wouldn't change much as the years went by. In her play, *The Way the Money Goes* (1910), with the famous actress Sybil Thorndike in the leading role, she had already pointed at some of the ideas that she would continue to hold during the coming years.

The issues under debate in the 1920s, following the passage of the suffrage law in 1918 were birth control and a woman's right not to have her identity defined through her association with a man or through motherhood. Women were in the process of redefining their role in the family circle, in personal relations, and in society in general.[32]

Lisa, very famous now as an actress and playwright, and as the embattled president of the Women Writers' Suffrage League during the war, was now active in the PEN (Poets, Essayists, Novelists) Club and the Society of Authors. She also served on the board of the Give and Take Club, an exclusive women's luncheon club, that met at the St James Hotel in London. Florence Bell was a member of both clubs as well. In addition, Lisa was a regular at the Ladies Athenaeum Club and frequently reported to Florence about its cultural activities. After a visit from Charlie Chaplin, Lisa wrote to her, 'The effect was of a man playing the clown . . . While the clown played the gentleman . . . Everybody delighted with Charlie'.[33]

Gertrude listened to Molly's stories with a mixture of interest and detachment. Molly would, during the years, update her with important cultural events: André Gide's new book of essays and Grieg's *Peer Gynt Suite* (1923), a musical work carrying the same title as Ibsen's earlier play (1867). She also told Gertrude about George Trevelyan's latest books and his vision of history, explaining how George and Charles Trevelyan differed in their approaches to family traditions – George describing them in words and Charles translating them into political action.

Politics ran in the family, Molly reiterated, asking Gertrude why she shouldn't engage in politics once her mission in Iraq was finished. 'How very glad I am that I am not in the House', Gertrude wrote after her visit to Northumberland, revealing that she had at least embryonic thoughts about developing a political career in England, an ironic turnround for a previous opponent to women suffrage. Gertrude however, was growing more doubtful about the results to be achieved by political action and had come to question the practice of politics on a more philosophical level. Was politics a term to be redefined? she wondered?

Although somewhat sceptical about Labour's ideals and its ability to make radical changes in the pattern of political life in England, Gertrude greeted Charles Trevelyan's nomination as secretary of education in 1923 with enthusiasm. When Charles and Molly headed the procession that paraded through the streets of Newcastle after the Labour success in the elections, it was an apotheosis for the Bells. 'Crowds cheering them in the streets, wherever they went. What a thing for their children to remember',[34] Florence commented at the occasion. 'Charles owed it all to Molly . . . the vindication of the public they care about',[35] Lisa responded, underscoring the Trevelyans' debt to the Bells not just for new connections in local politics and London circles, but also for Molly's more personal touch when interacting with Charles' constituency.

'Governments are not Gods Almighty to make and unmake worlds, but if they are honest and sincere they can do a great deal of making', Gertrude wrote to Charles Trevelyan in January 1924. She was back in Baghdad, reappraising politics in England and in the Middle East, the two poles of her life.

> It is my conviction that we are doing an honest and useful piece of work [in the Middle East], one that tends to make the world more just and more stable . . . For it is here that we have stated a policy which is imperial only in the very widest sense. Yes, wider than imperial, if you like.[36]

She truly believed that it was not just for Britain's sake that she was meeting her obligations as oriental secretary, but also for the wellbeing of Iraq. 'But I am enough of an English woman to be glad that it's we English who, as usual, lead the way'.[37] She obviously overstated her role and Britain's capability to 'run the world', as she understood it.

From Baghdad, Gertrude thanked Molly for a warm welcome and for letting her catch a glimpse of their lives. 'You have been very clever, I think, in managing your life well and win, and you deserve all you have got out of it . . .'.[38] While praising Molly's talent for happiness, Gertrude looked ahead to her own unsettled future with some apprehension. Her professional and private life seemed uncertain, and her place of influence in the court of King Faysal to be regained. Much water had flowed under the bridges of the Tigris and past the palace since the previous spring, when the king had asked for her advice. At that time, she was able to speak her mind freely. 'I told the King clearly how very mistaken I thought he had been, my style rather cramped by the fact that he held my hand most of the time!', she had reported then. This ambiguity in their relationship underlay Gertrude and Cornwallis' attempts to persuade the king to take a harder line with the nationalists: 'We all argued eagerly, in complete disagreement [but] unbroken affection'. At the end of the debate, the king had led her into his bedroom, 'where we sat solemnly side by side on a sofa and we swore on a Qur'an – which he detached from the head of his bed – that he had never done anything without the very best of intentions'. She thought then that their relationship, which included Cornwallis and Nuri Saʿid and Captain [Iltyd] Clayton, was stable: 'nothing can go very far astray'.[39]

She was wrong, however. The king had also made new friends. Among them, Mme Safwat Pasha, the chamberlain's wife, whose closeness to the king had given rise to gossip in the court. Mme Safwat had decorated the palace with 'abominable curtains and things at her pleasure',[40] and the king only turned back to Gertrude when Mme Safwat was away 'busy having a daughter'.[41]

After her return to Baghdad, Gertrude was occupied for a while with dinners, receptions, bridge games and, culminating with a dinner party at the palace in honour of Sir Henry Dobbs' effective appointment to the post of high commissioner. Tired of all this excitement, she reported home, 'Ken Cornwallis and I dined with ourselves on Sunday'.[42] They were having good moments together, by themselves and in the company of other people.

The autumn of 1923 was delightful, she wrote. The chrysanthemums in the garden 'exploded in shades of white, yellow, red, and brown'. Gertrude would sit on a bench, admiring the two guinea pigs the Emir Zayd had sent to her as a present. Playing with the animals made her feel as though she was retreating to the remotest corners of her childhood. The cool weather also inspired Gertrude and Cornwallis to dine outdoors. Invited by the naqib's son, they left for Turjmaniyya garden, toward the Diyala. 'It was [a] full moon and we loved motoring down the peaceful garden. We dined on the roof with the famous eucalyptus trees towering over us, and the sweet silence broken only by the gentle ripple of the Sayyid's talk'. Their host had many plans in his mind, but 'we didn't want steering. We just wanted to sit under the moon in the mild air with bunches of roses at our elbows'.[43]

Her friendship with Ken, as she now called Cornwallis in her letters, was a source of happiness in this transitional period of her life. 'I spent the whole day on Sunday helping Ken to get into his new house', Gertrude reported home in November 1923. 'It's amusing furnishing houses and we have made the new one quite nice'. Together they played bridge, drove into the desert, and rode camels at the crack of dawn.

On Christmas Day they went shooting in the gardens of Hajji Shukri Beg near the canal that followed the Hilla branch of the Euphrates. 'You remember the desolate water of the Hilla road, don't you?', Gertrude asked her father. 'Well, you motor half an hour down the Mahawil canal and you come into a paradise. Peopled villages, golden poplars along the canal, gardens, cornfields, and quantities of birds'. The crisp weather and the East's clear sky enchanted her. They 'shot at the edges of the palm gardens and the desert scrub along the canal '. . . It's beautiful to see him shoot',[44] Gertrude wrote then, proving how infatuated she already was. They carried with them sandwiches and bottles of beer, returning to Hajji Shukri Beg's house only late in the afternoon.

One day Gertrude and Ken drove down to 'Abbasiyya, in the early morning: 'The sun grew hotter and hotter as we walked through the golden poplar thickets and the green tamarisk scrub and thorns where the partridge lie'. They traversed the marshes, 'ankle deep, knee deep in mud and water and reeds'. On another occasion, they accompanied 'Umran al-Hajji Sa'dun, shaykh of the northern Banu Hasan, to the point where the Hindiyya River divided into three tributaries. After the beaters made the birds fly, they shot the birds and little boats picked them up.[45]

Ken was a remarkable athlete, and Gertrude liked to see him riding, playing tennis and running. 'Tall, rugged, imperturbable [he] seemed cast in the

great aristocratic mould', and when necessary he could assume all the aristocratic manners. For her he was always easy to access, simple, humorous
and abounding in common sense. 'A tower of strength and wisdom', she
once called him, and they laughed together at her description. His Olym-
pian height, prominent nose, deep voice, and quiet manner were most
impressive.[46] Lawrence regarded Cornwallis with respect: '[A] man rude to
look upon but apparently forged from one of these incredible metals with a
melting point of thousands degrees'.[47]

They had great talks. Not just on Iraqi politics and Faysal's future, but
also on their personal roles in Britain's Middle Eastern adventure. They
would sit near the fire in Gertrude's living room and tell each other about
their past exploits,[48] their similar experiences and backgrounds. Their times
at Oxford had shaped both their philosophical outlook and their practical
approach to the world. A student of jurisprudence at University College,
Cornwallis had also been president of the Oxford Athletic Club between
1904 and 1906.

Gertrude and Cornwallis tended to see things eye to eye, despite their
fifteen-year age difference. Now fifty-three (while Cornwallis was only
thirty-eight), Gertrude and Ken supported each other through hard times.
When Gertrude once asked Cornwallis for his advice on whether to stay or
leave the country, he begged her to stay, convincing her that they were the
only people among those who served the king who had no ulterior motives
except, obviously, for Britain's interests, which also became their own.[49] In
moments of loneliness, they sought each other out, the distance from their
respective families bringing them closer. By then, Cornwallis was already
separated from his wife and children and despite the personal price he paid,
'he thinks it is worth doing and does not reckon the cost to himself'.[50]

Occasionally, they differed on how to handle negotiations over the treaty
with the Iraqi government. Gertrude tended to sympathise with the Iraqi
side in the debates over the ratification of the treaty and its annexes. Especially in the case of the military agreement, she was much more critical than
her British colleagues, including Cornwallis. The treaty 'consists exclusively
in injunctions to the Iraq, harshly worded as to what [Iraq] may not do;
not a syllable as to what we will do except that we shall rapidly reduce our
forces as occasion serves'.[51] Cornwallis defended Britain's right to control
Iraq's network of communications providing free movement for British
troops in times of war. He also supported the idea of having a small, well-
trained army supported by the RAF instead of British land forces. Gertrude

sided with the nationalists who saw in a large conscripted army a sign of sovereignty.

Their differences spilled over into the debate about the future of the railways, the main cog in Iraq's communication network. Britain refused to give the railways away, considering the network as a British military asset. Thy also disagreed on the question of frontiers, of military control of the RAF airbases and other major and minor issues, Gertrude taking on, more often than not, the position of the nationalists.

Despite their differences, Gertrude and Cornwallis believed in the need to lead Iraq to political emancipation. 'This is a sign of progress', Cornwallis said when 'Ali Jawdat, the minister of the interior, took command of negotiations with the insurgent tribes and the Iraqi army took control of the railways, bridges, and aerodromes in the Samawa area.[52]

Cornwallis and Gertrude considered Faysal's role in unifying the country, while increasing his influence among the tribes, as pivotal.[53] She reported then 'the most beautiful Oriental scene' that illustrated her opinion: The king, dressed in 'the white and gold of Mecca princes', sat in his garden near a fountain. With him, sitting on the verges of the fountain were:

> Nuri Sha'lan, grim and scowling with his red kaffiya drawn up over his mouth and chin; 'Ajil al Yawar, shaykh of the Shammar, six feet six inches of huge body, long, fine hands holding a chain of amber . . . and 'Ali Sulaiman, the sturdy peasant shaykh whose word runs from Falluja along all Euphrates to the frontier . . . Around them . . . waves and waves of gold and orange marigolds, with the white and yellow of chrysanthemums above them echoing the King's white and gold. And the low sun sending long soft beams between the willow bushes and the palms . . . brushing the gold and the orange, the white and yellow into a brighter glow.[54]

In this setting, Nuri Sha'lan was trying to persuade the king to recapture some of the tribal lands held by Ibn Sa'ud. The king laughed at Nuri Sha'lan, the tribal leader, for his allegiance seemed to shift from Iraq to Syria, to Trans-Jordan, according to his changing moods. 'Whose subject are you, Nuri?' teased Faysal. 'When you want a passport, do you go to the French or to Sidi 'Abdullah or to whom? Or is your camel your passport or your sword and lance?' Nuri Sha'lan could not answer him, and 'his face grew blacker and he drew the red kerchief closer round his mouth'. 'Ajil smiled and Gertrude laughed, 'for we both knew Nuri's antecedents' and how difficult it was for him to believe in the advantages of modern citizenship.[55]

Nonetheless modern Iraq was taking shape as the year of 1923 ended with two important events. The first was an official dinner given by the king for the cabinet and his advisers. It was a 'male dinner', but Gertrude had been invited. She went to see the king and asked him, 'man to man if he wanted me to come. "Yes, of course,"' the king answered. Defining herself as a sexless high official,[56] Gertrude went to the reception wearing a pale blue velvet dress, her diamond tiara, and all her orders, making a statement of dignified equality with all the men present at the occasion. 'Ali Jawdat wore the Hijaz Nahdha. Ken Cornwallis wore his CBE (Commander of the British Empire) and DSO (Distinguished Service Order) medals. 'The King wore a blue uniform with the Hijaz Star and the collar of the Victoria Order; Sir Henry Dobbs with the pale blue ribbon of the Star of India; Ja'far al-'Askari and Nuri al-Sa'id wore their orders'.

She felt more feminine, however, when Marie, her French servant, packed a pink crêpe-de-chine night-gown for a hunting party with Ken on New Year's Eve. 'It's a hunting party, *Nuri-a-din les verra*' (Nuri-a-din will see them), Marie explained). She was referring to Ken's Sudanese servant. 'Hope [Nuri-a-din] was duly impressed', concluded Gertrude once back home.

The new year, 1924, would be a year of conclusions. Pending questions would be resolved, or at least come into clearer focus. The main questions still to be dealt with were again the treaty's ratification by the Constituent Assembly, Mosul's future and the Shi'i mujtahids' opposition to the treaty and to Britain's vision of Iraq as a secular state dominated by Faysal and his Sunni Sharifians.

Throughout these momentous negotiations over Iraq's future, there was Ken, with whom Gertrude shared her opinions, ideas, confidences, and even letters from home.[57] He visited her almost daily at the archaeological department of the museum, where Gertrude had started to spend her free time. From there they went together to other events. They would walk along the bank of the Tigris and talk of things 'outside Iraq', play tennis, croquet, bridge, read poems, or entertain mutual friends such as Lionel Smith, Nigel Davidson, the Bourdillons, and even the Dobbses.

But all was not amusement and social events. Ken, directly involved in the negotiations for the ratification of the treaty, was exhausted. 'If the acceptance of the Treaty is delayed much longer, he will break away', Gertrude worried.[58] The anti-British campaign in the nationalist press continued to shape public opinion in Baghdad and other towns. 'The intruders! The intruders! who have become a burden, competing with us for bread and water', claimed *Al Istiqlal* in September 1923[59] while explaining nationality in modern terms, as in Egypt, where, Sa'd Zaghlul claimed, there were no minorities, or majorities.[60]

In April 1924 Dobbs sent a telegram to Faysal warning him that if the treaty were not ratified in time, the British would go home.[61] Gertrude's understanding of the problem was slightly different. 'If we intend to stay at any price, which is scarcely conceivable', she commented, 'then we must be prepared to give the Iraqi government easier terms than those laid down in the subsidiary agreements'.[62]

She was again a step ahead of her male colleagues, Cornwallis among them. Closer to the population, Gertrude would update Cornwallis about the bargaining around the treaty. The Shi'is saw the treaty as advantageous to the Sunni Arabs. One of the strongest opponents of the treaty was 'Abd al-Wahid al-Hajj Sikkar, the Shi'i tribal leader of the 1920 rebellion. 'We fought the English, we shed our blood, and now we are asked to hand ourselves over to them like slaves by this treaty', he told members of the committee of deputies appointed to examine the issue.[63]

Kurdish delegations also came to Baghdad, some supporting, others rejecting the treaty. The main opposition came, however, from the Sunni nationalists headed by Yasin al-Hashimi. Appointed president of the committee negotiating the treaty, he tried to postpone its ratification for as long as possible. Gertrude's relationship with Yasin al-Hashimi dated from their early meeting in Damascus in 1919. She recognised now his abilities as a politician, with a pragmatic vision and an assertive manner to push his agenda forward. She still did not trust him and yet he was 'the ablest man in the town',[64] as she once described him. In her view it was essential to have a man such as Yasin, who knew his mind and was not afraid to express it, in the government. The question was, she wondered again, 'What Yasin's mind is?'. Intellectually superior, realistic, ambitious and driven by a strong belief in Iraq's political future, Yasin was also reserved and difficult to understand.[65] His reserve further fuelled Gertrude's concerns about his 'loyalty' as she defined his ambiguous position toward the British.

She remembered Yasin's constant changes of heart, and the letter he had sent in 1922 to Ja'far Abu al-Timman, the Shi'i leader of the anti-British camp, expressing his willingness to join in the efforts to 'drive out the oppressor . . . i.e., *us*', from the country, as Gertrude explained later to her father.[66] It was, however, somewhat preposterous to expect this kind of loyalty from an Arab officer who was, above all, loyal to himself and to his own ideas on how to promote the Arab cause, sometimes by taking paths less evident to others.[67] He would still opt for the possibility of having the Turks back as Iraq's mandatory power if certain clauses of the treaty with Britain weren't modified. As the president of the treaty committee, Yasin was the only man able to move the assembly to ratify the 1922 treaty given the agitation against it, led mainly by the press and urban parties.

As the Constituent Assembly convened to ratify the treaty and approve the constitution, demonstrations took place in the bazaar. As the deputies began to arrive, demonstrators stopped their cars, shouting 'Don't sign the Treaty!'. Letters signed by the 'Secret Society of Iraq' had already menaced the deputies, adding to the atmosphere of fear and panic.[68] One tribal deputy was shot. Cornwallis appeared 'unusually grave and Gertrude Bell had dark rings round her eyes', as C. J. Edmonds, the adviser to the Ministry of Interior, reported later.[69]

As the king rose to start his speech, shouts of the crowds in the streets made his voice shake.[70] A regiment of cavalry ordered by Ja'far al-'Askari, head of the cabinet, and Nuri al-Sa'id, minister of defence, dispersed the crowds. The treaty was finally ratified on 10 June 1924 at 11:30 p.m.[71] 'We beat Cinderella by half an hour', Gertrude later quipped. Once the treaty was ratified, leaving only the amendments of the subsidiary agreements to be further discussed, Gertrude managed to persuade Ja'far al-'Askari, then prime minister, to include Yasin in the cabinet. 'He is a force', she explained, 'safer in the Cabinet than outside it'.[72]

Yasin was mainly concerned then by the burden on Iraq's budget claimed by the British (full payment for military installations and equipment left behind by Britain's occupational forces), linking his rejection of the financial agreement with the need to abolish the military agreement, as the two were indirectly linked. He also wanted a conscripted army – less expensive and less dependent on the British – that would become the exponent of Iraq's sovereignty. Without agreeing, Gertrude now understood his position well.

As minister of antiquities he had passed the Antiquity Law two days before Gertrude returned from her annual leave to England, increasing the Iraqi minister's authority and circumventing the department's former prerogative to permit the export of antiquities. The department of antiquities, 'i.e., *me*', Gertrude explained then, would now have to consult with the minister before Iraq's historic treasures were allowed to leave the country. 'And yet I like the man', Gertrude wrote then, 'He has a curious charm and gives one a sense of power'. Less affected by any possible harm caused to her personally than by her interest in developing the department and increasing public awareness of the country's heritage, Gertrude complied with Yasin's initiatives. At the time, she had also developed a friendship with his wife. 'His family life is beautiful', Gertrude commented after one of her visits to his home. Their antagonistic views regarding the ratification of the treaty put aside, Gertrude and Yasin were able to joke privately about their differences of opinion. 'Yasin Pasha and his wife came to tea on Saturday', she wrote to her father some time later. Seeing Gertrude's piano, Yasin's wife complained that the Pasha would not buy her one. 'After the Treaty', Yasin replied then with a wink, 'and we both laughed'.[73]

The day following the ratification, Ken came to Gertrude's house. 'We have enjoyed these little dinners by ourselves; we dine and talk and go to bed at ten. Tonight we have the last one, for he leaves tomorrow; though I shall miss him dreadfully, I am glad he is going for he is so tired and worn out'. She wrote to her sister Molly, asking her to be kind to Ken: 'I have a great affection for him and think him [one] of the finest creatures I have known. To him, more than to anyone else, is due the ratification of the Treaty . . .'. Gertrude needed Molly's support. 'Except fathers, sisters are the greatest gifts in the world',[74] she admitted.

The sympathy Gertrude expected from her sisters regarding her relationship with Cornwallis could not be so easily obtained from Florence. Gertrude wrote to her explaining the difficulties Cornwallis was having with his wife, but Florence was not convinced: 'What does enlist my role and interest is Gertrude's interest in the matter and her friendship with Cornwallis', Florence explained in a letter to Lisa.[75] As for the rest, Florence thought very little of the affair, in fact, she had heard another side to the story from Lisa, and asked her permission to bring this version to Gertrude's attention.[76] The following version of events is what Florence learned.

Gertrude-Dorothy Cornwallis, Ken's wife, lived at Onslow Gardens, South Kensington, from 1920 onwards, when she returned from Egypt. The daughter of Albert Edward Bowen, first baronet, Gertrude-Dorothy was only twenty-two when she married Kinahan Cornwallis in 1911. Cornwallis was then twenty-eight, a political officer in the Sudan Civil Service. The couple's first two children, Elizabeth and Richard, were born in 1912 and 1915 and the third, Peter Brownell, came into the world only a couple of weeks before his parents went their separate ways. Gertrude-Dorothy did not want to follow her husband to Baghdad after the hardship and loneliness she had endured at his side in Khartoum and Cairo. She felt she had paid her dues for Britain's imperial adventure, and now she wanted to go home. It had not been easy to raise the children on a political officer's salary, and she had no other source of income at the time. Estranged from her father, she was deprived of the extra allowance that eased the lives of many officers' wives abroad. But what eventually drove Gertrude-Dorothy and Cornwallis apart was the emotional distance and coldness that both partners felt. It would be easier, she thought, to cope with it from England, where physical separation could help explain the widening gap between them.

Nothing was as hard as living together and feeling apart, living as they did in close quarters, where Ken's aloofness and reserve constantly kept her at arm's length, and where the control and discipline he had acquired during his years of training and service spilled over into their daily life. Gertrude-Dorothy Cornwallis did not want to live a life bound by customs and restraints and wanted the right to make her life over again.

Meanwhile, Gertrude Bell had only heard Ken's side of the story. 'There is no more affection between them', she explained 'the other Gertrude' to her father. In her view, Ken had tried to hold on for the sake of the children, but it was impossible. He finally relented, playing by the rules of the day, and gave his wife the evidence necessary to obtain a quick divorce – 'what one sees in *The Times* daily and knows that it is trumped up'.[77] The reputed grounds for divorce were adultery. The precipitating incident allegedly took place on the night of 23 October 1924, when Ken had been 'caught' in a small hotel on Shaftesbury Avenue with an unknown woman. Within a week, Gertrude-Dorothy's solicitors had filed for divorce. In a behind-the-scenes agreement, the solicitors had probably hired private detectives 'to catch Cornwallis in the act', and to ensure that the evidence was sufficient for a court hearing. Gertrude-Dorothy's lawyers attested that she did not know the woman; Cornwallis probably did not either.

The set-up was a scheme to obtain a quick divorce and was a common custom of the time. Cornwallis did not appear in court, nor did he take the opportunity to rebut the contents of his wife's petition of divorce. As the delinquent party, he would not have any legal right to the children. Although his wife had promised to let him pay for their education and maintenance, he did not feel certain that she would keep her promises. He could not even visit them as frequently as he would have liked. The children would continue to live with their mother at South Kensington while he, when visiting London, would stay at the Royal Automobile Club in Pall Mall.[78]

'She really, I am convinced, wants to marry someone else', Gertrude explained to her father, surprised by the hastiness with which the divorce had been planned and carried out.[79] Gertrude-Dorothy never remarried, however. Perhaps the death of her father in September 1924 released her from the need to keep up with appearances, making her feel freer to defy conventions and arrange the divorce. A sudden bequest from her father's estate brought her freedom from a strained and tiresome life shaped by the imperial designs of the Crown. She would finally be able to take the time to be bluntly and openly unhappy. Gertrude Bell felt sorry for the pain the divorce caused to both Ken and Gertrude-Dorothy. 'I am dreadfully sorry for my dear Ken', she lamented in a letter to her father,[80] asking Florence to pay Ken some attention and to let him and his children spend the summer at the Bells' property in Mount Grace.[81]

Florence talked the matter over with Lisa. Complaining that Gertrude's temperament was 'equal to anything', and that she had a rather presumptuous way of imposing her will on others, Florence engaged in a frank discussion about Gertrude's manners and behaviour. She was also referring, without saying it bluntly, to Gertrude's 'morals' as an unmarried woman having 'inconclusive' affairs with married men. Feeling that Florence's judgemental position also inadvertently pointed an accusing finger at her, Lisa refused to agree with Florence's arguments, but she would not tolerate Gertrude's attitude either.[82] She could understand Gertrude's pain and suffering linked to her liaison with Ken, as she herself was still caught emotionally in her past affair with William Archer, also a married man.[83]

Some weeks later, reading in *The Times* of William Archer's death, Lisa wrote in her well-kept diary: 'A strange day . . . a new moon . . . Good night, my friend . . .'.[84]

Gertrude's solitary life ran along parallel lines, as she also always became embroiled in impossible relationships. One could still wonder what the reason was for this. From today's perspective, one could say that her inconclusive relations had much to do with the emotional intimacy she had developed with her father; a closeness, dependency and identification that wouldn't leave enough space for other relationships to flourish. It was not just the puritanical mentality of the time that prevented her from getting really closer to other men, but it was mainly the incessant need to get her father's approval that prevented her from achieving a more mature attitude regarding personal affairs without permanently seeking for consent.

Self-centred and unable to liberate herself from the inhibitions that she had once called 'inner demons' or 'ghosts', Gertrude would, without understanding it fully, keep men at arms' length. In some aspects she would even envisage relationships as an incessant and yet an evanescent quest. The irony of her life stems perhaps from the fact that she was so daring and self sufficient in her professional endeavours and yet so dependent and fragile in her emotional life. It was her attraction to Ken, to his charismatic personality, his reserved smile and aristocratic manners that made her forget his way of minimising the differences between them. But these differences existed.

Ken also admired Gertrude in his way. He obviously valued her intellect, her sharp insights and was amused by her temperament and by the way she managed to keep his interest in her alive. He was attracted by her intricate mixture of 'feminine' spirituality and 'masculine' rationality, and by her energy and enthusiasm. Intuitive, emotional, and verbal, Gertrude counterbalanced his logical, rational, and controlled countenance. He liked her flamboyance and her ability to take refuge in the elusiveness of the moment as reflected in her sharp swings of mood. They had great moments together with the complicity in a twinkle, a gesture, a joke. On rare occasions, he would shed his armour and the more amusing facets of his personality emerged.

One of these rare occasions was a dinner in honour of Sir John Norton Griffith, the winner of a concession to build the Habbaniyya dam at Ramadi and a large canal system on the Tigris. 'How would you punctuate this sentence: "Mary ran out into the garden naked"?', Sir John asked the other guests. 'With a full stop, I hope', Ken answered without blinking.[85]

When the conversation finally turned serious, the issue of Mosul vilayet and Turkey's claim over it was brought up again. Gertrude should go to London and persuade the government not to give up Mosul, Sir John suggested. 'Without Mosul the treaty is valueless', he insisted. And, in his opinion, nobody but Gertrude would be able to do the job, not even Cornwallis with his assurance and calm authority.

The problem of Mosul vilayet was a complex one. Britain's well-known dependence on oil for its navy dictated its search for political control or influence over territories where oil was or could be found. Although the existence of oil in Mosul had not yet been established, there were previous surveys hinting at commercial quantities to be found in Mesopotamia, turning oil into a most important factor in Britain's strategic interests. The question of Mosul, transferred to the League of Nations after the impasse reached at the Lausanne Conference, focused now on the attempts made to link the question of the vilayet's frontier to Iraq's share in the future gains of the Turkish Petroleum Company (TPC, the main concessionaire). The

British were trying to convince the Iraqi government to hand over the twenty per cent of the shares to Turkey in exchange for Turkey's recognition of Mosul as part of Iraq's territory.[86]

The debate evolved, encompassing other facets of the problem. It also became a subject of international dispute as the USA continued to press for legal rights in former Ottoman territories in the name of the 'open door' principle.[87] It was not just the prominent question of oil shares and Britain's control of potential oil commercial areas, it was also concerned, although in a lesser measure, with no less complicated issues regarding Mosul's mixed population. The mounting pressures caused by the Assyrian refugees and the need to settle them after their expulsion from Turkey during the war, occupied now the minds of the British officials, given the urgency of the matter. The divergent policies of the Colonial and Foreign offices made the problem seem even less soluble, however. The Colonial Office started pressuring Iraq to exchange its part of the TPC shares, while the Foreign Office tried to undermine Britain's interests in Mosul's oil. Both were sending contradictory and, perhaps purposely, misguiding messages.

At the same time, there were the pressures related to the Kurdish claims for autonomy and Turkey's growing prestige among the Kurds, in spite of Turkey's dismissal of Kurdish aspirations and its temporary loss of authority after Mustafa Kemal's abolition of the caliphate in March 1924. Cornwallis commented on Faysal's proposal, namely, cultural autonomy for the Kurdish areas in Iraq's territory on the condition that the Kurds remained attached to Baghdad economically and politically. 'Something of the nature of Austria-Hungary absit omen', Gertrude would certainly repeat again.[88] Cornwallis believed that the Kurds' refusal to negotiate with Baghdad on Faysal's terms had created an impasse. The implications were far reaching, he explained, especially when the pro-Turkish position of the Turkmen, and the wish of the Arab Sunni population of the town of Mosul to become part of the Iraqi state, were taken into account.

Gertrude kept very much in mind the Arabs' interests in Mosul during the debates. For her, it was obvious that Mosul should be attached to Baghdad. The Iraqi nationalists would never acknowledge Mustapha Kemal's claims that Mosul was not an Arab province, but an ancient Ottoman vilayet with important Kurdish and Turkman populations and therefore not part of the Arab territories Turkey had given away at Lausanne.[89]

Mosul's unsolved future 'was a sign of Britain's weariness', Gertrude commented later, 'as even the Foreign Office seemed indifferent to the task of finding a solution to a question so vital to Iraq's existence'.[90] But more than anything else, Gertrude was concerned with the problem of Mosul's defence, and the Iraqi army's inability to guard the frontiers as Ja'far al-'Askari himself recognised. The problem had become even more acute now that Britain kept only RAF squadrons in Iraq and no land forces.[91] But even so, Gertrude was against the idea of building on the Assyrian Levies (created at the Cairo conference as a cheap substitute for British land troops) as Iraq's main land force, however. In her view, the maintenance of Christian troops, led by British officers and employed against Muslims, heightened the animosity between Christian and Muslims and increased the jealousy of the Iraqi army officers. Therefore, she claimed, the Levies should be disbanded or used only in their own areas and Britain should not interfere with the problem created by the Assyrian refugees. The Assyrians would come to terms with the Arabs if Britain stayed out of the conflict, Gertrude believed. They would have to settle in Iraq, become Iraqi citizens, and forget any plan to return to the Hakkari Mountains that had been excluded from Iraq's territory at Sèvres.[92] In this issue, as in others, Gertrude proved again that she was more attuned to the Arabs' opinions than her male colleagues were.

At the end of July 1924, Sir Henry Dobbs asked Gertrude to write an answer to an article published in the *Westminster Gazette* on 28 July, days after the reoccupation of Sulaymaniyya from Shaykh Mahmud by British and Iraqi troops. In her letter, Gertrude refuted the accusations made by a 'high authority' (probably A. T. Wilson) that the majority of Mosul's population wished to return to Turkey. They did not want the Turks back, Gertrude explained in her letter to the editor. 'The population in Mosul have said so by sending deputies to the Constituent Assembly and by passing the Treaty'.[93] The deputies of Kirkuk and Sulaymaniyya to the assembly were, in fact, representatives of the most important families in their districts: the Naftchizade, the Babans, and the Talabanis.[94] Gertrude had met most of them and was convinced that they wanted to see Mosul become part of Iraq. The idea of organising a plebiscite to appraise the population's wishes (a project launched in June 1924, after negotiations between Britain and Turkey had broken down) would not make it easier. The plebiscite would also be a problem, Gertrude believed, because the Turks would try to intimidate the population, and prevent the possible repercussions of a Kurdish nationalist campaign spreading from Mosul to the Kurdish areas in Anatolia.

'I need not bother much with the rest of the "high authority's allega-tions"', Gertrude continued in her letter to the editor, referring possibly to A. T. Wilson or even to T. E. Lawrence. 'I am here and he is not'. She punc-tuated the end of the letter with one of the incisive statements for which she became so famous: 'There! I am done. Forgive me for this enormous letter. Truth is usually longer than lies'.[95]

The campaign in the Iraqi press focused on three main arguments for keeping Mosul within the borders of Iraq: Mosul was an Arab and not a Turkish province; Mosul was incapable of surviving economically without being attached to Iraq; and no oil concessions should be given to foreign companies, especially to the TPC, which was being operated with Turkish and British capital.[96] 'This company . . . invites us to become motor drivers and tinsmiths and stokers and will give us four shillings for a ton or about 1 percent of the profit', claimed *Al Istiqlal*.[97] Who was to decide if the TPC or other foreign companies should be granted concessions? the nationalists asked, and why were the decisions made behind their backs? The national-ists were against the agreement with the TPC, finding it detrimental to the Iraqis, as they couldn't participate in the company's investments and management.

In spite of her ambivalence toward Yasin al-Hashimi, Gertrude was very much against the possibility of seeing him as prime minister. Her mixed feelings towards him stemmed not only from her admiration for his leader-ship, his ability and outspoken way of conducting politics, but also from his astute ability to adapt views and positions and circumvent confrontations. She believed that he was needed to move things forward, yet not as a prime minister. Overhearing a conversation between Cornwallis and Dobbs in support of Yasin's appointment to the post after Ja'far al-'Askari's resigna-tion in August 1924, Gertrude overreacted, 'falling into a furious passion that raged round the head of the luckless Ken for half an hour', leaving them 'barely on speaking terms'.[98] Yasin al-Hashimi's refused the job, at first for fear of being accused of having been won over by the British. His decision was, for Gertrude, a temporary relief. He would accept it later, however, and demonstrate a special talent for dealing with the vicissitudes of an ambiguous situation – *al-wadha' al-shadd*, as it was then called – in which the implementation of nationalist aims depended on British support.[99]

During his short term in office (until June 1925), Yasin would continue to push for an anti-British policy. Nonetheless, he would have to comply with Britain's pressures too, and grant a concession to Norton Griffith to build a dam in Habbaniyya, leaving himself open to gossip relating to possible shares in the company's future profits.

*   *   *

The intense debates made Gertrude feel even more discouraged, as the evolving problems seemed to underscore Britain's impossible mission.

On New Year's Eve 1925, Gertrude sat in her empty office, wrapped in a fur coat, finding it more difficult to concentrate on 'the impediments born of the insanity of Britain's Near Eastern policy',[100] as she had already called Britain's political blunders some years before. She preferred to stay at work and to skip the ball that followed the high commissioner's official dinner. Tired and worn out, she remembered the apprehension that had marked the same event in past years, when disillusionment and despair had been tempered by hope.[101] This time she could not make herself believe in promises ahead. 'I have grown so much of a recluse', she admitted once. 'After all, these years I have had of being alone are bound to alter one's character . . . not for the better', she then concluded.

Florence's letter describing the 1924 Christmas party at Rounton increased Gertrude's sense of loneliness. 'You bring us all together in your letter', Gertrude wrote back, 'but I don't feel I could fit in a Christmas party anymore'. She envisioned her nephews and nieces sitting in the library listening to Florence playing the piano; she could even guess that Pauline and George Lowthian, Molly's eldest children, had preferred to stay in the drawing room, reading poetry, rather than join the younger cousins in their games. Gertrude felt, however, that she did not belong to this perfect scene of domestic harmony. 'I do not have children or grandchildren growing around me',[102] she explained in her letter, as if this was the only reason for her low spirits.

The freezing winds blowing at night, sneaking in through the cracks in the windows made up this particularly cold winter. Seeming even sadder in the countryside, the 'lime and orange trees frozen dead'[103] added to the anxiety caused by the bad harvest, and the post-war depression, 'Sheep were dying like flies. People had lost all hope', Gertrude reported then.

In January 1925, the commission appointed by the League of Nations, headed by de Wirzen, arrived in Baghdad. A honest Swede, 'sans plus', reported Gertrude after the cold reception to the commission members. 'The live wire is Count Teleki, a Hungarian, he is the danger; the third is Colonel Paulis, a Belgian, half way between the two others . . . After din-

8. Gertrude Bell at the age of fifty-three.

ner, de Wirzen and Paulis started asking questions' but Teleki, as soon as the talk turned on Iraq, 'lost all interest'.[104]

Touring Sulaymaniyya in their cars, the commissioners moved among shopkeepers in the bazaar, asking the 'secret question',[105] 'Iraq or Turkey?'[106] Badly formulated by a less articulate translator, who sometimes missed the accurate meanings of the questions formulated by the commission members, the questions received evasive answers, also because 'government *farrashes* [spies] had been caught listening at doors', cutting short spontaneous and candid opinions.

Colonel Paulis suggestion was to create two separate administrative systems, one Arab, one Kurd, inside Iraq's state.[107] It was necessary to preserve the rights of the Kurds, the commission members believed, and to guarantee Assyrians that they would be better off staying in Mosul under Iraqi rule than going back to Turkey.[108] It was an alternative endorsed later by the Assyrians themselves. Given the choice, Arbil's inhabitants finally expressed their desire to be included in Iraq. Kirkuk, by contrast, had wanted to return to Turkey,[109] but its Turkmen inhabitants now considered the Iraqi option if Turkish remained Kirkuk's official language and if Turkmen officials would administer the town.[110]

Perhaps ignoring the contents of the early surveys, Gertrude believed that the fate of the Assyrian refugees was more urgent at that particular moment than oil in the debates on Mosul's future. In this regard, she aligned herself with C. J. Edmonds, now the liaison officer to the commission,[111] who perhaps was also less attuned to what was really at stake in London's corridors of power.

Her personal problems may also have affected her vision of events. In February Gertrude mourned her two little cocker spaniels, which had died of pneumonia; Sally, Ken's dog, left in Gertrude's care when he returned to England, and her own remaining dog, Peter, 'who danced around me all day', trying, so it seems, to appease her sadness. Alone at home with the 'two little ghosts', after the dogs' burial in the garden, Gertrude wondered about her life and her friendship with Ken. Things had developed in a different way to what she had hoped, and she would never be able to make Ken understand the way she herself had contemplated their relationship. She would have wanted more from him than just the evanescent moments of togetherness they shared. And Cornwallis, by all accounts, was the man who could give a woman as emotionally knotty and vulnerable as Gertrude, the strength to purge her 'inner demons'. But all seemed now unpromising and ephemeral.

In England, prospects were also dim. The coal crisis affected the Bells' fortune and their social position. With a heavy heart, Gertrude summed up the year's expenditures. She had spent £560 above her annual salary, an extravagance she could no longer afford. How could she survive on the £830 she earned as a civil servant abroad? Her salary did not cover the cost of food, books, papers, plant bulbs, and other amenities sent to her from London in order to make life in Baghdad somewhat easier. This did not include the clothes she needed to keep up with the weather in the Middle East.

But also the clothes – which were part of her image abroad and which had provoked mixed reactions at home – had lost their appeal. Boxes of hats, gloves and shoes lay unopened in her living room, waiting for Marie to take care of them. Gertrude's heart wasn't in it anymore. Her thoughts and feelings were with the affairs of the country and the changes occurring around her. Iraq had lost the candour of its earlier years. Scenes of scout parades, of hundreds of youngsters exercising and pitching tents, drawing a map of Iraq's borders 'stretching north, far beyond the present boundaries', she reported on 28 January 1925. Other displays of growing anti-British feeling made her feel even more estranged.

The League of Nations' commission was still meeting in Mosul, collect- ing facts and opinions. Turkey declared that whatever territorial borders were finally traced, the concession awarded to the TPC to search for oil in Mosul would not be affected. 'Maybe now the commission members would understand that Britain wasn't pressing for the inclusion of Mosul in the Iraq because of interests in Mosul's oil', Gertrude still believed. Things were not so simple, however. Negotiations would be resumed in the spring, but whatever their outcome, Mosul had to be assigned to Iraq because it was impossible to move the Assyrian refugees back to Turkey, so she explained again, underestimating the importance oil was gaining and the way in which both problems (oil and Mosul's frontier) were intertwined.[112]

The debate centred now over the Brussels Line (drawn by the Council of the League of Nations in October 1924) as the borderline that included Mosul in Iraq. Britain preferred the line demarcated in Istanbul in 1924, which ran through ranges of high, impassable mountains to prevent an easy passage of tribes from both sides and better defend Iraq's frontiers.[113] Fur- thermore, in Britain's view the Brussels Line did not permit an easy solution to the Assyrian problem. In effect, it prevented the access of 20,000 to 30,000 Assyrian refugees (almost half of the displaced Assyrian population) living north of the Brussels Line to a Turkish market or to the town of Mosul itself.[114] But it was mainly Britain's and Iraq's interest in ensuring that the oil fields remained on the Iraqi side of the frontier that determined the final drawing of the northern frontier's line.

Another major factor that persuaded the commission to leave the former vilayet of Mosul to Iraq was the fact that the town of Mosul, the centre of the vilayet with its 200,000 inhabitants was Arab, with lesser Ottoman influence than Baghdad. Mosul's aristocratic Sunni Arab families wanted to see the former vilayet, with its 600,000 inhabitants, linked to Baghdad. Its less eloquent Kurdish population could not counter the pressure of the Arab elites.

The question whether Mosul needed Baghdad as a market for its wheat, rice and tobacco was dismissed by the fact that Aleppo was Mosul's natural market, however. Colonel Paulis disputed the argument, making the three vilayets a single economic unit in one of the commission's sessions.[115] But the problem, again, was more complex than the way in which Colonel Paulis and his fellow commissioners perceived it.

The question of Mosul's oil arose again at the end of the commission's work. The Iraqi government still pressed for twenty-five per cent of equity participation in the company, claiming that payment on a royalty basis, as was now suggested, left Iraq more dependent on the company's decisions. In effect, an equity participation would give Iraq a greater say about the quantity of oil to be produced and, proportionately a higher dividend.[116] It was Count Teleki that mediated between both sides. Sliding royalties would be paid in gold (not in sterling), accommodating the nationalists only partially. It wasn't enough, however, as they wanted greater control over the company's gains.

The commission left Iraq in March 1925. In a dinner held in Baghdad before their departure, Teleki and Colonel Paulis revealed some of the commission's recommendations. Mosul was to be included in Iraq's territory, and the Brussels Line would be established as Iraq's northern frontier. The terms of Britain's presence would be extended to twenty-five years (not four years as established in the 1923 protocol). Finally, Iraq's Kurdish areas would be administered by Kurds and in Kurdish.

The report was presented to the Council of the League in September 1925 and, at the end of December, the Brussels Line was officially confirmed. A new treaty between Britain and Iraq was signed in January 1926, extending the alliance with Britain for twenty-five more years, unless, in the meantime, Iraq was admitted as a member to the League of Nations. The Iraq Petrol Company (IPC) as the TPC would later be called, was granted a concession for seventy-five years, and a pipeline was planned to bring oil across Iraq to the Mediterranean. A provision in the Turco-Iraqi treaty of June 1926 gave Turkey ten per cent of Iraq's oil royalties for twenty-five years.

In October 1927, after months of extensive digging, oil was found at Baba Gurgur, north of Kirkuk.[117] This discovery would affect Iraq in a way that Gertrude Bell, or her colleagues, could never have foreseen.

CHAPTER 9

'We Had Awakened and Become a Nation'

Spring would be rainy too. The Tigris River spilled over its banks, and the Maude Bridge was closed to traffic. Gertrude described the situation in the country in her famous intelligence reports. Homes were flooded, and the water inundated gardens. Dried citrus fruits hung on frozen branches. Inside the house, pots and bowls couldn't contain the water pouring from the ceiling.

When a pale sun appeared, Marie laid out the wet carpets on the lawn. 'The world was drying up wonderfully fast';[1] the bridges opened to traffic, allowing Gertrude, Ken Cornwallis, and Lionel Smith (now adviser to the Ministry of Education) to go for a visit to Faysal's farm near Ba'quba. The 'King's Marsh' was still muddy but spring was in the air. It was a perfect day to shoot wild ducks, letting the party forget, for this one day, the difficult moments of the last few months.

In April 1925, a Iraqi military expedition was launched against the Yazidis in Jebel Sinjar. Believed to be worshippers of the devil, whom they called Malik Ta'us (the Peacock King), the Yazidis followed a religion that combined precepts of Zoroastrianism, ancient Christian doctrines and Islam. They believed that the spirit of evil was part of the divinity, and that the devil was a fallen angel who would one day return to his ancient form. Gertrude had once visited the Yazidi shrine at Shaykh 'Adi ibn Musafir's tomb in Lalish, Mosul, on a summer pilgrimage that culminated in a great feast attended by Yazidis from all parts of the former Ottoman Empire: Mardin, Diyarbekr, Aleppo, Caucasia and Mosul itself. She described in her official reports their religious costumes, and their hierarchy of *pirs* (spiritual dignitaries), with the *mir* as their leader and including the *shaykhs* (religious teachers), the *qawwals* (attendants of the seven sacred golden peacocks), and the *faqirs* (lay brothers).[2] The mysteries of the Yazidis' religion were laid out in their Black Book[3] – a Qur'an in which the name of Shaytan (the devil) had been erased from the text. Any Yazidi who pronounced the name of Shaytan, it was believed, would be struck blind, and be punished if pronouncing any word with 'sh—t—' sounds.[4]

Shaykh 'Adi's sanctuary was quiet and empty when she came to visit. Passing through the doorway, Gertrude entered into a 'small paved court, still and peaceful and half-shaded by mulberries'. A black snake painted on a stony wall caught her eye 'in a kind of magnetic attraction'. 'Yazidis lived in close juxtaposition' with Kurds and Arabs, creating 'a Yazidi fringe running along the foothills while the mountains were entirely Kurdish',[5] Gertrude had written years earlier explaining how to distinguish the Yazidis from the surrounding population: Their unveiled women wore red cotton dresses, as red was considered a 'beneficent hue', while blue was to be avoided. Women kept in their coloured costumes many of the secret symbols of the different sects and religions.

There were other heterodox sects in northern Iraq, among them the Ahl al-Haqq (the People of the Absolute Truth) and the 'Ali Ilahis (the Deifiers of 'Ali) also called the Seveners (al Sab'iyya).[6] Gertrude was familiar with their rituals and with the Seveners' ceremony of sacrificing cocks at daybreak, symbolising the polarisation of dark and light; and with the ceremony of *sabz namudar* (making green), which derived from the belief that the divine light is hidden in plants, prohibiting followers to eat lettuce.

The question of whether and how these cults would survive and become a part of a modern secular state remained unanswered at that stage. But the main question that preoccupied Gertrude now was how to integrate the Kurds 'qua Kurds', in Iraq. In April 1925 Shaykh Mahmud's properties were seized by the government under Section 27 of the Tribal Criminal and Civil Disputes Regulations (TCCDR – the judicial code for the tribal areas) causing great concern among the Kurds. For other reasons it also concerned the nationalists, who considered the TCCDR as an instrument of British control[7] created to drive a wedge between the tribal and rural population and the town dwellers.

In June 1925, a new administration was established in Sulaymaniyya, and Shaykh Mahmud's episode would be forgotten, together with his too bold message of Kurdish autonomy. Troubles involving the Kurdish tribe of the Goyan would cause some stir along the frontier with Turkey. At the time, however, Turkey's prestige was too low to serve as counterweight to the Arabs. In effect, the abolition of the caliphate would reinforce the Arabs' position and threaten the Kurds even further.

Gertrude was not happy with the idea of having Britain stay in Iraq for twenty-five more years to protect Mosul's minorities. Although Britain was used 'to eat and retain cakes at the same time',[8] Gertrude had hoped that Iraq's acceptance as a member of the League of Nations would hasten the process and relieve Britain of the costs of an effective presence in the country. It was, one could argue, more for Britain's than for Iraq's sake that Gertrude wanted Britain to leave earlier. However, Iraq's faster path to independence also depended on the ability of Baghdad's politicians to bridge differences.

Yasin was the leader of the opposition after having left office in June 1925. The constituency of his party, Hizb al-Sha'b, formed primarily by urban Sunnis, supported him in his anti-British campaign, in a more extreme stance than the position of the Taqaddum (Progress) Party, a parliamentary bloc formed by more moderate nationalists, or the Nahda (Resurrection) Party, representing urban Shi'is.

Gertrude had followed Yasin's relationship with the Shi'is from the days of his collaboration with Ja'far 'Abu Timman, the Shi'i nationalist from Baghdad who had actively incited the Shi'i tribes to rebellion in 1920. As leader of Hizb al-Watani, Yasin continued to fight a valiant campaign against the British. In principle, the British believed Yasin was not opposed to collaboration with the Shi'is as long as their interests converged with his own. Although his major intent was to reduce tribal representation in parliament in order to strengthen the Sunnis, he gained their cooperation by remunerating them with land grants, water quotas and immunity from taxes. The patterns thus established would prevail in the decades to come, fostering Sunni–Shi'i alliances also based on personal ties and shifting interests, apart from the growing feelings of common destiny fuelled by their mutual antagonism to Britain's presence in the country.

The problem of Sunni–Shi'i relations, so vital to Iraq's political survival, was not a new one. Already by 1922, Gertrude explained to Sir Percy Loraine, Britain's resident in Teheran, the origins of dissension between Sunnis and Shi'is as they had manifested themselves in Iraq. The appointment of young Arab officials, who were often ex-military officers, to administrative posts in the Hilla and Nasiriyya divisions (the area stretching from the Hindiyya Dam to the junction of the Euphrates and the Tigris) introduced new patterns in Sunni–Shi'i relations. In Gertrude's views, the problems emerged from the young officials' tendency to judge tribesmen by their 'party affiliation' (as she defined pro- or anti-British positions), overlooking traditional rivalries and agrarian quarrels that emerged again as inequities at the root of renewed local conflicts.[9] The tribes' discontent spilled over into their relations with Baghdad's representatives. Yasin al-Hashimi himself, when mutasarrif of the Muntafiq in 1922, was almost turned out by rebellious tribesmen resentful of their Sunni landlords, the Sa'duns.

But the problem between Sunnis and Shi'is was deeper than just urban versus tribal divisions. Already in her *Review of the Administration of Mesopotamia*, Gertrude Bell exposed her views on the basic disagreements between both parts and the way it was reflected in Iraq's politics at the time. In Iraq, the centuries old rift between the Sunnis and the Shi'is regarding the selection of the right successor to the Prophet Muhammad,[10] had been also influenced by the presence of Persian mujtahids in the sacred towns of Najaf, Karbala and Kazimiya.

In 1920 Sunni–Shi'i collaboration to rid Iraq of the British seemed to have laid the basis for a long-term alliance. 'If they worked together, Shi'is and Sunnis would find their own salvation', Gertrude had explained then to her father.[11] She had had visions about what the future could hold for the country, she added. In fact, the basic agreement on three of the five principles (*'usul al-din*) of Shi'ism – *tawhid* (belief in divine unity), *nubuwwa* (prophecy), *ma'ad* (resurrection), *imama* (guidance), and *'adl* (divine justice) – could bolster the similarities between Sunni and Shi'i and downplay the differences, that stemmed mainly from religious disagreements on the function attributed to the Imam 'Ali as the intermediary between human beings and God.

Gertrude was also curious about the *hadith* (the account of the Prophet Muhammad's deeds as told by his companions), and the way it evolved among Sunnis and Shi'is. The *hadith al-nabawi* (the hadith of the Prophet followed by the Sunnis) and the *hadith al-'alawi* or *khabar* (news transmitted through 'Ali and followed by the Shi'is) had 'form, style and perfume of their own'.[12] Familiar with the richness of the language in two classical Shi'i works: *Nahj al-Balagha* (The Path of Eloquence), attributed to 'Ali himself, and *Al Sahifa al-Sajjadiyya* (The Scroll of al Sajjad, the Fourth Imam) Gertrude certainly saw them, a great linguist that she was, as parallel to the *Sahihan*, (The Authentics), the two most authoritative collections of Sunni hadiths.

From her visits to Najaf and Karbala, Gertrude had become acquainted with the rituals, festivals, and religious practices of Iraq's Shi'is, observing how these had contributed to the development of the two communities. She had witnessed how the *qraya* (readings of the Qur'an), the lamentations of grief, and the eulogies delivered in Karbala and Najaf differed from the recitations in the Sunni centres of Baghdad and Mosul. She had seen how the themes of *shahada* (martyrdom), *gha'iba* (occultation), and *jihad* (combat), corresponding to daily motifs of Iraq's Shi'i tribesmen, still shaped their approach to life. She had observed the rituals of physical drama contained in Shi'i Muharram festivities and noticed how they contrasted with the Sunni approach to the tenth of Muharram, the date of Husayn's martyrdom, as a beneficent day of prayer and blessings.

There were variations on these differences, however, for Shi'ism in Iraq was interwoven with Arab tribal motifs, which contrasted with the Shi'i rituals in Persia. The *ta'ziya* (condolence), the passion play performed during Muharram festivities, acquired a different dimension when performed in Iraq. Called *shabih* (allegory), because the actors dressed themselves up as personifications of the charaters they were playing, the play had taken on in Iraq more popular features than the ta'ziya in Persia. Performed on stages erected in public places, 'hung in black or ornamented with squares covered with large awnings', the play evoked different reactions from the public. In the passages emulating hunger and thirst of the martyrs the spectators pressed their foreheads onto a *muhr* or *turba*, a cake of baked clay representing the earth from Karbala.[13] The Arab roots of Shi'ism in Iraq would become the basis for the Shi'is' collaboration with the Sunnis, adding a new dimension to what the British had tried to emphasise at first. The British had been misled by their romantic vision of the East, on one hand, and by immediate interests in the country on the other.

However, Gertrude's initial romantic vision of the tribes as the backbone of the country evolved, over the years, into a more pragmatic approach, leading her to see the Sunni elites as the country's natural leaders. Some of the problems she still remembered, dated from the first attempts to include the Shi'is in the council and the reluctance of the naqib to accept them. The debates that followed on the need for Shi'i leaders to adopt Iraqi nationality before being allowed to take official positions in the administration, added a new aspect to the question. But it wasn't just a matter of appointing Shi'is to fifty per cent of the governmental posts, a claim that was often heard as the main reason for Shi'i discontent and further tension between the communities, but, as Gertrude noted in 1922, the need to help Shi'i tribal leaders to overcome their apprehension of the mujtahids' possible reaction if they accepted these appointments. She realised then the pressure of the mujtahids on the tribal leaders not to collaborate with secular authorities.[14] The fatwas issued by Shi'i mujtahids (Mahdi al-Khalisi, 'Abd al-Hasan

Isfahani and Muhammad Husayn al-Naʿini) were a sign of protest against the 1923 elections, and a reaction against a sovereign that hadn't been appointed by the ulama,[15] pushing the king then to deport them to Persia. Nonetheless the creation, in December 1923, of the Supreme Shariʿa Diwan, a body representing the unity of the two Muslim communities, was, in Gertrude's view, a step in the right direction. The nationalist press campaign against the debate on 'majorities and minorities',[16] which created opportunities for Britain's interference in Iraqi politics, was disputed by Britain's attack on the newspapers. But the ongoing clashes between the Shiʿi mujtahids and the Iraqi police during the holy month of Muharram[17] seemed to place the whole debate in a different perspective.

Despite the political disagreements, it was in the Shiʿi countryside that Gertrude found refuge from Baghdad's ordeals. The vast expanses of land running from the gardens south of Baghdad, 'where the brown leaves falling from the fruit trees [contrasted] with the green barley springing between the palms', to the marshes, where the *mashufs* (canoes) returned at sunset to reed houses built upon water, were inhabited by Shiʿis. 'From Qurna to Nasiriyya, marshes' rice swamps, palm groves and desert [were] occupied by some fifty distinct tribes of different origins, all of whom had at one time formed part of the Muntafiq League, under the once powerful Hijaz family of the Saʿdun',[18] Gertrude had described in her *Review*, giving the impression of an immutable and mystic countryside.

But this part of the country was also changing. The main themes of debate referred now to the extension of modern education to the Shiʿi provinces[19] and the clashes between the Shiʿi ministers of education and Satiʿ al-Husri, the department's director general. Gertrude was well acquainted with the different aspects of the debate, as Lionel Smith updated her weekly on the latest events. As adviser to the Ministry of Education, Lionel Smith still tried to stick to Britain's main policy lines. He wanted to expand elementary education to the provinces and create a network of technical institutions and a training school for teachers that reflected, in his view, the country's real needs and possibilities. He was, however, attacked by the nationalists who still insisted on the need to get secondary schools and universities that would prepare Iraq's future political and administrative cadres.[20]

In July 1924, Lionel Smith presented a letter of resignation, 'one of many he would submit in the years to come', after a clash he had had with Satiʿ al-Husri on how to adapt the curriculum to the particular needs of the Shiʿi rural population and how to allow the Kurds to teach in Kurdish without infringing on the state's sovereignty. He was trying to resolve this while at the same time trying to exercise greater control over the system itself: 'To have a shadow of control without the substance is useless', he explained to Gertrude, underestimating the reactions of the nationalists to such an attempt.

The issue was very sensitive, as it entailed much more than a simple debate on how to build a better educational system, Gertrude understood it well. It was with great personal satisfaction, therefore that she witnessed the laying of the foundations of the Aal al-Bayt University and the opening of its Divinity School in spring 1924. The campus was located in a charming spot, she reported then, 'growing under palms and nabk trees, thick evergreen trees, and the road running through the middle [leading] to the great dome of your imagination'.[21] Crossing through lines of British officials, Iraqi notables and boy scouts, King Faysal walked down the aisle formed by the palm trees. 'It was memorable, for after His Majesty had laid the stone, Sayyid Muhammad, the Naqib's son, read a prayer in the name of His Majesty King Faysal, son of His Majesty King Husayn ibn 'Ali, Amir al-Mu'minin and Khalifat al-Muslimin'.

The fact that Shi'is did not oppose the reading of King Husayn's name as caliph during the laying of the first brick for the Aal al-Bayt University turned, in Gertrude's eyes, the whole event into 'a wonderful experience'. 'We had awakened and become a nation', she commented later, as Aal al-Bayt opened Iraq's road to modernity.

PART III

DEPARTURES

CHAPTER 10

'Dust . . .'

In the spring of 1925, Gertrude and Ken drove to the desert to see the new Iraqi artillery forces 'firing star shells under the instruction of Colonel Iltyd Clayton'. 'Almost blinded by dust' by a sudden desert storm, they got back to Baghdad. The heavy wind was so hot that people could not even sleep outdoors, as was the custom in nights of *hamsin*. Gertrude couldn't sleep indoors either. It was a weather that could not be described, she explained, only experienced. The next day, a dust storm enveloped the whole country 'like a yellow London fog'. Gertrude hurried to the Museum of Antiquities, where she was now spending most of her time. One of her aides was restoring Ur antiquities in plaster 'with such ineptitude that the stone petals quite disappeared'. Falling into 'one of the worst passions I've ever been in', Gertrude had to explain her tempestuous mood. It wasn't just the damage to the artefacts, but 'the heaviness, the dust, the feeling of hopelessness in the face of nature's authority'. Dust storms whirled during the spring, enveloping the antiquities with a 'yellow grey film of fine sand'.[1]

On hot days Gertrude got up early to leave for the office before seven. She drove to work in the summer. She would ride her horse only in early spring and autumn. She returned home from the museum at two and rested for a few hours. The heat was so heavy that no sound was heard. Lying on a big sofa under a fan, she read novels or papers she had brought from the office. The windows were shut, to keep the room's coolness. Gertrude allowed her mind to wander and seek refuge in visions of distant, limpid waters. Then, suddenly, the calm waters would turn stormy, and Gertrude could hear voices – men preparing to land, protected by the darkness of night.

These imaginary scenes of that day in Gallipoli would bring back old memories. These visions, of Dick's landing at Sidd al-Bahr, were becoming more frequent as the years went by. Whenever it occurred, Gertrude rushed to the garden for relief. Among the apricot trees, the little gazelle followed her like a shadow. Memories were all she had left. Exhausted by the weather, weak and pale, Gertrude was 'mithl-a-rish', like a feather, as one of her Arab friends once described her, her wavy auburn hair now white and thin. Gertrude would sit in the garden for hours, the gazelle gently leaning against her knees. At dusk, when the garden's yellowish colours turned pink and red, she would return to the house for a light dinner, and then sit down to write letters. If she felt a breeze through the window, she would take a blanket and lie on the roof, trying to fall asleep, counting the stars.

Sometimes she swam by herself in the river, resting on the bank opposite the palace. Ken was still in England, and Lionel was too busy with the debate over higher education to join her. The river waters flowed silently, the calm interrupted only by the *mu'azin's* call for the sunset prayers. 'The dusty air hung heavily until a sudden southern wind stirred the motionless picture, raising the ashes of an extinguished campfire, filling the air with scents of roasted fish.' Once the king appeared on the veranda, and Gertrude curtsied in her wet bathing suit. Not as graceful as in the past, she well knew. The king responded with a smile and retired silently to his chambers.

Faysal had changed. His smile was sadder than ever. Queen Hazayma's arrival from Mecca had not made him any less lonely in Baghdad, for a barrier of silence stood between them. Gertrude never learned the reason. The queen was charming. Her delicate, sensitive face reflected her roots in one of the Hashemite branches: 'Not particularly pretty but looking so well-bred', Gertrude had remarked, in one of her earlier letters.[2] The queen looked smart in a gown that had been modelled on one of Gertrude's own dresses. A long string of pearls and a splendid aquamarine pendant enhanced the gown's brown colour. The two young princesses, as delicate and shy as the queen, were attempting to adjust to their new environment. The king felt more relaxed in their company than in the queen's presence, while trying to make them sense the ways of a Western-style court. How different their lives were in Baghdad compared with their placid existence in Mecca, where women and eunuchs had surrounded them, Gertrude noted in a letter home. In Baghdad they were forced to play an unfamiliar role and dared not even speak in Faysal's presence. Little Prince Ghazi, however, amused himself and played around. Gertrude supervised the education of the heir of the throne and would send him, some years later, to the best schools and academies in England.

'It is not a good plan for a widow to marry the nephew of her first husband', Florence wrote in her answer to one of Gertrude's letters, commenting on the circumstances, as she understood them, which framed the relationship between the king and queen. 'Even in a cooked state, a wild goose seems to stand for dreams and plans and projects', Florence wrote then.[3] Gertrude particularly resented Florence's snobbish and presumptuous remarks, but felt she was too far away to explain the situation properly, to convey the sense that the king was, in spite of everything, growing in the people's estimation. The royal family was gaining legitimacy along with him.

The queen would eventually get used to the country's customs. Gertrude helped her organise her first reception for Arab and English women. This task had its challenges, for the English 'wives', as Gertrude called them, condescendingly, spoke no Arabic, and few of the Arab ladies spoke English. Gertrude would have to mediate between the two groups and try to find common subjects of interest. But the women lived in two different worlds making it difficult to find similarities, or create a basis for understanding. Women were not any less attuned to the problems of their own societies than men, a fact that Gertrude had taken into account when trying to bridge gaps. But the women were prone to feelings of jealousy and rivalry as they tried to anchor their identities on their liaisons with men. Once, Gertrude intercepted the queen's oblique glance in the direction of Mme Safwat, the chamberlain's wife, whom the queen had barred from returning to the palace. The queen was fighting for supremacy in her territory, and the king would have to comply. Times were changing, Gertrude realised, affecting personal and collective destinies alike.

At the end of July 1925, Gertrude returned to England for a visit to her family. First, she drove to Haifa to board the train to Alexandria; from there she embarked on a cruise ship to Venice. In the taxi that took her from Victoria Station to Sloane Street, where she would find King Faysal, Sir Percy Cox, and Valentine Chirol invited for dinner, she left behind her black umbrella with its crooked bamboo handle, trimmed with a silver band engraved with the initials GLB. It had been a present from Ken, brought to her after a visit to England.

Ken was also in London at that time, but he had not been invited to the dinner party at the Bells' house. Tension had developed between him and Gertrude, caused in part by Gertrude's expectation that their relationship would grow closer than mere friendship. Further shadows were cast over their liaison by the gossip circulating in London circles about the 'real' causes for Ken's divorce. Lisa, who had heard it from Lady Bonin Bowen, Cornwallis' mother-in-law, had reported one version of it to Florence. 'What an extraordinary hazard that you should come to the knowledge of it all from another quarter', Florence wrote to Lisa, asking for permission to tell Gertrude the story 'as you have heard it'. Gertrude had given her own version of the affair to Florence, but 'I think very little of what she has told me', Florence told Lisa, 'my interest only aroused by her interest in the matter'. She added, with a hint of irony, 'Would you, Cornwallis or not, feel inclined to dine with me?'[4] trying to persuade Lisa to visit in the summer and be her 'salvation' during Gertrude's stay at Rounton.

Rounton was no longer the same. The tension bred by the economic crisis spilled over into the Bells' familiar life. As the coal strike continued far beyond anyone's expectations, Hugh and Florence wondered whether to change their lifestyle and move permanently to Mount Grace, where they usually spent part of the summer. Florence liked to write in the silent rooms of the seventeenth-century manor house built from the stones of a demolished priory, but to abandon Rounton meant openly admitting their financial difficulties.

Upon her arrival at Rounton, Gertrude felt the tension and the silence. Even Lisa seemed distant this time. Lisa still grieved for William Archer, feeling that a large part of her life had been swept away with his death. The epithet on the wreath she had sent to the funeral: 'From Hedda and Hilda, grateful memories', alluded to the Ibsen plays that had brought them together, in an anonymous homage to the circumstances under which their friendship had grown.

Lisa found some consolation in her talks with Florence, who had shared William and Lisa's admiration for Ibsen and knew of their feelings for each other. Florence, in turn, confided to Lisa her difficulties in resuming a creative life after years spent raising a family. It was only to Lisa that she could talk about Sir Hugh's aloofness during the last two years. 'Himself', as she called Sir Hugh in her letters to Lisa, had grown strange and distant, and apparently indifferent to her need to devote herself entirely to her writing.[5]

Gertrude's moods and manners became even more difficult to tolerate, Florence reported, 'Gertrude proved once again to be impossible'.[6] Gertrude's depression, which many attributed to the events in Iraq had, in fact, deeper roots, Florence explained. She would again refer to Gertrude's loneliness and inability to rebuild her life, ignoring the emotional dissonance inside the family itself. Although the endless deliberations of the League of

Nations' commission on Mosul's annexation to Iraq had deeply affected all of those whose destinies were in a way or another connected with the events. Gertrude was more concerned with the future of her relationship with Ken at that particular moment, on which hinged her decision either to remain in Iraq or to return to England permanently.

What she would do in England was an unsolved question, one of many she wanted to discuss with Lisa. On Lisa's night-table, she noticed the dates and dried figs she had sent some weeks earlier from Baghdad and, at their side, E. M. Forster's *A Passage to India* and Lowell Thomas' *With Lawrence in Arabia*. The romantic idea of the British Empire still inspired people, Gertrude perceived, perhaps less convinced then of the worthiness of the adventure. Not many words were exchanged in her first encounter with Lisa this time, nor in the walk they took later in the afternoon. A cloud of sadness enveloped both women as they slowly walked along the promenade that had been witness to much laughter in the past. 'It is rather terrible', Lisa commented, watching Gertrude's struggle to control her tears. 'What will become of us?'[7] The whole affair seemed like a bad performance: actors playing real people playing characters on the stage. Gertrude, supposedly free as the wind, was in fact chained and bound by unavoidable expectations, making it difficult for Lisa to get closer and share with her the intimacy that usually brings women together.

At the dinner table, Gertrude sat with a gaze of 'white fixed despair until she burst into tears'. But even in her misery, she kept her distance, as if not totally convinced of her family's unconditional acceptance of her private pain. 'God save us',[8] Lisa wrote, having not only Gertrude's, but her own fate in mind. She wasn't so sure that they would know how to cope with the reversal of fortunes and the changing times. All those feelings also pervaded Florence's writings and the poems, written in French, perhaps to keep them private.

> *Esperance qui m'accompagnes*
> *Par vallons et par montagnes*
> *Esperance qui guide mes pas*
> *Marchons toujours – n'arrivons pas.*[9]

> Hope that keeps me company
> Through valleys, over mountains
> Hope that sets my pace
> Never to reach – the final phase.

Only the visit of Lionel Smith, who had come to Northumberland to see his father, the former master of Balliol College, A. L. Smith, brought

Gertrude back to her senses for a while. Revived by the echoes of events in Iraq, Gertrude talked freely about Ken and their encounter in London before she came back to Rounton. She had invited Ken's parents to the dinner at Sloane Street with King Faysal and Lloyd George to add a note of familiarity to the occasion. It was only the day after that she and Ken had had an opportunity to see each other alone and talk things over: 'It was all easier than before . . . Somehow I felt as if we had set out a real basis of friendship. I can't [help] hoping that as far as I am concerned, the fire has burnt out',[10] Gertrude confessed to Molly then.

'Not yet over it', she could now say to Lisa during their long walks in the woods surrounding the mansion. But Lionel's cheerful presence dissipated some of the tension, allowing the members of the family to return, even if momentarily, to their normal activities. Florence had just finished writing a new play, *Angela* (1926), that was greeted by the family with enthusiasm, even by the depressed Gertrude. Florence had clearly come a long way when she expressed in her play the conviction that the ideal mate for the 'new woman' should be her match, 'not her master or slave'. Lisa encouraged Florence to engage Sybil Thorndike, the well-known actress, to play the principal part if the play were to be staged in London. Lisa, for her part, had just finished writing a new novel, entitled *Fear*, a story of a well-kept secret.

The cooperation and support Florence and Lisa enjoyed on a literary level did not reflect the strain that clouded their friendship with stifled resentment. The subjects they could not bring themselves to discuss openly prevented them from becoming closer. Lisa's appreciation of the Bells' open-hearted hospitality did not prevent her from asking some questions about Sir Hugh. 'Is this the man I thought I knew?', reads an entry in her diaries at an earlier stage in their friendship.[11] In effect much of the facade of self-control and restraint Sir Hugh maintained in public crumbled in the face of Lisa's perceptiveness. Lisa, more than others, could read between the lines, distinguish between his different expressions and the required mannerisms. She, more than others, knew about ambiguities, double-edged games, and the complementary effect of strength and weakness. She was well above the false prudishness and affectation so common in their social milieu. To Lisa, Sir Hugh could reveal his thoughts and worries and display the vulnerability he could not show to Florence. He could talk to her more openly about the Cornwallis affair and reveal the thoughts and worries that assailed him on sleepless nights, when the burdens of his industrial empire seemed even more pressing. How would all this end? he asked Lisa. What would be Gertrude's future, and how and where would she find some peace of mind?[12]

Personally involved with Gertrude's political activities, Sir Hugh Bell often found himself actively defending Iraq's cause in London's official circles. In his view, Iraq's future and Gertrude's destiny were so intertwined that he felt responsible for the former as a function of the latter. In the last few months, he had found himself promoting Iraq's designs on Mosul, explaining to government authorities the importance of Gertrude's unofficial opinions, those she could share only with her family in confidential letters.[13] Without Mosul, Iraq's 'granary', the country's fate was uncertain and possibly Gertrude's mission void, he feared. Knowing Gertrude, Sir Hugh did not believe she was serious about coming back home and going into local politics, 'beginning at the bottom', as she once claimed. He also knew she would be unwilling to live in London, given the memories she still worked diligently to avoid. Where would she go and what would she do? he asked Lisa.

Sir Hugh's talks with Lisa spilled over into other subjects that could not be shared so easily with Florence. He understood Lisa's special relationship with Octavia and accepted it without judgement. Both Florence and Gertrude rarely mentioned Octavia, each for her own reasons. Gertrude was too entangled in her own problems, while Florence's feelings were expressed obliquely by the fact that Octavia was rarely included on the guest lists at the Bells' family gatherings and other events.

Still opposed to the idea of women's rights, Florence dealt with the friendship between Lisa and Octavia by avoiding the subject altogether. Gertrude sometimes agreed to discuss the main issues in the women's rights debate, reacting, as was her way, with outbursts of anger. 'I burnt the book!', Gertrude replied to Lisa's question about Marie Stopes' *Married Love*. 'I understood her . . . she has [a] right to read it and, as the world is constituted, right to burn it', Lisa wrote in her diary after Gertrude's explosive reaction to Stopes' views on contraception and the rights of women over their bodies.[14] Gertrude's overreactions proved, perhaps, her deep fears for all that was related to her own femininity.

Gertrude stayed in England when the summer was over. She had missed the misty weather, the drizzle, and the long walks in Northumberland woods. She wanted to smell the autumn, to touch the falling leaves, and to see Mount Grace's walls coloured red with ivy climbing up the old stones. She had missed autumn's browns and greys and the yellow crocuses 'fearing to bud', as she once described it.

But by the end of September, Gertrude had grown impatient. She could not remain in England while the League of Nations still debated Mosul's fate. 'I couldn't [stay away]', she explained to Molly later. 'For I am one of the few "old ones", and if I had stayed away, the Arabs could have taken it as a sign that the British government had changed its policy'.[15]

But after returning to Baghdad, she realised that the atmosphere had calmed considerably. 'I begin to think I need not have come back; it would have gone quite well without me'.[16] This sense of being unneeded made Gertrude wonder where she really belonged. In her distress, she reached out to Florence:

> I do so love to think that you liked me to come into the library in the mornings, even though I was interrupting you horribly . . . I feel as if I had never known you before, not in all these years . . . but whatever it was, I feel certain that I have never loved you so much, however much I have loved you, and I am so thankful that we were together last summer and that we both have the sense of its having been a wonderful experience.[17]

As if not quite sure of Florence's approval, Gertrude added: 'So it was, wasn't it, darling?' As no record remains of Florence's response, it is impossible to know whether they were finally able to pull down the barriers between them, liberated by age and experience from the tensions that had plagued them in the past. In her rather distant way Florence seemed to ignore the sometimes forced complicity with which Gertrude tried to bridge the barriers between them. It was this lack of warmth, of unconditional love that contributed most of all to Gertrude's constant quest for new sources of emotional loyalty. But then again, it would be a futile attempt to consider this relationship as the only reason for her restrained behaviour.

In spite of the change in her official position in Iraq, which removed her from mainstream politics, leaving her only officially responsible for the Department of Antiquities, Gertrude tried to remain involved in affairs of state. The major topic of interest to her now was the political unrest in Syria, the rebellion in the Jabal Druze, and the growing disenchantment with France's colonial policy. In a secret memorandum, she elaborated the reasons for the impasse created by France's mismanagement of Syrian affairs. Faysal had even been invited to the Quai d'Orsay and was asked by Berthelot, 'the man who had insulted him in Paris in 1919', how to remedy the situation. 'I think of him telling His Majesty that we had interpreted our mandate rightly and the French theirs wrongly . . . Oh life, oh time!'.[18]

On a few occasions, she still displayed a sense of righteousness when defending Britain's intentions even if she wasn't so sure of it any more.

Indeed, times had changed, and she now viewed the union of Iraq and Syria under Faysal's crown as a possible resolution to the impasse. Sir Henry Dobbs, well-entrenched in his position of high commissioner, dismissed her views in his correspondence with London. It was 'déjà vu', Gertrude mused, to find herself once again more attuned to the views of her Arab nationalist friends than to those of her British superiors.

A young Syrian nationalist, George Antonius, 'a Christian of the Lebanon who speaks wonderfully good English', employed in the department of education in Palestine, paid Gertrude a visit on November 1925 to explain the terms of what became later known as the Bahra Agreement. Antonius had come to Baghdad with Sir Gilbert Clayton on a mission to negotiate the demarcation of the frontier between Iraq and the territory occupied by Ibn Sa'ud. Their objective was to persuade Ibn Sa'ud to agree to the notion of a fixed frontier, to abstain from inciting the tribes that now belonged to Iraq (the 'Anaza and part of the Shammar) to cross the border in both directions, and to prevent a 'sheikh living in one country from displaying the flag of the other', Gertrude explained in a monthly intelligence report.[19] Ibn Sa'ud, however, claimed that the tribes considered the frontier an artificial barrier, raised by colonialists to deny them access to wells and other sources they had relied on to water their flocks for generations. The frontier should move with the tribes in their perennial migration between the 'desert and the sown', as Gertrude explained Ibn Sa'ud's position. In her view, the nomad tribesmen should be persuaded to respect frontiers and accept the laws of the country they lived in. But all these problems related to modern notions of citizenship and territory were yet to be solved.

Other problems looming large in Gertrude's personal life seemed irresolvable. She felt lonely and discouraged. 'The truth is that I care for Ken as much as I can', she finally confessed to Molly.[20] They had had a terribly bitter talk after she came back to Baghdad, and she was avoiding seeing him alone. But now she had decided 'to show him what he really knows: that he can't do without me . . . I have given him inspiration after inspiration'.[21] Ken would have to realise what the next nine years would be like if she decided to leave. 'But if he let me, I can make him very happy and he can make me happier than I could be any other way'.

Gertrude wanted to stay in Baghdad and 'do nothing but archaeology' and work at the museum, without being involved in daily politics. 'But I can't, except on my own terms with him'. If he would not accept her terms, she would go home and 'try to make something of life with the family . . . a half life'. She loved her family, she explained to Molly, 'but the other sort of love is so overwhelming. It is that of the lover and the mother and the sister all combined'. She would not write again until she had something definite to tell, 'whether I go or whether I stay you will know what either means'.[22] While Gertrude was fighting her misery and loneliness, Emir Zayd came to see her to ask her to look after his brother, King Faysal. 'You know how lonely the King is ... he is the loneliest man in the world',[23] Zayd explained, asking Gertrude not to leave the king or the country, as there were many challenges ahead that only she could address.

On several occasions, Faysal still felt like an outsider, accepted by neither traditional local leaders nor extreme nationalists, Zayd explained. Yasin al-Hashimi, still acting as the main opposition leader, was conducting a campaign against King Faysal and was now calling for an immediate revision of the 1922 treaty and its annexes.

The nationalists' campaign for total independence could not be resolved on these terms, Gertrude still believed. She was referring again to the League of Nations' commission and their recommendations regarding the extension of the British mandate for twenty-five years, if Mosul was annexed to Iraq. The one was linked to the other, Gertrude explained. But this wasn't an easy pill to swallow for either Iraqi nationalists or British taxpayers. The only escape would be to recommend Iraq for membership in the League of Nations and have the treaty revised after four years. 'You need not be alarmed about the 25-years mandate', Gertrude explained again to her parents. 'If we go on as fast as we've gone for the last two years, Iraq will be a member of the League before five or six years have passed and our direct responsibility will have ceased'.[24]

After the League accepted the recommendations of the Mosul commission, the amended treaty had to be ratified by the assembly. 'Bernard [Bourdillon] and Ken have done an excellent work; to "cook" a treaty through in sixteen days is perhaps a record', Gertrude commented. She admired 'Ken's skills in guiding the institutions of the Arabs', Gertrude wrote in a rather patronising tone from her hospital bed where she was taken after catching pneumonia.[25] Although feeling like a 'broken reed',[26] Gertrude was still instrumental in persuading the acting high commissioner, Bernard Bourdillon, to invite Yasin al-Hashimi to the state dinner celebrating the passage of the 1926 treaty.[27]

Official dinners were political occasions. One year earlier, all the invited Iraqi officials appeared bareheaded in protest against the Turkish headdress. 'I wonder if they now intend to abandon it altogether',[28] Gertrude commented at the time. Mustafa Kemal's decree on the compulsory use of the 'Pahlavi hat', an effort to signal Turkey's more western orientation, had been received with mixed feelings in both Iraq and Turkey, provoking waves of unrest. Peasants in north-east Anatolia did not want to wear hats, whereas villagers in Mosul, persuaded perhaps by Turkish soldiers, started wearing 'all that could pass as a hat, baskets or anything that looked least like a fez or a turban . . . but the minds underneath were surging in revolt'. Gertrude reported in January 1926, while believing that 'Mustafa Kemal was going too far and too fast'.[29]

European hat or not, the unrest in Anatolia appeared to have contributed to Turkey's compliance with the League of Nations' decision to transfer Mosul to Iraq, in spite of the comments of Jawad Pasha, the famous Turkish general. 'This Iraq is going to be to us another Bulgaria', he said, referring to Bulgaria's irredentist nationalist campaigns and their role in inciting the Balkan wars.[30] Having coped with Bulgaria's nationalism in the past, Turkey was now dealing with Iraq's new nationalist messages and their repercussions in the Middle East.

*   *   *

The Middle East was in turmoil, however. The situation in Syria was alarming. 'Syria is heading straight to chaos. Muslims against Christians and *tout le bataclan*. When you have forced an Oriental country into complete confusion, it takes time and knowledge to pull it straight. The French have neither',[31] Gertrude commented in January 1926. Syrian nationalists wanted to send a commission to the League of Nations to declare their independence from France. 'The French want them to be a bad imitation of several French departments. What I ask is what you asked A. T. Wilson in April 1920. Can the mandatory power afford to hold onto direct control? We found we couldn't', Gertrude wrote.[32] The Syrians would agree neither to France's terms of armistice nor to its proposals for the Constituent Assembly elections.

Ibn Sa'ud had proclaimed himself King of the Hijaz at the end of January. The old King Husayn from Mecca and Medina had abdicated, and Ibn Sa'ud had entered into Jedda on the departure of King 'Ali, King Husayn's son. Was this Britain's reward to King Husayn for having helped the Allies during the war? Gertrude certainly wondered. Was King Husayn going to foot the bill and pay the price of Britain's adventure in Arabia? But even King Husayn's sons, now rulers of the fragmented parts of the once promised Arab state, preferred to see him out of the way. A possible source of embarrassment for Faysal and 'Abdallah in their relations with Britain, the once legendary Sharif of Mecca would finish his days in Cyprus. Even Ken, who had followed Husayn and Faysal so closely, now seemed to keep his distance from the old man. Another reversal of fortunes in the Middle East had transferred Islam's holy places from the hands of the Hashemites to those of the Wahhabis.

In February 1926 Gertrude received a telegram from her parents notifying her that her brother Hugo had passed away. A brilliant but rather weak young man, Hugo apparently had died from a bronchial attack a few weeks after arriving in England with his wife, Frances, and their children on a visit from Australia, where the couple had settled. His death struck the Bells like a thunderbolt. Hugo was the youngest of Florence and Hugh's children and the one with whom Florence could communicate on a special level – music. The most musically talented of the Bells' children, Hugo had had the sensitivity and the frailty of a child whose spirit was stronger than his body. This sensitivity, wrongly attributed to nervousness, had been the reason for his admittance to a clinic where he would be treated for more than a month, 'cut from the outside environment', a fashionable therapy at the time. Hugo's frailty and acute perceptiveness had made him more attuned to 'things of [the] spirit', so it did not surprise the Bells when he announced his desire to join a religious order.

In many respects, Hugo was Gertrude's opposite. A rational atheist, Gertrude sometimes lost her temper when confronted with Hugo's deep religious feelings. Their divergent views on the essence of religion, divine inspiration, and comparative faiths, carefully restrained during family gatherings, emerged in full flower during their trip together to India. Memories of the durbar invaded Gertrude again when the sad news reached her in Baghdad. 'It comes stabbing like a sharp sword', she wrote to her parents, feeling as though she had been through it twice: once some days earlier when she had a dream that he was dead, and now when her parents' telegram confirmed her foreboding.

The shock of Hugo's sudden death forced Gertrude to reconnect with her own perceptions of life itself. 'He had a complete life. A perfect marriage and the joy of his children and then, at last, his seeing you again', Gertrude comforted her parents while asking, 'I wonder if we should be happier too if we thought we were all to meet again'. But she found it hard to believe in such a possibility: 'Even when I lost what was dearest to me . . . [I understood that] the spirit without the body would be as strange as the body without a spirit. One feels the lovely mind behind, but what one knows are the little gestures, the sweet smile, the expression of the mind'. But it was not worth wondering 'why one can't believe in the unbelievable; one just can't'.[33]

Death itself did not mean a thing to Gertrude, but the nothingness that came after, the idea of death as a mere event, underpinned her belief in life as the true value. But the value of life depended on the guidelines that defined it, she certainly believed. It was not worth living in chains, when mind or body was denied basic freedom, she once said. And the courage to take one's own life, to dedicate the last moment to the mere thought of freedom, or to the desire for it was the highest act that one could aspire to. Apparently, Gertrude considered death not as the epitome of life, but as a prosaic event that could not affect Britain's continuous moment in the East.

The blow of Hugo's death was hardest on Florence. After his burial at the Rounton churchyard, Florence wrote to Lisa, 'Nothing could have made Hugo pervade my life more than he has done ever and always. We were looking forward to playing the piano together, picking up the threads . . . None of this will happen . . . Voila! . . . That's all'.[34] Would the former master of the college still remember Hugo and his music? Florence asked Lisa, her thoughts wandering to the happy times when Hugo was at Eton. Her thoughts were reflected in Rossini's *Stabat Mater* or the Chopin she used to play with Hugo. 'That Chopin thing you've made me know [Nocturne 12, op. 37, no. 2] . . . Think of me when you play it next, for I will be with you when I hear it', Lisa consoled Florence.[35]

Hugo's wife took up residence in the north of London, near her relatives the Furses and the Ponsonbys, Sir Hugh informed Lisa. He felt close to Frances, as her grief had taken him back with painful vividness 'to my own suffering 55 years ago, to the agonies I underwent', when his own wife died suddenly. In a letter he sent to Lisa from Sloane Street, Sir Hugh mentioned that he was 'overwhelmed with work and the other thing you will know of'.[36] Even to Lisa, Sir Hugh could not openly admit how the tensions caused by the coal crisis and Hugo's death were affecting his family life. She knew, however, that strain and loneliness could strike even happy marriages such as his and Florence's.

CHAPTER 11

'Flood . . .'

'In the spring of 1926 even the skies wept, dropping endless tears. Incessant rains seemed to announce the end of times', Gertrude reported home. 'A south wind blew, rapidly melting the snow in the mountains. The runoff mounted high in the rivers, spilling over their banks'. All traffic had stopped – the bridges were empty. Sandbags were left on the river's banks to prevent the waters from uprooting shrubs and plants. 'The waters sounded as if they were pushing into the foundations under our feet', Gertrude wrote. 'Palm trees lay naked on the banks, their roots exposed to the fury of the unflinching waters'.[1]

After the dyke broke on the left bank of the Tigris, 'the waters rushed over the eastern desert, . . . menacing to flood the lower parts of Baghdad', she wrote. The king's family had to be moved from the palace while the king himself was away in Khaniqin. Gertrude rode along the river to see thousands of peasants, struggling to stop the waters by reinforcing the banks with reed mats and sandbags. The waters, continuously infiltrating the banks' lower layers, would not be held back. Baghdad was flooded. Near the abandoned railway station drenched bags of rice and flour lay on the floor, like heavy corpses adding to the sense of men's lost battle against unknown forces.[2]

The road to Ba'quba was closed. Only a temporary road across the desert saved Baghdad from its isolation. Iltyd Clayton's house was inundated. Open houses had their soaked ruined furniture exposed and unclaimed. Luxury houses near the banks broke down, parts of them falling into the Tigris. Gertrude rode into the desert. The desert was a lake '. . . This is a country of extremes, it's either dying of thirst, or dying of being drowned . . . The endlessly changing moods of the river and the deluge', as told in the epic of Gilgamesh, Gertrude realised as she mailed home her 'flood letter'.[3]

'A flood will sweep over the cult-centres for seven days and seven nights and destroy mankind', read a poem found among Ashurbanipal's tablets assembled at the British Museum by George Smith, a young Assyriologist. Gertrude remembered how the story of the discovery and deciphering had made the news. She was then a very young girl but had heard the story repeated again and again, people fascinated by the similarity of the Gilgamesh epic to the account of the Great Flood in the Bible: Gilgamesh, King of 'Uruk, in search for the secret of immortality, found an old man, Ut-napishtim, who told him the story of the flood as he had survived it. 'The Gods sat bowed, weeping, while the wind blew, the rivers submerged the lands and the earth shrouded in darkness'.[4] On the seventh day, when the great thunderstorm finally abated, Ut-napishtim opened a window in the vessel in which he had gathered his family, servants and animals. He looked upon the sea '. . . all was silence and mankind had turned to clay'.[5]

The myth of the deluge, transmitted from ancient Mesopotamia through the Hebrews to future generations, was just a hint of the kinds of artefacts that might be found by digging in Iraq's soil, Gertrude knew well. Layer after layer would reveal the secrets of a buried past like closed books opening to the light of day. Their secrets would reveal things as they were, and hint at things to come: a continuity of history, fables, myths. The unveiled past would prove that the northern steppes and the southern marshes were local variants of the great Mesopotamian plain. It would also prove Iraq's unity, one comprised of contrasts. It would connect the tells dotted around cornfields and gardens along the rivers to those clustered around the springs and wells of the valleys, and extend to the settlements of the Ma'dan, 'among the shallow lakes and narrow waterways' of the marshes. Past would explain present, and the history of the Land, as Mesopotamia was once called, would emerge again.

The earth's exposed secrets would set Iraq's roots in the depth of time and inspire its future. For now it was a history shaped by a yet unknown past. To find the threads, to prove that things had not changed much was a real challenge. The sun, the moon, the winds and the rivers dictating the rhythm of life and death, shepherds driving their flocks in the hills, Bedouins wandering between wells in the desert, and peasants finding refuge from daily labour in their mud huts on the plains were timeless images. The unearthed past would reveal the commonalties, the uniformity, the power of social codes, of religious beliefs, of myths and legends that sprang from the rivers and spread through the orchards of palm trees to the Upper Tigris, and from there to Syria. The unveiled past would prove that the commonalties between Ur, 'Uruk, Nippur, Babylon, and Nineveh were stronger than the political rivalries separating the self-ruling cities, with their own kings and gods.

But all this had yet to be proven. Archaeology in Iraq was still in its infancy. The excavations at Tell al-Muqayyar, conducted by Charles Leonard Woolley, were still in their preliminary stages. Was Tell al-Muqayyar the legendary Ur of the Chaldeans, where Terah took his son Abraham, as written in the Bible? And was Birs Nimrud the supposed Tower of Babel? But it was 'Uruk, the Biblical Erech, now Warqa, that gave Iraq its name. When her tents 'were pitched on the slopes of a mound, [Gertrude] watched the Bedouins watering their flocks. Then the moon rose over Assyria and found it, I expect, little changed' as she had already commented in one of her first visits to the area.[6] She would now dedicate her life to find the connections, to attach Iraq back to its glorious past.

Tell al-Muqayyar, the Mount of Pitch – so-called by the Bedouins, who pitched their tents at its base, seeking protection from sand storms, seemed no more than a massive red hillock rising from a monotonous yellowish-grey emptiness. Endless stretches of sand extended from the improvised railway station where Woolley and his British-American team unloaded their digging equipment. Discovered in 1854 by J. G. Taylor, the British consul in Basra, and rediscovered by Campbell Thompson of the intelligence staff of the British army during the war, Tell al-Muqayyar was named Ur when the first archaeological findings – engraved cylinders – revealed its past. Ur Namu, King of Ur, so the story goes, had built a tower on the top of the ziggurat, the four-tiered truncated pyramid, filled to its top with the debris and waste of past generations. To verify whether Tell al-Muqayyar was really the Ur mentioned in the Bible, Woolley's team excavated the surrounding sites for ruins of settlements. Woolley could not have guessed, as the excavation began, that his search for Ur would lead to the discovery of a civilisation older than the one that had flourished in ancient Egypt.

As the excavations proceeded, the world discovered the Sumerians, the bearers of a culture that left an indelible imprint on the city-states of ancient Mesopotamia. Who were the Sumerians? Where had they come from? Were there features common to the Sumerians in the south and the Akkadians in central Mesopotamia? These were the questions still asked at the time. 'Black-headed' Sumerians living in the region spoke a language similar to old Turkish, but their origins were unknown. It would be difficult to answer these questions by examining the artefacts being exposed to the light of day for the first time in centuries. The physical features of the people depicted on them were typical of the Mediterranean basin, but this was just a hint. It would take Woolley years of research to identify the similarities and differences between the Sumerians and the Akkadians and to understand how the loose bonds created by the need to control irrigation would eventually result in the submission of the Sumerians to the Akkadians in 2400 BC and in the unification of Mesopotamia under the kings of 'Sumeria and Akkadia'. It would take Woolley years of digging and archaeological research to reconstruct the texts that mentioned the kings and the cities that existed before the Great Flood, suggesting the possibility that the Sumerians occupied Mesopotamia before the deluge.[7] It would also take some time for Woolley to reaffirm the idea that the flood (whose expected geological markers harmonised so well with local conditions in Lower Mesopotamia) was more than a myth. In Woolley's mind, it was a historic fact, and he was determined to prove it.

But these were still hypotheses. The debates during the first stages of Woolley's work at Ur were no different in substance from those that had marked his work at Carchemish twelve years earlier. What was the right method to dig a tell? Cut a long trench on the side of the mound from summit to base, to see how one civilisation built upon the ruins of another? Or divide the site into squares, dig each square to a certain level, than dig deeper in the middle to discover the site's layered past? Gertrude thought the second method was better, but she was careful not to guess. An admirer of the meticulous German methodology, she tried to convince her British colleagues of the importance of Dr Jordan's archaeological mission. Her debates with Woolley centred not only on the technical aspects of the excavations at Ur, but also on their accuracy and on their predominance over other work taking place simultaneously at other archaeological sites.

The excavations at Nimrud, a site explored in the 1850s by Austen Henry Layard, the famous archaeologist, were again attracting attention. The findings at Ashurbanipal's palace – the colossal winged bull-men, the winged lions, the stone slabs covered with inscriptions telling about the Assyrian civilisation (953–605 BC) with its autocratic monarchy and centralised bureaucracy – remained a subject as important and interesting in archaeological circles as did Ur.

Other archaeological missions were working at the Sumerian city of 'Uruk, at 'Ubaid, Nineveh and Kish. They boasted walls of hieroglyphs and depicted corn and barley fields, market gardens, fruit orchards, and date groves irrigated over hundreds of years by the waters of Mesopotamia's rivers, canals and ditches. These sites had been visited for centuries by

228 • A QUEST IN THE MIDDLE EAST

Bedouins and their flocks seeking relief from the desolation of the desert in the cool grass sprouting after the winter rains.

Continuity would also be found through an archaeological study of Babylon, the capital of Babylonia on the Euphrates. For Gertrude, the wonders of Babylon were modern Iraq's patrimony: the Hanging Gardens, as described by Herodotus; the palaces, temples, gates and city walls; and the imposing monuments paved with blue-glazed bricks or embellished with cuneiform inscriptions telling of the achievements of Babylon's kings or of Hammurabi's Code of Laws.

But closest to Gertrude's heart was Ukhaydir (the 'little green place', as Bedouins called it), a site located near Wadi al-'Ubaid, on the west bank of the Tigris, south-west of Karbala, whose origins had not yet been definitively established. Although belonging to a group of fortress-palaces found in the western frontiers of the Syrian Desert, Ukhaydir was the only building of the type discovered on the desert's eastern side. Built by the Lakhmides (the pre-Islamic Arab dynasty that ruled over southern Iraq at the time of the Sassanides), Ukhaydir's importance lay in its upper floor, rebuilt by the Abbasids in the eighth century AD. Gertrude had visited the palace in March 1909 and again in 1911 and had devoted her book *Ukhaidir*, published in 1914, to describing it: Ukhaydir, with its parabolic arches and squat piers, its vaults of brick, and its central court marked by an *iwan*, a large vault open at the front, accentuated by a rectangular frame, the *pishtaq*; with its central gateways, audience chambers and four *bayts*, each with its own courtyard.[8] It was to Ukhaydir, 'the finest monument of such an earlier date', that Gertrude took Faysal to bring him closer to the history of his new country.

Although a typical 'Gertrudesque' tirade, it spoke volumes about how she envisaged her role as a bearer of knowledge who was entitled to pass it on to the inhabitants of the land. She didn't seem to realise though, that it wasn't her story that she was, patronisingly, adopting as hers to tell. Although her mischievousness and ironic observations had already caused her trouble in the past and would be further misunderstood by humourless readers, she couldn't avoid seeing it that way. For after all, with all her more advanced views and clever insights, she still believed in the validity of the imperial enterprise.

During her first years in Iraq, Gertrude had been busy with daily politics, but now she became totally absorbed in her work at the museum. She promised her parents that, once she had put 'this gigantic task and other things into enough order', she would return to England. Although she would have preferred to take a leave of absence and then return to Iraq, she could no longer afford such a move. Money had become a problem, and applying to the British government for a permanent post somewhere other than Iraq did not appeal to her. But these were not the only reasons. 'You have to understand', she explained to her family, 'how difficult it is to leave everything that I have been doing here and find myself rather loose in the world'.[9]

In the meantime, work was all there was. Gertrude catalogued the Ur and Kush findings pouring in from the sites: the little statues of the Inanna, the goddess of love and war; the weapons, the jewels, the wooden boxes, a frog stand found at Kush; and a little statue of a gazelle, dating from 2,600 BC, found at Ur. She was trying to arrange a mandate to supervise the excavations at Babylon, started by the Germans, and the excavations at Warqa, the ancient Erech, the biggest mound in Iraq, where a team from Yale was currently 'nibbling'.

Mornings were very busy, but she complained that afternoons 'hang heavy in my hands'. No longer involved in the high commissioner's office, Gertrude was waiting for Bernard Bourdillon to come back from leave to officially take over her post of oriental secretary. Politics had now given way to resolving administrative questions, matters 'in which I am not concerned and in which I am not good', she explained.[10] Her only involvement in politics was advising Lionel Smith in the formulation of a university curriculum. Sir Henry Dobbs wanted to create a faculty of fine arts, whereas Lionel's idea was to combine languages and literature with history and political economy in a three-year course. The question under debate was whether Iraqi students would gain any advantages from the study of Victor Hugo, Balzac, de Maupassant and Zola. Gertrude was convinced that Iraq's educational system should focus mainly on the Arab language and heritage and that the educational institutions should prepare students technically and administratively to take over governing functions from the British.[11]

By the spring of 1926 Gertrude was almost ready to return to England. In England, the coal strike continued, affecting Sir Hugh Bell personally, and he expressed his opinions about the government's proposals that could lead to 'unworkable compromises'.[12] King George V had proclaimed a state of emergency, given the unprecedented effects of the continuous strike on the economy. Sir Hugh, in his remarks to a meeting at the Bishop Auckland Rotary Club in June 1926, launched a dramatic appeal to the workers to get back to work. 'I am being ruined',[13] he announced. 'It doesn't matter to the country whether I live in a palace or a hovel, but what does matter is whether my investments and the industry in which I am engaged, prosper'. He suggested that all it involved was to submit themselves to difficult conditions 'in the hope that progress will again be made'.[14] Gertrude wrote to her father some days later: 'That was a very vigorous speech of yours at Bishop Auckland', wondering what his reaction would be to the newly proposed legislation. Gertrude believed that the new '7 hours bill' would enable Sir Hugh to make his own proposal to the workers, in the hope that they would get back to work on 'the owners' terms'. That would not be so easily accomplished, however. The Bells' financial problems were even more serious than Sir Hugh had acknowledged. The Bells' collection of Charles Dickens' books and letters had to be sold to finance the staging of a pageant written and directed by Florence. Gertrude consoled her father. 'On the whole, . . . the pageant is worth more than the satisfaction of knowing that [the papers] were reposing on shelves and in drawers. Still I am sure that it cost mother a pang to part with them'.[15]

This was to be one of Gertrude's last letters to her parents from abroad. It was not very eloquent or tuned to how she was feeling. She could more easily open her heart to Molly, and to her she confessed, 'I don't think I have any other strong feelings left, but just a great gratitude for the kindness and friendship which had been shown me here . . . I carry on with the present and try to feel as happy as I can'.[16]

*   *   *

Dusk shaded the white walls of Gertrude's living room. Above the fireplace hung the Bell family's coat of arms with their motto: 'Perseverance'. How many times had this word been invoked? On the table, Florence's letter from Mount Grace, sent in March when things still seemed hopeful, spoke of their move there on a soft, fragrant evening 'flooded with misty moonlight' and the sight of the garden's arches and vines. Gertrude sat quietly holding the letter, dreaming in silence. Solitude had grown on her, become a habit, an acquired and cherished taste. She now lived through memories. Memories of morning light in the desert, of round hills eroded by the winds, of black tents stretching on white dunes far beyond the horizon. She could feel the dust, the desert winds, the thin air in early mornings, the gravity of silent nights. She could follow her thoughts in the 'paths they had taken',[17] follow them through the desert and to Baghdad, compare the contrasts, the drought and the flood. In her thoughts she went back to

Petra, where sunset pink and purple tones coloured the sandy walls of the Nabataean kings' palace. From there to Wadi Musa, the valley of Moses, where the Prophet drew water from the rocks. And then north, to the road leading to Damascus, leaving Petra behind.

In her imagination, Gertrude followed the caravans of camels and donkeys through the forest of shady palms along the Euphrates. And from there to Ur, to Kush, to Ukhaydir – to the buried past 'with roots in the darkness of time and blossoms at the dawn of history'. She remembered the waning and waxing of armies, the ruins that for centuries 'watched the procession of victors and the plight of the vanquished over plains which now lie vacant round their slowly perishing bulk'.[18] She followed the waterways winding through the reeds, pouring into the shallow lakes where water buffalo and wild birds lived side by side. And the Tigris' muddy waters spread through marshes and swamps, while the Euphrates slowly rolled down the canals, reviving the sown fields. And she remembered the rivulets rolling down the slopes of the Damavend, their waters shimmering softly at sunset, Hafiz's poetry read aloud, and the Book of Kings – *Shahname* – with its stories of courage and earthly ambitions.

She travelled back to the Persia of her beginnings. To the mountains, the ruins and the splendours of Farsi Sassanian palaces and the capital city of Ctesiphon. And again to Hafiz's poems:

> Thus said the Poet: 'When Death comes to you,
> All ye whose life-sand through the hour-glass slips,
> He lays two fingers on your ears, and two
> Upon your eyes he lays, one on your lips,
> Whispering: "Silence!"'
> . . . .
>
> The songs thou sangest still all men may hear.
> Songs of dead laughter, songs of love once hot,
> Songs of a cup flushed rose-red with wine,
> Songs of a rose whose beauty is forgot.[19]

Gertrude remembered that spring day in Konya, when the frozen waters dissolved into tiny streams running down the slopes. When the passage of the seasons corresponded to the states of the body, and the *khalwa* (the period of retirement) announced the *jilwa* (God's first manifestations), pointing to the renewal of spiritual life. The dervishes then emerged from their black cloaks and whirled their way to God. Al-Rumi's song of the reed echoed then in the *zikr* at Mawlana's tomb:[20] 'Oh, hear the reed flute, how it does complain and how it tells of separation's pain'.

Gertrude searched for answers by assembling contrasts, the hidden connections that could unravel the tangled motifs of her life. She searched for the little girl of her early years by wandering in thoughts with Molly on Redcar's High Street, shopping for Christmas presents, 'stockings, sweets, and four cards for a penny'.[21] Or in her earlier memories of the 'reception' she and Maurice had prepared for Florence upon her arrival at Redbarns after marrying their father. Hats had been thrown then on the newcomer before she and Maurice hurried to hide in the closets. She searched for better answers in the woman who once broke bonds with the world when entering the 'path that stretches across the rounded shoulder of the earth'. And she remembered Basra as seen from the sea.

'One can't do much more than sit and record if one is of my sex', Gertrude had written in December 1916, hoping unconsciously 'that people would judge events as you think they ought to be judged'. But the recording of events was 'very small change for doing things'. And she had wanted to 'do things', to find the threads, to discover affinities lost somewhere in the past. Was this what had brought her to the East? Her affinity with those who preceded her? With H. C. Rawlinson, the pioneer who had deciphered the cuneiform? With Lady Hester Stanhope, who had visited Palmira, defying both the Emir Bashir in Lebanon and Muhammad Ali in Egypt? Or was it the image of Lady Stanhope's solitary life and death that had appealed to her the most? Or even her affinity with Isabella Bird and her journeys through Persia and Kurdistan that had linked her with the predicament of women in the East?[22] They were all accounts of travellers searching in the certitudes of the East for a response to the uncertainties of the West.

This was valid too, Gertrude still believed. The need to revive traditions. To recreate, even in thoughts, Babylon and its Hanging Gardens, where the roots of the trees were also embedded in upper terraces, not in the earth. But many questions remained. Was the Tower of Babel Babylon's ziggurat? And were the temples, palaces, walls and gates in the East the remains of the rulers' desire to compete with gods and to make up for their own failures?[23]

*   *   *

Gertrude looked at it now from a different perspective. Perhaps the monuments silhouetted against Mesopotamia's skies had more value in people's hearts than self-evident truths dawning in their minds. And in the end, geography would tell as much as history. There were the same densely populated areas separated by vast stretching, empty, spaces; the same fables and traditions shaping men's beliefs in modern times as they have done in the past. This was the East she knew: an intertwining of opposites, of contrasts, tightly woven into her own life. 'I have known the terrific contrast between light and darkness', she once wrote to Elsa, 'when I lost everything at once'. She had tried to find answers in the failed and futile attempts to work out destinies, realising at the end the fleetingness of her adventure and the weariness of the struggle itself. 'Now I know it, I know it . . . but with what anguish I have bought learning'.

Tonight, she thought, she could not stand eyes and faces, 'nor men, nor talk, nor anything', as she had once written to Dick. She wanted the ghosts, and the solitude protecting her from the world – to cherish the idea that, at the end, there was solitude again. Nothing would happen, nor would the silence be broken or the solitude interrupted. There were only Dick's ever-present words and the memories 'of a day as long as a lifetime and a lifetime as short as a day'. The memories of that night at Rounton.

Dick's words followed her wherever she went. To London, distant and empty as if she were a stranger. 'Don't come', he had warned her. But she had taken the chance, believing that they would be able to brush away conventions. Yet she knew how chained they were to their own destinies. 'Someday . . . perhaps in a whisper, in a kiss, I will tell you', he had promised. But when the precious moments were slipping away, they sat silent. And what was the omen? 'The days of absence and the bitter nights of separation, all are at an end: where is the influence of the star that blights my hope? The omen answers: at the end!'[24]

The end seemed near when his last letter crossed with hers. 'My dear, my dear', Gertrude asked then,

> what can I write to you in this room? . . . Your safe return and then . . . that's all I think of . . . for against any other alternatives I have made myself secure. Do you remember that my doctor made me take morphium with me on the last journey? I never used it, and now I have sent for it from home, and have it always by me . . . Two full tubes . . . enough to cut a thread even as strong as mine . . . That's why I feel safe, whatever happens . . . When my heart quakes, I remember the morphium tubes and know there is a way out, smooth and easy as sleep . . . to wake where? . . .[25]

*　　*　　*

On a Sunday afternoon in July 1926, sitting at the window of the Forum Club at Grosvenor Place, Lisa watched dozens of women march by for a demonstration in Hyde Park. Having partially won the suffrage battle after the war, women were now fighting for their place in society. A law according suffrage to women over thirty with property was passed into law in 1918. In 1923, a new law facilitated the procedures for divorce, yet divorce remained an unacceptable solution to marital problems. Much had yet to be changed, Lisa thought, and the outcome of this movement would, in the end, testify to the character of British society itself. Lisa knew that the next generations of women would take over, and she herself might not see the battle through to its conclusion. She had taken her part in this struggle, but now she wanted some time out, time to concentrate on her life and the lives of her close friends. And yet, her heart was heavy with apprehension.

'We are going to get a sign', Lisa wrote then in her diary without specifying exactly what she meant. In fact, she did not really know herself what to expect. Was it to be a good omen, a sign auguring the successful end of women's long journey? She expected a sign, predicting the liberation of men and women from false pretensions, unwritten rules, and worn out conventions. Women would then be able to play an equal role in society without having to pay for it with their own life experiences, Lisa still believed. While hoping that this state of affairs would come to pass, Lisa was also aware of the problems that women might encounter in the process. Sometimes, the struggle to attain this freedom seemed to be a contest lost from the outset, lost in the trap set by pre-established dependencies, lost in the heavier price paid by women in the still uneven exchange between the sexes. Doughty-Wylie had not been afraid of Gertrude's strength, Lisa realised, but by the freedom of a relationship that had outgrown him. At the end, it was the strength of weakness that won over strength itself. And yet she felt that something would happen. Would it augur well?

Elsa's letter arrived at the Forum Club the next day. Gertrude had died in her sleep on Saturday night. The rumour was that she had taken an overdose of sleeping pills, but Elsa wondered if it wasn't the morphine that Gertrude had referred to during their walk in Rounton's woods, the morphine vials from Ha'il that Elsa sent her to Boulogne as the war was raging. Was this the 'sign' that Lisa referred to in her writings? It was, she well knew, the inevitable end to an overly ambitious adventure. Immersed in sadness, Lisa called Elsa and wired a telegram to Sir Hugh. She could not yet face Florence.

Some days later, Florence broke the silence herself: 'Autumn suddenly fell on us . . . Hugo's dead and now there is Gertrude . . . it isn't real. Or, if so, autumn then true'. An autumn letter in mid-August, Lisa thought to her-self. Dead leaves wafting in a bright and flawless sky, evanescent lives intertwined in vanishing historic moments. It was the last act telling of the impossible attempt to shape the desert sands and shape lives in the process.

Was this the bad omen, the '*absit omen*' of Gertrude's letters? The merging in death of contrasting lives like Hugo's and Gertrude's, lives shaped by contradictions in Britain, and the controversies of the empire? It was, Lisa then realised, the end of the 'might have beens', as Gertrude used to say.

*   *   *

Gertrude Bell was buried in Baghdad on Monday evening, 12 July 1926. Iraq's unbearable heat forcing the hurried last arrangements. Her colleagues, the British officers that were part of her adventure, presided over the brief ceremony. A large crowd followed the 'Khatun's' coffin to Baghdad's British cemetery, where British officers and soldiers killed in the line of duty had been buried during and after the war.

The king himself, it was told, watched the procession from his private balcony at the palace, his face half concealed by his white *agal*. Among the wreaths of flowers surrounding Gertrude Bell's fresh grave lay a basket of fruit, the one usually brought to her in the early morning by Hajji Naji, her Shi'i friend of Karrada.

Sadness fell on the Bells after Gertrude's and Hugo's deaths and the different ways they grieved for each of their children confirmed Lisa's impression that parents unconsciously admire most the children they never quite succeeded in taming. Gertrude had rebelled by fleeing, by deliberately defying, from as far away as possible, the inconsistencies and contradictions in British society. Hugo, for his part, had found a refuge in God, a spiritual shelter from the rationalism and enlightened liberalism that could not touch the secret grooves of his sensitive soul. The merging in death of two divergent, yet complementary lives, left Lisa wondering about their significance at that particular moment in Britain's history. More intrigued by the outcome of Gertrude's life, Lisa wondered whether Gertrude, as a woman, perceived Britain's presence in the East differently from the way her male colleagues did. Gertrude had certainly lived it more intensely, and her personal experiences had changed her own perception of the mission in which she had been so deeply involved.

Could the 'bad omen' be found in Gertrude's death? Lisa wondered. She remembered vividly the many talks they had had about life and death. 'I am not afraid of this other crossing', Gertrude once said referring also to moments that epitomise whole lives. Moments, as Dick used to say, in which one sits at the top of a mountain 'watching others climb their way through thorny paths . . . ' 'We then become that moment', when the end of life is a choice, an outcome of the feeling that one's presence is not needed as before, when one can gaze into the dark without fear and leave this world with a shrug of indifference. 'When Death comes to you . . . Whispering: Silence'.[26]

Gertrude's fascination with death was not news to Lisa. She still remembered one of Florence's letters written during the war, after Gertrude had learned of Dick's death. Gertrude's reaction was to go to Serbia, 'with the primary object of catching some illness of which she would die'. Only the appointment of Lord Robert Cecil, the head of her office in Boulogne, to a post in the coalition government formed in the summer of 1915, prevented Gertrude from realising her plans. She felt that she could not leave her place in Boulogne with the bureau's mission unaccomplished. But as time passed, she discovered that she had been unable 'to build up anything out of the ruins left to her'. This was, Florence explained then, the reason for 'Gertrude's resentment toward everything'.[27] But this was not all, Lisa realised, remembering fragments of a letter that Gertrude had sent to her father some years later. 'The older one grows, the more one lives in other people's lives . . . well, I have got plenty of lives to live in'. It had been best that way, Gertrude concluded. She did not regret her destiny. 'I have got the love and confidence of a whole nation'. It might not have been the intimate happiness that she had missed in her personal life, but her work in Iraq was, again, a 'wonderful and absorbing thing . . . almost too absorbing, perhaps'.[28]

*   *   *

As soon as news of Gertrude's death became public, condolences began to arrive at the Bells' Sloane Street residence. Among the messages of grief was King George's letter, deeply regretting the passing of the empire's 'gifted daughter . . . who had won by her intellectual powers, force of character and personal courage'.[29] Reports, articles, lectures and letters written by David G. Hogarth, Vita Sackville-West, Leo Amery, A. T. Wilson, Sir Percy Cox and Sir Henry Dobbs, among others, poured into Sloane Street. A service was held at St Margaret's Church in Westminster, in spite of the fact that the ceremony was far from being consonant with 'what we all know of Gertrude's views', Florence commented.[30]

T. E. Lawrence sent a personal message to Elsa from his hotel on Baker Street: 'She stood out as the one person who, thinking clearly, saw the true ultimate goal of our work with the Arabs and, daunted by nothing, worked unsparing of herself toward it'. Lawrence continued by telling Elsa about a gathering of comrades two days after Gertrude's death: 'Her name came up and there was a heavy feeling, and silence for nearly five minutes . . . We had lost a friend, Iraq had lost a guide and the country had lost, possibly has found, a beacon'.[31] An open secret was Lawrence's admission that he owed Gertrude Bell much of the information that had helped him to rally the Arab tribes in the desert at a critical moment in the war.[32]

Newspapers in Iraq and Britain printed eulogies on Iraq's uncrowned queen, 'Guide, Philosopher and Friend of the Arabs', echoing much of what had been written about her when her *Review on the Administration of Mesopotamia* was published in December 1920.[33] Gertrude Bell had accomplished a 'man's work', reported the press, 'the work of an army of men . . . when not unearthing those secrets of older civilisations which the desert had swallowed up'.[34] She had told the story of 'the cities destroyed in [the] course of history and those that had received all the embellishment that powerful monarchs could bestow, only to be abandoned and finally left in ruins'.[35] She had been able to build a bridge between the British and Iraqi people with a 'faith preventing her from being discouraged by what she sometimes found in her way'.[36] But, above all, Gertrude had been able to seize the moment and turn it to the advantage of the mission she believed in.

Lisa delivered a radio broadcast some months later punctuated by her deep, perceptive descriptions of Gertrude Bell, her life, and her deeds. Gertrude had the 'habit of success', Lisa said, and 'if she hadn't had the call to be and do so many other things, she would have been a poet the world would remember'.[37] Great sorrows had come to her over the years, but she had remained a 'passionate lover of life'. In spite of her losses, Lisa stressed, 'Gertrude Bell has won, . . . *comme celui qui vince* [like the one who conquers]',[38] ending her address with Gertrude's chosen quotation from Dante.

'I love to think of you alone in that strange veiled room, telling the story of Gertrude to the universe . . . the red light summoning your thousands of hearers and then suddenly disappearing. And you being alone again. That seems to me a fitting setting for what is still to me a supernatural achievement', Florence wrote to Lisa after the broadcast.[39] Gertrude Bell had lived to tell the story, Lisa answered, by means of the memories, the reports, and mainly the letters she sent weekly to her family, letters that told more about the atmosphere of Iraq's early days than all the official documents put together. Florence assembled, reread, classified, and prepared Gertrude's letters for publication. Much was left out – '2,400 pages of letters to be reduced to 400 pages'[40] – largely for reasons of security or discretion. Florence's zeal in the selection task was confirmed by the fact that censors at the Foreign Office and the Colonial Office (Sir John Shuckburg, Sir Henry Dobbs, and Sir Percy Cox) removed no more than three pages from Florence's proposed final draft. Sir John made his cuts using a pen with an unmistakable thick black line. 'It is a rather poor compliment to me to suppose that I was going to take any risks in giving the world things that had better not be given', Florence wrote to Lisa. She admitted that she might not have chosen the most interesting letters for publication, but she would bring the censored letters to London 'for your interest and for your [subject] of conversation when I am not present!'.[41] Florence had also left out Gertrude's 'adverse criticisms and Good Lord! what numbers of them'.[42]

The final product was a collection of letters that evoked memories of times past and images deeply rooted in the minds of those who had shared in the adventure. Letters that blended substance with flashes of humour and wit, letters that painted history not just as a thought but as a wish. Letters that spoke of the invention of a modern nation on the very spot once inhabited by civilisations which the desert had swallowed up.

'Progress in Iraq', Gertrude once explained, 'is a blend of old and new, of change' and replacement 'of the *mashuf* for the petrodriven launch and of the creaking irrigation lift for a petrol pump'.[43] 'In the future', she continued, 'taxis for hire would run in the larger towns, and the shaykhs of the desert would come to Baghdad to conduct their affairs with the government in cars laden with followers, tribesmen, and then return to their black tents in spring pasturages.[44]

> What a country this is! I fear I shall spend the rest of my life travelling in it. Race after race, one on the top of the other, the whole land strewn with the mighty relics of them. We in Europe are accustomed to think that civilisation is an advancing flood that has gone steadily forward since the beginning of time. I believe we are wrong. It is a tide that ebbs and flows, reaches a high water mark and turns back again. Do you think that from age to age it rises higher than before? I wonder – and I doubt . . . But it is a fine world for those who are on the top of the wave'.[45]

This letter, sent by Gertrude from Konya to her cousin Florence Lascelles in April 1905, was included in Florence Bell's selection. As work on the collection advanced, publishers lined up at Sloane Street to take a look at the proofs, and Ernest Benn finally acquired the rights to publish the letters. Florence was exultant. But, thrilled as she was by Gertrude's letter of 1921 and her role as 'the King maker', Florence also wondered, in a comment so typical of her, whether the revelation of how Faysal had been pulled and pushed onto the throne by Gertrude Bell and Sir Percy Cox would make Faysal 'more likely to tumble off it now'.[46] Other omissions were necessary as well, Florence realised. 'For you only', she wrote Lisa, 'I will remark that the less said of a very high-handed action taken with regard to Sayyid Talib for instance or indeed (I say *this* in a whisper) to some of the engineering of the plebiscite, the better!'[47] Hugh Bell and Valentine Chirol pressed Florence to be less rigid with some references to Gertrude's personal life, 'otherwise people might think of her as being a sort of hard, brilliant creature without the softer womanly things'.[48] However, Gertrude's relationship with Dick Doughty-Wylie would not even be hinted at, nor would her stillborn affair with Ken Cornwallis. Only her juvenile affair with Henry Cadogan was considered socially acceptable enough to underscore the 'womanly' aspects of her personality.

Gertrude Bell's original correspondence in its entirety was sent to Armstrong College, to be opened in fifteen or thirty years. Meantime, the first extracts of the book of letters, finished in a 'frenzy of haste', were to be published on the front page of *The Times* on 12 August 1927, during King Faysal's visit to England.

'Lisa! King Feisal is coming for dinner! It's rather agitating', Florence wrote some weeks later. 'I am not accustomed to having kings of the East to dine or indeed of the West for that matter. King Feisal, his Prime Minister Ja'far, his aide of camp, the Dobbses, the Coxes, the Richmonds',[49] were driven to the Bells' residence by the impact of the publication of Gertrude Bell's letters. It was a posthumous homage, a token of admiration and an expression of sadness for her absence, for she was sorely missed. In addition to the dinner, a number of ceremonies to launch the book had been planned, among them an opening at the Winter Gardens in the presence of Lord Grey. When the uproar caused by the book quietened down, a letter from India, dated 4 November 1927, reached Sir Hugh Bell's office at Middlesbrough.

Dear Sir Hugh,
You will probably remember me as Lawrence, my wartime name: we met several times in Cairo when Gertrude and myself were playing a tune on the political conference there in 1921. I've just been reading the 'Letters' which

Mrs. Bernard Shaw sent me, and they have been so great a pleasure to me that I felt I must write to you and thank you for letting them come out.

Lawrence had left politics and enlisted in the RAF, serving near Karachi, India:

I think she was very happy in her death, for her political work – one of the biggest things a woman has ever had to do – was as finished as mine . . . [But] it seems such a very doubtful benefit – a government – to give a people who have long done without.

Her letters are exactly herself – eager, interested, always excited about her company and the day's events. She kept an everlasting freshness or, at least, however tired she was, she could always get up enough interest to match that of anyone who came to see her . . . leap out in the direction of any expert who had engaged her mind.

Her loss must be nearly unbearable but I am so grateful to you for giving so much of her personality to the world.[50]

The letter was signed, 'T. E. Shaw', Lawrence's newly adopted identity.

Lawrence's letter was as pleasant a surprise as his new name was puzzling. Rumours about his ongoing friendship with Mrs Charlotte Shaw were making the rounds. 'I thought the burlesque of the love affair, amusing and original', Florence commented to Lisa, mentioning some days later that Bernard Shaw himself was planning to visit.[51]

As the number of book-launching ceremonies dwindled, life at the Bells' slowed down, recovering its quiet routine. Occasionally, they would attend public functions like the annual trooping of the colours by the first battalion of Green Howards in the British army in commemoration of the regiment's victorious battles. In his capacity as lord lieutenant of the North Riding Yorkshire Regiment, Sir Hugh Bell presided over the ceremony, attended by hundreds of Yorkshire residents. Another event that brought some colour into their drab existence was the armistice parade, which the Bells attended in the company of their grandchildren. Elsa's and Molly's children remained the focus of Florence's attention and the source of inspiration for two booklets of children's poems Florence had written recently. 'Nora is Four and Hugh is No More' was the title of one poem. Nora, among the youngest of Elsa's children, had been named after the leading character in Ibsen's *A Doll's House*, translated by Florence years earlier. Ibsen's plays remained theatrical hits, as were Bernard Shaw's. Shaw was now mentioned frequently in Florence's and Lisa's correspondence, given his stormy work relationship with Lisa. Although still very active, Lisa could not escape some considerations about her age. She mentioned death as Gertrude's way of avoiding old age,[52] to which Florence answered: 'Neither age by itself nor youth by itself is solely good', ending her letter with a quote from a poem by Victor Hugo:

> Et l'on voit de la flamme aux yeux des jeunes gens
> Mais dans l'oeil du vieillard on voit de la lumière.[53]

> One sees fire in a young man's eyes
> But in an old man's, light shines.

*   *   *

Raindrops fell on the windows of the townhouse on Sloane Street. The autumn of 1927 was almost over, and winter colours painted the sky grey. The trees and bushes in the square in front of the house were bare. A few brown leaves hung on the branches, some of which were broken by the sweeping wind.

An official carriage stopped at the entrance to the townhouse, and the coachman in livery brought down a wooden chest and knocked on the door. Gertrude Bell's belongings, shipped months earlier from Baghdad, had arrived that morning at the warehouse of the Colonial Office. Among the gowns, silk blouses, hats and boots carefully packed by Marie was Gertrude's embattled fur coat. The mud stains that had escaped Marie's attention reminded the Bells of Gertrude's account of the modern version of Gilgamesh's myth: her ankles deep in mud, she had traversed flooded Baghdad to try to save Lionel's belongings from the fury of the waters. 'To the best of comrades', read the tiny inscription in the corner of Sir Percy Cox's photograph in a silver frame. Deeper in the wooden chest was a copy of Gertrude's portrait, painted by John Sargeant and dedicated to one of her Baghdadi friends. At its side lay a silver cigarette case and an old snuff box, a present from a niece, and an umbrella with a crooked bamboo handle and a silver band marked GLB, sent some months earlier to Baghdad from the headquarters of Scotland Yard. A folder with papers was there, too – last letters, one unfinished, that she would have sent to her parents had she not died.

One of these letters described the state dinner party celebrating King Faysal's birthday. At the reception that followed the dinner, Iraq's ministers, deputies and senators appeared hatless, in European evening dress, in reaction to the 'occidental' Pahlavi hat. The shaykhs came dressed in their robes and coloured turbans. 'Wonderful diversity!',[54] Gertrude concluded in what

was to be her last homage to the country whose modern institutions she
had helped create.

*   *   *

Among Gertrude's belongings were two letters from Lord Hardinge of
Penshurst, written in 1920 and 1921 from his post at the British embassy
in Paris.

> I have not forgotten that I was really instrumental in your going to Baghdad.
> I really think that [this] was one of the best bits of business I ever did in the
> interest of H.M.G . . . What a tremendous change in your life and outlook
> was occasioned by that visit you paid me at Delhi and how wonderful it is to
> think what splendid use you have made of the opening that then presented
> itself.[55]

In the same folder were the yellowing pages of a manuscript for a book that
was never to be published. Chapter 6 of the unfinished manuscript was
entitled *Romance*:

> I have written of politics and commerce, of steamship and of locomotive
> engines, but I have not pronounced the word which is the key note of the
> 'Iraq. It is romance, wherever you may look for it, you shall find it. The great
> twin rivers, gloriously named; the huge Babylonian plains, now desert, which
> were once a garden of the world; the story stretching back into the dark
> recesses of time – they shout romance. No less insistent on the imagination
> and no less brilliantly coloured are the later chapters on the history of the
> 'Iraq. The echoing name of Alexander haunts them, the jewelled splendours
> of the Sassanian King of Kings, the clanging fame of the Muhammadan Kha-
> lifate, the tragic dissolution of the Mongol invasion and last (to English ears
> not least) the enterprise, the vigour, the courage of our seamen and mer-
> chants who forced their path through the gates of the 'Iraq and brought the
> Pax Britannica to the torrid seas of the Persian Gulf.[56]

Was this the Iraq Gertrude knew, or the Iraq she thought she knew? Gertrude demonstrated in this and in other pieces she authored how personal
passions and perceived images blended in her mind, at times preventing her
from making dispassionate judgements of men and situations. But even if
her writings seem too emotional to later readers, the witty remarks sprinkled throughout the text give it a sharpness that brings things back to
proportion, for those readers who have already caught the flavour of her
style. Endearing for some, exasperating for others, Gertrude's writings are
full of life reflecting not just her intellectual energy and eye for detail but

also a conceptual subtlety that proves, again, how futile any attempt to define her as a proponent of a single cause could be. She reminds us, time and again, that 'texts exist in contexts', and that she should be understood in the context of her time. Again, her sense of humour proves that Gertrude herself was able to see beyond the moment she was describing, by underscoring the 'grain of salt' that would make her (and us) see it all from a different perspective.

The sense of desolating uncertainty that seized her at other moments, and the feeling that she was at a loose end and lonely in an affair that was drifting to a close, spilled over from her personal life into her work, and by extension, into her vision of both worlds in which she acted. Having been launched into the adventure of reshaping the Middle East by Doughty-Wylie's death, she understood too well the outcome of the 'dreadful story of broken promises and friends abandoned'[57] that took unforeseen developments in different directions. She understood the sense of betrayal felt by her Arab friends as she understood other, more complex and no less painful, consequences of this inestimable adventure.

If asked, she might have wanted to prove Meinertzhagen wrong. Not just in relation to the Arabs' primordial role in making their own destinies, but also in the overemphasis of her role and her ability to change the Arabs' fate by simply recording events and pulling some strings when she saw it fit; not always the right strings and not always at the right moment. Or was it the fact that she wasn't entitled to pull strings at all? But she wasn't asked, and she herself disliked interviews and other types of personal promotion and unsolicited self-exposure. She would leave that to Lawrence.

Given the fact that their ways diverged in the aftermath of the Cairo Conference, it seems that Lawrence would never have admitted that the Arabs might have rebelled against the Turks without Britain's (and his own) help. Gertrude seemed to have understood it better than him. She also realised that papers (however brilliant), making the rounds of London's corridors of power could not change the reality on the ground. In the end, the Middle East would challenge not just the knowledge displayed in the papers they had both written but also the ambitions of those who had commissioned them.

Again, if asked, she might have downplayed her own ambition, perhaps because she herself did not view it that way. She might have defined her mission as a duty, a commitment, even as a privilege. The awareness that came 'after the fact', that she had fallen into the trap of Britain's unresolved adventures, made Gertrude grow even more disillusioned. Added to it was the sense that, whatever she did, she would, at the end, feel herself shut off from the world she had helped to create. All this contributed to her erratic behaviour and her increasing outbursts of bad temper. The depression that developed at the end was the mechanism that counterbalanced the sense of omnipotence with which she began her adventure.

But above all, it was the vulnerability underlying her display of the 'stiff upper lip' that makes it easier to understand her need to become 'a person', a 'transformation' that happened to her only in the East. It was not just the power to break social conventions, the prestige and authority that came with the status, but also the freedom to become herself.

Also as a sign of self-defence, she tried to differentiate herself from the 'wives' that challenged her with their femininity. That did not prevent her from connecting with women of the Middle East and from seeing them as factors of change in their own societies. This disparate approach was just one of the many contradictions that defined Gertrude's vision of the differences between West and East. In effect, in spite of the anti-suffrage position she endorsed, Gertrude found herself as 'the other voice' that tried to answer, with her life's example, other contradictions in a woman's life. The contradictions in her own life could, however, be seen as an outcome of imagined relationships and, possibly, of no less imagined missions.

A victim of her own contradictory self-image, as a link in a chain connecting her two worlds, Gertrude Bell ended up falling into the very gap she had tried to bridge.

Epilogue

In the early 1990s, Britain's National Trust organised a tour to Mount Grace, a former monastery in North Yorkshire to which Hugh and Florence Bell had retired after being forced to leave Rounton Grange following the coal-mining crisis. In the priory gardens, the tourists expected to find the herbs used to prepare Chartreuse liqueurs, the silky yellow and green elixirs prepared by Carthusian monks in the French Alps. The secret recipe had been passed down to only two monks in each generation, and one of them, so the story goes, had been transferred to Mount Grace before the monastery had become the Bells' summer residence and Florence's study. There, among the shrubs growing over the garden's abandoned pathways, visitors could find vestiges of many herbs, such as yellow gentian and wormwood which, when distilled and added to the locally prepared liqueur, created the taste, smell, and texture of the famous Chartreuse. Some of the herbs still could be found lining the garden paths or climbing among the vines elegantly festooning the ruins of the ancient monastery. The recipe itself, possibly hidden behind the stones of the abbey's vaulted hallways, was never found. It seemed to have faded like the memory of the monks, who had sipped the liqueur during northern England's long and cold winter nights.

Decades after the Bells had left Mount Grace and the old monastery was handed over to the trust, a stack of notes was found in a dark drawer in Florence's study. The hand-written notes, half eaten away by the years, meant nothing to visitors unacquainted with the Bells' personal and public heritage. They meant more, however, to those familiar with the family's saga and Gertrude Bell's special mission to the Middle East, where no liqueurs were needed to warm people's hearts and enliven their imagination.

The undated letters, addressed to Florence, seemed to have been written in a hurry, Gertrude's illegible handwriting leaving much room for imagination. Some words, however, familiar to those who knew about her adventures, could be easily spotted. These words seemed to spring out from the rather faint text. Among them the usual 'omens' and 'absit omens' refer-ring to many issues in which she had been involved during her life. There were also names of colleagues and friends that Gertrude used to mention when writing home. Lawrence and Cornwallis, whose adventures in the Middle East intertwined with hers, were alluded to frequently. One can only try to guess the themes of their conversations, had they had the oppor-tunity of meeting with Gertrude again before her death.

Gertrude's imagined conversation with Lawrence (years after their encounter in Cairo in 1921) would have been enlivened by reminiscences of the little daily pleasures and simple rituals at the archaeological sites they had both visited before starting their involvement in the politics of the area. They would have remembered the working men at Carchemish when they displaced the huge stones at the ruins, while moving to the rhythmic cry of 'Yalla', and the complicity of women chatting when preparing breakfast. Their coloured handkerchiefs wrapped around freshly baked pitas con-trasted with the earthy tones of clay jugs and jars containing milk and leben,[1] the sour curd that became Gertrude's main meal when wandering in the desert. These colours, textures, sounds, and rhythms would become part of the memories Gertrude and Lawrence would carry with them when away from the Middle East.

Had they met during the year before her death, Lawrence and Gertrude would have gossiped about people they knew in the East, some of them already gone. They would have remembered Charles Doughty and *Arabia Deserta*, the book that had inspired them in the beginning of their travelling careers, and they would have worried about their ailing friend, David Hog-arth, who had brought them to Cairo during the war and changed the trend of their lives. They would have recalled Lawrence's articles in the 1920s[2] and reconsidered the implications of his suggestions. Although refuting Wilson's plans to 'Indianise' Mesopotamia, they would still have disagreed about the measure of 'advice' that Britain should retain before control of the country's affairs was handed over to the Iraqis themselves. They would have remembered how Gertrude had helped Lawrence 'to swing the British officials'[3] to accept Faysal as Iraq's future king. And they would have relived the whispered conversations they had held in Basra in 1916.

And yet, Gertrude and Lawrence would not have totally grasped what had really brought them together. It wasn't just the need to escape from the oppressive rules of English society that had drawn them to the desert. For them, so they still wanted to believe, 'It was the sweep of open places, the

taste of wide winds, the sunlight and the hopes in which we worked, and
. . . the morning freshness of the world-to-be'.[4] Carried away by the memories of these moments, they forgot, at times, the overwhelming weight of
Britain's interests in the area, and the way in which their own agendas were
framed by it.

But they certainly remembered other personal reasons, though some of
them had dwindled with the end of the war. For Lawrence, there was his
affection for Dahum, the Bedouin boy from Carchemish, his intellectual
curiosity and personal ambition to create a British-led Commonwealth of
Nations after the war. But these 'sensations of mind', Lawrence had once
explained, could not be repeated, once he realised what had been Britain's
aims before the war.[5] For Gertrude it was perhaps her need of the 'love of a
whole [and yet single] nation', that prevented her from taking upon herself
the 'whole trusteeship' over Britain's mission in the East', as Lawrence had
done.[6] Had Gertrude's imaginary encounter with Lawrence actually taken
place, it would have served as a comparison between their parallel lives and
as a chronicle of the ideas and trends that seem today to be the very source
of the problems they tried to solve.

Other parallel lives symbolised for Gertrude either conflict or harmony.
Florence represented conflict. 'The antagonism between mothers and
daughters poisons the whole existence', Florence had written in *The Minor
Moralist*, 'if the normal severing of ties that occurs with marriage does not
occur when a daughter remains single . . .'.[7] In this single line Florence
revealed the reason for her own conflict with Gertrude. She had wanted
perhaps, to see Gertrude sever the emotional ties linking her to the family:
links that, paradoxically, grew tighter with physical distance. It was an irony
that Florence herself would be the one to edit 'The Letters', the very
embodiment of these connecting threads.

For Gertrude, however, especially at the end of her life, Elsa and Molly
represented harmony. The same was true of Lisa, despite their diverging
opinions on women's issues during less harmonious times. Gertrude's inner
conflict, caused by the discrepancies between her assigned role in society
and her impulse to defy it, therefore led to clashes with both sexes, and
attempts to compensate for her 'masculine' attitudes by concentrating on
clothes, not always very successfully.

It was easier for Gertrude to leap over cultural hurdles than over class
barriers, as her work with women in the East seemed to prove. Among
other things, the creation of a women's club in Baghdad,[8] the opening of
girls' schools, initiated by Faysal's Madrasat Banat al-Shuhada (School for

the Daughters of the Martyrs) in Damascus, and the women's movement in Jerusalem[9] were examples of a trend that was seen by Gertrude in a very positive light. Kurdish women, however, seemed to have discovered, earlier than others in the Middle East, how to manage their affairs, without totally relinquishing conventions like this report of the 1940s suggests: Wearing 'quilted coats slim at waist and jewelled huge slanting turbans and tinsel brocaded shawls . . . they sat equal in the evening gathering with their men'.[10]

Among Gertrude's other parallel lives, there was Ken Cornwallis. 'He could remain for months, hotter than other men and yet look cold and hard'. Thus Lawrence had described Cornwallis in his book.[11] To others, however, Cornwallis was 'tall, rugged, imperturbable, cast in the great pro-consular mould and manners. But he was always easy to access, simple, humorous and abounding in common sense'.[12] For Gertrude, he had been 'a tower of strength and wisdom' in the years they shared memories and vision while working together in Iraq.

Officially identified with King Faysal, to whom he had offered, with Curzon's approval, the throne of Iraq in December 1920 (an offer formalised later by Lawrence and Churchill), Cornwallis remained at Faysal's side until the king's sudden death in September 1933 in Geneva. Less then two years after Faysal's death, he was asked to leave the country. In the new regime under King Ghazi, the services of the 'elder statesman', as young and impetuous nationalists now called Cornwallis, were no longer needed.[13] In May 1935, Yasin al-Hashimi asked Cornwallis to retire. For the 'old guard', however, he would remain the exemplar of the pragmatism and efficiency that replaced the faltering romanticism of the Sir Percy Cox era.

The Order of Rafidayn awarded to him for his long service did not appease him, however. 'Sir Kinahan Cornwallis left Baghdad on 30 May somewhat disgruntled', reads a Foreign Office minute in June 1935.[14] Cornwallis' bitterness was attributed to the sense of having left his task unfinished. 'I cannot say we entirely share his gloom', Archibald Clark Kerr reported from Baghdad after Cornwallis's departure, 'hoping that Yasin al-Hashimi would be able to redress the situation created by the 1935 tribal uprising . . . If Yasin cannot do this, I do not see who the hell can'.[15]

Yasin al-Hashimi, 'the ablest man in town', was now stronger than ever, having had established a more independent attitude toward the British and the palace.[16] But it was precisely his too independent position and centralist policies that led, at the end, to his own downfall. A military coup in October 1936, led by General Baker Sidqi and Hikmat Sulayman, a pro-Turkish politician, removed Yasin from power and opened an era of direct military intervention in Iraqi politics.[17]

Cornwallis came back to Iraq as the British ambassador in April 1941 to try to convince Iraq to abandon its pro-Axis orientation. He was besieged together with other British officials and members of the British community in the embassy until British troops released them. Unwilling to clash with the Iraqi police forces Cornwallis did not interfere in order to stop the mob and the retreating rebel units in their attack on Jewish and Christians lives and properties during the Farhud on 1 June. Explaining, some years later, to his superiors at the Foreign Office the concrete implications of the political choices made in 1921, he noted how difficult Iraq was to govern, torn between the different interests of its communities. 'A complex society',[18] he concluded, underestimating the power of nationalism, when rightly defined, as a glue that could possibly bind them all together. Years later, Cornwallis still asked himself how these antagonisms could be resolved.

Iraqi politics had, in the meantime, taken a different direction. Gone were the years marked by the end of official British dominance. Those were followed by years of instability defined by reactions to the new state on the part of groups and factions that felt threatened by it or underrepresented in its institutions.[19] During these years, several attempts to better define the Shi'i–Sunni relations would emerge, reflecting Gertrude Bell's hopeful observation at the launching of Aal al-Bayt University years earlier. Cornwallis was less optimistic, however.[20]

In 1945 Sir Kinahan Cornwallis returned to England, with the Grand Cross of St Michael and St George (GCMG) he had received in 1943. Appointed chairman of the Middle East Committee at the Foreign Office, he did not believe much in a possible resumption of Arab–British relations in the Middle East. 'It is a sad commentary on all our work of the last twenty years', Cornwallis wrote to Elsa Richmond from Baghdad. 'How terribly Gertrude would have felt it',[21] he concluded. Cornwallis wrote to Elsa again in September 1945 from his London Club, the Athenaeum, asking her to be careful with the new selection of Gertrude's letters she planned to publish, which would follow the 1937 edition of her early letters.[22] Worried about their content and the possible effects of Gertrude's 'frank remarks' on some of the leading Iraqi figures who 'are still alive and are our best friends now',[23] Cornwallis asked Elsa to have them cleared by the Foreign Office. 'My wife joins me in kindest wishes', he added at the end of his letter.

Cornwallis had married Madge B. Clark of Lymington in 1937. A former headmistress of a government school for girls in Khartum, Lady Cornwallis had an 'old-fashioned concern for protocol and a sense of ambassadorial dignity'.[24]

*   *   *

Cornwallis' letter of September 1945 reached the Richmonds' residence in Cambridge some weeks later. As the sunlight faded and a gloomy autumn afternoon closed in, the living room darkened with invading shadows. Children's voices interrupted Elsa's thoughts, bringing her back to her usually controlled countenance. Elsa's husband, still known as Admiral Herbert Richmond, in spite of his now academic activities, was away on one of his missions. Sitting by herself near the fire, Elsa certainly remembered a line in one of Gertrude's letters to Molly:

> We all work out our destiny differently . . . We all wonder what sort of destiny the other is aiming at . . . and find no answer.[25]

Now, the answers to 'all questions and all wonderings' had come, Elsa certainly realised, to which Florence would have added, 'and for Gertrude, so peacefully'.[26]

Afterword

Reading about Gertrude Bell's life may pique the reader's curiosity about the tangible evidence that remains of her incomparable adventure. Indeed, the letters, diaries, maps, and folk objects she brought home from the East have been assembled in England at the Robinson Library, University of Newcastle. Hundreds of photographs, carefully organised in folders, lie in wooden drawers in the archives of the Department of Archaeology. But as revealing as these artefacts may be of the story of Gertrude Bell and Iraq's creation, they can only partly detail the truth, for they lack the context, the environment, the feel, and the romance of both the settings and the buildings where the memories of these events remain. What remnants of the lives once lived can still be found in these places? The curious reader might journey to these places to fill in the missing pieces of the story, to sense where the events and circumstances of Gertrude Bell's life unfolded like the lives of those tangential to her great adventure.

We begin our journey, reaching Newcastle-upon-Tyne by train after leaving London's King's Cross station in the morning. We cross over the Tyne after a couple of hours and perceive Newcastle's shadowy profile in the skyline. Houses and monuments frame the broad main street of a city wrapped by the green woodlands. Near the University of Newcastle, we discover the 'neo-gothic' tower built by Sir Hugh Bell, a reminder of the Bell family's position in town. Turning left, we enter the gated campus of the university and see Armstrong Hall and the red brick buildings that together comprise Armstrong College, the first institution to receive Gertrude Bell's letters. A view of the Northumbrian coast leaves us once again impressed with the majesty of Bamburgh and Dustumburgh castles and with Hadrian's Wall still controlling the surrounding hills and empty shores.[1]

A visit to Northallerton helps us visualise Rounton Grange before its destruction by fire in the 1950s. Red Barns, at Redcar, the Bells' former residence, which still remains, is a red brick manor that serves today as a hotel. By visiting its terrace and gardens, we can reconstruct the scenes of family life so well described in the Bell family's letters. In our mind's eye, the long table is set for dinner, with the hot dishes placed on the sideboard. We can almost hear Lisa, in her deep theatrical voice, telling Brer Rabbit tales, in an authentic American southern accent, to the children of the house. Her accent at times was so heavy, Sir Geoffrey Trevelyan and Dame Val Richmond Vester would later tell us, that the youngest among the Trevelyans and Richmonds could hardly understand a word she said. But they liked her intonations and theatrical gestures without ever realising that their storyteller was one of London's greatest actresses. To them she was just 'Granny's friend' – very special and intense, with stunning bright eyes. Granny was special, too, they still remember, always acting as if she were in a stage production in which she played the leading role. Never wearing outdoor clothes or walking shoes, she seemed to belong not quite to England's countryside but rather to a *fin-de-siècle* Parisian salon. Her grandchildren still remember Florence always dressed in black and practising her piano, addressing them in French and teaching them good manners.[2]

A visit to Wallington in Northumberland brings the memory of Molly and Charles Trevelyan, who remained so much the same over the years – he idealistic and intense, with frequent flashes of hot temper, she vivacious and agile of mind. Wallington, bequeathed to the National Trust in 1958 after Sir Charles died, opened again to the public in 1966 following Molly's death. The mansion reveals much about the Trevelyan's family life and heritage. Approaching it from Paine Bridge, following the path leading to the clock tower and the portico house that overlooks 'a large kitchen garden sloping down to the pond',[3] we see two stone griffin heads watching over the east front of the manor's exterior. Little of its austere architecture hints at the splendours inside – magnificent plasterwork, seventeenth- and eighteenth-century Chinese and Japanese porcelain, and superb needlework panels, among them Molly's embroidered portrait of the first Trevelyan swimming ashore on his white horse with the family motto – *Tyne-Tryeth-Troth* – as his guide. We learn then that Sir Charles and Lady Trevelyan opened Wallington on several occasions to the Tyneside workers, transforming it, by turns, into a centre for adult education, a youth hostel and a home for local theatre, making an additional point to the historical threads linking the Trevelyan family to the region.

A visit to Cambo village, a mile to the north, brings us to the house standing at the end of a row of eighteenth-century cottages built for the coal miners. In this little house, Charles and Molly Trevelyan spent their happiest years, as their children grew and Charles launched his political career.

From Cambo, still a Trevelyan residence, we easily travel to Sledmere, Mark Sykes' manor in Yorkshire. The mansion remains a silent witness to the splendours of years gone by. 'Sheltered by belts of woodlands',[4] Sledmere is an eighteenth-century house with its exterior walls adorned with busts of famous post-Renaissance and mythological figures. An elaborate Triton on high and heavily decorated gates lead us into a large garden. To the left of the entrance hall is the Oriental room, resplendent with turquoise-glazed floor tiles, Persian rugs, copper lamps, Turkish sofas and chairs upholstered in white and blue brocade. The room reminds us of Mark Sykes' other world, the world he so well depicted in his drawings, but failed to seize in his political actions. On one of the shelves at the entrance we find copies of Sykes' incisive caricatures that captured the contemptuous attitudes of his fellow officials when dealing with the subjects of the empire. With an insightful penstrokes he had depicted, in one of his most famous drawings, Sharif Husayn's ironic glance when confronting a British envoy anxiously attempting to explain the inexplicable.

Heading back to London, we pass Oxford and Cambridge, whose houses remain the epitome of 'unostentatious living'.[5] A modest red-brick townhouse at 2 Polstead Road, Oxford, was the Lawrence family residence until the First World War. In Cambridge, on a corner of West Road, near the History faculty, stands a dull brick house.[6] Here, Charles Trevelyan's brother, the famous historian George Macaulay Trevelyan, reflected on his book *Grey of Fallodon* (1937), which became a 'requiem and a lament not just for a man but for a class . . . not just for a life but for a way of living'.[7] Not far from George Trevelyan's house was the residence of the third brother, Robert, where Bertrand Russell and other 'apostles' used to assemble. Also in Cambridge stands the house that served as the Richmonds' residence when Sir Herbert fulfilled the functions of master of Downing College.

In the Sussex village of Henfield stands Backsettown, a pretty fifteenth-century house whose plaque reads: 'Elizabeth Robins, 1862–1952, Actress–Writer, lived here'. Lisa and Dr Octavia Wilberforce lived in the house until 1927, when it was converted from a private country home to a 'rest place for overworked women and for women with heavy domestic responsibility'.[8] It still serves this purpose.

The townhouse at 95 Sloane Street, where the Bells lived their London life, was never opened to the public. Not much happened there, it seems, after Florence's death in 1930 and Sir Hugh's death in 1931. Only Lisa's diaries, written during its glory days in the late 1920s, note Gertrude's last visit in the summer of 1926. We can imagine her, in the last years of her life, rereading Dick's letters sent from the officers' club at Half Moon Street, near Hyde Park, before he left for Addis Ababa and later to Gallipoli from where he would not return. Farther on, somewhat ironically, we find Cadogan Place, named after the Earl of Cadogan, Henry Cadogan's more fortunate relative.

Following Gertrude Bell to the Middle East we discover Gertrude's other world, with its churches, temples and ruins of all times. We reach Jordan with Gertrude's Belqa castles. We get to the Mushatta a palace of the seventh century. with its brick walls and columned entrance. Gertrude revisited Qasr al-Mushatta 'or the ghosts of it' in January 1914.[9] The palace has not changed much with the years.

From the empty palace we go to Petra, the rose city, 'half as old as Time'[10] that had taken the 'power of its artistic impulse from Hellenized Egypt and Syria'.[11] From Petra 'almost transparent at dawn . . .' we continue to Jalul, a ruined village from where 'miles and miles of rolling grass stretched far away to a dim horizon of low hills, dotted with black tents and white flocks . . .' And from there to Damascus 'with its gardens, domes and minarets . . . and the rustling water, deep green corn and the grey shades of olive trees'.[12] From there to Aleppo, which Gertrude visited in her way back from the Peace Conference in Paris. There we search for Fattuh's tiny house, the one in which he found refuge after having lost his fortune because he had served 'the Englishwoman'.[13]

From there, we reach Baghdad, 'after a heat wave has lifted and a political crisis has dissipated'. We then search for a little house near South Gate with no plaques on its walls or in the gardens. Moistened *argoub*s (rough curtains of camel-thorn) hanging from the windows, had protected its owners from Baghdad's pitiless heat.[14] The garden flowers, we still visualise, have already turned into weeds, and no light could now be seen from the outside. As we approach we learn that the house has already been destroyed. And yet, we can still imagine Gertrude strolling in the garden, her gazelle always at her side. During summer afternoons, when nobody came to visit, she certainly reminisced about other times and places, and still remembered that in the mountains 'one can still find snow in the high pass which divides the headwaters of the Tigris from the Euphrates'.[15]

She would recall the long journeys, and the 'ghosts which were once me, riding about on camels, before the world which was my world crashed together and foundered'. She didn't like the look of these ghosts, she explained once 'they are too happy and confident. It's I who feel a ghost beside them . . .'.[16]

From Baghdad we go to Jerusalem. In the heart of East Jerusalem, an impressive white mansion stands sun-drenched and bleached with desert hues. In the patio of the American Colony Hotel, a fountain bubble, surrounded by lemon trees and geranium flowers, its bottom agleam with Turkish coins tossed decades earlier into its waters by visitors making their wish. A small plaque at the entrance celebrates the hotel as the host to some of the Middle East's most influential guests, among them Winston Churchill and T. E. Lawrence. Gertrude Bell's name somewhat escaped them. Her name had been mentioned in the original plaque, however. Here, so the story goes, Lowell Thomas heard about Colonel Lawrence's adventures for the first time. Right or wrong, the story remains another reminder of the region's numerous myths. Dame Val Vester, the hotel's proprietor, formerly Valentine Richmond (Elsa's daughter, named after her godfather, Sir Valentine Chirol), kindly shares with us some reminiscences of her famous aunt, Gertrude Bell.

Sitting around the fountain, a soothing wellspring of momentary calm in rather tumultuous surroundings, we contemplate the hotel's guests throwing their coins in its gurgling waters. We then ponder on the real meaning of 'the omen', so often evoked by Gertrude in her writings. What was it, we still wonder. Was it the 'magic word' in Dick's letters that remained unspoken? Or a line in Rupert Brooke's poem evoking 'the other crossing'? Or again 'Safe Baghdad', Gertrude's message to Dick, which augured a Middle East of orchards, after crossing deserts of fears and horrors.

Or was it the creation of a state in a region not quite acquainted with the price and gains of independence and modern institutions? 'It would be the beginning of a quite new thing which will serve as an example' – Gertrude once wrote. 'Let's hope not as a warning',[17] she concluded. And the 'bad omen', what did it refer to? Were these the bad prospects of what could happen if not enough precautions were taken?

While still pondering about the obstacles to be avoided, and the certitudes to be reappraised, we rethink the meaning of successful or failed lives and missions. Was it all written? Gertrude had believed in the country that had given her so much before its own contradictions started to emerge. Gertrude didn't want to see Iraq as a kind of 'Austria-Hungary'[18] nor reverted to any kind of Turkish rule.[19] While sticking to her conviction regarding the need to integrate Baghdad, Basra and Mosul and create a modern Iraq, Gertrude met three different kinds of reaction:

The Sunnis had accused her of having a patronising attitude toward the Arabs, when trying to shape Iraq according to Britain's imperial designs;

the Shi'is had accused her of having given the country away to the Sunnis to comply with Britain's interests; the Kurds accused her of forgetting the promises of autonomy made to them after the war by actively bringing to the annexation of Arbil, Kirkuk and Sulaymaniyya to Baghdad.[20]

And yet, beyond these accusations, there was much admiration for the 'Khatun', as she is still fondly called. That is because, so we are inclined to believe, she had 'an extraordinary power of tearing the heart out of a thing, whether it was a book, a person or a nation'. Not just a 'queen of words' but also a 'queen of impressions', 'reacting more vividly than others to certain sides, certain shades',[21] Gertrude, so her supporters claim, reflected all the nuances of a determined situation with an unequalled rapidity, leaving her colleagues pondering about the accuracy of her conclusions well after these had been made.

Sitting around the fountain, the sound of the rustling leaves of the lemon trees brings us back to the Middle East of nowadays. As the age of empire has passed, we wonder about the lessons to be drawn from Gertrude Bell's story and the settings in which she operated that seemed to capture all the irreconcilable contradictions of her role. She acted in a country that would never be hers and yet, by leaving an indelible mark on it, she would lose her own. The exercise of empire was so overwhelming, and yet so frustrating, that she had to take drastic decisions, and at the end, detach herself from this untenable position. And again, we ponder about Gertrude's legacy, 'the omen', and the wishes embodied in the coins gleaming at the fountain's bottom. When throwing our own coin in the fountain's waters we also make a wish.

Still searching for the unspoken, bridging words that would encompass the different wishes silently formulated at the fountain's border, we will again turn to Hafiz and ask ourselves when could hopes and aspirations supersede bad auguries and premonitions. Reminding ourselves that 'not all is written' we will still try to find answers in the poet's lines:

> Where is the influence of the stars that blights my hope?
> The Omen answers:
> At the end . . .

More familiar with Gertrude Bell, her understanding of the peoples in the Middle East, and the sometimes amusing and less amusing ambiguities with which they confront otherwise impossible situations, we can imagine Gertrude's smile when concluding, with a twinkle, that the 'Omen's end' might also augur new beginnings.

Notes

The following abbreviations have been used in the notes:

SAD – Sudan Archive, University of Durham

GBP – Gertrude Bell Papers, Special Collections, Robinson Library, University of Newcastle-upon-Tyne

ERP – Elizabeth Robins Papers, Special Collections, Fales Library, New York University

LP&S – Correspondence of the Political and Secret Department, India Office

DW – Charles ('Dick') Doughty-Wylie

ER – Elizabeth ('Lisa') Robins

FB – Florence Bell

GB – Gertrude Bell

HB – Hugh Bell

All the letters come from GBP unless otherwise stated.

Molly's Diaries are in Trevelyan Papers, Special Collections, Robinson Library, University of Newcastle-upon-Tyne.

To avoid cluttering the text, where consecutive quotations are taken from the same source, only the last of these is annotated. Some quotations are taken from GB's unedited letters and papers.

The opening epigraph is from Clifford Geertz, *After the Fact: Two countries, Four Decades, One Anthropologist* (Cambridge, MA: Harvard University Press, 1995) p.131.

PREFACE

1 Elizabeth Monroe, *Britain's Moment in the Middle East 1914–1956* (London: Chatto & Windus, 1963), p. 20.

2 Seton Dearden, 'Gertrude Bell: A Journey to the Heart', *Cornhill*, 1062 (Winter 1969–70), pp. 457–510.

3 T. E. Shaw (T. E. Lawrence) to J. G. Wilson, 4 October 1927, *The Letters of T. E. Lawrence*, ed. David Garnett (London: Jonathan Cape, 1938), p. 240.

4 Edward Said *Orientalism* (1st edn 1978; New York: Peregrine Books; Middlesex: Penguin, 1985), p. 118.

5 Elie Kedourie, *In The Anglo-Arab Labyrinth: The McMahon–Husayn Correspondence and its Interpretation, 1914–1939* (Cambridge: CUP, 1976). Also quote in Elie Kedourie, 'The Genesis of History', *The Anglo-Arab Labyrinth* (London: Frank Cass, 2000), p. 343.

PROLOGUE

1 James Morris, *Pax Britannica: The Climax of an Empire* (London: Faber & Faber, 1968), pp. 22–34.
2 Lawrence James, *The Rise and Fall of the British Empire* (London: Little, Brown, 1994; London: Abacus, 1998), pp. 172, 173.
3 Ibid.
4 Ibid, pp. 200–3.
5 Ibid, p. 204.
6 Monroe, *Britain's Moment*, p. 13. The shorter sea route ran from Alexandria to Suez and then to the Red Sea. The longer overland route cut across the northern Syrian desert. From there it went to the Euphrates and the Persian Gulf.
7 Said, *Orientalism*, p. 5.
8 Morris, *Pax Britannica*, pp. 220–2.
9 James, *Rise and Fall*, pp. 204–5.
10 David Cannadine, *The Decline and Fall of the British Aristocracy* (New Haven, CT: Yale University Press, 1990), pp. 2, 6, 13, 327, 340.
11 Ibid., p. 2.
12 Ibid.
13 Morris, *Pax Britannica* (1979), pp. 31–3.
14 H. V. F. Winstone, *Gertrude Bell* (London: Jonathan Cape, 1978; paperback edition London: Constable, 1993), p. 2.
15 Gertrude was ten years older than Hugo, eleven years older than Elsa and thirteen years older than Molly. *The Letters of Gertrude Bell* ed. by Lady Bell, vol. 1 (first published September 1927; London: Pelican Books, 1939), p. 20.
16 Quoted in Winstone, *Gertrude Bell* (1993), p. 16.
17 *Letters of GB*, p. 21.
18 Ibid.
19 Quoted in ibid, p. 22.
20 Edward Said, *Orientalism*, pp. 4-5.

1 'LIGHT OF MINE EYES AND HARVEST OF MY HEART'

1 GB to HB, Damascus, 29 November 1913.
2 David Divine, *Hadrian's Wall: The Northwest Frontier of Rome* (New York: Barnes and Noble, 1995), pp. 9, 10.
3 GBP.
4 GB to her family, Petra, 29 March and 20 May 1900.
5 Elizabeth Burgoyne, *Gertrude Bell: From Her Personal Papers*, vol. 1 (London: E. Benn, 1958), pp. 296–7.
6 Ibid.
7 Theodore Fyfe, 'Review of Sir William M. Ramsay's and Miss Gertrude Bell's *The Thousand and One Churches*', *Archaeological Journal*, 67 (1910–11), pp. 204–7.
8 E.G. Browne on Hafiz, *Encyclopedia of Islam*, vol. 4 (1971), pp. 55–7.
9 Born in the 1326 in Shiraz, in the province of Fars, Shams al-Din Muhammad Hafiz, best known as Hafiz (the Memoriser of the Qur'an) was also known as the Tongue of the Hidden (*Lisan al-Gha'ib*) and the Interpreter of Secrets (*Tarjuman al-Asrar*), agnomens that described his attempt to instill the *ghazal* (love lyrics) with mystical dimensions. Originating from the Arabic *qasida* (classic Arab poems), or even from Persian folk songs antedating Arabic influence, the ghazal acquired in Hafiz's time the mystical quality that distinguished it from other gen-

res of Islamic literature. The call for a direct communication with God, widened its appeal in spite of the opposition of the Orthodox ulama.

10 Idris Shah, 'Introduction' to Gertrude Bell, *The Teachings of Hafiz* (London: Octagon Press, 1979), pp. 15, 16.

11 The diwan's verses were arranged in alphabetical order with mid-couplet cycles of rhymes.

12 Bell, *The Teachings of Hafiz*, pp. 78, 79.

13 Ibid.

14 Denison Ross, the director of London's School of Oriental and African Studies, offered a comparison between a grammatical translation and Gertrude Bell's versatile and flamboyant version of ghazal 38.

> *Dast az talab nadaram ta kam-i dil bar ayad*
> *Ya tan rasad bijanan, ya jan xi tan bar ayad.*

should read

> I will not hold back from seeking till my desire is realised,
> Either my soul will reach the beloved, or my soul will leave its body.

But it is rendered by Gertrude Bell with more than a pint of poetical license:

> I cease not from desire till my desire
> Is satisfied; or let my mouth attain
> My love's red mouth, or let my soul expire
> Sighed from those lips that sought her lips in vain.

15 Bell, *The Teachings of Hafiz*, pp. 86, 87.

16 E. G. Browne (ed.), *The Hafez Poems of Gertrude Bell: by Sham ad-Din Hafez* (Bethesda, MD: Ibex Publishers, 1995).

17 GB to HB, Jerusalem, 22 April 1900

18 DW to GB, 13 August 1913.

19 DW to GB, 16 August 1913, as quoted in Dearden, 'Gertrude Bell', pp. 457–510.

20 Also quoted in Winstone, *Gertrude Bell* (1993), pp. 123–4. Other questions have been drawn from the sources directly if not specified otherwise.

21 GB to Valentine Chirol, Damascus, 11 December 1913, SAD 303/4/155.

2 'SHE HAD KNOWN RUPTURES, SHE HAD KNOWN THE WHOLE'

1 James, *Rise and Fall*, pp. 217–22. Queen Victoria's interest in the overseas domains surpassed what was then called 'the legitimacy of the three 'Cs' – Christianity, Civilisation and Commerce – the three-fold message that had served to depict, for domestic purposes, Britain's overseas endeavours and justified, so to speak, their imperialistic nature.

2 GB to Valentine Chirol, 3 February 1901, SAD 303/4/34-36.

3 William Manchester, *Winston Spencer Churchill, The Last Lion*, Vol. 1: *Visions of Glory 1874–1932* (New York: Delta Publishing, 1989), pp. 234–7.

4 GB to FB, 18 January 1903.

5 GB to FB, 31 December 1902 and 1 January 1903.

6 David Cannadine, *Aspects of Aristocracy: Grandeur and Decline in Modern Britain* (New Haven, CT: Yale University Press, 1994), pp. 77–84.

7 GB to FB, 31 December 1902 and 1 January 1903, and GB Diaries, 1 January 1903.

8 James Morris, *Farewell the Trumpets* (London: Faber and Faber, 1978), pp. 60, 61.

9 GB to FB, Delhi, 2 January 1903.
10 Cannadine, *Aspects of Aristocracy*, ibid.
11 GB to FB, 2 January 1903.
12 Manchester, *Winston Spencer Churchill*, pp. 234–6.
13 GB to her family, 4 and 5 January 1903.
14 James, *Rise and Fall*, pp. 219–21, 232.
15 Manchester, *Winston Spencer Churchill*, p. 47.
16 GB to her family, spring 1892, quoted in Bourgoyne, *Gertrude Bell*, p. 26.
17 GB to FB, July 1892, quoted in Burgoyne, *Gertrude Bell*, p. 28.
18 Winstone, *Gertrude Bell* (1993), pp. 15–16.
19 GB to FB, Zermatt, 31 August 1904.
20 Dea Burkett, *Spinsters Abroad, Victorian Lady Explorers* (London: Gollancz, 1991), p. 19.
21 Winstone, *Gertrude Bell* (London: Quartet, 1980), pp. 93, 96.
22 Ibid.
23 David Cannadine, *G. M. Trevelyan: A Life in History* (London: HarperCollins, 1992), p. 11; quotation from Beatrice Webb's diaries.
24 Molly's Diaries 1902.
25 Molly's Diaries 1903.
26 Cannadine, *G. M. Trevelyan*, pp. 6, 7.
27 Ibid, pp. 8, 9.
28 *The Letters of Gertrude Bell* (second edition), p. 72.
29 Molly's Diaries, September 1899.
30 Cannadine, *G. M. Trevelyan*, p. 95.
31 Ibid., pp. 8, 9.
32 Molly's Diaries, 1903–4 and Cannadine, *G. M Trevelyan*, p. 40.
33 Molly' Diaries, 1904.
34 Ibid.
35 William Blake, *Selected Poems* (London: Penguin, 1996), pp. 74, 140, 178, and William Blake's *Songs of Innocence and Songs of Experience* (New York: Dover Publications, 1992), pp. 20–2.
36 Molly's Diaries, September 1903.
37 Ibid.
38 Cannadine, *G. M. Trevelyan*, p. 40.
39 May 1907, Miscellaneous 23a, GBP.
40 Britain's economy in the late decades of the nineteenth century was very much based on coal and iron, basic raw materials of an early industrial era. Britain's coal and iron were also supplied to the continent, speeding up the process of industrialisation of other countries in Europe.
41 May 1907, Miscellaneous 23a, GBP.
42 Ibid.
43 Ibid.
44 Cannadine, *Aspects of Aristocracy*, pp. 57, 58; and Cannadine, *G. M. Trevelyan*, p. 162.
45 Hugh Bell's alignment with the Unionists (the 1895 coalition of the Tories and Liberal Unionists) wasn't so surprising after all. While subscribing to the old principle of free trade, the Unionists also believed in the need to promote greater cooperation between industry and technical education in view of Britain's growing competition with Germany and the US.
  Following the split of the Liberal Party in 1886 on the question of Home Rule,

Hugh Bell had turned Unionist as other Liberals in the area, returning, however, to the Liberals some years later.

46 James, *Rise and Fall*, p. 207.

47 During the first Boer War (1881) the Boers surrendered their autonomy after a brief conflict, in exchange for Britain's protection against the Zulus. Defeating the British at Majuba in 1881, they regained their autonomy by the Convention of Pretoria, but restarted their strife in 1889 with an attack on Cape Colony. The Boer War ended in May 1902, but self-government was granted to the Transvaal in December 1906; to the Orange Free State in July 1907.

48 Asa Briggs, *Victorian Cities*, (London: Odham Books, 1963), pp. 253–82. The coming of Bell Brothers to Middlesbrough some decades earlier had followed the establishment there of other firms of pioneer ironmasters led by Henry Bolckow, John Vaugham, Joseph Pease, Arthur Dorman, Albert de Lande-Long, William Hopkins, Thomas Snowdon and Bernhard Samuelson. The influence of the 'owners' in town was illustrated by their full-length portraits hanging at the Council Chamber in the Clock Tower of Middlesbrough Town Hall, the impressive gothic building opened in 1887 by Mayor Dixon, Middlesbrough's largest shipmaker. The relations between the 'owners' were not only connected to business, but they also had social ties. The Bells' position in town, already very prominent with Thomas Hugh Bell's nomination as Mayor in 1874, grew even stronger after the merger of manufacturers of iron bars and angles for shipment between the Bell Brothers with Dorman-Long and the appointment of Sir Isaac Lowthian Bell as chairman of Dorman-Long in 1902.

49 From Lady Florence Bell, *At the Works* (London, 1907; republished 1969, 1985), quoted in Kenneth O. Morgan (ed.), *The Oxford History of Britain* (Oxford: Oxford University Press, 1993), pp. 530–1.

Charles Booth's *Life and Labour of the People in London* (33 vols, 1889–1903) and Seebohm Rowntree's *Poverty: A Study of Town and Life* (1901) had defined poverty as a social phenomenon. By revealing the living conditions of the working classes in London and in York, Booth and Rowntree raised public awareness to a much-needed social reform. See Briggs, *Victorian Cities*, p. 276.

50 Briggs, *Victorian Cities*, pp. 262–70.

51 Morgan, *The Oxford History of Britain*, pp. 530–1.

52 Ibid.

53 See Gertrude Himmelfeld, *The De-Moralization of Society: From Victorian Virtues to Modern Values* (New York: Knopf, 1995; London: Vintage, 1996), pp. 143–60.

54 A report about a society on the brink of social reforms, Bell's *At the Works*, remains a classic still included in British universities' reading lists. The second edition shows the effects of Edwardian welfare reforms. See the introduction by Angela V. John to the Virago edition (1985).

55 Norman Emory, *The Coalminers of Durham* (Durham: Sutton Publishing, 1992), p. 100.

56 GB to HB, 25 June 1916, also quoted in Lesley Gordon (ed.), *Gertrude Bell 1868–1926* (Newcastle-upon-Tyne: University of Newcastle-upon Tyne, 1994).

57 Molly's Diaries, February 1905.

58 See Joan Perkins, *Victorian Women* (London: J. Murray, 1993; New York: New York University Press, 1995), pp. 16, 17, 31.

59 See Revel Guest and Angela V. John, *Lady Charlotte: A Biography of the Nineteenth Century* (London: Weidenfeld and Nicolson, 1989), p. 31.

60 Winstone, *Gertrude Bell* (1993), pp. 134–6.

61 Guest and John, *Lady Charlotte*, ibid.
62 Manchester, *Winston Spencer Churchill*, pp. 374–5.
63 Norman Rose, *Churchill, The Unruly Giant*, The Free Press, New York, 1994, p. 46.
64 Published in *Nineteenth Century Magazine*, 1889; quoted in Perkins, *Victorian Women*.
65 Perkins, *Victorian Women*, p. 215.
66 Ibid.
67 Brian Harrison, *Separate Spheres: The Opposition to Women's Suffrage in Britain* (New York: Helmes & Meir Publishers, 1978), p. 60.
68 GB to Lord Cromer, 2 February 1913.
69 Although women's colleges had been founded in Oxford, Cambridge and London from the late 1870s, no full university degrees were awarded to women at the time. Oxford would award degrees to women in 1920 and Cambridge only in 1947.
70 GB to Lord Cromer, 2 February 1913.
71 Harrison, *Separate Spheres*, p. 79.
72 Angela V. John, *Elizabeth Robins: Staging a Life, 1862–1952* (London: Routledge, 1995).
73 FB to ER, 5 November 1905, Series 5B, Box 8, ERP.
74 John, *Elizabeth Robins*, p. 142.
75 Harrison, *Separate Spheres*, p. 13, 18.
76 Ibid., p. 114.
77 Ibid., pp. 23, 33.
78 Ibid., p. 59.
79 Perkins, *Victorian Women*, p. 213. Despite the serious aspects of the debate, there were anecdotes illustrating the early stages of the campaign when the movement still seemed no more than a social diversion. Among them Queen Victoria's reaction to Lady Amberley's (Bertrand Russell's grandmother) position. The queen had said a 'good whipping [should] to be inflicted to Lady Amberley [for her support of] the horrors that would certainly arise from the overturn of the status quo between the sexes'.
80 Molly's Diaries, November 1908.
81 Harrison, *Separate Spheres*, p. 33.
82 Rose, *Churchill, The Unruly Giant*, pp. 80–2.
83 Manchester, *Winston Spencer Churchill*, pp. 374–5.
84 FB to ER, 6 April 1908, Series 5B, Box 8, File 4, ERP.
85 Harrison, *Separate Spheres*, p. 120.
86 Ibid., p. 75.
87 Bell, *At the Works*, 'Introduction'.
88 FB to ER, 16 January 1908, Series 5B, Box 8, File 5, ERP.
89 FB to ER, 6 September 1911.
90 Quoted in Winstone, *Gertrude Bell* (1993), pp. 30–1.
91 John, *Elizabeth Robins*, pp. 53–68.
92 Ibid.
93 Ibid., pp. 87–90.
94 Ibid., pp. 31–41.
95 Ibid., pp. 92–5.
96 A series of strikes had shaken the already flimsy relations in England's industrial infrastructure: the dock strike, and the railways strike, of August 1921 were fol-

lowed by the miners strike of February 1912 calling for national minimal wages. This strike ended in April after the Bells established minimal distinct wages for the miners.
97 Molly's Diaries, April 1912.
98 Florence Bell, *The Minor Moralist: Some Essays on the Art of Everyday Conduct* (London: E. Arnold, 1900, 1903).
99 FB to Elsa, 7 July 1907, Miscellaneous F.
100 Genevieve Fraisse and Michelle Perrot (eds), *A History of Women in the West*, Vol. 4: *Emergence of Feminism from Revolution to War* (Cambridge, MA: Belknap Press, 1993), pp. 135–6, 441–2.
101 FB to ER, 25 August 1911, Series 5B, Box 8, ERP.
102 FB to ER, 22 April 1919, Series 5B, Box 8, ERP.

3 'THE SHADOW OF A STONE'

1 Molly's Diaries, 30 December 1909 and 28 December 1911.
2 Ibid.
3 Ibid.
4 Molly's Diaries, 2 January 1911.
5 Ibid.
6 GB to Valentine Chirol, March 1911, SAD 303/4/108-110.
7 GB to her family, 20 January 1911.
8 GB to HB, Baghdad, 18 March 1911
9 The general discontent with the sultan's policies, the insurgency in the Balkans, the growing indebtedness of the empire to the Western powers and the popular claims for freedom and reform fuelled a movement calling for the restoration of the 1876 Constitution. The spreading of the anti-Hamidian movement to the Ottoman troops stationed in Macedonia and Edirne the adoption of the mutineers by the CUP (Committee of Union and Progress) forced the sultan to announce on 23 July 1908 the restitution of the 1876 Constitution.
10 GB to Florence Spring Rice, Qara Dagh, 30 June 1909, Miscellaneous 34.
11 'Syria under the Constitution', *The Times*, 13 April 1909, Miscellaneous 22, GBP.
12 'The Desert under the Constitution', *The Times*, 22 May 1909, Miscellaneous 22, GBP.
13 GB Diaries, 22 March 1909.
14 GB Diaries, 9 April 1909.
15 Bernard Lewis, *The Emergence of Modern Turkey* (2nd edn, Oxford: Oxford University Press, 1968), pp. 210–11.
16 The construction of the Hindiyya Canal (1803) was made possible by the contributions from Indian Shi'is and was meant to improve water distribution to Najaf to sustain a growing number of Shi'i pilgrims and help to establish Najaf as the major Shi'i academic centre in Iraq.
    The impact of the Hindiyya on the socio-economic situation of Najaf was manifold. After its completion, Najaf emerged as one of Iraq's major market towns attracting a larger number of tribesmen to the area and accelerating their conversion to Shi'ism. See Yitzhak Nakash, *The Shi'is of Iraq*, (Princeton, NJ: Princeton University Press, 1994), pp. 19–20.
17 GB to FB, 21 March 1911.
    Sir William Willcocks – the famous irrigation engineer from Egypt – was appointed the consultant for Iraq's irrigation in 1908 and was trying to convince

the Turkish government of the need to undertake large-scale works in order to prevent flooding. Euphrates waters would flow into Lake Habbaniyya and to Abu Dibis valley. The Tigris flooding waters would be assembled in the Tharthar depression. Barrages would be erected above Baghdad and Kut al-'Amara and Qarmat 'Ali near Barna to raise water levels in the low season and restore irrigable lands in Gharraf (Hayy). Although costly and too ambitious a plan, Willcocks managed to forward his projects starting with the construction of the new Hindiyya barrage that began in September 1910 by Sir John Jackson and Co. See Stephen Hemsley Longrigg, *Iraq, 1900 to 1950. A Political, Social and Economic History* (Oxford: Oxford University Press, 1953), pp. 63–4.

18 An agreement in 1903 between Turkey and the Berlin–Baghdad Railway Company extended the line to the Persian frontier, the Mediterranean and the Persian Gulf. The railway represented a menace to Britain's commercial interests (by holding navigation rights on the Tigris and threatening British control of the Euphrates and Tigris Steam Navigation) securing port rights at Baghdad and Basra, envisaging oil concessions in Mosul and Baghdad provinces, threatening British trade with India and the visit of Indian pilgrims to Shi'i holy places. In fact, it was a major threat to British strategic interests, Britain's supremacy on the Persian Gulf.

The problem was only solved to Britain's satisfaction in 1913 by the signing of the Railway Agreement by which the British directors would sit on the board of directors of the railways and by the introduction of a clause specifying that the extension of the railway beyond Basra to the Gulf area could be only executed with Britain's approval. See Marian Kent, *Oil and Empire British Policy and Mesopotamian Oil 1900–1920* (Houndmills: Palgrave, 1976), pp. 10–11.

19 'Baghdad under the Constitution', *The Times*, 5 June 1909, Miscellaneous 22, GBP, and GB Diaries, March 1909.

20 GB to HB, Baghdad, 18 March 1911.

21 Burgoyne, *Gertrude Bell*, vol. 1, p. 278.

22 Leonard Woolley, quoted in T. E. Lawrence, *Seven Pillars of Wisdom*, and in J. Mack's *A Prince of Our Disorder: The Life of T. E. Lawrence* (Boston: Little, Brown, 1976), p. 39.

23 Mack, *Prince of Our Disorder*, ibid.

24 Isaiah X.9 and Jeremiah XI VI.2, which tells about a battle won by Nebuchadnezzer II in 604 BC against the Egyptian troops that invaded Syria. See C. L. Woolley, *Carchemish, Report on the Excavations at Jerbulus on Behalf of the British Museum*, pt. II; *The Town Defences* (London, 1921).

25 Other sources identify Carchemish with Circesium (Karkis in ancient Egyptian records). Ibid.

26 D. G. Hogarth, 'Revealing the Civilisation of the Hittites of Syria: Excavations at Carchemish', *The Illustrated London News*, 24 January 1914; and Jeremy Wilson, *T. E. Lawrence* (London: National Portrait Gallery Publications, 1988).

27 Woolley, Carchemish, chapter I, p. 13.

28 T. E. Lawrence to his family, 13 May 1911; also quoted in Jeremy Wilson's *Lawrence of Arabia, The Authorised Biography of T. E. Lawrence* (New York: Athenaeum, 1990), p. 88.

29 T. E. Lawrence to his family, 13 September 1912, also quoted in Wilson, *Lawrence of Arabia*, p. 109.

30 Burgoyne, *Gertrude Bell*, p. 275.

31 GB to HB, Binbirkilisse, 13 May 1905.

32 DW to GB, 11 August 1913.
33 DW to GB, London, 22 August 1913.
34 DW to GB, 15 August 1913.
35 Misha Glenny, *The Balkans Nationalism, War and the Great Powers 1804–1999* (New York: Viking Penguin, 2000), 'Introduction', p. XXIII.
36 DW to GB, 23 August 1913.
37 DW to GB, Monastir, 25 September 1913; Miranda Vickers, *The Albanians – A Modern History* (London: I.B. Tauris, 1997), p. 15.
38 DW to GB, Leskovik, 21 November 1913.
39 DW to GB, Brindisi, 3 September 1913.
40 Monastir was the main town of the ancient vilayet of Monastir that, with Shkoder, Janina and later Kosova (added in 1878), formed what was still vaguely defined as 'Albania'. The population in these areas was heterogeneous and the Ottomans (and later the Young Turks) tried to avoid the crystallisation of an Albanian identity. Also Greece continued to have claims on Albania's territory. Vickers, *The Albanians*, pp. 26, 55–6.
41 DW to GB, 22 September 1913.
42 DW to GB, Colonia, 31 October 1913.
43 A previous attempt to define Albania's territory and nationality by using language as a criterion had been made in 1877 by F. Hippich, the Austrian consul in Shkoder. The Ottomans refused, however, to recognise the Albanians (especially the Muslims) as non-Turks, preventing any attempt to define the Albanians as a nation. See Vickers, *The Albanians*, pp. 30–1.
44 DW to GB, 31 October 1913.
45 DW to GB, Colonia, 31 October 1913.
46 DW to GB, Florence, 14 December 1913.
47 DW to GB, Monastir, 29 December 1913.
48 'Les Atrocités des Coalisés Balkaniques', Constantinople, 1913, Miscellaneous 23, GBP.
49 DW to GB, Monastir, 29 September 1913.
50 DW to GB, Leskovik, 23 November 1913.
    The Bektashis were a heterodox sect whose creed was pantheistic (finding god in nature and in men). Their popularity in the Balkans was mainly due to their tolerance toward Christians, as their own religion included elements of Shi'ism, Christianity and possibly Buddhism. The sect was widespread among the Janissaries, the military corps made up of converted boys recruited from among the empire's Christian minorities (which explains the vestiges of Christianity in their practices).
    After the rebellion of the Janissaries in 1826 (in reaction to the creation of a new regiment called *muallem eshkinji*) the Bektashi order was considered as a threat for the Sunni Ottoman authorities and was forced to take refuge in mountainous areas. The Bektashi *tekkes* were considered thereafter a 'subversive' element struggling for Albanian cultural affirmation. See Vickers, *The Albanians*, pp. 22–3, 46.
51 Ibid.
52 The alliance, based on a secret treaty contracted by Germany, Austria-Hungary and Italy (to be ratified every five years until 1915), aimed at the protection of the signatory members in case of attack on one of them by France, Britain or Russia. Italy's antagonism to France was also due to France's occupation of Tunis in 1881. In October 1913, after Austria's ultimatum to Serbia, related to Serbia's occupation of Albania, secret negotiations were taking place between Britain and

Germany regarding control of Mozambique and Angola. It is possible that Doughty-Wylie alluded to these secret negotiations in his comment on the perils to the Triple Alliance posed by its members' uncoordinated policies. See Martin Gilbert, *The First World War, A Complete History, 1914–1918* (New York, Henry and Holt, 1994), pp. 11–12.

53 DW to GB, 23 August 1913.
54 DW to GB, 18 December 1913.
55 DW to GB, 26 August 1913.
56 DW to GB, Leskovik, 23 November 1913.
57 DW to GB, Leskovik, 18 December 1913.
58 Ibid.
59 DW to GB, 22 August 1913.
60 DW to GB, 18 December 1913.
61 DW to GB, 31 October 1913.
62 DW to GB, Suffolk, 5 January 1914.
63 DW to GB, Colonia, 26 October 1913.
64 DW to GB, Leskovik, 21 November 1913.
65 GB to Valentine Chirol, Damascus, 11 December 1913, SAD 303/4/155-157.
66 Ibid.
67 Miscellaneous 34, GBP. The last European travellers to reach Ha'il and Riyadh were Sir Wilfred and Lady Anne Blunt in the late 1880s and Barons Wolde and Krenz in the early 1890s. Charles Doughty, Dick's uncle, and Charles Huber had reached the interior of Arabia in the 1880s, but their journey had already been forgotten.
68 GB to FB, Damascus, 12 December 1913; and Miscellaneous 34, GBP. After only two hours, it was attacked by Druze horsemen as it approached the mountains of Jabal Druze. Gertrude was finally recognised by the colour of her camel – 'a negro' – and was greeted with respect, she reported. Already a legend in the desert and beyond, Gertrude had learned how to deal with tribal practices. She would hire a man from each belligerent tribe in order to secure the safety of her caravan as it moved through the desert.
69 GB Diaries, 25 to 28 January 1914.
70 Ibid.
71 GB to her family, 4 February 1914 and GB Diaries, 4 February 1914.
72 GB to DW, February 1914. and ibid.
73 GB to DW, 27 January 1914.
74 GB to DW, 24 February 1914.
75 Sir Louis Mallet to Sir Edward Grey, Constantinople, 20 May 1914, PRO, Kew Gardens, CP 355, FO 371/2127.
76 Notes on Arabia, June 1907, A 1194. Confidential. General Staff, War Office, Miscellaneous 23, GBP.
77 Ibid.
78 GB to Valentine Chirol, Damascus, 5 December 1913, SAD 303/4/152-154.
79 GB Diaries and Letters, 24 February to 8 March 1914.
80 Ibid.
81 Ibid.
82 Ibid.
83 Charles Montagu Doughty, *Travels in Arabia Deserta* (1st edn 1888; London: Cambridge University Press, 1979), pp. 658–9.
84 GB Diaries, February and March 1914.

85 GB to her family, 7 March 1914.
86 Ibid.
87 GB Diaries, 17 March 1914.
88 GB Diaries, 2 March 1914. The expulsion of the Saudi emirs from Riyadh in 1890 by the Rashidis of Ha'il ended the second Saudi-Wahhabi dynasty and opened a new phase in the relations with the neighbouring tribes. Alliances were formed and Ha'il's rulers tried to find the balance between the Saudi emirs, the Egyptians and the Ottomans and explore it to their advantage. See Madawi al-Rashid, *Politics in an Arabian Oasis: The Rashidis of Saudi Arabia* (London: I.B. Tauris, 1991), pp. 39–48.
89 DW to GB, Theberton Hall, Leiston, Suffolk, 31 December 1914.
90 Ibid.
91 DW to GB, Suffolk, 31 December 1914.
92 DW to GB, 15 May 1914.
93 DW to GB, 22 January 1914.
94 DW to GB, Leskovik, 16 December 1913 and Theberton Hall, Leiston, Suffolk, 26 January 1914.
95 DW to GB, 8 December 1913.
96 DW to GB, Suffolk and London, 22 January 1914.
97 DW to GB, 26 January 1914.
98 DW to GB Suffolk, 31 December 1914.
99 DW to GB, Suffolk, 22 December 1914.
100 DW to GB, Suffolk, 15 and 23 January 1914.
101 DW to GB, Suffolk, 22 January 1914.
102 DW to GB, 15 August 1913.
103 DW to GB, 28 January 1914.
104 Also quoted in Winstone, *Gertrude Bell* (1993), p. 144.

4 'I WILL DEDICATE THIS YEAR TO YOU'

1 GB to DW, Baghdad, 14 April 1914.
2 Ibid.
3 GB to DW, 1 May 1914.
4 Nakash, *The Shi'is of Iraq*, p. 185.
5 Ibid., p. 191.
6 Ibid., pp. 18–20.
7 GB to DW, 26 March 1914.
8 Ibid. Also quoted by Dearden, 'Gertrude Bell', p. 473.
9 'Irrigation' in draft of an unpublished manuscript, n.d., Miscellaneous – item 20, GBP.
10 Ibid.
11 When writing these lines in March 1914 Gertrude was not yet aware, so it seems, of the agreement signed in 1913 between Turkey and Britain by which two British directors would sit on the board of the Baghdad railways, so as to get more control over its administration and permit the preservation of Britain's strategic and commercial interests in the Tigris, securing port construction rights in Baghdad and in Basra and controlling the railway terminus in Basra and the outlet for the railway on the Persian Gulf. This agreement ended a years-long negotiation between Britain and Turkey permitting the British to gain the competition with Germany over the control of the Berlin–Baghdad railway (a German concession

from 1903). See Kent, *Oil and Empire*, pp. 9–11.

12 GB to DW, 13 April 1914 and GB Diaries 13 April 1914.

13 GB to DW, May 1913 and GB Diaries 1 May 1914.

14 Sir Louis Mallet to Sir Edward Grey, Constantinople, 25 May 1914, CP Turkey 23205 no. 355, FO 371/2127.

15 DW to GB, Suffolk, 15 January 1914.

16 Ibid.

17 DW to GB, Addis Ababa, 26 April 1914.

18 DW to GB, Suffolk, 15 January 1914.

19 DW to GB, 23 January 1914.

20 DW to GB, Suffolk, 15 January 1914.

21 Birkett, *Spinsters Abroad*, pp. 263–4.

22 DW to GB, 30 May 1914.

23 Ibid.

24 Manchester, *Winston Spencer Churchill*, p. 427.

25 Rose, *Churchill*, pp. 108–9.

26 Ibid.

27 Home Rule was a movement in favour of the establishment of a parliament in Dublin to deal with Irish domestic affairs. Two attempts to pass a Home Rule Bill (in 1886 and in 1893) were rejected by the House of Lords. After the Parliament Act of 1911, limiting the power of the Lords, the Liberals tried to introduce a third Home Rule Bill which was opposed by the Protestants at Ulster, almost leading to a civil war between them and the Catholics of Dublin.

28 Rose, *Churchill*, p. 123.

29 Manchester, *Winston Spencer Churchill*, p. 434.

30 Monroe, *Britain's Moment*, pp. 23–4.

31 Ibid.

32 Ibid.

33 Rose, *Churchill*, p. 124.

34 Ibid., pp. 124–6, and Gilbert, *First World War*, pp. 9–11.

35 DW to GB, 30 May 1914.

36 Gilbert, *The First World War*, pp. 32–3, and Manchester, *Winston Spencer Churchill*, pp. 379 and 467–8.

37 DW to GB, Abyssinia, May 1914.

38 DW to GB, 14 and 15 June 1914

39 Correspondence regarding the European Crisis Q 7467, House of Parliament, August 1914, GBP.

40 Ibid.

41 Monroe, *Britain's Moment*, pp. 24–5.

42 DW to GB, Addis Ababa, 6 November 1914.

43 Ibid.

44 DW to GB, Addis Ababa, 6 November 1914, 21 November 1914, and 20 December 1914.

45 DW to GB, 15 November 1914.

46 DW to GB, 18 December 1914.

47 DW to GB, 15 November 1914.

48 DW to GB, 6 November 1914.

49 DW to GB, 27 December 1914.

50 FB to ER, 14 August 1914, ERP.

51 Manchester, *Winston Spencer Churchill*, pp. 503, 516.

52 GB to DW, Boulogne, 30 December 1914.
53 GB to DW, 20 January 1915.
54 GB to DW, 2 January 1915.
55 Gilbert, *The First World War*, pp. 100–24.
56 GB to DW, Boulogne, 20 January 1915.
57 GB to DW, Boulogne, 16 January 1915.
58 GB to DW, 5 January 1915.
59 GB to DW, 25 January 1915.
60 DW to GB, 14 January 1915.
61 Ibid.
62 GB to DW, 17 February 1915.
63 GB to DW, 26 February 1915.
64 Ibid.
65 GB to DW, 4 March 1915.
66 Manchester, *Winston Spencer Churchill*, pp. 527–8.
67 Ibid., p. 522.
68 Rose, *Churchill*, pp. 137–8.
69 If Greece, Bulgaria, and Romania were to join the Triple Entente, they would acquire ports on the Sea of Marmara and other areas. Greece would annex West Anatolia's province of Smyrna with its large Greek population; Bulgaria would retain its port on the Aegean; Italy would get the South Anatolia province of Adana; and Russia would acquire the province of Armenia and perhaps Constantinople.
70 Monroe, *Britain's Moment*, pp. 28–9.
71 Manchester, *Winston Spencer Churchill*, p. 518.
72 Ibid.
73 Gilbert, *The First World War*, p. 135.
74 GB to DW, 17 February 1915.
75 GB to DW, 2 January 1915.
76 GB to DW, 10 January 1915.
77 Manchester, *Winston Spencer Churchill*, pp. 533–4; Gilbert, *The First World War*, p. 134.
78 DW to GB, 10 March 1915.
79 Ibid.
80 GB to DW, 4 and 7 March 1915.
81 GB to DW, 11 March 1915.
82 DW to GB, 4 March 1915.
83 GB to DW, 12 March 1915.
84 GB to DW, 20 March 1915.
85 GB to DW, 19 March 1915.
86 GB to DW, 20 March 1915.
87 GB to DW, 16 March 1915.
88 GB to DW, 25 March 1915.
89 GB to DW, 19 March 1915.
90 GB to DW, 10 March 1915.
91 Gilbert, *The First World War*, pp. 132–5.
92 GB to DW, 15 March 1915.
93 Valentine Chirol to GB, Persian Gulf, 10 February 1915, enclosed in GB to DW, 15 March 1915.
94 Ibid.

95 Ibid.
96 Ibid.
97 Ibid.
98 Gilbert, *The First World War*, p. 135.
99 Monroe, *Britain's Moment*, pp. 28–30.
100 DW to GB, 30 March 1915.
101 DW to GB, 2 April 1915.
102 DW to GB, 1 April 1915.
103 Italy would get Addis Ababa in 1936, in the territorial arrangements preceding the Second World War. King Victorio Emmanuel would then become emperor. In 1941, British troops and the Ethiopian Levies reconquered the country and brought Emperor Haile Selassie back from exile. Italy would, however, remain in Eritrea and Somalia for many more years.
104 Gilbert, *The First World War*, p. 151.
105 GB to DW, 20 April 1915.
106 DW to GB, 20 April 1915.
107 GB to DW, 16 March 1915 and 26 February 1915.
108 DW to GB, 21 April 1915.
109 GB to DW, 24 and 25 April 1915.
110 Ibid.
111 Rose, *Churchill*, p. 146.
112 O'Moore Creagh and E. M. Humphris (eds), *The Victoria Cross* (Suffolk: J. B. Hayward, 1985), pp. 169–70; and *The Times*, 4 May 1915, in H. W. C. Davis and J. R. H. Weaver (eds), *Dictionary of National Biography, 1912–1921* (New York: Oxford University Press, 1927).
113 Ibid.
114 Manchester, *Winston Spencer Churchill*, p. 550.
115 Creagh and Humphris, *The Victoria Cross*, ibid.
116 GB to DW, 1 May 1915.
117 *The Times*, 4 May 1915.
118 Creagh and Humphris, *Victoria Cross*, ibid.
119 Colonel Charles (Dick) Doughty-Wylie's will, November 1909.
120 February 1915, FO 327/639 14633, .
121 Lt. Col. Doughty-Wylie's Diaries, L/2657/25, November 1907, Regimental Museum of the Royal Welch Fusiliers, Caernafon Castle, Caernafon, Gwynedd, Wales.
122 Lt. Col. Doughty-Wylie's Diaries, L/2651/19, November 1907.
123 Ibid.
124 Lt. Col. Doughty-Wylie's Diaries, L/2651/19, and L/2651/20.
125 Lt. Col. Doughty-Wylie's Diaries, 1 November 1913, L/2651/45.
126 Lt. Col. Doughty-Wylie's Diaries, 22 May 1908, L/2651/19.

5 'ON THE EDGE OF IMPORTANT THINGS'

1 GB to FB, Cairo, 10 January 1916.
2 Bruce Westrate, *The Arab Bureau British Policy in the Middle East 1916–1920* (Pennsylvania: Pennsylvania State University Press, 1992), pp. 27–8.
3 Egypt was, at the time, a centre of numerous commands. Together with General Murray in Isma'iliya there was General Sir Ian Hamilton commanding the Mediterranean Expeditionary Force in Alexandria and General Sir John Maxwell in

Cairo commanding the British Army in Egypt. Sir F. Reginald Wingate was then *sirdar* of the Egyptian army in the Sudan. Westrate, *The Arab Bureau*, p. 24.

4 Ibid., p. 36.

5 Ibid.

6 R. Storrs, *Orientations* (1st edn London: Nicholson and Watson, 1937; London, 1954), p. 154.

7 Shane Leslie, *Mark Sykes: His Life and Letters* (New York and London: Cassell, 1923), p. 285.

8 Monroe, *Britain's Moment*, p. 41.

9 Westrate, *The Arab Bureau*, pp. 27, 29, 32.

10 Ibid., pp. 4, 25.

11 GB to FB, Basra, 9 March 1916.

12 According to Britain's previous agreements with the Allies the districts of Mersina and Adana, the Syrian littoral, were to go to France, and the vilayets of Baghdad and Basra were to go to Britain and would be excluded from the territory promised to the Arabs; Liora Lukitz, 'The Antonius Papers and *The Arab Awakening* over Forty Years on', *Middle Eastern Studies*, 30: 4 (October 1994), pp. 883–95. But there were different interpretations of the intentional vagueness of the agreements. Also the fact that at the time of their formulation these agreements seemed less binding than after the war. See Monroe, *Britain's Moment*, pp. 32–7.

13 GB to HB, Basra, 22 May 1916

14 GB to HB, Basra, 24 March and 16 April 1916.

15 GB to her family, 18 March 1916.

16 GB to HB, Basra, 24 March 1916.

17 GB to FB, Basra, 9 April 1916.

18 The *waqf* (pl. *awqaf*) was money or property given in perpetuity to Muslim authorities for pious purposes or for public good. Originally created to protect inheritors from rulers or to prevent fragmentation of real estate, the waqf became an institution used to avoid property from being expropriated by the state. During Ottoman times, the Ottoman Awqaf Department transferred to itself the profits also from the awqaf of Shi'i properties handing back only small percentages to Shi'i shrines.

In 1917 the British diverted Shi'i awqaf monies to Shi'i mosques and institutions. After the creation of the Iraqi state, the control of the revenues went to the Iraqi Ministry of Awqaf, turned in 1929 into a general directorate, controlling Sunni and Shi'i waqf revenues alike.

19 T. E. Lawrence, report to Clayton, Arab Bureau, Cairo, undated, enclosed in letter from Clayton to Wingate, 12 June 1916, SAD 137/7/3-23/ Lawrence's views regarding the creation of the Shi'i waqf are in SAD 137/7/22-23.

20 Nakash, *The Shi'is of Iraq*, pp. 236, 237. The question of the Shi'i *waqf* properties in Mesopotamia was more complex than Lawrence had perceived. The Shi'is' claims over the revenues of their *waqf* properties dated back to Ottoman times and the Tanzimat reforms of 1838. Already then the Shi'is turned to the British agent in Baghdad asking him to intervene in their favour and return to their hands the *waqf* revenues that were used by the Sunni authorities. The creation by the British of a public Shi'i *waqf* during the war was a step taken to reinforce Britain's ties with the local Shi'i population while defying the Sunni Ottoman authorities in Baghdad.

21 GB to FB, G.H.W. Basra, 29 April 1916.

22 Peter Sluglett, *Britain in Iraq* (Ithaca, NY: Ithaca Press, 1976), pp. 9–16 and ibid.

23 W. F. Stirling, *Safety Last* (London: Hollis & Carter, 1953), pp. 67–8, also quoted in Westrate, *The Arab Bureau*, p. 89.

24 Clayton Papers, Reports 143.7.22, 16 November 1916; 160.2.87, 17 August 1916; and 201.1.95, July 1916, Durham.

25 Philip Graves, *The Life of Sir Percy Cox* (London, 1941), p. 211.

26 GB to HB, Basra, 23 November 1916.

27 Ibid.

28 GB to HB, Basra, 23 November 1916.

29 GB to HB, 'Amara, 1 January 1917.

30 GB to HB, Hilla, 10 January 1918.

31 GB to HB, Basra, 23 November 1916.

32 GBP.

33 Graves, *Life of Sir Percy Cox*, p. 214.

34 A. T. Wilson, *Loyalties in Mesopotamia: A Personal and Historical Record* (Oxford: Oxford University Press, 1950), vol. 1, p. 160.

35 GB to HB, 1 December 1916 and *Arab Bulletin*, 12 January 1917. Also quoted in Winstone, *Gertrude Bell* (1993), pp. 191–2. .

36 Philby to Wilson, Report on the Operations of the Najd Mission, 2 November 1918, FO 371/4144/4370.

37 The Wahhabis invaded Iraq several times raiding the Muntafiq and the Khaz'al tribes. The Wahhabis had also besieged Najaf and ravaged Karbala in 1801. See Nakash, *The Shi'is of Iraq*, p. 28.

38 GB to HB, Basra, 10 March 1917.

39 GB to HB, 1 December 1916.

40 Gertrude L. Bell, 'Syrian Report', 23 June 1917; 18 August 1917, no. 162432, FO 371/3059.

41 Ibid.

42 GB to FB, 25 January 1918.

43 T. E. Lawrence's letter to *The Times*, 11 September 1919; and Lukitz, 'The Antonius Papers', ibid.

44 Monroe, *Britain's Moment*, pp. 32–8.

45 Ibid., p. 32.

46 F. C. C. Balfour, 'Mesopotamia 1917–1918', January 1958, F. C. C. Balfour Papers, SAD 303/3/3.

47 GB to HB, Baghdad, 8 June 1917.

48 GB to HB, Baghdad, 3 May 1917. Conversion to Shi'ism cut across confederations and tribes – the examples were many: the Banu Lam were mostly Shi'is, but few sections had remained Sunnis. The Jubur on the Euphrates were Shi'is, whereas sections of the Jubur on the Tigris were Sunnis.
    The Dulayim north of Baghdad were Sunnis and the Fatla settled on the Hindiyya were Shi'is. The tribesmen conversion to Shi'ism was a consequence of many factors: among them the influence of Shi'i pilgrimage to the holy cities and the increasing need of tribesmen to identify with their social environment after the dismemberment of the tribal structure. See Nakash, *The Shi'is of Iraq*, pp. 45–6.

49 Suq al-Shuyukh together with Diwaniyya, Zabayn, Hayy, 'Asmara and Nasiriyya had been established early in the nineteenth century. Their rapid expansion could point to the hasty settlement of tribes as a result of the breaking of tribal confederations. See Nakash, *The Shi'is of Iraq*, p. 35.

50 18 August 1917, no. 162433, FO 371/3059, Report by G. L. Bell, 10 July 1917; and GB to Valentine Chirol, 12 June 1916, SAD 307/4/189-193.

51 GB to Valentine Chirol, 12 June 1916, SAD 307/4/189-193.
52 See Nakash, *The Shi'is of Iraq*, pp. 33–5. In the early nineteenth century a great part of the cultivated areas of Central and Southern Iraq was collective tribal domain. At the end of the century, following the Ottoman Land Code of 1869 leading families managed to get title deeds and asked the fallahin to pay the *mallakiyya*. Although the tribal shaykhs still maintained some of their traditional functions – keeping order and security, arbitrating disputes among fallahin and organising labour and distribution of water – their new function as landlords affected their traditional relations with their tribesmen.
53 See Stephen Hemsley Longrigg, *Four Centuries of Modern Iraq* (Oxford: Clarendon Press, 1925), pp. 288–90, 305–9.
54 F. C. C. Balfour, 'Mesopotamia 1917–1918', January 1958, F. C. C. Balfour Papers, SAD 303/3/5.
55 Ibid., SAD 303/3/6.
56 See Nakash, *The Shi'is of Iraq*, pp. 29–31, 94–6.
57 GB to Valentine Chirol, 29 January 1918, SAD 303/4/207-209.
58 See Nakash, *The Shi'is of Iraq*, pp. 94–6.
59 E. B. Soane, *To Mesopotamia and Kurdistan in Disguise* (London, 1912). In October 1918 the British troops under the command of General Marshall (who had succeeded Sir Stanley Maude as commander-in-chief in Mesopotamia) attacked Turkish positions across the Tigris, reaching Mosul in November 1918, after the armistice.
60 GB to Valentine Chirol, 29 December 1917, SAD 303/4/204-206.
61 See Marian Kent, *Oil and Empire*, pp. 13–14.
62 GB to HB, Baghdad, 28 November 1918.
63 GB to FB, 5 December 1918.
64 Ibid.
65 Ibid.
66 GB to HB, 27 December 1918.
67 Also quoted in Gordon, *Gertrude Bell*.
68 Sluglett, *Britain in Iraq*, pp. 32–3.
69 Gertrude L. Bell, *Self-Determination in Mesopotamia*, memorandum no. 524, Baghdad, 22 February 1919, issued by Lieutenant Colonel Wilson, acting civil commissioner to under secretary of India, London, and Government of India, Delhi. In GBP and quoted in Wilson, *Loyalties*, vol. 2, pp. 330–41
70 The most important measure supporting this move was the Tribal Criminal and Civil Disputes Regulation (TCCDR), introduced a few months earlier. The regulation stipulated that tribal disputes should not be referred to the courts but rather should be dealt with by the shaykhs themselves, with the assistance of the British political officer in the area. Although inspired by the colonialist trend that tended to romanticise the spirit of native institutions, the regulation was to stir future debates regarding Britain's intent and whether it denoted a strategy to drive a wedge between the urban and rural areas to prevent unification of the country. See Hanna Batatu, *The Old Social Classes and the Revolutionary Movements of Iraq: A Study of Iraq's Old Landed and Commercial Classes and its Communists, Bathists, and Free Officers* (Princeton, NJ: Princeton University Press, 1978), p. 24, and Lukitz, 'The Antonius Papers', p. 69.
71 Bell, *Self-Determination in Mesopotamia*,1919, 'Appendix I: Political Views of the Naqib of Baghdad',. Also quoted in Elie Kedourie, 'The Kingdom of Iraq: a Retrospect', in *The Chatham House Version and Other Middle Eastern Studies* (1st edn

London: Praeger, 1970; reprinted Hanover: University Press of New England, 1984), pp. 236–82.

72 GB to Valentine Chirol, 22 February 1918, SAD 303/4/210-212; GB to her family, 23 June 1921; and Wilson, *Loyalties*, vol. 2, pp. 314–15.

73 Sluglett, *Britain in Iraq*, pp. 3, 23–8.

74 GB to HB, Paris, 7 March 1919.

75 In the Husayn–McMahon correspondence the British promised a unified Arab state in the Arab-speaking ex-Ottoman provinces. The 1916 Sykes–Picot agreement endorsed France's designs over Syria. The debate over the legality of Britain's presence in Mosul vilayet (also formerly promised to France) drew from the fact that the British had entered the town some days after the signing of the armistice at Moudros on 31 October 1918. It involved the political future of the Kurdish population in the whole area. But contradictions remained.

76 Also quoted in Gordon, *Gertrude Bell*.

77 GBP.

78 Gertrude Bell to her family, Aleppo, 17 October 1919.

6 'FATHER, THINK!'

1 Dispatch from Civil Commissioner, Mesopotamia, to Secretary of State for India, 15 November 1919, LP&S/10/756 P 8253/19/B337; and LP&S/18/B 337 in F. C. C. Balfour Papers, SAD 303/1/67-76.

2 LP&S/10/756 P 8253/19/B337, .

3 Ibid.

4 Ibid.

5 Ibid.

6 Gertrude Bell, 'Syria in 1919'. The question of Mosul's oil was a complex one, however: under the Sykes-Picot Agreement, the area of Mosul was granted to France, indicating perhaps that Britain's main interests were not guided exclusively by economic imperatives, but also by strategic and defence planning. See Kent, *Oil and Empire*, pp. 12–14.

7 Phebe Marr, *The Modern History of Iraq* (Boulder, CO, and London: Westview, 1985), p. 32, and Sluglett, *Britain in Iraq*, pp. 34–7.

8 Military: £44,110,000; civil: £2,125,712; total £46,235,712. 'Estimated Expenditure in Mesopotamia, 1921–1922', LP&S/11/193-P593.

9 Sluglett, *Britain in Iraq*, p. 37.

10 Secret B317 A. T. Wilson to Memorandum 'Future Constitution' Secretary of State for India, 6 April 1919, LP&S/10/758 P 2023. Wilson was a representative of the 'Indian' school who assumed that efficient administration was a substitute for self-government and independence.

11 G. L. Bell, 'Self-Determination in Mesopotamia', February 1919, Memorandum no. 524, in letter by A. T. Wilson to Under-Secretary of State for India, 22 February 1919, F. C. C. Balfour Papers, SAD 303/1/60. Also quoted in Wilson, *Loyalties*, vol. 2, pp. 330–41

12 The question of tribal representation, in her view, should be solved by appointing twenty representatives of the twenty main tribes and the other ten representatives by grouping the small tribes together in the ten divisions. It was an innovative step. In Turkish times, tribes would not be represented, as tribesmen feared to be conscripted in the army when registering themselves to elections. GB to HB, 12 December 1920.

In fact, even if the population's unfamiliarity with public affairs made the creation of political institutions difficult, the plebiscite showed that a large majority of the population was in favour of the integration of Mosul in Iraq and of an Arab government.

13 'The Problems of Mesopotamia', note by H. E. Bowman, addendum to letter from A. T. Wilson to Stephenson, 20 September 1920, A. T. Wilson's Papers, British Library; and Nakash, *The Shi'is of Iraq*, pp. 61–6.

14 Nakash, *The Shi'is of Iraq*, p. 62.

15 A. T. Wilson to Captain G.C. Stephenson, Baghdad, 15 September 1919, A. T. Wilson's Papers, no. 28106, British Library.

16 A. T. Wilson to Captain G.C. Stephenson, c/o Political Secretary India Office, Baghdad, 20 September 1919, no. 28610; A. T. Wilson to Stephenson, 8 October 1919, no. 30361 (Private and Personal), A. T. Wilson's Papers, British Library.

17 Sluglett, *Britain in Iraq*, pp. 26, 32.

18 'The Problems of Mesopotamia', note by H. E. Bowman, addendum to letter by A. T. Wilson to Stephenson, 20 September 1920, A. T. Wilson's Papers, British Library.

19 GB to her family, 12 October 1919.

20 GB to her family, Damascus, 12 October 1919.

21 Gertrude Bell, 'Syria in 1919', October 1919, ibid., also Sluglett, *Britain in Iraq*, pp. 38–9.

22 GB to HB, 25 December 1919.

23 GB to HB, 30 January 1921.

24 240,000 British soldiers were needed to keep order and control of Mesopotamia whereas only 20,000 were used to the same purposes in Persia.

25 GB to HB, 4 January 1920.

26 GB to FB, 14 March 1920.

27 Ibid.

28 Ibid.

29 Wilfred Thesiger, *The Marsh Arabs* (1st edn London: Longmans, Green, 1964; London: Penguin, 1967).

30 Ibid.

31 GB to HB, 4 January 1920.

32 Ibid.

33 Bell, *Review of the Civil Administration*, p. 132.

34 GB to FB, 10 April 1920.

35 GB to FB, 12 January 1920.

36 Monroe, *Britain's Moment*, pp. 56–8.

37 GB to FB, 12 January 1920.

38 GB to FB, 24 March 1920.

39 A. T. Wilson to Stephenson, 12 April 1920 (not numbered), A. T. Wilson's Papers, British Library.

40 GB to FB, 23 May 1920.

41 Mesopotamian Constitution, E. Bonham-Carter Committee, Summary of Proposals, July 1920, LP&S/11/174 P 4709 B343. Charles Tripp, *A History of Iraq*, (Cambridge, Cambridge University Press, 2000) pp. 40–1. The mandate given to Britain by the League of Nations at San Remo in 1920 specified Britain's obligation to prepare Iraq for self-rule but conditioned it to the submission of a constitutional draft prepared by the council of state (set by the constitutional committee headed by Sir Edgar Bonham-Carter) to the League. A legislative assembly appointed by local councils was meant to give the whole process a stamp of

legitimacy. The opposition to the mandate brought to its substitution by the 1922 treaty. Sluglett, *Britain in Iraq*, pp. 139–40.

42 Mesopotamian Constitution, Memorandum by Mr. H. R. C. Dobbs, Foreign Secretary to the Government of India, on the proposals of the Bonham-Carter Committee, 26 May 1920, LP&S/11/174 P 342.

Sir Henry Dobbs, who had laid the foundations for British administration in Basra and now served as foreign secretary to the government of India, made two suggestions: make the council's Arab members technically responsible for their departments, leaving in the hands of the British political officers the right to refer matters of discord to the High Commissioner. Dobbs also suggested that they preserve the authority of the shaykhs by letting them appoint the representatives in tribal areas rather than having the candidates elected by the heads of tribal subsections.

43 GB to HB, 1 June 1920; note by Gertrude Bell regarding Syrian Affairs, 7 May 1920, LP&S/11/174 P 4801.

44 Ibid.

45 Nakash, *The Shi'is of Iraq*, pp. 66-72.

46 Bell, *Review of the Civil Administration of Mesopotamia*, p. 140, and Nakash, *The Shi'is of Iraq*, pp. 68–70. The leaders of the movement and organisers of the *mawlids* were largely Sunnis, among them Yusuf Effendi Suwaydi, Shaykh Ahmad al-Da'ud, and 'Ali Effendi Bazirgan. The three leading Shi'is in the movement were Sayyid Muhammad al-Sadr, whom Gertrude Bell had met in January when invited to Kazimayn by his father, Sayyid Hasan al-Sadr, Muhammad Baqr al-Shabibi and Ja'far Abu Timman, a young lawyer she knew from Baghdad.

47 GB to HB, 7 and 14 June 1920.

48 Ibid.

49 Sluglett, *Britain in Iraq*, pp. 26, 39.

50 Telegram of 17 November 1918, quoted in Sluglett, *Britain in Iraq*, p. 28.

51 Ibid., p. 38.

52 F. C. C. Balfour Papers, Civil Commission Baghdad to GHQ, 21 September 1920, SAD 303/1/50.

53 Memorandum, 'The Outbreak of Disturbances – Rumaytha' by Major Daly (PO Diwaniyya), LP&S/10/761, July 1920. For the location of the tribes (the Fatla and the Banu Hasan, the Banu Zurayyij, Banu 'Ard, Albu Hasan and the Khaz'al) in the area see Great Britain Admiralty Naval Intelligence Division, *Iraq and the Persian Gulf*, Geographic Handbook Series (London, 1944), p. 366.

54 GB to HB, 11 July 1920.

55 GB to HB, 26 July 1920.

56 Batatu, *The Old Social Classes* p. 174. The tribesmen of Samawa had been incited by Muhsin Abu Tabikh (a wealthy landowner from the Muntafiq), Sayyid Hadi al-Muqatar of Sharafiyya, and Sha'lan Albu Chon from the Zawalim. Among the most palpable reasons for the open rebellion was the confiscation of rifles, the abolition of allowances to the shaykhs, mismanagement of Euphrates waters and the anti-British propaganda that flowed into the area. According to Batatu, the British irrigation scheme of weekly distribution of water, in a rotating schedule between Hilla and Shamiyya deprived the tribes from the Shamiyya area from their quote of water, stirring up the rebellion; Memorandum by Major Daly (PO Diwaniyya), June 1920, and report of FCC Balfour, 18 June 1920, SAD, LP&S/110/761. The tribesmen were helped by the *sarākil* (*sarkals*, or minor shaykhs) whose hostility against the British was a result of Britain's tribal policy that permitted the exploita-

tion of the cultivators and the *sarkals* themselves by the big shaykhs.

57 A. T. Wilson to Stephenson, 26 July 1920 (not numbered), A. T. Wilson Papers, British Library.
58 Ibid.
59 GB to HB, 2 August 1920.
60 Telegram, Civil Commissioner's Office, Baghdad, to Secretary of State, India, no. 11081, 11 September 1920; and Memorandum, Civil Commissioner Baghdad, to POs in the divisions, no. 10/223, in F. C. C. Balfour Papers, SAD 303/1/44; and Marr, *The Modern History of Iraq*, p. 33.
61 Longrigg's reports on Arbil and Kirkuk during the uprising and report of Civil Commissioner's Office, Baghdad, to Secretary of State, India, 16 July 1920, no. 8563, LP&S/10/761 P8625. The Surchi Kurds from 'Aqra invaded Desht i-Harir, and discontented aghas from Koi Sanjaq, led by Mulla Ahmed Agha-i Mann and Rasul Agha, caused a great deal of trouble for the British forces. In Arbil the disturbances were led by Mulla Effendi of the Bait section of the Diza'i, who had been inspired, as were other aghas, by the anti-British campaign led by Mustapha Kemal. Given the impact of the rebellion, the British were forced to revise their policy by attempting to buy the support of the aghas. Those who wanted to collaborate with Britain were rewarded with a percentage of the land revenues, farm taxes, and cash subsidies.
62 Gertrude Bell, 'An Account of Col. Leachman', Miscellaneous, GBP. Leachman was PO of Mosul from November 1918 until February 1920 and Military Governor part of the period.
63 GB to HB, 23 August 1920 (Private).
64 Marr, *The Modern History of Iraq*, p. 33 and Tripp, *The History of Iraq*, p. 44. Tripp rightly concludes that the 1920 rebellion is still 'claimed by different group used to assert their own roles in the foundation of the state'.
65 E. Kedourie, 'Mesopotamia, 1918–1921', in E. Kedourie, *England and the Middle East: The Destruction of the Ottoman Empire, 1914–1921* (1st edn 1956; London: Mansell, 1987), pp. 175–213, 190–1.
66 GB to HB, 30 August 1920.
67 GB to HB, 2 August 1920.
68 GB to HB, 14 June 1920.
69 GB to HB, 26 July 1920.
70 GB to HB, 1 June 1920.
71 A Case for Frankness', *The Times*, 15 June 1920, LP&S/10/761.
72 Quoted in A. T. Wilson's memorandum to POs in the divisions, 1 October 1920, no. 10/223, A. T. Wilson Papers, British Library, also at SAD 303/1/43-52.
73 Ibid.
74 Ibid.
75 Ibid. Faysal wanted to gather two more divisions to the new Iraqi army.
76 GB to HB, 9 May 1920 and 19 September 1920.
77 GB to HB, 19 September 1920.
78 GB to FB, 5 September 1920.
79 Ibid.
80 Ibid.
81 See also Kedourie, 'Mesopotamia, 1918–1921', ibid., p. 193.
82 The clash of views between the 'India school' to which A. T. Wilson and Edwin Montagu belonged and the more liberal views of the Inter-Departmental Committee of Middle Eastern Affairs was reflected in the debates between A. T. Wilson

and Lawrence and Gertrude Bell. See Longrigg, *Iraq – 1900–1950*, p. 116.

83 Memorandum by A. T. Wilson, 1 September 1920, no. 10/223, LP&S/10/761 P 7638, Civil Commissioner's Office, Baghdad, 1 October 1920, P 8230.

84 *The Times*, 19 August 1920, attached to Memorandum by A. T. Wilson, no. 10/223 (strictly confidential), Civil Commissioner's Office, Baghdad, 1 October 1920, LP&S/10/761, ibid.

85 GB to HB, 27 September 1920.

86 Monroe, *Britain's* Moment, pp. 66–7.

87 19 September 1920, GBP; and Ottoman Law for Selection of Deputies to Parliament Office, Civil Commissioner's Office, Baghdad, 25 August 1920, LP&S/10/759 P 7366/1920 Re: P 7422/1918.

88 GB to HB, 17 October 1920.

89 Monroe, *Britain's Moment*, p. 67.

90 GB to HB, 1 November 1920.

91 Percy Cox, *Iraq: Report on Iraq Administration, October 1920–March 1922* (London: H.M. Stationery Office, 1922).

  The council also included, as minister of justice, Mustafa Effendi Alusi, a *qadi* from a well-known family of ulama, and Ja'far al-'Askari, whose fame as an officer and as a governor of Aleppo during Faysal's term in Syria was great. Ja'far al-'Askari would serve as minister of defence on the Provisional Council. Other members included 'Izzat Pasha, a Turkman from Kirkuk, as minister of public works; Sayyid Muhammad Mahdi Tabataba'i, a Shi'i *'alim* from Karbala as minister of health; 'Abd al-Latif Pasha, a notable from Basra, as mnister of commerce; and Muhammad 'Ali Effendi, an ex-deputy in the Ottoman parliament, representing Mosul.

  Nine ministers without portfolio were also given seats in the council, including the mayor of Baghdad, 'Abd al-Majid Beg Shawi, two prominent shaykhs of large Shi'i tribal confederations, Christians from Mosul and Baghdad, and Sunni notables from Baghdad and Basra.

92 Ibid.

93 GB to HB, 7 February 1921.

94 Cox, *Iraq*. The administrative scheme followed along the lines of the former Ottoman administrative units; namely, 10 *liwas*, 35 *qadas*, and 85 *nahiyas*. The council would also have to reorganise administrative divisions in the Kurdish areas in order to address the interests of other ethnic groups, among them the Turkmen and the Christians, regarding education and revenue. The problem of Shi'i political representation was more complex, however, reflecting the different interests of the various sectors in the Shi'i community: the leading Shi'is of Baghdad refused to join the provisional council before the election of a Constituent Assembly, and the leading mujtahids of Najaf and Karbala, who were Persian subjects, were required to adopt Iraqi nationality before filling official positions. In addition, the prominent tribal leaders felt that the question of tribal representation had not been fully addressed.

95 GB to HB, 12 December 1920.

96 GB to HB, 7 November 1920. This scheme would also help end the stalemate created by the Shi'is' refusal to collaborate with the council on the grounds of Shi'i under-representation, and would circumvent the idea of a Shi'i autonomous enclave under Turkish suzerainty and British advisers still entertained by some Shi'i leaders.

97 GB to HB, 3 October 1920.

98 Nakash, *The Shi'is of Iraq*, p. 72.
99 GB to HB, 18 December 1920. The reality was more complex however. The Arab tribes converted to Shi'ism during the nineteenth century retained their Arab culture, language and values. Gertrude Bell's use of the term 'Arabisch' in the historical context in question (namely the establishment of the first Arab administrative council in Iraq) meant the alignment of Iraq's Shi'is with the Sunni dominated Arab Iraqi national movement.
100 Memorandum, 'Arab National Movement', September 1920, Miscellaneous 2, GBP; and Wilson, *Loyalties*, pp. 305–6.
101 Note by Gertrude Bell, 'The Settlement of the Arab Provinces', 1919, Miscellaneous 2, GBP; Conversation, F. C. C. Balfour with General Haddad, autumn 1920, F. C. C. Balfour Papers, SAD 303/1/77; see also Sluglett, *Britain in Iraq*, pp. 43–4, 45.
102 Ibid., pp. 43–4.
103 GB to HB, 18 December 1920.
104 GB to HB, 'Extremely Confidential', 10 January 1921.
105 Marr, *The Modern History of Iraq*, p. 34.
106 GB to HB, 'Extremely Confidential', 10 January 1921.
107 Ibid.
108 Said, *Orientalism*, p. 40.

7 'TO MAKE KINGS, TO INVENT KINGDOMS'

1 A. T. Wilson to F. C. C. Balfour, 20 January 1921, F.C.C. Balfour Papers, SAD, 303/1/95–100.
2 'Mesopotamia', lecture by Lieutenant Colonel A. T. Wilson, 15 April 1921, F. C. C. Balfour Papers, SAD 303/1/92-95.
3 Sluglett, *Britain in Iraq*, pp. 48, 49.
4 Short memorandum, 'Near East Department', by G. L. Bell, 1921, Miscellaneous 1, GBP. The department was organised in five subsections: Egypt (including Sudan, Cyprus and Malta), Palestine, Arabia, Mesopotamia, and East Africa.
5 Sluglett, *Britain in Iraq*, pp. 44, 49.
6 Iraq's territory (116,600 square miles) would be defended by the RAF, saving the Treasury £25 millions a year. See Manchester, *Winston Spencer Churchill*, p. 701 and Sluglett, *Britain in Iraq*, p. 49.
7 Quoted in Wilson, *Lawrence of Arabia*, (1990), p. 648.
8 Ibid.
9 Manchester, *Winston Spencer Churchill*, pp. 701–3.
10 Martin Swartz, *The Union of Democratic Control in British Politics during the First World War* (Oxford: Clarendon Press, 1971), pp. 203–4.
11 A. T. Wilson to Frank Balfour, Cairo, 25 March 1921, F. C. C. Balfour Papers, SAD 303/1/96-98.
12 Secretary of State, Foreign Office to Secretary of State, India, 2 March 1921, LP&S/10/556 E 2276/382/93.
13 Kinahan Cornwallis, *Asia before World War I*, (1st edn Arab Bureau, 1916; reproduced New York and Cambridge: Oleander Press, 1976).
14 Churchill to Colonel Lawrence, 19 April 1921, FO 371/6365 CP E4700/4531/93, 20 April 1921, Enclosure 1; and 24 May 1921, FO 371/6366 E5983.
15 GB to HB, 23 June 1921.
16 H. Bullard's minute of 4 March 1921, CO730/1/9829, quoted in Sluglett, *Britain*

in Iraq, p. 44.

17 GB to HB, 17 April 1921.
18 GB to HB, 23 June 1921.
19 Ibid.
20 GB to HB, 28 August 1921.
21 Ibid.; and G. L. Bell, 'The Fealty of the Tribes: A Chapter in the History of Iraq', Miscellaneous 20, GBP.
22 GB to HB, 30 June 1921.
23 GB to her family, 8 July 1921.
24 Ibid.
25 GB to HB, 12 June 1921.
26 See Marr, *The Modern History of Iraq*, pp. 34, 35.
27 Intelligence Reports, 1921, FO371/6353.
28 *Al Dijla*, 10 July 1921, quoted in Intelligence Report, July 1921, FO371/6353.
29 *Al 'Iraq*, 16 July 1921, Intelligence Report 18, July 1921, FO371/6353.
30 Ibid.
31 *Al 'Iraq*, 16 July 1921, Intelligence Report 18, July 1921, FO371/6353; and Intelligence Report 17, July 1921, FO371/6353; and GB to her family, 8 July 1921; GB to HB 30 June 1921.
32 GB to HB, 6 August 1921.
33 GB to HB, 20 July 1921.
34 The Jewish community amounted to approximately 90,000 people, of which 50,000 lived in Baghdad. See Sylvia G. Haim, 'Aspects of Jewish Life in Baghdad under the Monarchy', *Middle Eastern Studies*, 12 (1976).
35 Bell, 'The Fealty of the Tribes, A Chapter in the History of Iraq', in Miscellaneous 20, GBP.
36 Ibid.
37 Ibid.
38 GB to HB, 17 October 1921; Marr, *The Modern History of Iraq*, pp. 34–5; Batatu, *The Old Social Classes*, pp. 100–1.
39 Bell, 'The Fealty of the Tribes', ibid.
40 GB to HB, 6 August 1921.
41 GB to HB, 21 August 1921.
42 Bell, *Review of the Civil Administration of Mesopotamia*, GBP.
43 Ibid.
44 GB to her family, 17 October 1921; 'Britain's Relations with Kurdistan', 27 August 1919, LP&S/18/332. Many Kurdish leaders had, in the past, tried to fulfil this role. Among them was Sharif Pasha, who had headed a delegation of the Committee of Kurdish Independence at the Peace Conference. Another leader was Hamid Beg, whose vision focused on the resurrection of the Baban's principalities that had flourished in the area during Ottoman times. In view of the personal rivalries and the difficulty of delineating a model of administration that would satisfy the various demands, Britain had, after the war, proposed the idea of creating a strip of autonomous Kurdish emirates under British guidance. Sayyid Taha would control the territory stretching from Arbil to Van, Isma'il 'Simko' would control the area bordering Persia, and the Badr Khans would control the area of 'Urfa, Diyarbekr, and Mardin. Establishing this fringe of 'autonomous states' would serve two purposes: it would appease the different demands for autonomy and [it would] leave Mosul's interior to Iraq. However, Britain's 1919 commitment to Persia territory's integrity rendered the scheme impracticable. As a result

Britain gradually abandoned the idea of playing a more active role in the Kurdish areas across the Turkish border where a movement toward Kurdish autonomy was taking shape. Pamphlets translated by Jalal 'Ali Badr of the Central Committee for the Administration of Kurdistan. LP&S/18/330. LP&S/11/168 P1487/20, 20 February 1920, Reports from Cairo to Lloyd George, 9 December 1919.

45 GB to HB, 7 February 1921.

46 GB to HB, 29 May and 14 August 1921.

47 Intelligence Report 19, August 1921, and Intelligence Report 23, September 1921, in FO 371/6353. Other delegations poured into the capital, including representatives of the Jami'at Tashkilat Kurdiyya, headed by Khaled Rami Badr Khan and Rif'at Beg Mawlan Zada (former Mutasarrif of Malatiya and editor of the newspaper *Sarbasti*), and delegates of Jami'at Ta'ali Kurdiyya, founded by Sayyid 'Abd al Khadr of Neri. All of them asked to be granted independence and the right not to be subjugated by the Arabs as they had been by the Turks. Given the remote possibility that an autonomous Kurdish state would be created, Kirkuk's Turkoman population decided not to take part in the plebiscite either. They preferred to wait and see if an independent Kurdistan would be established 'and decide later'.

48 GB to HB, 28 August 1921.

49 Intelligence Reports 22 and 23, September 1921, FO371/6353.

50 But things were more complex. In effect, an anonymous letter written by an Iraqi army officer, which quoted Mirza Muhammad and Hamid Khan, Mutasarrif of Karbala, warned against the possible problems that would emerge from centralist administration under Faysal and the excessive costs of keeping an Arab army officered mainly by Sunnis. There were also reactions to the appointment of Sunni effendis as administrators in Shi'i tribal areas and, as the letter concluded, a general disbelief in *istiqlal* and *hurriyya* (independence and freedom). A. T. Wilson to Frank Balfour, London, 20 January 1921, F. C. C. Balfour Papers, SAD 303/1/95. Anonymous letter to Col. Wilson, Basra, 5 October 1921, F. C. C. Balfour Papers, SAD 303/1/101-103.

51 GB to HB, 11 September 1921.

52 Ibid.

53 Ibid., and GB to her family, 17 September 1921.

54 GB to HB, 18 December 1920.

55 See Nakash, *The Shi'is of Iraq*.

56 GB to Frank Balfour, 13 May 1921, F. C. C. Balfour's Papers, SAD 303/1/41-42(v).

57 A. T. Wilson to Frank Balfour, Muhammara, 17 June 1922, F. C. C. Balfour's Papers, SAD 303/1/109-110.

58 GB to HB, 11 and 25 September 1921.

59 Ibid.

60 Also quoted in Gordon, *Gertrude Bell*.

61 Ibid.

62 GB to HB, 31 July 1921.

63 21 March 1921, FO 371/6365 E 4347. Among them were Yusuf and Tawfiq al-Suwaydi and Mawlud Mukhlis.

64 GB to Lord Hardinge of Penshurst, 6 August 1921, Correspondence, GB to Lord Hardinge, 1920–2, GBP.

65 Lord Hardinge to GB, 27 December 1920.

66 GB to Lord Hardinge, 24 November 1921.

67 GB to HB, 13 October 1921.
68 GB to HB, 18 December 1921.
69 Batatu, *The Old Social Classes*, p. 177; and Marr, *The Modern History of Iraq*, pp. 34–9.
70 SS Colonies to High Commission, telegram, 16 August 1921, FO 371/6352 E 9483/100/93. Also quoted by Batatu, *The Old Social Classes*, p. 324.
71 GB to HB, 9 November 1921.
72 Ibid.
73 Ibid.
74 GB to HB, 17 September 1921.
75 Ibid.
76 GB to HB, 17 October 1921.
77 See Liora Lukitz, *Iraq: The Search for National Identity* (London: Frank Cass, 1995), pp. 23–4.
78 The Christians in Iraq represented sixty per cent of the population in Mosul area (comprising mainly peasants scattered in valleys and plains of the Kurdish highlands; twenty per cent in Baghdad also comprising Armenians. They were mainly merchants. The Chaldeans (Nestorians united to Rome) and Jacobins had a patriarch in Mosul. See Marr, *The Modern History of Iraq*, pp. 11, 39, 51, 57-59; Batatu, *The Old Social Classes*, pp. 40, 312.
79 GB to her parents, 10 October 1920.
80 GB to her parents, 12 and 13 November 1921.
81 Ibid.
82 Ibid.
83 Ibid.
84 Ibid.
85 See Lukitz, *Iraq*, p. 84.
86 GB to HB, 2 January and 16 February 1922.
87 GB to HB, 31 January 1922.
88 Marr, *The Modern History of Iraq*, p. 110.
89 Sluglett, *Britain in Iraq*, pp. 75–82.
90 Telegram, High Commissioner Percy Cox to Secretary of State for Colonies, 12 March 1922, LP&S/11/212.
91 GB to HB, 30 March 1922.
92 GB to HB, 16 February 1922.
93 GB to HB, 22 June 1922.
94 Ibid.
95 GB to HB, 16 February 1922.
96 GB to HB, 6 July 1922, and GB to her family, 4 June 1922.
97 Ibid.
98 Batatu, *The Old Social Classes*, pp. 25–7.
99 GB to her family, 4 June 1922.
100 GB to HB, 30 July 1922.
101 *Public Opinion and Affairs in Baghdad*, 1922, Miscellaneous 2, GBP.
102 GB to Percy Loraine, 25 March 1922.
103 Monroe, *Britain's Moment*, p. 26.
104 Ibid., p. 76. Britain would condition Egypt's independence on its ability to guarantee the security of the Suez Canal, the Sudan, the minorities and the country's defence. Egypt's 'failure' to comply with the requirements implied a continuous British presence also after formal independence was achieved.

105 GB to Percy Loraine, 25 March 1922.
106 Monroe, *Britain's Moment*, p. 72.
107 GB to Percy Loraine, 19 August 1922.
108 Ibid.
109 GB to her family, 27 August 1922. See also Burgoyne, *Gertrude Bell*, pp. 292–3.
110 Ibid.
111 Sluglett, *Britain in Iraq*, pp. 76–9.
112 The 1922 treaty had two annexes: a Judicial Agreement to safeguard the interests of foreigners, allowing them to retain some of the advantages and privileges they enjoyed under the system of capitulations; and a Financial Agreement that transferred all public works built by the British to Iraq. The railway system and the port of Basra – considered strategic assets – would, however, remain under British control. The signing of the treaty did not diminish the dangers pressing from all directions. Threats from outside (the Turks from the north and the Wahhabi Ikhwan from the south-west) and threats from inside (the Kurds and the Shi'is) would continue to shape Iraq's politics and challenge the new Iraqi leaders. Ibid. The treaty stipulated that the king and the members of his cabinet would be Iraqis, but that the advisers attached to the ministries would be British. Arab officials and British inspectors in the provinces would send reports to the British adviser at the Ministry of the Interior (initially, Kinahan Cornwallis), who would then report to the high commissioner. The high commissioner would report to the Air Officer Commanding (AOC), the functionary responsible for maintaining internal order. British forces would defend the country against external attacks and help the Arab army to preserve domestic tranquillity. Iraq would pay a half share of the high commissioner's costs and those of his staff. The system permitted Britain's control on both financial and military levels, as well as the country's foreign affairs. A protocol to be signed in April 1923 would reduce the period of mutual engagement to four years, conditional on the enforcement of peace with Turkey. A clause would further reduce the treaty's extension, provided that Iraq was admitted to the League of Nations. See Marr, *The Modern History of Iraq*, pp. 38–40, Lukitz, *Iraq*, pp. 14–17 and Monroe, *Britain's Moment*, pp. 76–7.
113 As in 1918–19 and the plebiscite leading to Faysal's election in 1921. Sluglett, *Britain in Iraq*, pp. 79–90.

8 'A TOWER OF STRENGTH AND WISDOM

1 GB to Percy Loraine, 3 March 1923.
2 GB to Percy Loraine, 16 April 1923.
3 GB to Percy Loraine, 19 August 1922.
4 GB to HB, 6 July 1922.
5 AIR 23/2, 'Situation in Iraq', 30 September 1922.
6 Memorandum by G. L. Bell, 'Kurdish Situation', 1922, Confidential, in Miscellaneous 2, GBP.
7 AIR 23/2, 'Situation in Iraq'; and Bell, 'Kurdish Situation', ibid.
8 Ibid.
9 GB to HB, 8 October 1922.
10 C. J. Edmonds, *Kurds, Turks, and Arabs* (London: Oxford University Press, 1957), pp. 280, 301–2, and GBP.
11 Ibid., p. 280.
12 Lukitz, *Iraq*, p. 42.

13 GB to HB 8, 10 and 24 September 1922, and Edmonds, *Kurds, Turks, and Arabs*.
14 Lukitz, *Iraq*, pp. 36, 37.
15 The first Kurdish newspaper, *Kurdistan*, appeared in Cairo in 1989, and *Roja Kurd* (Kurdish Day), and *Jin* (Life) appeared in the 1910s in Istanbul.
16 Kirmanji (or the northern dialect) was spoken in Turkey, Armenia, Azerbaijan and Bahdinan (in Mosul liwa); Sorani or Kurdi was spoken in the centre (Arbil, Sulaymaniyya, Kirkuk, and Mahahad); and Gorani was sandwiched between the central and southern group of dialects.
17 GB to Percy Loraine, 16 April 1923.
18 GB to Percy Loraine, 27 May 1922.
19 GB to Molly Trevelyan, 29 December 1922.
20 Ibid.
21 GB to Percy Loraine, Baghdad, 15 September 1923.
22 See Cannadine, *Decline and Fall*, pp. 504, 539, 540, 542.
23 GB to HB, 24 October 1922.
24 Cannadine, *Decline and Fall*, pp. 229–30.
25 GB to Percy Loraine, 15 September 1923.
26 Cannadine, *G. M. Trevelyan*, p. 4.
27 Cannadine, *Decline and Fall*, pp. 4–6.
28 See John, *Elizabeth Robins*, p. 199.
29 Ibid.
30 ER to FB, 22 February 1922, Series 5A, ERP.
31 ER to FB, 3 March 1922, Series 5AF, ERP.
32 John, *Elizabeth Robins*, pp. 206, 207.
33 ER to FB, 31 August 1921, Series 5A, ERP.
34 FB to ER, 1923, Series B17, ERP.
35 ER to FB, 17 November 1923, ERP.
36 GB to Charles Trevelyan, 30 January 1924.
37 Ibid.
38 GB to Molly Trevelyan, 9 August 1923.
39 GB to FB, 27 April 1922.
40 GB to HB, 25 September 1923.
41 Ibid.
42 Ibid.
43 Ibid.
44 GB to HB and her family, 29 November, 5 and 31 December 1923.
45 Ibid.
46 E. T. Williams and H. M. Palmer (eds), *The Dictionary of National Biography, 1957–1960* (Oxford: Oxford University Press, 1971); and *The New York Times*, 5 June 1959.
47 T. E. Lawrence, *The Seven Pillars of Wisdom* (London and New York: Dorset Press, 1926; 1935; New York: Doubleday, 1991), p. 58.
48 Kinahan Cornwallis' Obituary, *The New York Times*, 5 June 1959; and Williams and Palmer, *Dictionary of National Biography*, pp. 256–7 and Telegram, Lord Allenby to Foreign Office, Cairo, 12 December 1920, FO 371/5197 E 15591/800/44.
    Cornwallis was thirty-eight when he first came to Iraq with Faysal in 1921. His acquaintance with Faysal dated from 1915 when, as a young member of the Arab Bureau, he was sent by Clayton to Jedda to obtain King Husayn's approval for the planned Arab revolt. Cornwallis later succeeded D. H. Hogarth and Gilbert Clay-

ton as director of the Arab Bureau and was appointed to the Distinguished Service Order (DSO) and Commander of the Order of the British Empire (CBE) before proceeding to Syria as a political officer. He then became Emir Faysal's close friend. Cornwallis served again as the head of the Arab Bureau during the years 1919–20. He had followed Faysal in his journey by sea from Jedda to Basra in 1921 after having been transferred from the Ministry of Finance in Egypt to the Middle East department at the Colonial Office, to Iraq.

49 GB to HB, 18 December 1921.
50 Ibid.
51 GB to her family, 18 September 1923.
52 GB to HB, 11 and 13 December 1923.
53 GB to HB, 20 February 1924.
54 GB to HB, 5 December 1923.
55 Ibid.
56 GB to HB, 31 December 1923.
57 GB to FB, 13 February 1924.
58 GB to HB, 4 May 1924.
59 Press supplements in Intelligence Reports for 1923, *Al Istiqlal*, 10 September 1923, FO 371/9010.
60 Ibid.
61 GB to HB, 21 April 1924.
62 Ibid.
63 GB to HB, 9 April 1924.
64 GB to HB, 24 September 1922, GB to FB, 13 July 1924, and GB to HB, 24 June 1925.
65 Ibid. A Sunni lawyer from Kirkuk (born in 1889), of Turkish descent, Yasin al-Hashimi saw in his tenure of office a natural instance to which he had been close from his childhood (his father has served as a *mukhtar* of Baghdad). After the fall of Faysal's administration in Syria (in which he served as C.G.S. of Faysal's army) he remained in Damascus until March 1922, when he returned to Baghdad. Appointed by Faysal to the post of mutasarrif of the Muntafiq at first, Yasin became minister of communication and works in Abdul Muhsin al-Sa'dun's cabinet. From this time on, Yasin became the staunchest opponent to the treaty, trying to avoid its ratification by the Constituent Assembly. He would later, in a typical pragmatic move, induce the Assembly members to accept it. Yasin al-Hashimi fulfilled different ministerial functions until 1935 when he became prime minister again (he had served shortly as prime minister in 1924). He is also remembered by the tribal rebellion that occurred during his premiership and by his dubious acquisition of government lands, while in power. Leading Personalities in Iraq, 18 January 1937, FO 371/20801 E 363/363/93 .
66 GB to HB, 24 September 1922.
67 Faysal himself was reluctant to embrace Yasin's conditional loyalty as he remembered Yasin's readiness to give in too quickly to General Gouraud's ultimatum in 1920.
68 GB to Alfred Spender, from *Westminster Gazette*, 20 August 1924.
69 Edmonds, *Kurds, Turks, and Arabs*, p. 384.
70 GB to HB, 1 April 1924.
71 19 November 1924, FO 371/10097 E 11170/232/65, CP, and E 10056/232/65, Ratification of Anglo-Iraqi Treaty; and Text of Treaty of Alliance between Britain and Iraq, 10 October 1922, FO 371/10834. Cmd. 2370/1925, enclosures Finan-

cial, Judicial and Military Agreements.
72 GB to HB, 18 June 1924.
73 GB to HB, 28 May 1924.
74 GB to Molly Trevelyan, June 1924.
75 FB to ER, 25 October 1924, ERP.
76 Ibid.
77 GB to HB, 26 November 1924.
78 Principal Probate Registry Divorce Files, J 77/2132 No. 12495, 1924, Public Record Office, Chancery Lane, London.
79 GB to HB, 26 November 1924.
80 Ibid.
81 GB to FB, 8 October 1924.
82 ER Diaries, 22 September 1924, Series 5A, File 33, ERP.
83 ER Diaries, 24 October 1924, ERP.
84 ER Diaries, 29 December 1924ERP.
85 GB to HB, 15 April 1924.
86 Sluglett, *Britain in Iraq*, pp. 105–16. The Mosul question in 1919–20 differed from the evolution of the problem in the 1920s. In 1919 Britain's differences with France on the issue were solved by the Berenger-Long oil agreement, which assigned to France the twenty-five per cent share in the TPC formerly retained by Germany. Sluglett, *Britain in Iraq*, p. 59, fn. 84.
87 The US interests were accommodated in 1923 when the US government received one-quarter of the TPC's share capital. Sluglett, *Britain in Iraq*, pp. 108–9.
88 GB to her family, 17 September 1921, and GB to HB, 5 January 1923. See Marr, *The Modern History of Iraq*, pp. 40–3; Sluglett, *Britain in Iraq*, pp. 110–14; and Lukitz, *Iraq*, pp. 17–19.
89 The Arab Cause and the Mosul Question', *Al Istiqlal*, 24 October 1923, Intelligence Report 21, November 1923, in FO 371/9010. The estimates then were 58 per cent Kurds, 23.5 per cent Arabs, 8.5 per cent Turkmen, 8 per cent Christian, 2 per cent Jews. The Turks claimed that the Kurds were of Turanian origin and therefore Ottomans.
90 GB to Percy Loraine, 15 September 1923.
91 GB to HB, 18 December 1920.
92 GB to HB, 28 May 1924.
93 GB to Alfred Spender, 20 August 1924.
94 Edmonds, *Kurds, Turks, and Arabs*, p. 383. Salih Beg Naftchizada (from Kirkuk), Jamil Beg Baban (from Kifri), Shaykh Habib Talabani (a leading tribal chief from Kirkuk), Ishaq Efrayim (from the Jewish community), Shaykh Qadir (brother of Shaykh Mahmud, representing the Barzinji), and 'Izzat Beg (son of 'Adlah Khanum of the Jaf tribe).
95 GB to Alfred Spender, 20 August 1924.
96 *Al Iraq*, 25 October 1923; *Al Istiqlal*, 24 October 1923; *Al Amal*, 8 November 1923. In Intelligence Report, November 1924, FO 371/9010. Also see Sluglett, *Britain in Iraq*, p. 59, fn. 84.
97 *Al Istiqlal*, 27 February 1924, Intelligence Report 5, 6 March 1924, FO 371/ 10097.
98 GB to FB, 13 July 1924.
99 See Sluglett, *Britain in Iraq*, pp. 161–70.
100 GB to HB, 3 January 1921.
101 GBP and GB to Molly Trevelyan, 29 December 1922.

102 Ibid.
103 GB to FB, 28 January 1925.
104 GB to FB, 21 January 1925.
105 Intelligence Reports, 1925, 3 March 1925, FO 371/10833 E 1283/126.
106 GB to FB, 4 February 1925.
107 Diary no. 3 of Liaison Officer to League of Nations Frontier Commission, C. J. Edmonds, Secret, 22 February 1925 to 3 March 1925, C. J. Edmonds' Papers, Middle East Centre, St Antony's College, Oxford.
108 See Sluglett, *Britain in Iraq*, pp. 123, 124.
109 GB to her family, 18 February 1925.
110 Intelligence Reports, 1923, Report no. 6, April 1925, FO 371/10833 E 12135.
111 Edmonds, *Kurds, Turks, and Arabs*, p. 398. For an opposite view, see Sluglett, *Britain in Iraq*, pp. 110, 111.
112 Sluglett, *Britain in Iraq*, ibid.
113 'The Geography of the Mosul Boundary', by Major H. I. Lloyd, Meeting of the Royal Geographic Society, 8 March 1926.
114 Ibid.
115 See Lukitz, *Iraq*, p. 44. Mosul's population was estimated then as 600,000 from which 300,000 were Kurds.
116 See Sluglett, *Britain in Iraq*, pp. 112, 113.
117 Ibid.; and Marr, *The Modern History of Iraq*, pp. 42, 43.

9 'WE HAD AWAKENED AND BECOME A NATION'

1 GB to HB, 18 February 1925.
2 Gertrude Bell, 'Review of the Administration of Mesopotamia', Cmd 1061, 1920.
3 Divided into seven sects, each with its own guardian angel, the Yazidis counted among their saints Malik Farah al-Din (the moon), Khatum Fakhrah (the keeper of the gate of Paradise), Shaykh Maud (the picker of vipers), and the Kochak (the diviners, the dreamers of dreams).
4 Bell, 'Review of the Administration', ibid.
5 Gertrude Bell, *Amurath to Amurath* (London: 1911).
6 The Seveners (al Sab'iyya) were followers of the seventh imam, Isma'il, whom they also called al-Tamm (the Final), in the last in the line of 'Ali's successors. The symbolism of the number seven permeated their whole approach, as it represented the sum of all possible directions in space: right, left, forward, backward, above, below, and centre. The Seveners comprised, among others, the Fatimids, the 'Alawis, and the Isma'ilis. Other heterodox sects Ahl al-Haqq (the People of the Absolute, the Divine Truth) and the 'Ali Ilahis (the Deifiers of 'Ali) believed that 'Ali ibn Abi Talib, the Prophet's cousin and son-in law was the final Imam.
7 See Sluglett, *Britain in Iraq*, pp. 239–43.
8 GB to HB, 10 January 1921.
9 GB to Sir Percy Loraine, 19 August 1922. See also Nakash, *The Shi'is in Iraq*, pp. 27–38, 45–8; Sluglett, *Britain in Iraq*, pp. 231–53; Marr, *The Modern History of Iraq*, pp. 43–6; and Lukitz, *Iraq*, pp. 50–8.
10 The Sunnis opted to choose from among the Prophet's companions, whereas the Shi'is asserted that the caliphate should pass down to his nephew 'Ali ibn Abi Talib.
11 GB to HB, 1 November 1920.
12 'Allamah Tabataba'i, *A Shi'ite Anthology*, trans. William C. Chittick (London:

Muhammadi Trust of Great Britain and Northern Ireland, 1981); 'Allamah Tabataba'i, *Shi'ite Islam,* trans. and ed., Sayyid Husayn Nasr (Albany, NY: State University of New York Press, 1975); and 'Allamat Reza Muzaffar, *The Beliefs of Shi'ite School* (London, New York, 1985).

13 See Nakash, *The Shi'is in Iraq,* pp. 146–7.

14 Memo on the Political Situation, 1922, Miscellaneous, GBP.

15 See Sluglett, *Britain in Iraq,* pp. 82–6, 306–14; Nakash, *The Shi'is in Iraq,* pp. 79–85, 110–11; and Marr, *The Modern History of Iraq,* pp. 44–7.

16 Intelligence Reports nos. 22, 24, 25 of November and December 1923, FO 371/10097, and *Al Istiqlal,* 10 October 1923, in Intelligence Report, 18 October 1923 in FO 371/9010.

17 Intelligence Report 18, 3 September 1925, FO 371/10833.

18 Bell, *Review of the Civil Administration of Mesopotamia,* p. 21.

19 See Abbas Kelidar, 'The Shi'i Imami Community and Politics in the Arab East', *Middle Eastern Studies,* 19 (1983); Nakash, *The Shi'is in Iraq,* pp. 111, 115; Lukitz, *Iraq,* pp. 110–21; Reeva Simon, 'The Teaching of History in Iraq before the Rashid 'Ali Coup of 1941', *Middle Eastern Studies* (Winter 1986), pp. 37–51, 82–5; Phebe Marr, 'The Development of a Nationalist Ideology in Iraq, 1920–1941', *Muslim World* (1985), p. 92; Sati' al Husri, *Mudhakkirati-fil-Iraq,* vol. 2 (Beirut, 1967).

20 See Sluglett, *Britain in Iraq,* pp. 273–91; Lukitz, *Iraq,* pp. 111–21; Marr 'The Development of a Nationalist Ideology', ibid.; Simon, 'The Teaching of History in Iraq', ibid.

21 GB to her family, 18 March 1924.

10 'DUST . . ',

1 GB to HB, 8 April 1925

2 GB to HB, 23 December 1924.

3 FB to ER, 29 December 1924, ERP.

4 FB to ER, 25 October 1924, Series 5B, Box 9, Folder 19, ERP.

5 Series 5A, File 33, 1924, ERP.

6 FB to ER, 17 July 1923, Folder 32, Series 5A, ERP.

7 ER Diaries, 30 July and 1 August 1925, ERP.

8 Ibid.

9 FB to ER, September 1925, Series B20, ERP.

10 GB to Molly Trevelyan, 9 September 1925.

11 ER Diaries, 1924–6, 1A, Box 7, Folders 6–8, ERP.

12 Ibid.

13 HB to Hon. J. H. Thomas, M.P., Colonial Office, Rounton, 5 July 1924, GBP.

14 ER Diaries, 31 August 1925, ERP.

15 GB to Molly Trevelyan, Rounton, 27 September 1925.

16 GB to FB, Baghdad, 21 October 1925.

17 Ibid.

18 GB to HB, 17 November 1925.

19 Intelligence Report, 12 November 1925, GBP. Ibn Sa'ud finally signed a first draft of the agreement with Clayton, who had been empowered by the Iraqi government to do so. Although not officially involved, Gertrude remained an authoritative figure to be consulted about, or at least informed of, the nascent state's difficulties.

20　GB to Molly Trevelyan, 25 November 1925.
21　Ibid.
22　Ibid.
23　GB to HB, 12 December 1925.
24　GB to HB, 13 January 1926.
25　GB to HB,30 December 1925
26　Ibid.
27　GB to HB, 27 January 1926.
28　GB to HB, 22 January 1925.
29　GB to HB, 13 January 1926.
30　GB to FB, 28 January 1925.
31　GB to HB, 13 January 1926.
32　GB to HB, 1 February 1926.
33　GB to FB, 16 February 1926.
34　FB to ER, 11 February 1926, ERP.
35　ER to FB, 18 May 1920, ERP.
36　HB to ER, 10 February 1926, ERP.

11 'FLOOD . . ',

1　GB to FB, 14 April 1926.
2　Ibid.
3　Ibid.
4　Georges Roux, *Ancient Iraq* (1964; reprint, London: Penguin Books, 1992), pp. 110–11.
5　Ibid.
6　GB to her family, 4 May 1909.
7　C. Leonard Woolley, *The Sumerians* (London: Norton, 1965).
8　Gertrude Bell, *Ukhaidir* (London: Clarendon Press, 1914).
9　GB to FB, 26 May 1926.
10　GB to HB, 26 May 1926.
11　GB to FB, 2 June 1926.
12　Ibid.
13　ER Diaries, June 1926, *The Express*, ERP.
14　Ibid.
15　GB to HB, 30 June 1926.
16　GB to Molly Trevelyan, 16 March 1926.
17　Gertrude Bell, *The Desert and the Sown* (1907; reprint, Boston: Beacon Press, 1987), p. 41.
18　Bell, 'The Fealty of the Tribes: A Chapter in the History of Iraq', Miscellaneous 20, GBP.
19　*Poems of the Divan of Hafiz*, translated by G. L. Bell (London: Heinemann, 1897).
20　Annemarie Schimel, *I am Wind, You are Fire: The Life and Work of Rumi* (Boston: Shambhala Dragons Edition, 1996), pp. 51–5, 58, 71, 195–202.
21　Letters from Molly Trevelyan, December 13, 1892, ERP.
22　Isabella Bird, *Journeys in Persia and Kurdistan* (London, 1891).
23　Peter A. Clayton and Martin J. Price, *The Seven Wonders of the Ancient World* (1980; reprint, London: Routledge, 1995).
24　*Poems of the Divan of Hafiz*, trans. Bell.
25　GB to DW, 15 March 1915.

26 *Poems of the Divan of Hafiz*, trans. Bell.
27 FB to ER, September 1915, ERP.
28 GB to HB, 16 February 1922
29 Also quoted in Winstone, *Gertrude Bell* (1993), p. 268.
30 FB to Molly Trevelyan, 19 July 1926.
31 T. E. Lawrence to Lady Richmond (Elsa), August 1926, Miscellaneous 7, GBP.
32 Elizabeth Robins' [radio] broadcast, 17 September 1927, Miscellaneous 14 and 36, GBP.
33 *The New York Herald*, 24 July 1921, GBP.
34 Ibid.
35 Preface by Sir Edmond Denison Ross to Gertrude L. Bell's *Persian Pictures* (London, 1928; reprinted by Ernest Benn after Gertrude Bell's death).
36 Ibid.
37 Elizabeth Robins' [radio] broadcast on Gertrude Bell.
38 Ibid.
39 FB to ER, 22 October 1927, series 7129, ERP.
40 FB to ER, 14 October 1927, ERP.
41 FB to ER, Mount Grace, 11 October 1927, File 22, ERP.
42 FB to ER, 23 October 1927, ERP.
43 Gertrude Bell, *The Iraq: An Experiment in Anglo-Asiatic Relations*, Miscellaneous 1923, GBP.
44 Ibid.
45 GB to Florence Lascelles, Konya, 4 April 1905.
46 FB to ER, 23 December 1926, ERP.
47 FB to ER, 23 October 1927, ERP.
48 FB to ER, 5 April 1927, Folder 22 5B, ERP.
49 FB to ER, 23 October 1927, ERP.
50 Malcolm Brown (ed.), *The Letters of T. E. Lawrence* (New York: Oxford University Press, 1991), pp. 352–3.
51 FB to ER, 23 and 26 November 1927, ERP.
52 Elizabeth Robins' [radio] broadcast on Gertrude Bell.
53 FB to ER, 29 September 1927, ERP.
54 GB to HB, 9 June 1926.
55 Lord Hardinge of Penshurst to GB, 20 December 1920 and 20 September 1921.
56 Chapter of an unfinished, undated manuscript by Gertrude L. Bell, Miscellaneous 20, GBP.
57 Monroe, *Britain's Moment*, p. 47.

EPILOGUE

1 T. E. Lawrence's letters to his mother, Jerabulus, 31 March 1911; Carchemish, 29 April 1911, from Brown, *The Letters of T. E. Lawrence*, pp. 33–6.
2 *The Times*, 22 July 1920; *Observer*, 8 August 1920; and *The Sunday Times*, 22 August 1920.
3 T. E. Lawrence to Charlotte Shaw, 13 October 1927, quoted in Mack, *Prince of Our Disorder*.
4 T. E. Lawrence's suppressed introduction to *Seven Pillars of Wisdom*, quoted in Mack, *A Prince of Our Disorder*, pp. 271–2.
5 T. E. Lawrence to G. J. Kidston, Foreign Office, quoted in Brown, *The Letters of T. E. Lawrence*, pp. 168–70.

6 Mack, quoting Anis Sayigh on T. E. Lawrence's personal reasons for his Middle Eastern campaigns, in *A Prince of Our Disorder*, pp. 194–5. Anis Sayigh, a well-known Arab nationalist writer, analysed Lawrence's role in the Middle East, as follows: 'Lawrence gave Britain the right of trusteeship over the East as he gave himself the trusteeship over the two', Anis Sayigh, 'Ra'y 'Arabi fi Lawrence' ['An Arab Opinion on Lawrence'], *Hiwar*, 5 (July–August 1963), pp. 15–23.
7 Florence Bell, *The Minor Moralist*, p. 385.
8 GB to HB, 22 January 1924.
9 Bell, memorandum, 'Syria in 1919', LP&S/18/B337 P 8253/19.
10 Freya Stark, *East Is West* (1945; reprint London: Century Travellers, Arrow Books, 1991), p. 186.
11 T. E. Lawrence, *The Seven Pillars of Wisdom* (New York: Doubleday, 1996), p. 58.
12 Sir Kinahan Cornwallis's obituary, *The Times*, 5 June 1959.
13 David Boyle on Sir Kinahan Cornwallis, in Williams and Palmer, *Dictionary of National Biography*, pp. 257–8.
14 Termination contract of Sir Kinahan Cornwallis, 5 June 1935, FO 371/18954 E 3592.
15 Archibald Clark Kerr, Baghdad, to George Rendel, Foreign Office, 30 May 1935, Private, FO371/18954 E 3592.
16 Marr, *The Modern History of Iraq*, pp. 67–8.
17 The pro-Axis coup headed by Rashid 'Ali al-Gaylani turned the British–Iraqi equation upside-down, as the terms of the Anglo-Iraqi Treaty of 1930 were put again into question. While the Russians advanced toward Persia and Afghanistan in the summer of 1941 the British reinforced their military presence in Iraq that started building from April also in response to Rashid 'Ali's flirtation with the Axis powers and the surrounding of the RAF bases at Habbaniyya and the British embassy in Baghdad by Iraqi troops.
18 Kinahan Cornwallis to Eden, Foreign Office, 30 March 1945, FO371/45302.
19 Cornwallis' departure from Iraq coincided with these changes in the country's political orientation and with reactions to Baghdad's growing control over the provinces. Under Yasin al-Hashimi's second ministry (March 1935 to October 1936), the tribes of Rumaytha and Diwaniyya rebelled (May 1935), followed by the tribes in Suq-al-Shuyukh, Nasiriyya, and the Muntafiq. In the summer of 1935 the rebellious Kurdish tribes of Barzan were subdued by the Iraqi army while another military contingent was on its way to Jabal Sanjar to control the Yazidis, who were resisting conscription to the Iraqi army. In April and June 1936, Rumaytha and Diwaniyya reignited and were bombarded from the air. This growing unrest had multi-layered reasons, ranging from religious and ethnic groups' claims for autonomy, to the revival of tribalism and the passage from a tribal to a settled society. It was also the outcome of the economic disparities aggravated by sectarian politics. On the surface, however, there were ongoing personal rivalries among Baghdad politicians: Nuri al-Sa'id and Ja'far al-'Askari, on the one hand, and Yasin al-Hashimi and Rashid 'Ali al-Gaylani, on the other. The rivalries between the two groups stemmed from their different positions on the need to comply with the British after independence and to what degree. Kedourie, 'The Kingdom of Iraq', in *The Chatham House Version* (1970), pp. 236–85; Lukitz, *Iraq*, pp. 50–81.
20 Ibid. The divisions in the Shi'i camp after independence differed in essence from the splits that had characterised the first years of Faysal's rule. The Shi'is who had contributed in such a large measure in the struggle against the mandate and fur-

ther against Britain's 'indirect rule' engaged, after Iraq's independence, in different contentions. Also the leaders of the Shi'i religious establishment (where the state-oriented, Arab-speaking ulama had grown in influence at the expense of the older, Persia oriented, guard) engaged after independence in a strife to shape Iraq, as an Arab state, but not exclusively Sunni in its definition. However, the main problem to the Sunni establishment after independence remained the Shi'i tribes. The tribal shaykhs, seeing their power diminished and their economic problems increased, continued to rebel during the 1930s. Also see Nakash, *The Shi'is of Iraq*, pp. 82–8 and Marr, *The Modern History of Iraq*, pp. 55–76. Also see GB to her family, 18 March 1924.

21 Kinahan Cornwallis to Elsa Richmond, 20 September 1941, Miscellaneous item 1, GBP.

22 Lady Elsa Richmond, *The Earlier Letters of Gertrude Bell* (London: Benn, 1937).

23 Kinahan Cornwallis to Elsa Richmond, September 1945, Miscellaneous item 7, GBP.

24 Molly Izard, *Freya Stark: A Biography* (London: Spectre, 1993). After serving as director of the British Bank in the Middle East, Sir Kinahan Cornwallis died in North Warnborough, Hampshire, on 3 June 1959.

25 GB to Molly Trevelyan, July 1922, Molly's Letters, GBP.

26 FB to Molly Trevelyan, 19 July 1926, Molly Trevelyan Papers.

AFTERWORD

1 Divine, *Hadrian's Wall*.

2 Interviews with Sir Geoffrey Trevelyan, youngest son of Sir Charles and Lady Mary (Molly) Trevelyan, St Albans, and Lady Bridget Plowden, daughter of Lady Elsa and Admiral Sir Herbert Richmond, Essex, August 1997.

3 Raleigh Trevelyan, *Wallington* (London: National Trust Publication, Penhurst Press, 1982).

4 Leslie, *Mark Sykes*.

5 Cannadine, *G. M. Trevelyan*, p. 8.

6 Ibid., p. 183.

7 Ibid., p. 164.

8 John, *Elizabeth Robins*.

9 GB to her family, 9 January 1914 and 22 March 1900.

10 From Dean Burgon's 1845 Newchgate Prize poem 'Petra', reprinted in Iain Browning, *Petra* (1st edn 1973; London: Chatto & Windus, 1994).

11 Gertrude Bell *Ukhaidir*, 'Preface'.

12 Also quoted in Gordon, *Gertrude Bell*.

13 M. R. Ridley, *Gertrude Bell* (1st edn 1941; London: Blackie & Son, 1943), pp. 164–5.

14 Dearden, 'A Journey to the Heart'.

15 Gertrude L. Bell, 'Report on British Expeditionary Forces "D" 1917', GBP.

16 GB to HB, 3 January 1921.

17 GB to Frank Balfour, Suez, 25 March 1921.

18 GB to her parents, 17 September 1921.

19 GB to HB, 22 January and 7 and 13 February 1921.

20 GB to HB, 22 January, 17 October and 7 February 1921.

21 Ridley, *Gertrude Bell*, pp. 65–6.

Selected Bibliography

PRIMARY SOURCES/DOCUMENTS

Gertrude Bell's Papers: letters, diaries, notebooks, memoranda and official papers assembled at the Robinson Library, Special Collections, University of Newcastle-upon-Tyne.

Gertrude Bell & Lord Hardinge Correspondence, Cambridge University Library.

Gertrude Bell's Papers at the Royal Geographical Society, London.

Molly Diaries, The Trevelyan Papers, Robinson Library, Special Collections, University of Newcastle-upon-Tyne.

Elizabeth Robins' Papers, Series 2 and 5, Fales Library, New York University.

C. J. Edmonds' Papers, St Antony's College, Oxford University.

India Office, Series L/P&S/10, L/P&S/11, L/P&S/18, Correspondence of the India Office's Political and Secret Department 1932–41.

Wingate's Papers, Sudan Archive, Gilbert Clayton's Papers and F. C. C. Balfour Papers, Library of School of Oriental Studies, Palace Green Section, University of Durham.

A. T. Wilson's Papers, British Library, London.

Lt. Charles Montagu Doughty-Wylie Diaries, Regimental Museum of the Royal Welch Fusiliers, Gwynedd, Wales.

R/15/6/34, India Office Records Memorandum by G. L. Bell, 23 February 1920.

PUBLISHED SOURCES

The Arab Bulletin, papers of the Arab Bureau 1916–18. Public Record Office and SOAS Library.

The Arab War, confidential information for GHQ from Gertrude L. Bell. London, 1940. Introduction by Kinahan Cornwallis.

Admiralty War Staff, Intelligence Division. *A Handbook of Mesopotamia*. Vols I and III. London, 1916–17.

Colonial Office. *Special Report by His Majesty's Government in the United Kingdom of Great Britain and Northern Ireland to the Council of the League of Nations on the Progress of Iraq during the Period 1920–1931*. London, 1931.

Colonial Office. *Reports by His Majesty's Government in the United Kingdom of Great Britain and Northern Ireland to the Council of the League of Nations on the Administration of Iraq for the period – January to October – 1925–1932*. London, 1933.

Cornwallis, Kinahan. *Asia Before World War I*. Arab Bureau 1916, Cambridge, New York, 1976.

Cox, Percy Z. *Iraq, Report on Administration*, October 1920–March 1922. London, 1922.

Foreign Office – Historical Section, *Mesopotamia*, by Gertrude L. Bell. London, 1920.

Lorimer, J. G. *Gazetteer of the Persian Gulf, Oman and Central Arabia*, 2 vols. Calcutta, 1908–15.

Reports by His Britannic Majesty's Government to the Council of the League of Nations on the Administration of Iraq for years 1922–1929.

Review of the Civil Administration of Mesopotamia, by Gertrude L. Bell. India Office, London, 1920.

BOOKS AND ARTICLES ON GERTRUDE L. BELL

'Gertrude Bell', review of E. Burgoyne's work by D. C., *Central Asiatic Society Journal*, 49: 1 (1962).

Bell, Lady. *The Letters of Gertrude Bell*, 2 vols. London, New York, 1928–7.

Burgoyne, Elizabeth. *Gertrude Bell from her Personal Papers 1914–1926*, 2 vols. London, 1961.

Dearden, Seaton. 'Gertrude Bell: A Journey of the Heart', *Cornhill Magazine*, 1062 (Winter 1969–70).

Edmonds, C. J. 'Gertrude Bell in the Near and Middle East', *Central Asiatic Society Journal (CASJ)*, 56: 3 (1969).

Fyfe, Theodore. 'Review of Sir William M. Ramsay's and Miss Gertrude Bell's *The Thousand and One Churches*', *Archaeological Journal*, 67 (1910–11).

Gordon, Lesley (ed.). *Gertrude Bell, 1868–1926*. University of Newcastle-upon-Tyne, 1994.

Hill, Stephen. *Gertrude Bell: A Selection from the Photographic Archive of an Archaeologist and Traveller*. University of Newcastle-upon-Tyne, 1976.

Hogarth, David G. 'Revealing the Civilization of the Hittites of Syria: Excavations at Carchemish', *Illustrated London News*, 24 January 1914.

———. 'Review of "A Journey in Northern Arabia", by G.L. Bell', *Geographical Journal*, 44.

———. 'Obituary of Gertrude Bell'. *Geographical Journal*, 68 (1926).

———. 'Paper on Journey to Hail with Remarks by Sir Hugh Bell', *Geographic Journal*, 70 (1927).

———. 'Review of *Letters of Gertrude Bell* edited by Lady Bell', *Geographical Journal*, 70 (1927).

Lukitz, Liora. 'Gertrude Bell', in *The New Dictionary of National Biography (NDNB)*. 2004.

———. 'Introduction' to reprint of Gertrude Bell, *Persian Pictures*. London, 2005.

McMunn, Lt. Gen. Sir G. F. 'Gertrude Bell and T. E. Lawrence: The Other Side of Their Stories', *The World Today* (November–December, 1927).

O'Brien, Rosmary (ed.). *Gertrude Bell: The Arabian Diaries 1913–1914*. Syracuse, 2000.

'Review of *Persian Pictures* re-issued', *Geographical Journal*, 72 (1928).

Richmond, Lady (ed.). *The Letters of Gertrude Bell*. New York, 1953.

———. *The Earlier Letters of Gertrude Bell*. London, 1937.

Ridley, M. R. *Gertrude Bell*. London, 1941.

Van Ess, Dorothy, 'Pioneers in the Arab World (Gertrude Bell)', in W. B. Erdmands (ed.), *Historical Series of the Reformed Church of America*. Michigan, 1974.

Wallach, Janet. *Desert Queen: The Extraordinary Life of Gertrude Bell*. New York, 1996.

Winstone, H. V. F. *Gertrude Bell*. London, 1978, 1980, 1993.

PUBLISHED WORKS BY GERTRUDE L. BELL

Safar Nameh, Persian Pictures, published anonymously. London, 1894. Subsequent editions with title *Persian Pictures*, foreword by Sir E. Denison Ross, London, 1928, reprint by Cape, 1937.

Poems from the Divan of Hafiz. London, 1897. Reprinted in 1928, foreword by Sir E. Denison Ross, and 1995, Bethesda, MD.

'Islam in India', *Nineteenth Century and After*, 60 (1906).

'Notes on a Journey through Cilicia and Lycaonia', *Revue Archaeologique*, 7 (1906–7).

The Desert and the Sown. London, 1907.

The Thousand and One Churches (with Sir William Ramsay). London, 1909.

'The Vaulting System at Ukhaidir', *Journal of Hellenic Studies*, 30 (1910).

Amurath to Amurath. London, 1911.

'Asiatic Turkey under the Constitution', *Blackwood's Magazine*, 190 (1911).

'Damascus', *Blackwood's Magazine*, 189 (1911).

'Postroad through the Syrian Desert', *Blackwood's Magazine*, 190 (1911).

'The Churches and Monasteries of the Tûr Abdin and Neighbouring Districts', in Max van Berchem, *Amida*. Heidelberg, 1910. Included in *Zeitschrift für Geschichte der Architektur*, No. 9. Heidell, 1913, new edition in 1982, with introduction by Marla Mundell Mango.

Palace and Mosque at Ukhaidir. Oxford, 1914.

The Arabs of Mesopotamia, published anonymously. Basra, 1918.

'Review of the Civil Administration of Mesopotamia', Cmd. 1061. HMS, 1920.

'Three Difficult Months in Iraq', from a correspondent in Baghdad, *CASJ*, 10: 1 (1922).

'The Early Days of the Arab Government in Iraq', from a correspondent in Baghdad, *CASJ*, 9: 4 (1922).

'Current Affairs in Iraq', from a correspondent in Baghdad, *CASJ*, 10 (1923).

'Great Britain and Iraq: An Experiment in Anglo-Asiatic Relations', published anonymously in *The Round Table* (1924).

Teachings of Hafiz, reprint with preface by E. Denison Ross. London, 1928, 1979, 1985.

The Arab War, confidential information for the General Head Quarters in Cairo from Gertrude L. Bell. Dispatches for the *Arab Bulletin*. Introduction by Sir Kinahan Cornwallis. London, 1940.

Bell, Gertrude. *Fusul min ta'rikh al 'iraq al qarib* (Episodes of the Recent History of Iraq), translated by Ja'far Khayat. Beirut, 1971.

'Iraq', in *Encyclopaedia Britannica* (14th edn).

ARTICLES

Browne, E. G. *Encyclopedia of Islam* (1971), vol. 4, pp. 55–7

Drower, Lady E. S. Stevens. 'Marsh People of South Iraq', *Journal of the Royal Central Asian Society*, 34 (1947), pp. 83–90.

Hodgkin, E. C. 'Lionel Smith on Education in Iraq', *Middle Eastern Studies* (*MES*), 19 (1983).

Husri, Khaldun. 'The Assyrian Affair of 1933', *International Journal of Middle Eastern Studies* (*IJMES*), 5 (1974).

Kedourie, Elie. 'Colonel Lawrence and his Biographers', in E. Kedourie and Sylvia G. Haim (eds) *Islam in the Modern World and Other Studies*. London, 1980.
———. 'Mesopotamia 1918–1921. in *England and the Middle East, The Destruction of the Ottoman Empire*. London, 1956.
———. 'Reflexions sur l'Histoire du Royaume d'Iraq 1921–1958', *Orient*, 11 (1959).
———. 'Sir Mark Sykes and Palestine 1915–1916', *MES* (October 1970).
———. 'The Kingdom of Iraq: A Retrospect', in *The Chatham House Version and Other Middle Eastern Studies*. New York, 1970.
———. 'Continuity and Change in Modern Iraqi History', *Asian Affairs*, 62 (1975), pp. 140–6.
Kelidar, Abbas. 'The Shi'i Imami Community and Politics in the Arab East', *MES*, 19 (1983), pp. 3–16.
———. 'Iraq, the Search for Stability', *Conflict Studies*, 59 (July 1975).
Lloyd, Major H. I. 'The Geography of the Mosul Boundary, Meeting of the Royal Geographical Society, 8 March 1926', *Geographical Journal* (1926).
Marr, Phebe. 'The Development of a Nationalist Ideology in Iraq 1920–1941', *Muslim World* (1985).
Simon, Reeva. 'The Teaching of History in Iraq before th Rashid 'Ali Coup of 1941', *MES* (1986), pp. 37–51.
Tibawi, A. L. 'Syria in the McMahon Correspondence', *Middle East Forum*, 42 (1966), pp. 20–1.
Trevelyan, Humphrey (Baron Trevelyan). 'Postscript to Asian Empire', *CASJ*, 60: 3 (1968).
Vinogradov, Amal. 'The 1920 Revolt in Iraq Reconsidered: The Role of Tribes in National Politics', *IJMES*, 3 (1972), pp. 123–39.
Wilson, Lt. Col Sir Arnold. 'The Peoples of the Persian Gulf', *Journal of the Geographical Society* (1927).
———. 'Mesopotamia: 1914–21', *CASJ*, 8: 3 (April 1921).
Woolley, Sir Leonard H. 'The Excavations at Ur of the Chaldeans, 1922–23', *CASJ*, 10: 4 (1923).
———. 'The Excavations at Ur 1924–1925', *CASJ*, 12: 4 (1925).

Books and Articles in Arabic

Al-'Azzawi, 'Abbas. *Ta'rikh al-'iraq bayn ihtilalayn* (The History of Iraq between Two Occupations), 8 vols. Baghdad, 1956.
Al-Fir'awn, Fariq al-Muzhir. *Al-Haqa'iq al-nasi'a fi-al-thawra-al-'iraqiyya sanat 1920 wa nata'ijiha* (The Forgotten Facts about the Iraqi Revolution of 1920 and its Results), Vol. 1. Baghdad, 1952.
Al-Hashimi, Taha. *Mudhakkirati* (Memoirs), 2 vols. Beirut, 1967 and 1969.
Al-Hassani, 'Abd al-Razzaq, *Ta'rikh al-wizarat al-'iraqiyya* (The History of Iraq's Cabinets). Sidon, 1953–67.
———. *Al Thawra al-'iraqiyya al-kubra sanat 1920* (The 1920 Great Iraqi Revolution). Sidon, 1952.
———. *Ta'rikh al-ta'lim fi al'' Iraq* (The History of Education in Iraq), 2 vols. Baghdad, 1959 and 1975.
Al-Husri, Sati'. *Mudhakkirati fi al-'iraq* (My Memoirs from Iraq), 2 vols. Beirut, 1966 and 1967.

Al Khattab, Raja'a Husayn. *Ta'sis al-jaish al-'iraqi wa tatawwur dawrihi al-siyasi 1921–1941* (The Establishment of the Iraqi Army and the Development of its Political Role 1921–1941). Baghdad, 1979.

Sayigh, Anis. 'Ra'y 'arabi fi lawrence' (An Arabic Opinion of Lawrence), *Hiwar*, 5 (July–August 1963), pp. 15–23.

Shahbandar, 'Abd al-Rahman. 'Al colonel lawrence', *Al Muqtataf*, 78 (March), pp. 269–76.

BOOKS

Batatu, Hanna. *The Old Social Classes and the Revolutionary Movements of Iraq: A Study of Iraq's Old Landed and Commercial Classes and its Communists, Bathists, and Free Officers*. Princeton, NJ, 1978.

Bell, Sir Hugh, *High Wages: Their Cause and Effect*, address to National Association of Merchants and Manufacturers. Reprinted in *Contemporary Review* (December 1920).

———. *Safeguarding and the Iron and Steel Industries*, address to Free Trade Union. London, 1925.

———, with Sir Swire Smith and Walter Runciman. *Protection and Industry*. London, 1904.

Bell, Sir Isaac Lowthian, *Chemical Phenomena of Iron Smelting*. London, 1872.

———. *Principles of the Manufacture of Iron and Steel*. London, 1884.

———. *The Iron Trade of Britain*. London, 1886.

———. *Report on Iron Manufacture in the United States*. London, 1887.

———, with Baron Armstrong. *The Industrial Resources of Tyne and Wear*, address to British Association. London, 1864.

Bell, Lady Florence. *The Minor Moralist; Some Essays on the Art of Everyday Conduct*. London, 1900, 1903.

———. *At the Works*. London, 1907. Republished with an introduction by Frederick Alderson, 1969; and with an introduction by Angela V. John, 1985.

———, and Elizabeth Robins. *Alan's Wife*. London, 1893.

Bird, Isabella. *Journeys in Persia and Kurdistan*. London, 1891, 1988.

Birkett, Dea. *Spinsters Abroad, Victorian Lady Explorers*. London, 1991.

Blake, W. *Selected Poems*. London, 1923 (reprint).

———. *Songs of Innocence and Songs of Experience*. New York, 1992 (reprint).

Bland, Lucy. *Banishing the Beast: English Feminism and Sexual Morality 1885–1914*. London, 1983.

Briggs, Asa. *Victorian Cities*. London, 1963.

———. *A Social History of England*. London, 1987.

Brown, Malcolm. *The Essential T. E. Lawrence. A Selection of His First Writings*. New York, 1992.

——— (ed.). *The Letters of T. E. Lawrence*. Oxford, 1951.

Bruinnessen von, M. M. *Aghas, Sheykhs and State*. Utrecht, 1978.

Burckhardt, Titus. *An Introduction to Sufism*. London, 1976.

Cannadine, David. *The Decline and Fall of the British Aristocracy*. New Haven, CT, 1990.

———. *G. M. Trevelyan, A Life in History*. London, 1993.

———. *Aspects of Aristocracy: Grandeur and Decline in Modern Britain*. New Haven, CT, and London, 1994.

Chirol, Sir Valentine I. *Indian Unrest*. London, 1910.

————. *50 Years in a Changing World*. London, 1927.

Clayton, Sir Gilbert. *An Arabian Diary*. Los Angeles, 1969.

Cleveland, William. *The Making of an Arab Nationalist: Ottomanism and Arabism in the Life and Thought of Sati' al-Husri*. Princeton, NJ, 1977.

Creagh, O'Moore, and E. M. Humphris (eds). *The Victoria Cross*. Suffolk, 1985.

Crow, James. *British Heritage Housestead*. London, 1995.

Divine, David. *Hadrian's Wall. The Northwest Frontier of Rome*. New York, 1995.

Doughty, Charles M. *Travels in Arabia Deserta*. London, 1921, 1979 (first published 1888).

Drower, Lady E. S. Stevens. *By Tigris and Euphrates*. London, 1923.

Edelman, Hope. *Motherless Daughters, the Legacy of Loss*. New York, 1994.

Edmonds, C. J. *Kurds, Turks and Arabs*. Oxford, London, 1957.

Emory, Norman. *The Coalminers of Durham*. Durham, 1992.

Erskine, S. *King Faisal of Iraq*. London, 1935.

Fernea, Elizabeth W. *Guests of the Sheik: An Ethnography of an Iraqi Village*. Garden City, NJ, 1969.

Fernea, Robert A. *Sheikh and Effendi: Changing Patterns of Authority among El-Shabana of Southern Iraq*. Cambridge, 1970.

Fisher, John. *Curzon and British Imperialism in the Middle East 1916–1919*. London, 1999.

Fraisse, Genevieve, and Michelle Perrot (eds). *A History of Women in the West: Emerging Feminism from Revolution to World War*. Cambridge, MA, and London, 1993.

Friedlander, Shems. *The Whirling Dervishes*. Albany, NY, 1992.

Fromkin, David. *A Peace to End All Peace. The Fall of the Ottoman Empire and the Creation of the Modern Middle East*. New York, 1989.

Garnett, David (ed.). *The Essential T. E. Lawrence*. Oxford, 1992.

Geertz, Clifford. *After the Fact : Two Countries, Four Decades, One Anthropologist*. Cambridge, MA, 1995.

Gilbert, Martin. *Churchill, a Life*. New York, 1991.

————. *The First World War: A Complete History*. New York, 1994

Glenny, Misha. *The Balkans Nationalism, War and the Great Powers 1804–1999*. New York, 2000.

Graves, Philip. *The Life of Sir Percy Cox*. Plymouth, 1941.

Guest, John S. *The Yezidis, A Study in Survival*. London, New York, 1987.

Guest, Ravel, and Angela V. John. *Lady Charlotte, A Biography of the 19th Century*. London, 1989.

Haldane, Lt. Gen. Sir Aylmer L. *The Insurrection in Mesopotamia, 1920*. Edinburgh, 1922.

Harrison, Brian. *Separate Spheres: The Opposition to Women's Suffrage in Britain*. New York, 1978.

Himmerfeld, Gertrude. *The Demoralization of Society: From Victorian Virtues to Modern Values*. New York, 1995.

Hobsbawm, Eric. *The Age of Empire 1875, 1914*. New York, 1987.

Hogarth, Janet. *The Women of My Time*. London, 1934.

Hopwood, Derek. *Sexual Encounters in the Middle East*, Ithaca, NY, 1999.

James, Lawrence. *The Golden Warrior: The Life and Legend of Lawrence of Arabia*. London, 1990, 1996, 1999, 2000.

————. *The Rise and Fall of the British Empire*. London, 1995, 1998.

John, Angela V. *Elizabeth Robins, Staging A Life, 1862–1952*. London, New York, 1995.
Keddie, Nikki. *Scholars, Saints and Sufis. Muslim Religious Institutions since 1500*. Los Angeles, 1978.
————, and Beth Baron. *Women in Middle Eastern History Shifting Boundaries in Sex and Gender*. New Haven, CT, and London, 1991.
Kedourie, Elie. *England and the Middle East: The Destruction of the Ottoman Empire 1914–1921*. London, 1956.
————. *The Chatham House Version and Other Middle Eastern Studies*. New York, 1970.
————. *Arabic Political Memoirs and Other Studies*. London, 1974.
————. *In the Anglo-Arab Labyrinth: The McMahon–Husayn Correspondence and Interpretations 1914–1939*. Cambridge, 1976, 1978.
Kent, Marian. *Oil and Empire: British Policy and Mesopotamian Oil 1900–1920*. London, 1973.
Klieman, Aaron. *Foundations of British Policy in the Arab World: The Cairo Conference of 1921*. Baltimore, 1970.
Kostiner, Joseph. *The Making of Saudi-Arabia. From Chieftancy to Monarchical State*. Oxford, 1993.
Kramer, Martin (ed.). *Middle Eastern Lives. The Practice of Biography and Self Narrative*. Syracuse, 1991.
Kunitz, Stanley (cd.). *The Essential Blake*. New Jersey, 1987.
Lawrence, Arnold W. (ed.). *T. E. Lawrence by his Friends*. London, 1937.
Lawrence, T. E. *The Seven Pillars of Wisdom: A Triumph*. London, 1926; London, New York, 1935, 1991, 1996 and further editions.
Leslie, Sir Shane. *Mark Sykes: His Life and Letters*. London, 1929.
Lewis, Bernard. *The Emergence of Modern Turkey*, Oxford, New York, 1961, and further editions.
Longrigg, S. H. *Iraq, 1900 to 1950. A Political, Social and Economic History*. Oxford, 1953.
————. *Four Centuries of Modern Iraq*. Oxford, Beirut, 1968.
Lorimer, J. G. *Gazetteer of the Persian Gulf*. Bombay, 1913.
Luizard, Jean Pierre. *La formation de l'Irak contemporain: le role politique des ulema Chiites à la fin de la domination Ottomane et au moment de la construction de l'état Irakien*. Paris, 1991.
Luke, M. *Mosul and its Minorities*. London, 1925.
Lukitz, Liora. *Iraq: The Search for National Identity*. London, 1995.
Mack, John E. *A Prince of Our Disorder: The Life of T. E. Lawrence*. Boston, Toronto, 1976.
Manchester, William. *Winston Spencer Churchill, The Last Lion, Vision of Glory 1874–1932*, Vol. 1. New York, 1989.
Marlowe, John. *Late Victorian: The Life of Sir Arnold Talbot Wilson*. London, 1967.
Marr, Phebe. *The Modern History of Iraq*. Boulder, CO, 1985.
Meinertzhagen, Richard. *Middle East Diary: 1917–1956*. London, 1959.
Mejcher, Helmut. *Imperial Quest for Oil, Iraq 1900–1928*. London, 1976.
Melman, Billie. *Women's Orient: English Women and the Middle East 1718–1918*. Ann Arbor, MI, 1992.
Monk, Ray. *Bertrand Russell, The Spirit of Solitude, 1872–1921*. New York, London, 1996.
Monroe, Elizabeth. *Britain's Moment in the Middle East 1914–1956*. London, 1963.

Moojan, Momen. *An Introduction to Shii Islam. The History and Doctrines of Twelver Shi'ism*. New Haven, CT, 1985.

Morris, A. J. A. *C. P. Trevelyan, Portrait of a Radical 1870–1958*. Belfast, 1977.

Morris, J. *Farewell the Trumpets: An Imperial Retreat*. London, New York, 1978.

———. (James). *Pax Britannica, the Climax of an Empire*. London, 1968, 1979.

Mousa, Suleiman. *T. E. Lawrence: An Arab View*. New York, 1966.

Nakash, Yitzhak. *The Shi'is of Iraq*. Princeton, NJ, 1994.

Nicholson, Harold, *Curzon: The Last Phase*, London, 1934.

Önder, Mehmet. *Mevlana and the Whirling Dervishes*. Ankara, 1977.

Perkins, Joan. *Victorian Women*. London, 1993.

Porter, Roy. *English Society in the 18th Century*. London, New York, 1990.

———. *London, A Social History*. Cambridge, MA, 1990.

Rasheed, Madawi al-. *Politics in an Arabian Oasis The Rashidis of Saudi Arabia*. London, 1991 (paperback edn 1997).

Rose, Norman. *Churchill, The Unruly Giant*. New York, 1995.

Roux, Georges. *Ancient Iraq*. Middlesex, New York, 1964, 1992.

Said, Edward W. *Orientalism*. New York, 1971.

Sandars, N. K. (introduction and translation). *The Epic of Gilgamesh*. New York, 1972.

Schimmel, Annemarie. *I Am Wind, You are Fire. The Life and Work of Rumi*. Boston, London, 1996.

Simon, Reeva. *Iraq Between the Two World Wars: The Creation and Implementation of a Nationalist Ideology*. New York, 1986.

Sluglett, Peter. *Britain in Iraq 1914–1932*. London, 1976.

Soane, E. B. *To Mesopotamia and Kurdistan in Disguise*. London, 1912.

Stafford, R. S. *The Tragedy of the Assyrians*. London, 1935.

Stark, Freya, *Baghdad Sketches* (introduction by Barbara Kreiger), Illinois, 1992 (1st edn 1938).

Storrs, Ronald. *Orientations*. New York, London, 1937, 1945.

Sykes, Sir Mark. *Through Five Turkish Provinces*. London, 1900.

———. *The Caliph's Last Heritage: A Short History of the Turkish Empire*. London, 1915.

Thesiger, Wilfred. *The Marsh Arabs*. London, 1964, 1967.

———. *Arabian Sands*, New York, 1991 (1st edn 1959).

Thomas, Lowell. *With Lawrence in Arabia*. New York, 1924.

Tripp, Charles. *A History of Iraq*. Cambridge, 2000.

Trevelyan, G. M. *A Shortened History of England*. London, 1942, 1987.

Trevelyan, Raleigh. *Wallington*. London, 1982.

Vester, Bertha Spafford. *Our Jerusalem. An American Family in the Holy City 1882–1949*. Jerusalem, 1988 (1st edn, 1950).

Vickers, Miranda. *The Albanians, A Modern History*. London, 1995.

Westrate, Bruce. *The Arab Bureau British Policy in the Middle East 1916–1920*, Pennsylvania, 1992.

Willcocks, Sir William. *The Irrigation of Mesopotamia*, 2 vols. London, 1914.

Wilson, A. T. *Loyalties in Mesopotamia: A Personal and Historical Record 1914–1917*. London, 1936.

———. *A Clash of Loyalties. Mesopotamia 1917–20*. London, 1937 (1st edn 1930 and 1931).

Wilson, Jeremy. *T. E. Lawrence, Lawrence of Arabia*. London, 1988.

————. *Lawrence of Arabia. The Authorized Biography of T. E. Lawrence*. New York, 1990.
Woolley Sir Leonard H. *Ur of the Chaldeans*. London, 1929.
————. *History Unearthed*. London, 1963.
————. *The Sumerians*. London, 1965.
————, and T. E. Lawrence. *The Wilderness of Zin*. London, 1914.
Yapp, M. E. *The Making of Modern Middle East, 1792–1923*. Essex, 1987.
Young, G. M. *Portrait of an Age: Victorian England*. Oxford, 1977.

Index